DATE DUE

~~1-10~~			
~~4-05-07~~			
12-06-07			
4-25-24			

Demco

DATE DUE

2/19/97			

Demco

HANDBOOK OF TREES FOR THE MIDWEST

Pamela Sue Stava

Horticulturist at the North Central Forest
Experiment Station—U.S. Forest Service,
Rhinelander, Wisconsin

2460 Kerper Boulevard,
Dubuque, Iowa 52001

Cover photo by George Taloumis

Copyright © 1978 by Kendall/Hunt Publishing Company

ISBN 0—8403—1851—0

All rights reserved. No part of this publication may be reproduced, stored in a retrieval system, or transmitted, in any form or by any means, electronic, mechanical, photocopying, recording, or otherwise, without the prior written permission of the copyright owner.

Printed in the United States of America

He who plants a tree plants love.

Taken from *Plant a Tree*, Lucy Larcom

With love to the Creator of trees and to those who have encouraged my career and this publication.

CONTENTS

Preface vii

Acknowledgment ix

Introduction xi

Key to Genera xvii

Tree Descriptions 1

Bibliography 319

Index 321

PREFACE

This text was designed to provide a quick and easy reference for the practical needs of all those people who have a special interest in trees. The subject matter presented provides a useful aid in tree identification, selection, culture, and propagation. The goal was not to present new material, but rather to compile known material in a new way. The text was condensed into phrase descriptions to provide ample space for illustrations. Also, much scientific terminology was eliminated to keep simplicity.

Although the data was collected in Northern Illinois and Central Iowa, the information is applicable wherever the included plant materials can be grown even though some characteristics may differ due to varying environmental factors.

ACKNOWLEDGMENT

The author would like to acknowledge the following sources: the hardiness zone map, used by permission of The Arnold Arboretum, Harvard University, Jamaica Plain, Massachusetts; the crown illustration of *Taxodium distichum* from **Handbook on Conifers**, Vol. XXV, No. 2, used by permission of Brooklyn Botanic Garden, Brooklyn, New York; the seed pretreatments and much of the flowering and fruiting dates from **Seeds of the Woody Plants** in the United States, U.S. Department of Agriculture-Forest Service, Agricultural Handbook 450; crabapple selection descriptions from **Disease Resistant Crabapples—1976** used by permission of Nichols, Lester, Pennsylvania State University Cooperative Extension Service, University Park.

The author would also like to special thanks to all those who provided their expertise in plant materials and propagation.

Finally, many thanks to my family for their special efforts and patience.

The research for this publication was partially funded by the Iowa State University Alumni Fund. This was granted through the Iowa State University Honors Program.

INTRODUCTION

Tree: a woody perennial that can be grown with a single trunk; in most cases is at least 15 feet in height; has a trunk diameter greater than 2 inches at maturity

Nomenclature: latin names are standardized according to Handbuch der Laubgehölze and Die Nadelgehölze by Gerd Krüssman; latin names are printed in italics; common names are those in general use in the Midwest

Foliage: most illustrations are actual size; for those species which have exceptionally large foliage, the illustrations are reduced to one half actual size; see page xiii and xiv for illustrated descriptions of terminology used in the key; size and color vary with environmental conditions; many trees are hybrids and the foliage may not appear identical to that described

Flowers: unless otherwise stated, male and female flower parts are produced in one flower; date of flowering depends on geographic location and weather conditions

Fruit: illustrations are actual size; see page xv for illustrated descriptions of terminology used in the key and text; time of ripening and persistence vary with weather and geographical location; size and color vary with environmental conditions

Buds and Twigs: illustrations are actual size; see page xiv for illustrated descriptions of terminology used in the key and text; color may vary with age and environmental conditions; "pith" is the central portion of the twig

Bark: texture and color may vary with age and environment

Roots: data derived under native conditions; structure may vary with depth of water table, soil structure and root pruning; generally, nursery grown trees are more readily transplanted than forest grown trees

Growth Habit: crown illustrations depict specimen trees; sketches are not scaled to one another; a marker on the right side of the crown illustration designates 6 feet or the approximate height of a person; habit can vary with age, amount of direct sun and proximity to buildings and other trees; all heights are approximate

Site: derived from the site on which a species is often found growing natively or other conditions under which a species appears to grow well

Growth Rate: derived under natural conditions; varies with age, environmental conditions and cultural practices

Hardiness: zones refer to the map on the inside front cover; determined by annual low temperature for an area; hardiness may vary due to seed source (example: seed produced from a northern source would be more hardy than the same type of seed produced from a southern source); zones are only approximate—a plant can extend outside its natural range when special care is taken to alter the local environment to meet the plant's specific needs

Maintenance: based on special attention required other than autumn raking; tolerance to pruning refers to shading out, sucker removal or pruning for Christmas trees, hedges, or use under utility lines

Propagation: methods of reproduction; seed treatments vary with seed source and hardness of seed coat

Selections: most are cultivars or cultivated varieties; this is a plant with a distinguishing characteristic which is significant to warrant propagation to maintain this characteristic;

botanical variety (designated as "var." in text) is a variation that causes a plant to be significantly different from the type

Note: a ruler is provided inside back cover for field use; key to genera page xvii-xx, is to aid in identification

Leaf Characteristics

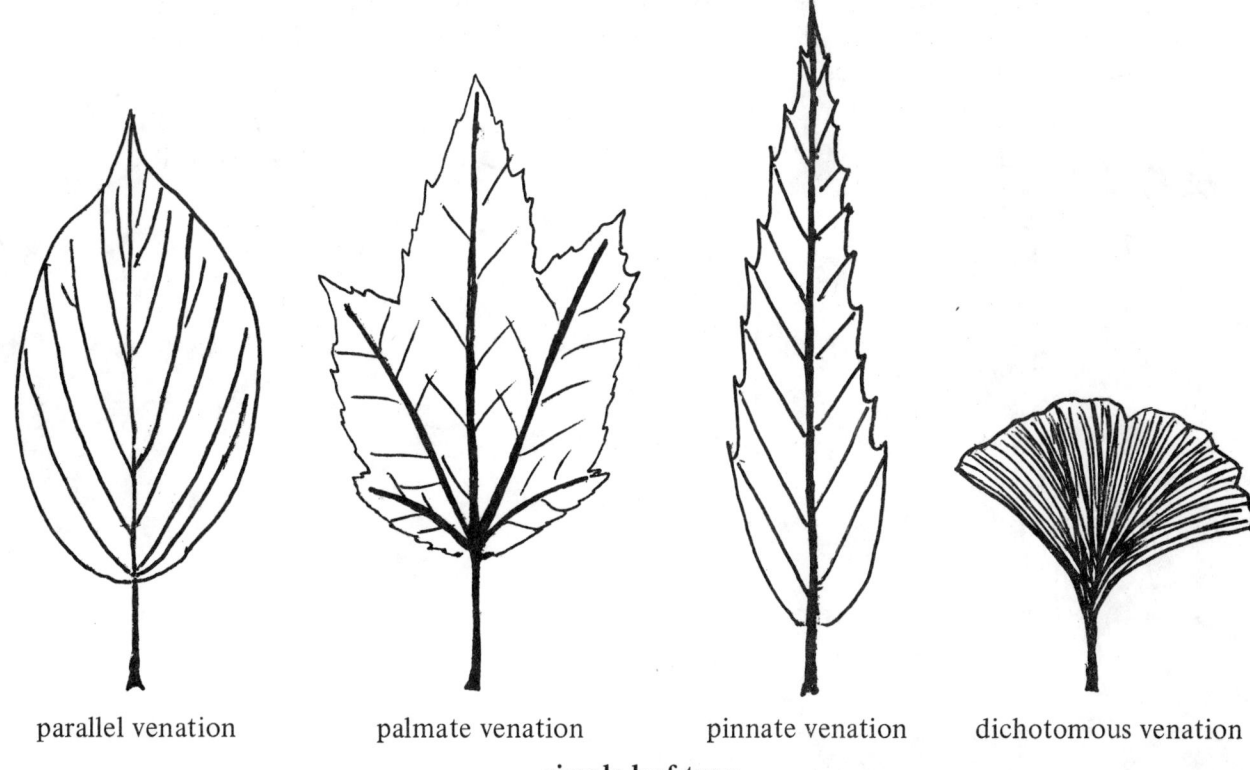

parallel venation — palmate venation — pinnate venation — dichotomous venation

simple leaf type

fascicle — palmately arranged — pinnately arranged

compound leaf type

Leaf Arrangement

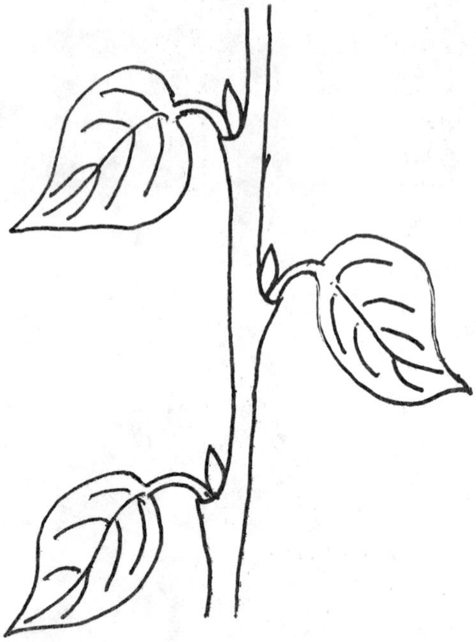

alternate

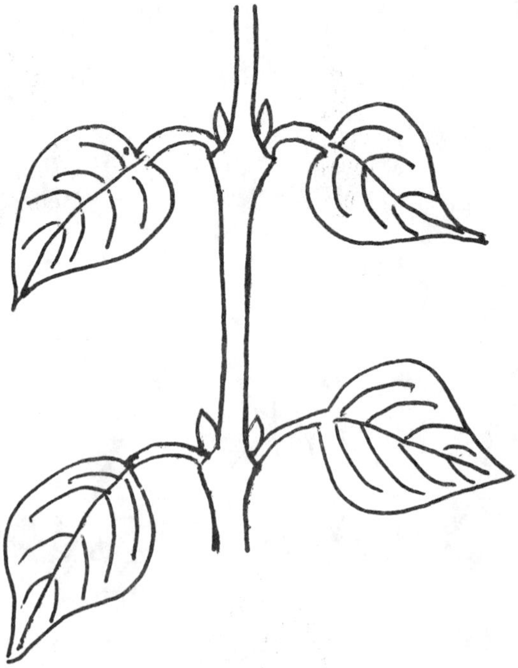

opposite

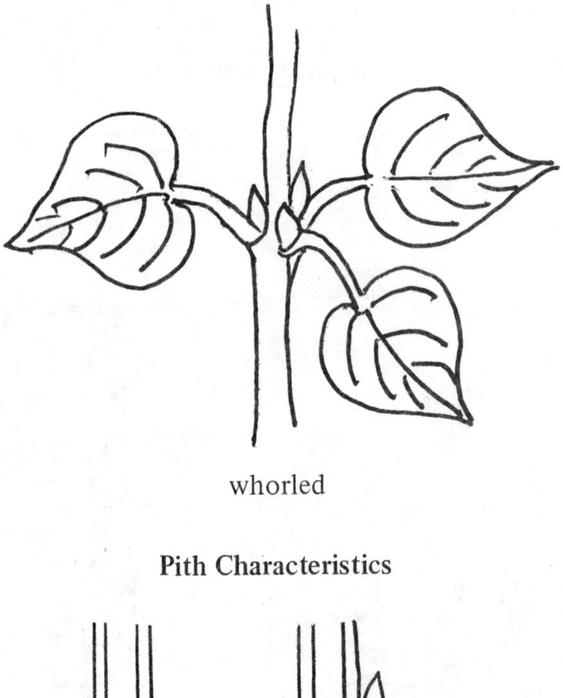

whorled

Pith Characteristics

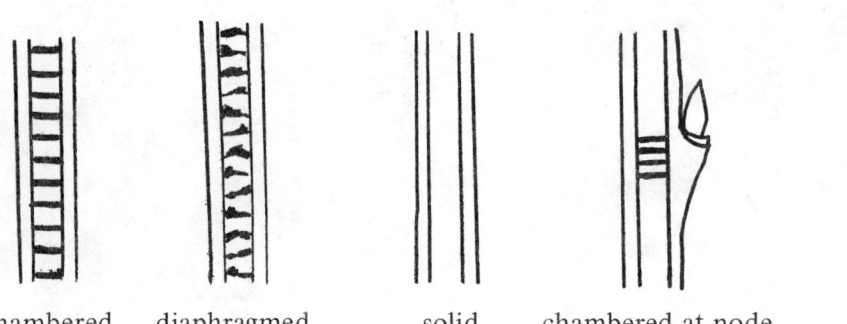

chambered   diaphragmed   solid   chambered at node    round    star shape

Fruit Types

 achene

 acorn

 capsule

 strobile

 berry

 drupe

 pome

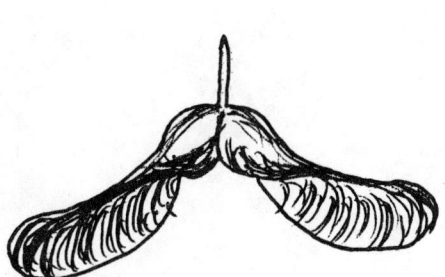   samara

 pod

Key to Genera

1. leaves needlelike or scalelike 2
1. leaves broad, not needlelike or scalelike 10
    2. leaves needlelike 3
    2. leaves not needlelike 9
3. leaves produced in fascicles 4
3. leaves produced singular, not in fascicles 5
    4. 2, 3, or 5 leaves per fascicle; evergreen; without spurs .... *PINUS*
    4. 10 or more leaves per fascicle; deciduous; produced on spurs .... *LARIX*
5. leaf base persistent on twigs when leaves fall; twigs feel rough 6
5. leaf base not persistant; twigs do not feel rough 7
    6. leaves usually 4 sided; no leaf stalk .... *PICEA*
    6. leaves usually flat; 2 white lines below; short leaf stalk .... *TSUGA*
7. leaves without leaf stalk; cones upright; circular leaf scars when leaves are removed
   .... *ABIES*
7. leaves with leaf stalks; cones pendent; without circular leaf scars when leaves are removed 8
    8. leaves airy and soft in appearance; deciduous; buds small; round cones ....
       .... *TAXODIUM*
    8. leaves not airy and soft; evergreen; terminal buds long and pointed; cone with extended bracts .... *PSEUDOTSUGA*
9. leaves all scalelike with glands; fruit an oval, upright cone .... *THUJA*
9. leaves scalelike and awllike without glands; fruit a berry .... *JUNIPERUS*
    10. leaves opposite or whorled 11
    10. leaves alternate 21
11. leaves sometimes in whorls of 3 .... *CATALPA*
11. leaves opposite, not whorled 12
    12. leaves simple 13
    12. leaves compound 17
13. leaves lobed .... (except *A. negundo*) *ACER*
13. leaves not lobed 14
    14. leaves with parallel venation 15
    14. leaves without parallel venation 16
15. leaves without teeth; twigs not spine tipped .... (except *C. alternifolia*) *CORNUS*
15. leaves with teeth; twigs often ending in a spine .... *RHAMNUS*
    16. leaves with round teeth; lateral spurs; small red flowers .. *CERCIDIPHYLLUM*
    16. leaves without teeth; no lateral spurs; showy, white, feathery flowers ....
        .... *CHIONANTHUS*
17. leaflets palmately arranged; fruit globular .... *AESCULUS*
17. leaflets pinnately arranged; fruit not globular 18
    18. 3-7 leaflets with coarse teeth; often lobed .... *ACER NEGUNDO*
    18. 5 or more leaflets without coarse teeth and lobes 19
19. leaflets with or without teeth; fruit a samara with a terminal wing; twigs with a wide terminal bud .... *FRAXINUS*

19. leaflets without teeth; fruit not a samara; terminal bud not wide 20
    20. leaflets 3-3 1/2 inches long with a long, pointed apex; fruit a persistent, bluish black drupe; raised corky bark .... *PHELLODENDRON*
    20. leaflets 1-1 1/2 inches long without a long, pointed apex; fruit a green pod; bark not corky .... *SOPHORA*
21. leaves simple 22
21. leaves compound 61
    22. leaves without teeth 23
    22. leaves with teeth 26
23. leaves fan shape with dichotomous venation; spur shoots .... *GINKGO*
23. leaves not fan shape or with dichotomous venation; without spur shoots 24
    24. leaves lobed 25
    24. leaves not lobed 33
25. 1-2 lobes; leaves and twigs with a spicy odor; pith solid .... *SASSAFRAS*
25. 4 lobes; leaves and twigs not spicy; pith diaphragmed .... *LIRIODENDRON*
    26. leaves with palmate venation 27
    26. leaves with pinnate venation 30
27. leaves with coarse teeth 28
27. leaves without coarse teeth 29
    28. dense, white hair on lower leaf surface; bark white with horizontal lenticels, not mottled .... *POPULUS ALBA*
    28. without hair on lower leaf surface; bark mottled, not with horizontal lenticels .... *PLATANUS*
29. star shaped leaves with 2-3 inch leaf stalks; without spines .... *LIQUIDAMBAR*
29. maple shaped leaves with leaf stalks up to 20 inches; many spines ... *KALOPANAX*
    30. milky sap; fleshy, mutliple fruit .... *MORUS*
    30. sap not milky; fruit not a fleshy multiple 31
31. star shaped pith; terminal buds clustered; fruit an acorn .... *QUERCUS*
31. pith round; fruit a pome 32
    32. twigs with sharp thorns; often with a round crown and low, horizontal branching .... *CRATAEGUS*
    32. twigs without sharp thorns; crown usually round with upright, spreading branches .... *MALUS*
33. without teeth 34
33. with teeth 41
    34. leaves, twigs and fruit with silvery bloom .... *ELAEAGNUS*
    34. leaves, twigs and fruit not silvery with bloom 35
35. leaves heart shape; fruit a pod .... *CERCIS*
35. leaves not heart shape; fruit not a pod 36
    36. pith diaphragmed 37
    36. pith not diaphragmed 38
37. leaves 2-5 inches long; fruit a small drupe .... *NYSSA*
37. leaves 6-12 inches long; fruit a 2-4 inch berry .... *ASIMINA*
    38. leaves with parallel veins; branches whorled in tiers .... *CORNUS ALTERNIFOLIA*
    38. leaves not with parallel veins; branches not in tiers 39

39. pith chambered; bark with irregular corky blocks; fruit an orange berry . . . . DIOSPYRUS
39. pith not chambered; bark not with corky blocks; fruit not a berry 40
    40. milky sap; green spines; green multiple fruit . . . . MACLURA
    40. sap clear; large, terminal bud that is often fuzzy; fruit a cucumber or conelike pod with red seeds . . . . MAGNOLIA
41. leaf stalk flattened . . . . POPULUS
41. leaf stalks not flattened 42
    42. milky sap . . . . MORUS
    42. sap clear 43
43. each leaf vein terminating in a coarse tooth; fruit a nut in a bur 44
43. leaf veins not terminating in teeth; fruit not a nut in a bur 45
    44. bark gray and very smooth; round pith . . . . FAGUS
    44. bark gray or brown becoming furrowed; star shaped pith . . . . CASTANEA
45. part or all of pith chambered 46
45. no part of pith chambered 47
    46. pith chambered throughout the twig; young bark green and white striped . . . . HALESIA
    46. pith chambered only at nodes; bark warty . . . . CELTIS
47. leaves heart shaped; fruit a nutlet on a leafy bract . . . . TILIA
47. leaves not heart shaped; fruit not on a leafy bract 48
    48. triangular pith . . . . ALNUS
    48. pith not triangular 49
49. twigs or leaves bitter to taste 50
49. twigs or leaves not bitter 52
    50. leaves bitter . . . . OXYDENDRON
    50. leaves not bitter; twigs bitter 51
51. buds covered by a single, caplike scale; fruit a capsule; leaves without glands . . . . SALIX
51. buds with 2 or more scales; fruit a drupe; leaves with 2 glands at base . . . . . PRUNUS
    52. pith star shaped; terminal buds clustered; fruit an acorn . . . . QUERCUS
    52. pith round; terminal buds not clustered; fruit not an acorn 53
53. bark often papery with horizontal lenticels; fruit a 2 winged nutlet in a strobile . . . . BETULA
53. bark not papery; fruit not a 2 winged nutlet in a strobile 54
    54. fruit a nutlet 55
    54. fruit not a nutlet 56
55. bark smooth; fruit a nutlet at the base of a trilobed, leafy bract . . . . CARPINUS
55. bark flaky and shaggy; fruit a nutlet in a cluster that looks like hops . . . . OSTRYA
    56. fruit a pome 57
    56. fruit not a pome 60
57. fruit pear shape . . . . PYRUS
57. fruit rounded 58
    58. twigs with thorns; crown usually round with low, horizontal branches . . . . CRATAEGUS
    58. twigs without thorn; crown often round with upright, spreading branches 59

59. pomes always less than 1/2 inch; long, pointed buds .... *AMELANCHIER*
59. pomes may be greater than 1/2 inch; buds usually rounded .... *MALUS*
    60. teeth often double and sharp; bark furrowed and without horizontal lenticels .... *ULMUS*
    60. teeth single and scalloped; bark with horizontal lenticels .... *ZELKOVA*
61. even number of leaflets 62
61. odd number of leaflets 64
    62. leaflets less than 1/2 inch in length; fine teeth .... *GLEDITSIA*
    62. leaflets greater than 1/2 inch long; without fine teeth 63
63. leaflets with 1-3 glandular teeth only at the base; leaflets with foul odor when crushed; fruit a samara .... *AILANTHUS*
63. leaflets without teeth or foul odor when crushed; fruit a pod .... *GYMNOCLADUS*
    64. leaflets without teeth 65
    64. leaflets with teeth 66
65. leaflets 1-1 1/2 inches long; spines on twigs; dark, coarse furrowed bark .... *ROBINIA*
65. leaflets 3-4 inches long; twigs without spines; very smooth, gray bark .... *CLADRASTIS*
    66. chambered pith .... *JUGLANS*
    66. pith solid 67
67. leaves and twigs have milky sap when broken .... *RHUS*
67. sap clear 68
    68. lobed leaflets; flower panicle up to 12 inches long; fruit triangular with inflated, papery walls .... *KOELREUTERIA*
    68. not as above 69
69. leaflets 2-7 inches long; fruit a nut in a husk .... *CARYA*
69. leaflets 1-1 1/2 inches long; fruit a cluster of red pomes .... *SORBUS*

HANDBOOK OF TREES
FOR THE MIDWEST

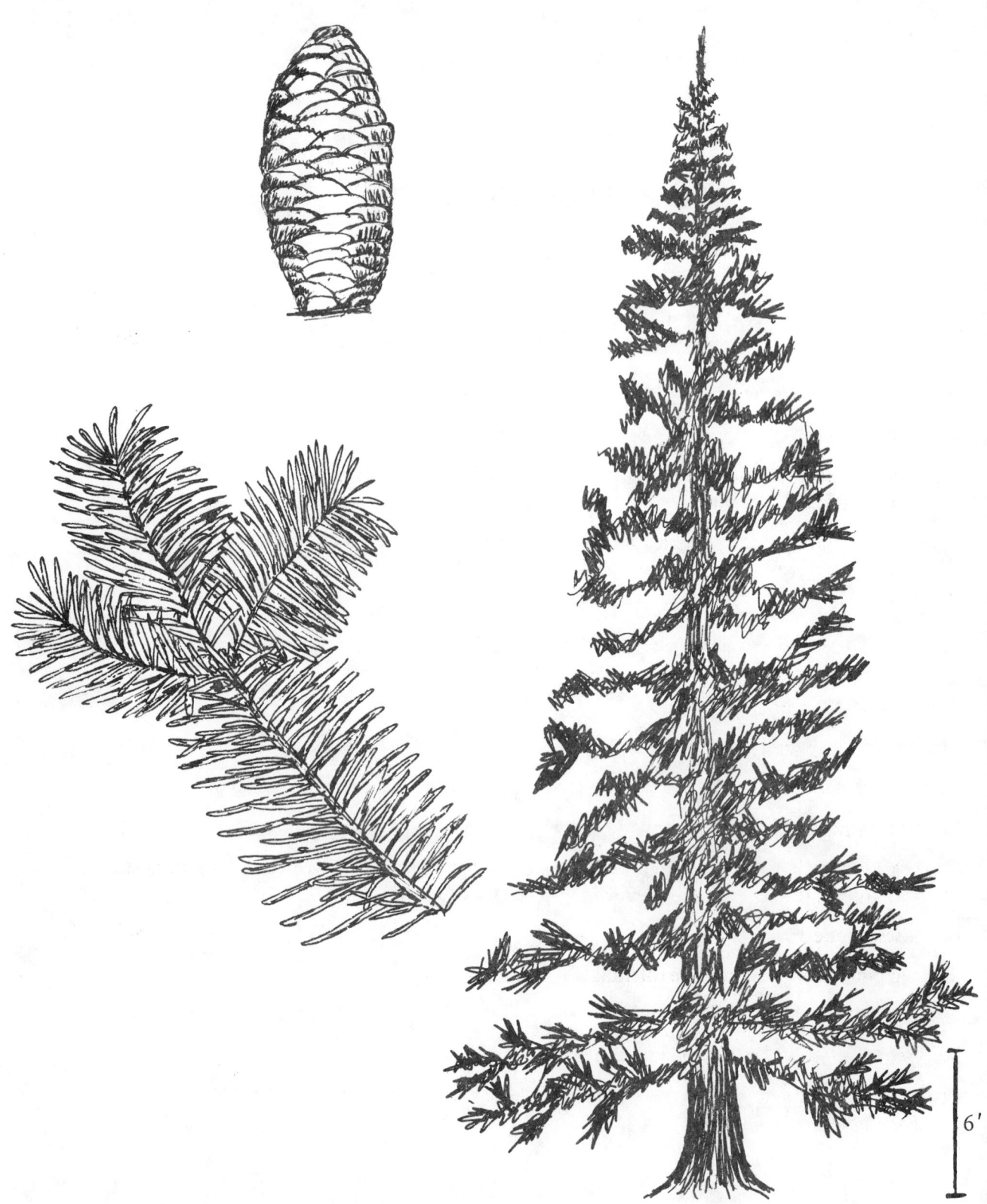
Abies balsamea

TREE DESCRIPTIONS

Abies balsamea

Common Name: Balsam Fir

Family: Pinaceae

Foliage: 3/4-1 inch, evergreen needles; flat; blunt tipped; 2 white lines below; fragrant; persists 7-10 years

Flowers: male and female separate on the same tree; axillary; male: yellow to red, on lower portion of tree; female: purple with green tips on bracts, on upper 1/4-1/3 of tree; mid to late May

Fruit: 2-4 inch cone; erect; thin, flat, deciduous scales; dark purple; ripens late August-early September

Buds: clustered; reddish; resinous

Twigs: light gray; hairy

Bark: gray turning reddish brown; scaly; resin blisters which have a balsam aroma

Roots: taproot; difficult to transplant

Growth Habit: 40-60 feet in height; dense; narrowly pyramidal crown; branching almost horizontal; lower limbs are shed with age and lack of light

Hardiness: zone 3

Site: rich, moist soil; sun; shade tolerant while young

Growth Rate: rapid

Maintenance: clean; limited tolerance to pruning

Propagation: seed—fall sow dry seed and mulch, or stratify in a moist medium at 34-41°F for 28 days

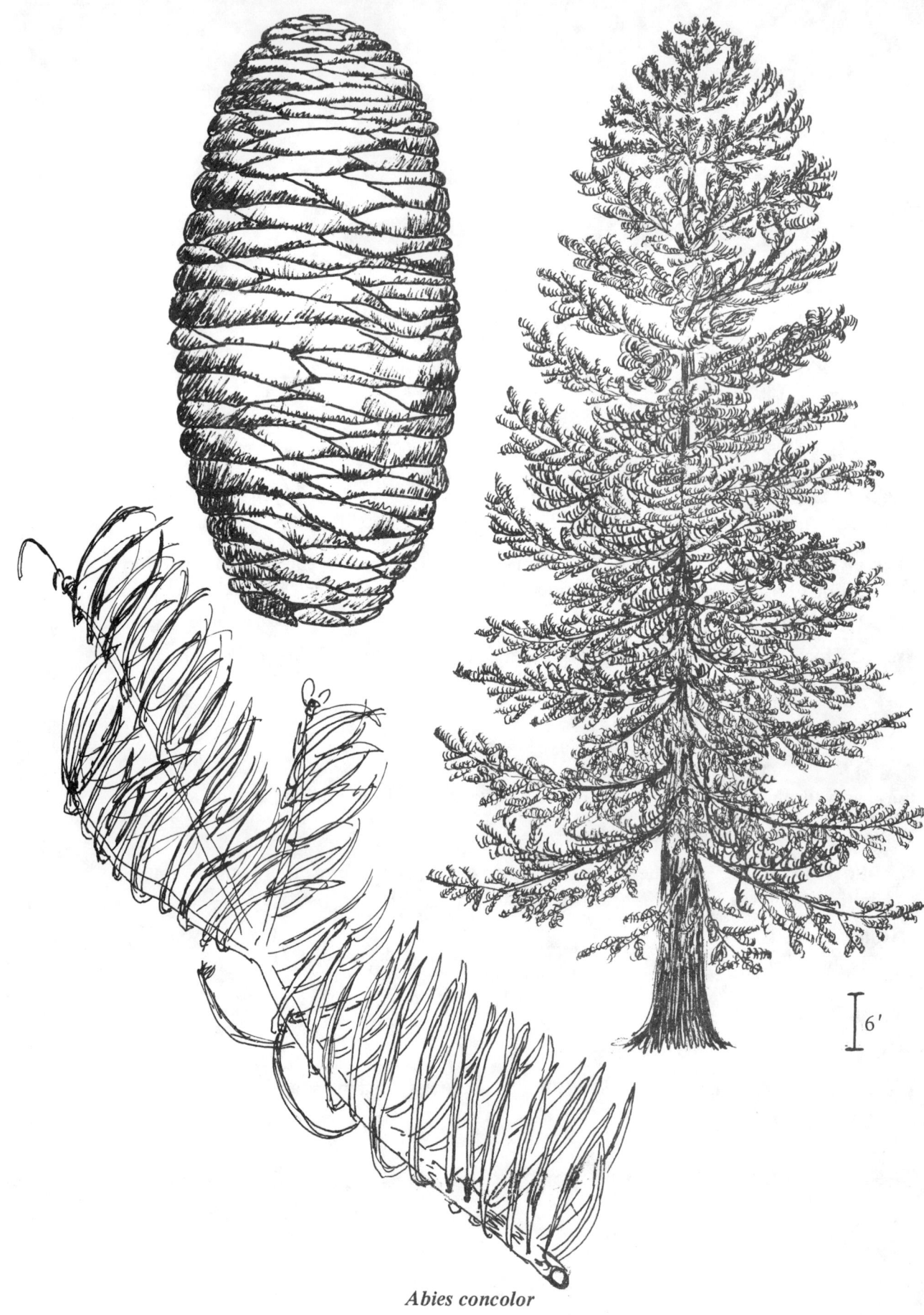

Abies concolor

Abies concolor

Common Name: Colorado Fir; White Fir

Family: Pinaceae

Foliage: 3/4-1 1/2 inch, evergreen needles; flat with a blunt tip; silvery blue to silvery green; scattered in double rows; erect; persists 7-10 years

Flowers: male and female separate but on the same tree; axillary; male: reddish purple, on lower portion of tree, female: reddish green, on upper 1/4-1/3 of tree; May-June

Fruit: 3-5 inch cone; erect; thin, deciduous scales; yellowish purple; ripens September-October

Buds: resinous; yellowish brown

Twigs: raised, circular leaf scars; yellowish green

Bark: gray; resin blisters on young trees; becomes thick with platelike scales

Roots: Taproot; transplants well if root pruned

Growth Habit: 100-120 feet in height; stiffly conical; short, horizontal branching; branches extend to the ground

Hardiness: zone 3

Site: prefers moist, well-drained soil; will tolerate dry; sun or partial shade; heat tolerant

Growth Rate: moderate-rapid

Maintenance: clean; tolerant to pruning

Propagation: seed—fall sow with dry seed and mulch, or stratify in a moist medium at 34-41° F for 21 days; soaking prior to stratification may be helpful; graft on *A. concolor* understock

Selections: 'Conica' — dwarf; conical habit
'Violacea' — bluish white foliage

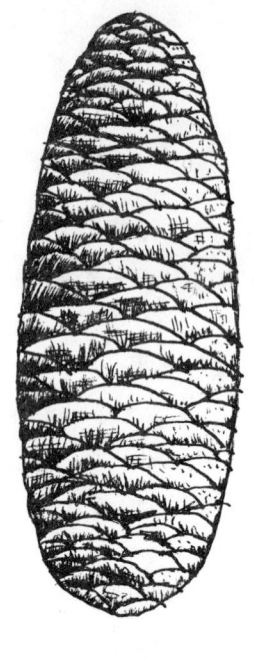

Abies homolepis

4

Abies homolepis

Common Name: Nikko Fir

Family: Pinaceae

Foliage: 1-1 1/4 inch, evergreen needles; flat with blunt tips; bright green and shiny above; white bands below; dense; persists 7-10 years

Flowers: male and female separate but on the same tree; axillary; male: pendent, on lower portion of tree; female: short, upright, on upper portion of tree; May-June

Fruit: 3 inch, oblong cone; erect; thin, flat, deciduous scales; resinous; purple ripening to brown; ripens September

Buds: resinous; pink

Twigs: leaf stubs persist; tan; separated with deep grooves

Bark: gray; flaky with cracks

Roots: taproot with fibrous laterals; transplants moderately well if root pruned

Growth Habit: 70-90 feet in height; pyramidal crown; horizontal branches that extend to the ground

Hardiness: zone 4

Site: rich, moist, well-drained soil; sun or partial shade

Growth Rate: moderate

Maintenance: clean; limited tolerance to pruning

Propagation: seed—stratify in a moist medium at 34-41° F for 30 days; soaking prior to stratification may be helpful; graft on *A. concolor* understock

Selections: var. *umbellata* — immature cones green

Acer campestre

Acer campestre

Common Name: Hedge Maple

Family: Aceraceae

Foliage: 2-4 inches long; 3-5 lobes; blunt; entire; downy beneath; milky sap when leaf stalks are crushed; yellow in autumn

Flowers: male and female in one flower or separate; greenish white; April-June

Fruit: 1/2-3/4 inch samara; wings horizontally spread; usually fuzzy; ripens August-October

Buds: several terminals; downy; dark brown

Twigs: slender; hairy; brown; branches may have corky ridges

Bark: gray; deep furrows with narrow, corky ridges

Roots: fibrous; transplants well

Growth Habit: 20-30 feet in height; dense, round crown; low branching; often with multiple trunks

Hardiness: zone 4

Site: dry, poor soil; sun or partial shade

Growth Rate: slow

Maintenance: clean; tolerant to pruning

Propagation: seed—fall sow dry seed and mulch, or stratify in sand for 30 days at 68-86°F then at 36-40°F for 90-180 days; graft or bud on *A. campestre* understock

Selections: 'Postelense' — young foliage yellow
  'Pulverulentum' — white specks on foliage
  'Schwernii' — young foliage purple

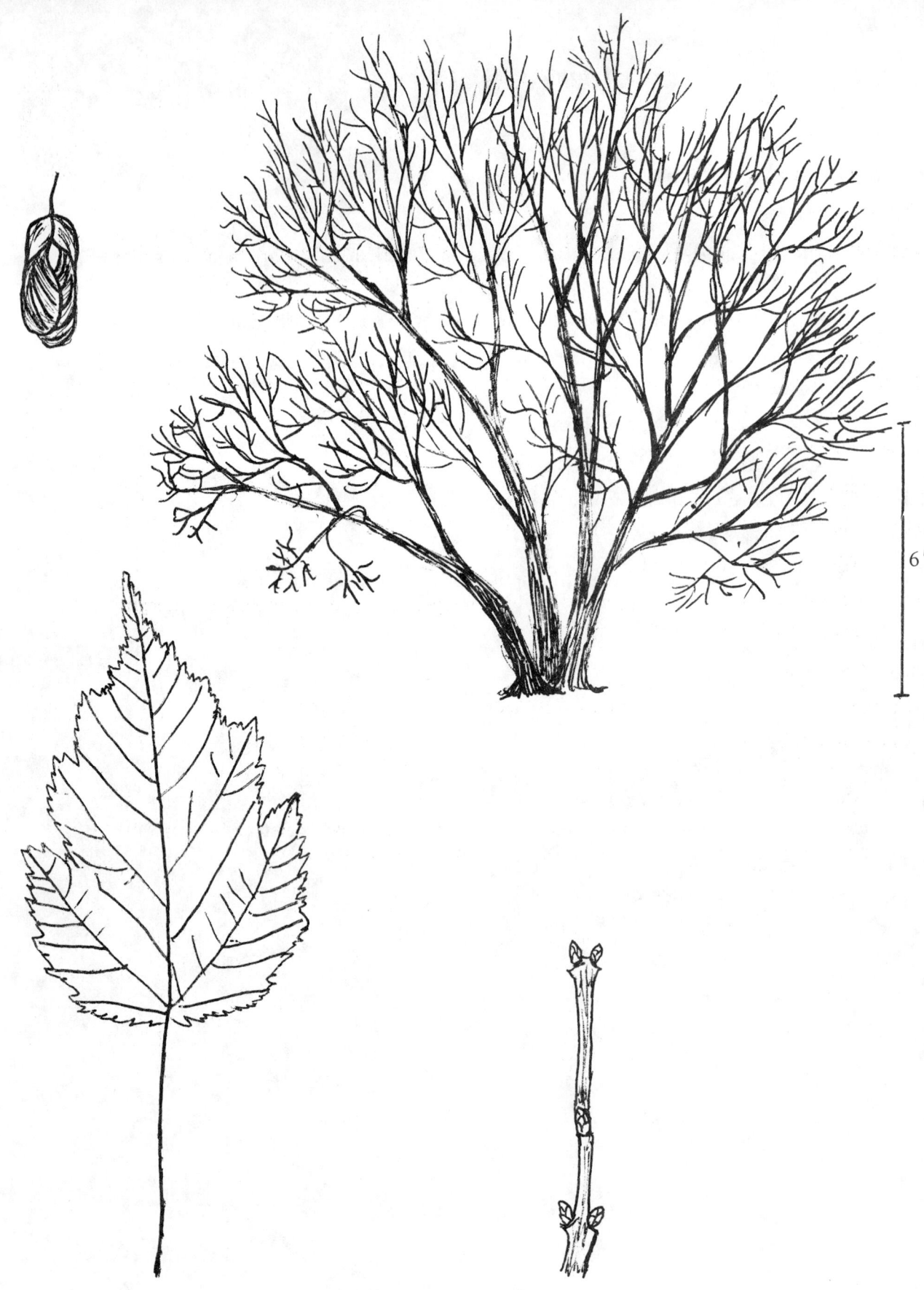

Acer ginnala

8

Acer ginnala

Common Name: Amur Maple

Family: Aceraceae

Foliage: 1 1/2-3 1/2 inches long; usually 3 lobes with the middle lobe elongated; double, irregular teeth; shiny above; red leaf stalk; scarlet or orange-yellow in autumn

Flowers: male and female separate but on the same tree; greenish yellow clusters; fragrant; April-June

Fruit: 1 inch samara; wings almost parallel; turns red in summer; ripens August-September; persists into winter

Buds: brown; several scales

Twigs: slender; reddish brown

Bark: thin; brownish gray

Roots: fibrous; transplants well

Growth Habit: 15-20 feet in height; round to vase shaped crown; dense branching; upright; often with multiple trunks

Hardiness: zone 2

Site: moist, well-drained soil; sun or partial shade

Growth Rate: moderate

Maintenance: clean; tolerant to pruning

Propagtion: seed—fall sow with dry seed and mulch, or mechanically scarify then stratify in sand at 68°F for 30 days, then at 36-40°F for 90-180 days

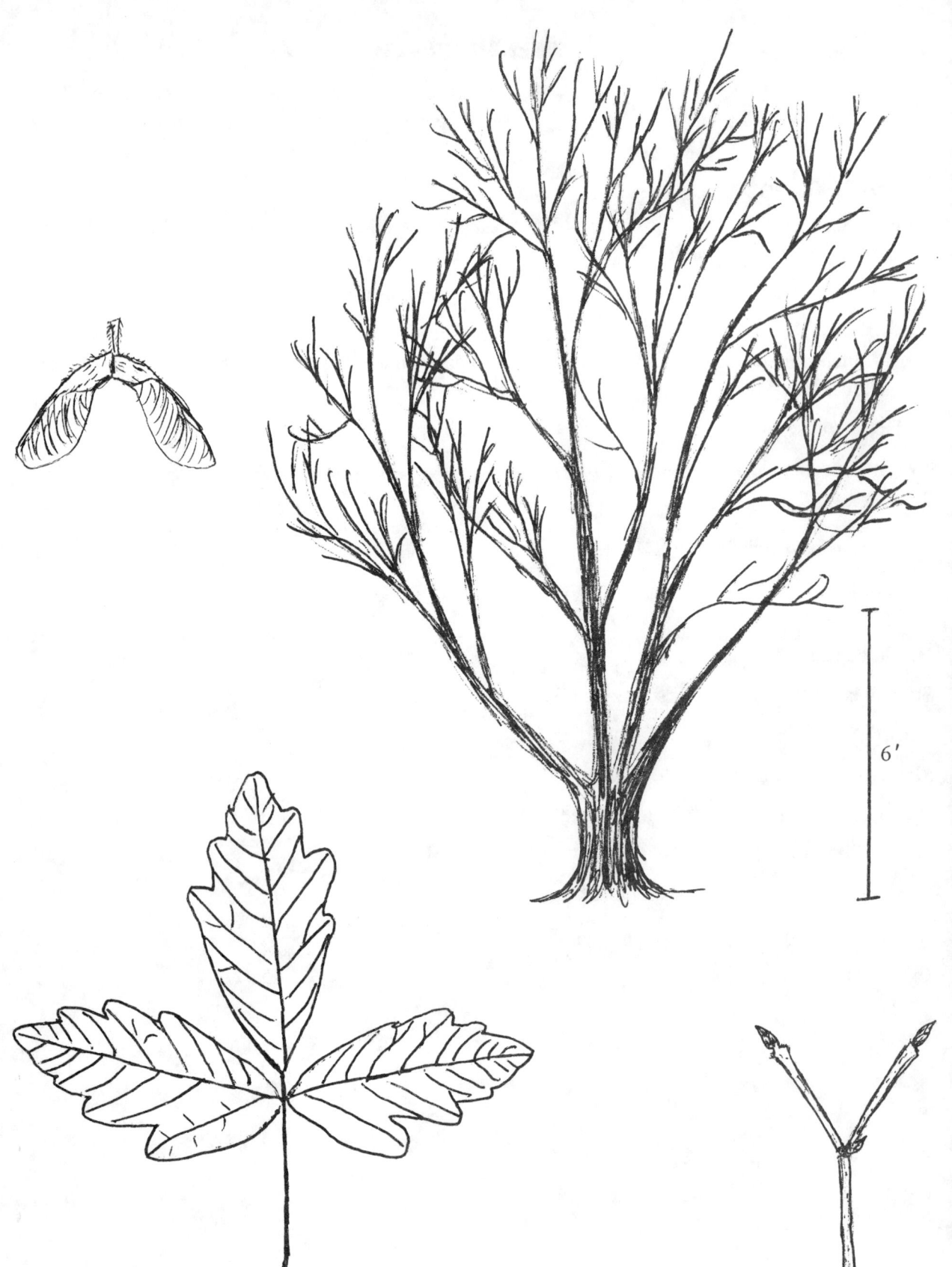

Acer griseum

Acer griseum

Common Name: Paperbark Maple

Family: Aceraceae

Foliage: 3 leaflets; each leaflet 2 inches long; middle leaflet with a short stalk; coarse, blunt teeth; gray-green beneath; hairy leaf stalk; orange-red to gold in autumn

Flowers: greenish yellow clusters; hairy; short stalked

Fruit: 1 inch samara; wings at right angle; pendulous

Buds: small; sharply pointed; dark brown

Twigs: slender; hairy above leaf scar; dark brown

Bark: cinnamon brown; peeling in thin strips

Roots: frequently taprooted; can be difficult to transplant

Growth Habit: 15-20 feet in height; open, round crown

Hardiness: zone 5

Site: tolerant to many soil types; prefers well-drained soil; sun or partial shade

Growth Rate: slow

Maintenance: clean; fairly tolerant to pruning

Propagation: seed is slow to develop and frequently not viable; softwood cuttings

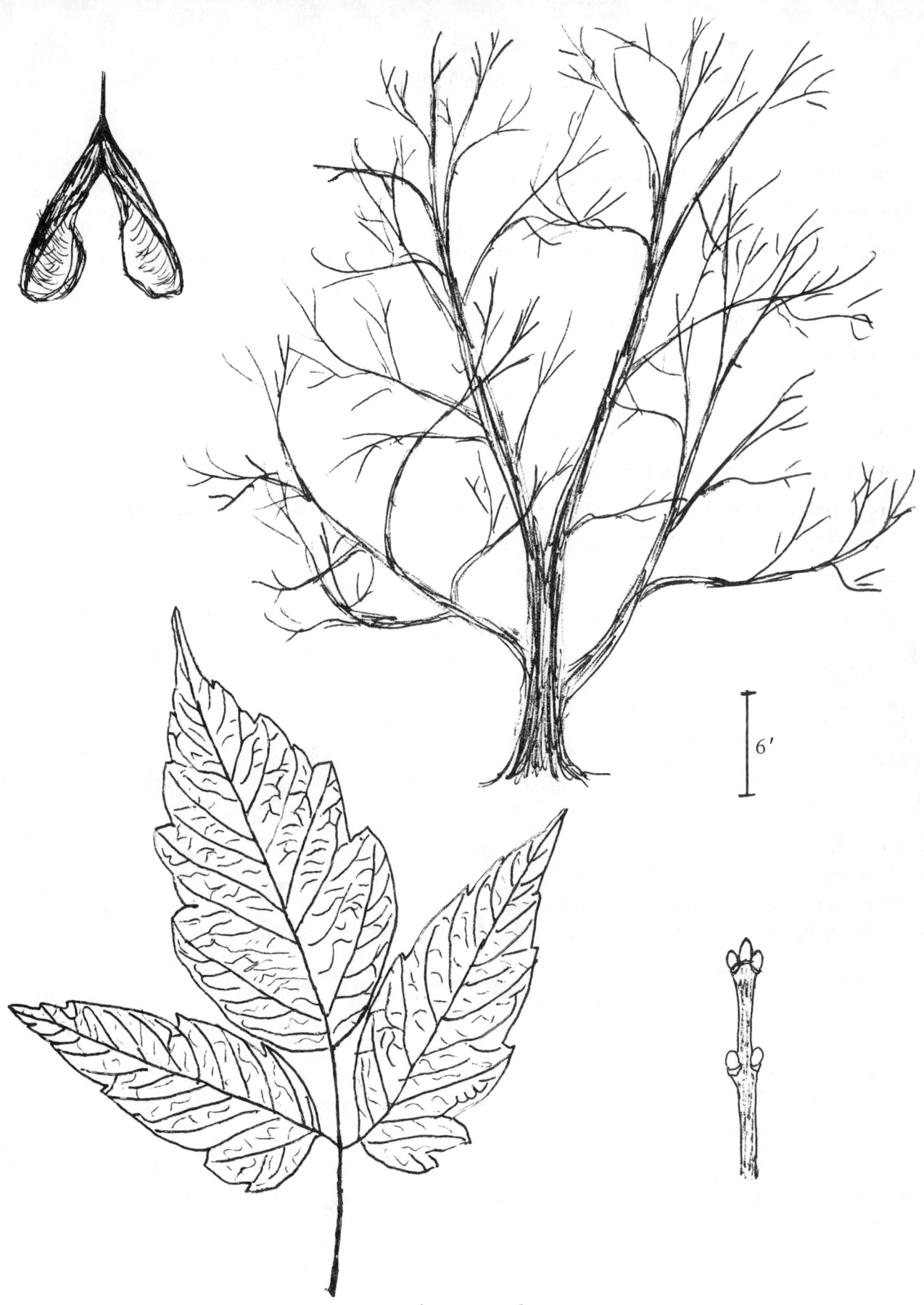

Acer negundo

Acer negundo

Common Name: Box-Elder; Ash-leaved Maple

Family: Aceraceae

Foliage: 3-7 leaflets; 3-4 inches long; coarse teeth; sometimes lobed; yellow in autumn

Fruit: 1-1 1/4 inch samara; V shaped; narrow wings; in drooping clusters; ripens August-October; often persists in winter

Buds: short stalked; 2 dull, red scales; more or less white fuzzy

Twigs: moderately stout; green; smooth; glossy or often with white bloom that rubs off

Bark: light gray; thin; furrows with round ridges

Roots: fibrous; shallow; transplants well

Growth Habit: 40-60 feet in height; broad crown that divides near the ground into several widespreading branches; usually very irregular

Hardiness: zone 2

Site: prefers moisture but is drought tolerant on poor soils; will tolerate flooding; sun or shade

Growth Rate: rapid

Maintenance: weak wood; fruit can be messy; tolerant to pruning

Propagation: seed—fall sow with dry seed and mulch, or mechanically scarify then stratify in sand/peat mixture at 34-41° F for 40-60 days; suckers; softwood cuttings; graft or bud on *A. negundo* or *A. saccharinum* understock

Selections: 'Crispum Variegatum' — wrinkled foliage with yellow variegations
'Rubescens' — young foliage reddish
'Variegatum' — white variegated foliage
var. *violaceum* — purplish twigs often with a white bloom; 5-7 leaflets

Acer nigrum

14

Acer nigrum

Common Name: Black Maple

Family: Aceraceae

Foliage: 3-6 inches long; 3 lobes; broad, shallow sinuses; more shallow sinuses than *A. saccharum;* thick; dark, dull green above; lighter and hairy beneath; drooping edges; hairy leaf stalk; yellow in autumn

Flowers: male and female in one flower or separate; yellowish green; April-May

Fruit: 1 inch samara; parallel wings; ripens in September

Buds: sharp terminal; hairy; black

Twigs: slender; brown; dull; pale lenticels

Bark: dark gray to black; furrowed and scaly

Roots: fibrous; transplants well

Growth Habit: 50-65 feet in height; oval, compact crown; upright, spreading branches

Hardiness: zone 3

Site: rich, moist, well-drained soil; tolerant to drought; sun or shade

Growth Rate: moderate

Maintenance: clean; fairly tolerant to pruning

Propagation: seed—fall sow with dry seed and mulch, or stratify in sand or peat at 33-41 °F for 40-90 days; seed may benefit by a warm stratification prior to cold; graft or bud on *A. nigrum* understock

Selections: 'Slavin's Upright' — upright habit; rapid growth rate

Acer palmatum

Acer palmatum

Common Name: Japanese Maple

Family: Aceraceae

Foliage: 4-5 inches long; 5-11 long pointed lobes; double teeth; sinuses reach more than halfway to the middle of the leaf; hairless or with axillary tufts; red in autumn

Flowers: erect cluster; purple; June

Fruit: 3/4 inch samara; widespreading wings; tinged with red; ripens September

Buds: small; plump; pointed; brown

Twigs: slender

Bark: dark reddish gray; tight and firm

Roots: fibrous; often difficult to transplant

Growth Habit: 10-20 feet in height; round crown; ascending, spreading branches; often as broad as it is high

Hardiness: zone 5

Site: rich, well-drained soil; sun or partial shade

Growth Rate: slow

Maintenance: frost injury; intolerant to pruning

Propagation: seed—fall sow dry seed and mulch, or soak in water at 110° F for 2 days and/or stratify in sand at 41° F for 90 days; softwood cuttings; graft or bud on *A. palmatum* understock

Selections: 'Atropurpureum' — very hardy; dark red foliage; small leaves with 5 main lobes
'Sanguineum' — 5 main lobes; small, scarlet red foliage with green beneath
var. *heptalobum* — 7 lobes; large leaves
var. *dissectum* — cutleaf foliage; pendulous branches; 7, 9, or 11 lobes

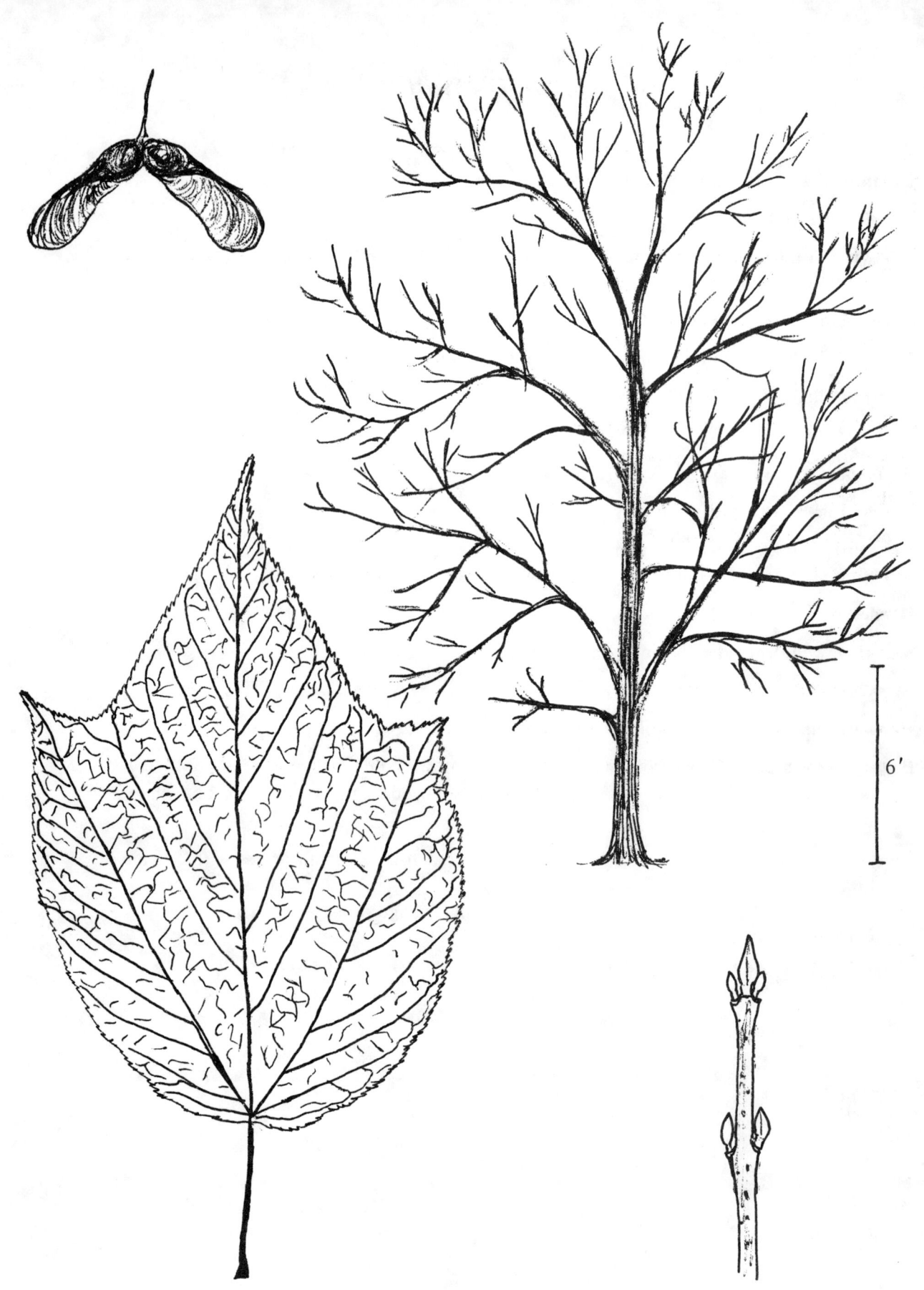

Acer pensylvanicum

Acer pensylvanicum

Common Name: Moosewood; Striped Maple

Family: Aceraceae

Foliage: 5-8 inches long; short lobes; 3 main veins; rounded base; slightly coarse; double teeth; thin; stout leaf stalks; yellow in autumn

Flowers: male and female separate but on the same tree; drooping clusters; yellow; May-June

Fruit: 1 inch samara; wings at a wide angle; red-brown; ripens September-October

Buds: 2 scales; on short stalks; green and red

Twigs: slender; smooth; mottled; green

Bark: thin; green with vertical white stripes

Roots: fibrous; difficult to transplant

Growth Habit: 20-30 feet in height; broad, oval crown; erect branches

Hardiness: zone 3

Site: moist, rich soil; cool; shade

Growth Rate: slow to moderate

Maintenance: clean; fairly tolerant to pruning

Propagation: seed—fall sow dry seed and mulch, or stratify 90-120 days at 41°F; seed may benefit by a warm stratification prior to cold treatment

Acer platanoides

20

Acer platanoides

Common Name: Norway Maple

Family: Aceraceae

Foliage: 3-6 inches long; 5-7 lobes; rectangular; more teeth than *A. saccharum;* wider than long; milky juice; bright green on both surfaces; yellow in autumn

Flowers: male and female in one flower or separate; yellowish green; in drooping clusters; late April

Fruit: 2 inch samara; widespreading wings which are almost horizontal; ripens September

Buds: blunt; plump and round; few scales; greenish brown

Twigs: stout; smooth; brown; milky sap

Bark: nearly black; shallow ridges

Roots: fibrous; shallow; transplants well

Growth Habit: 40-90 feet in height; broad, rounded, fairly symmetrical crown

Hardiness: zone 3

Site: rich, moist soil; tolerant to dry sites; sun

Growth Rate: moderate

Maintenance: clean; fairly tolerant to pruning

Propagation: seed—fall sow dry seed and mulch, or stratify in sand or peat at 41° F for 90-120 days; graft or bud on *A. platanoides* understock

Selections: 'Almira' — weeping branches
    'Charles F. Irish' — round crown
    'Cleveland' — upright, oval crown
    'Columnare' — compact, columnar habit
    'Crimson King' — deep red foliage
    'Crimson Sentry' — upright; red foliage
    'Drummondii' — white margins on foliage
    'Emerald Queen' — upright, oval habit; larger leaves; rapid growth rate
    'Erectum' — upright crown with short, erect branches
    'Faassen's Black' — reddish foliage
    'Globosum' — short, globose crown
    'Goldsworth Purple' — reddish purple foliage
    'Greenlace' — cut foliage; upright crown
    'Miller's Superform' — upright; rapid growth rate
    'Lorbergii' — cut foliage; round crown; slow growth rate
    'Palmatifidum' — cut foliage
    'Royal Red' — red foliage; more heat resistant than other red forms
    'Rubrum' — foliage dark red in autumn
    'Schwedleri' — reddish purple in spring becoming more green in summer
    'Summershade' — upright; leathery foliage; rapid growth rate
    'Undulatum' — upright; leaves in horizontal planes

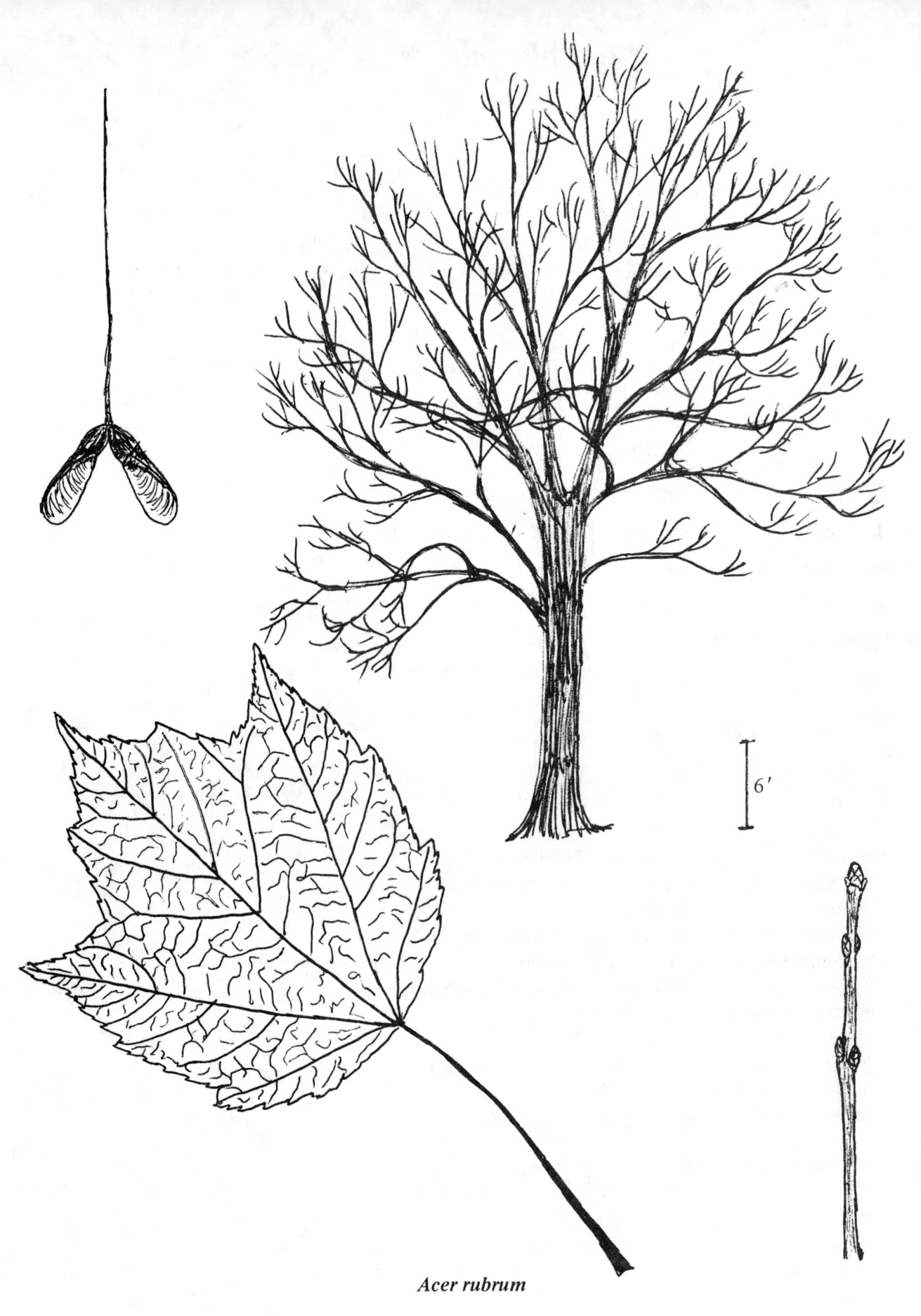

Acer rubrum

Acer rubrum

Common Name: Red Maple; Scarlet Maple; Swamp Maple

Family: Aceraceae

Foliage: 2-6 inches long; 3 triangular lobes; small teeth; wide sinuses; bright green above; pale and usually whitish below with hair; sometimes with reddish veins and leaf stalks; red in autumn

Flowers: male and female in one flower or in separate; reddish petals; clusters; March-May

Fruit: 3/4 inch samara; wings at right angles; scarlet; drooping stalk that may be 4-6 inches long; seed is dark red; ripens April-June

Buds: blunt; several scales; often clustered; reddish

Twigs: slender; reddish; shiny

Bark: smooth becoming roughened into long, scaly ridges; gray

Roots: fibrous; transplants well

Growth Habit: 50-70 feet in height; oval or round crown with upright branching

Hardiness: zone 3

Site: prefers moist, rich soil; shade

Growth Rate: moderate to rapid

Maintenance: clean; fairly tolerant to pruning

Propagation: seed—sow fresh; cuttings; graft or bud on *A. rubrum* or *A. saccharinum* understock

Selections: 'Armstrong' — narrow, upright crown; rapid growth rate
'Autumn Flame' — round crown; bright red autumn color
'Autumn Glory' — good fall color
'Bowhall' — pyramidal crown; good fall color
'Columnare' — upright, columnar habit
'October Glory' — red in autumn; retains foliage longer
'Schlesingeri' — early autumn color
'Tilford' — globose crown
'Wageri' — weeping twigs

Acer saccharinum

Acer saccharinum

Common Name: Silver Maple

Family: Aceraceae

Foliage: 4-5 inches long; 5-7 deep lobes; rounded sinuses; base of lobe ends narrowed; irregular teeth; pale green above; whitish below; reddish leaf stalk; yellow or orange in autumn

Flowers: male and female in one flower or separate; small; yellowish green; March-April

Fruit: 1 1/2-2 inch samara; thin wings; slender, drooping stalks; ripens May-June; pale brown when ripe; one embryo is often aborted

Buds: red; blunt; 2-4 scales with hairy margins

Twigs: slender; reddish; odor when broken

Bark: gray; smooth becoming loosely plated

Roots: fibrous; widespreading; transplants well

Growth Habit: 75-100 feet in height; low branched; widespreading, round or broad crown; lower branches droop

Hardiness: zone 3

Site: rich, moist, well-drained soil; will tolerate drought and heat; sun or partial shade

Growth Rate: rapid

Maintenance: brittle; fairly tolerant of pruning

Propagation: seed—spring sow only, do not allow the wings to dry out; cuttings; graft or bud on *A. rubrum* or *A. saccharinum* understock

Selections: 'Fastigiata' — upright columnar
'Laciniatum' — cut foliage; weeping branches
'Pendulum' — weeping branches
'Pyramidale' — pyramidal crown
'Silver Queen' — seedless; cut foliage
'Tripartitum' — large foliage divided into 3, broad lobes

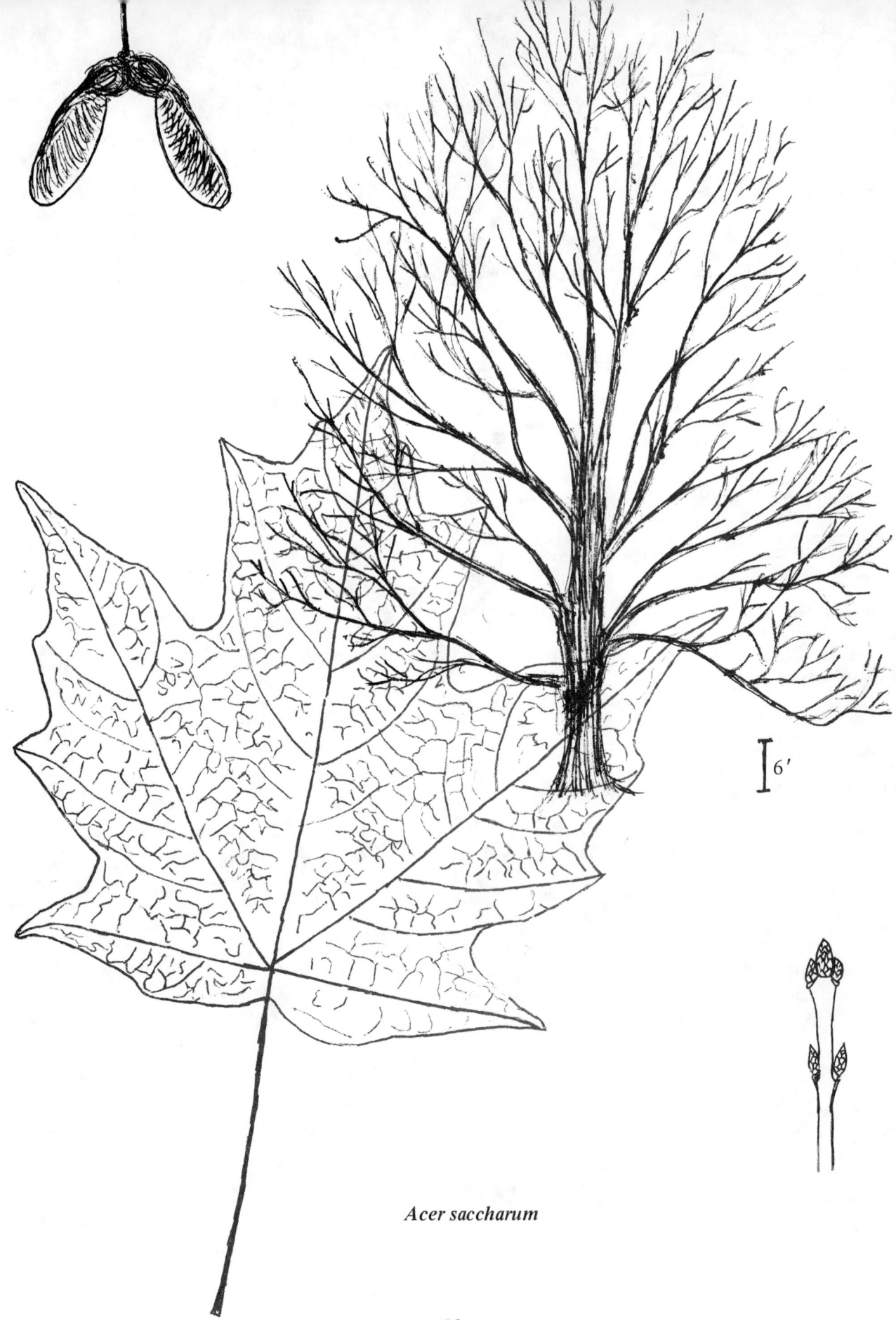

Acer saccharum

26

Acer saccharum

Common Name: Sugar Maple

Family: Aceraceae

Foliage: 3-6 inches long; 5 lobes; deep, round sinuses; large teeth; 5 main veins; paler green beneath; long, slender leaf stalks; yellow or orange in autumn

Flowers: male and female in one flower or separate flowers; yellowish green; March-May

Fruit: 1-1 1/4 inch samara; U shaped wings; long stalk; ripens September-October

Buds: sharp pointed; dark brown; scale edges hairy

Twigs: slender; smooth; shiny; brown

Bark: dark gray; smooth becoming furrowed and ridged

Roots: fibrous; transplants well

Growth Habit: 75-100 feet in height; upright branching; branching to ground; compact; broad, oval or oblong crown

Hardiness: zone 3

Site: prefers moist, rich well-drained soil, but will grow on poor soils; prefers sun but very shade tolerant

Growth Rate: slow-moderate

Maintenance: clean; fairly tolerant to pruning

Propagation: seed—fall sow dry seed and mulch, or stratify in sand or peat at 33-41°F for 40-90 days; graft or bud on *A. saccharum* understock

Selections: 'Columnare' — upright, dense crown
'Globosum' — dwarf; globular crown
'Green Mountain' — oval crown; retains color under adverse conditions
'Laciniatum' — cut foliage
'Newton Sentry' — columnar; central leader
'Sweet Shadow' — cut foliage
'Temple's Upright' — upright; without a central leader

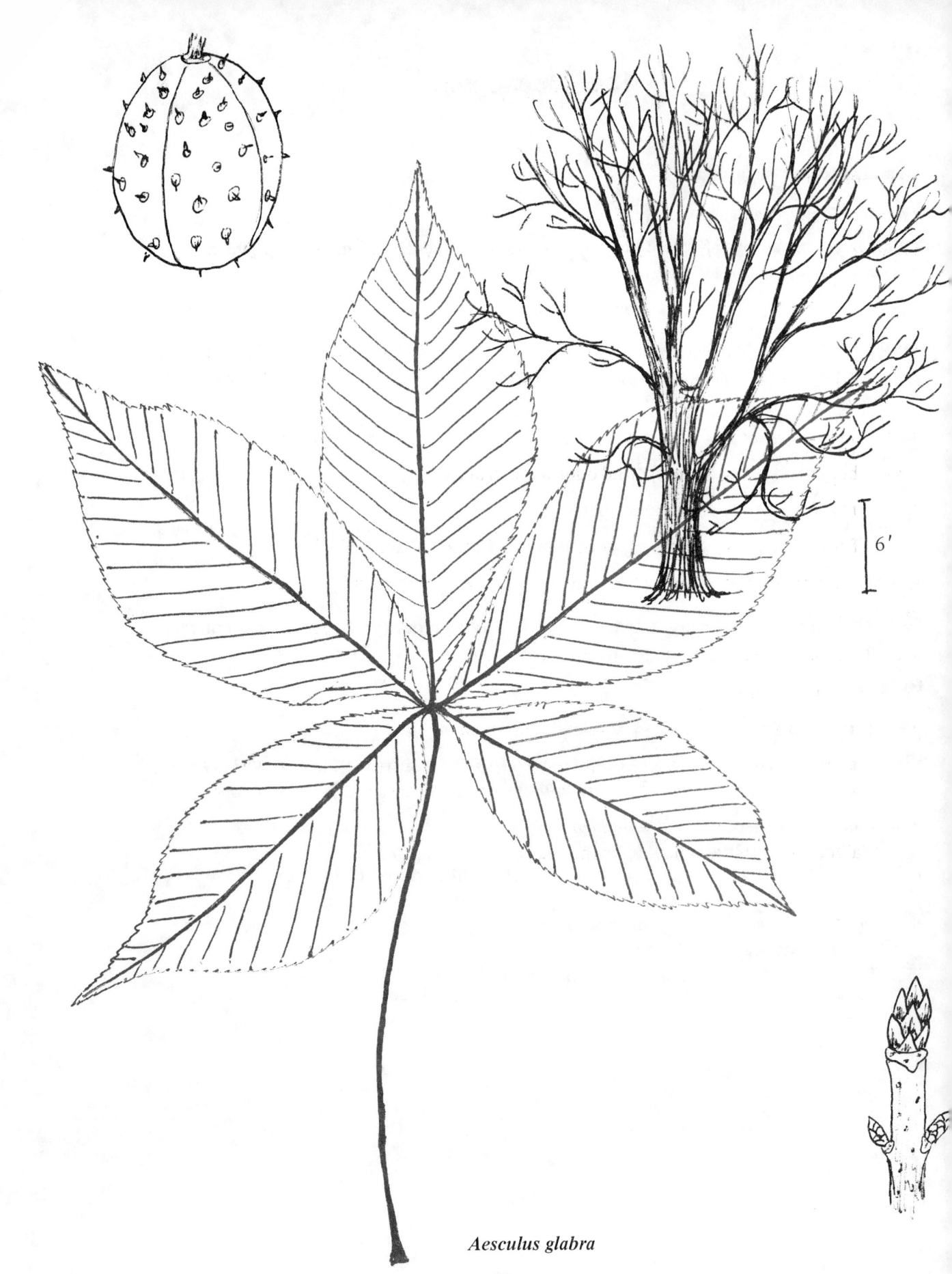

Aesculus glabra

Aesculus glabra

Common Name: Ohio Buckeye

Family: Hippocastanaceae

Foliage: 5 stalked leaflets; 3-5 inches long; fine teeth; hairy beneath when young; yellow or orange in late summer

Flowers: large, loose spikes, erect; white or yellow-green; May

Fruit: 1-1 1/2 inch in diameter; nutlike; irregular shape; small spines on young husks; warty and yellowish when old; 1-3 smooth, shiny seeds; poisonous; ripens September to mid-October

Buds: many ridged scales; underside of scales red; not shiny or gummy; brown

Twigs: brown; scattered lenticels; foul odor when broken

Bark: gray; fissured with roughened plates

Roots: fibrous; shallow; will form taproot in dry soil; transplants well

Growth Habit: 30-35 feet in height; round or oval crown; low branching

Hardiness: zone 3

Site: adaptable to many soils; full sun or parital shade

Growth Rate: moderate

Maintenance: fruit can be messy; will tolerate light pruning

Propagation: seed—fall sow and protect from rodents, or stratify in sand or sand/peat mixture at 41°F for 120 days; root cuttings; graft on *A. glabra* or *A. octandra* understock

Selections: var. *leucodermis* — whitened bark
'Pallida' — persistent hair beneath foliage

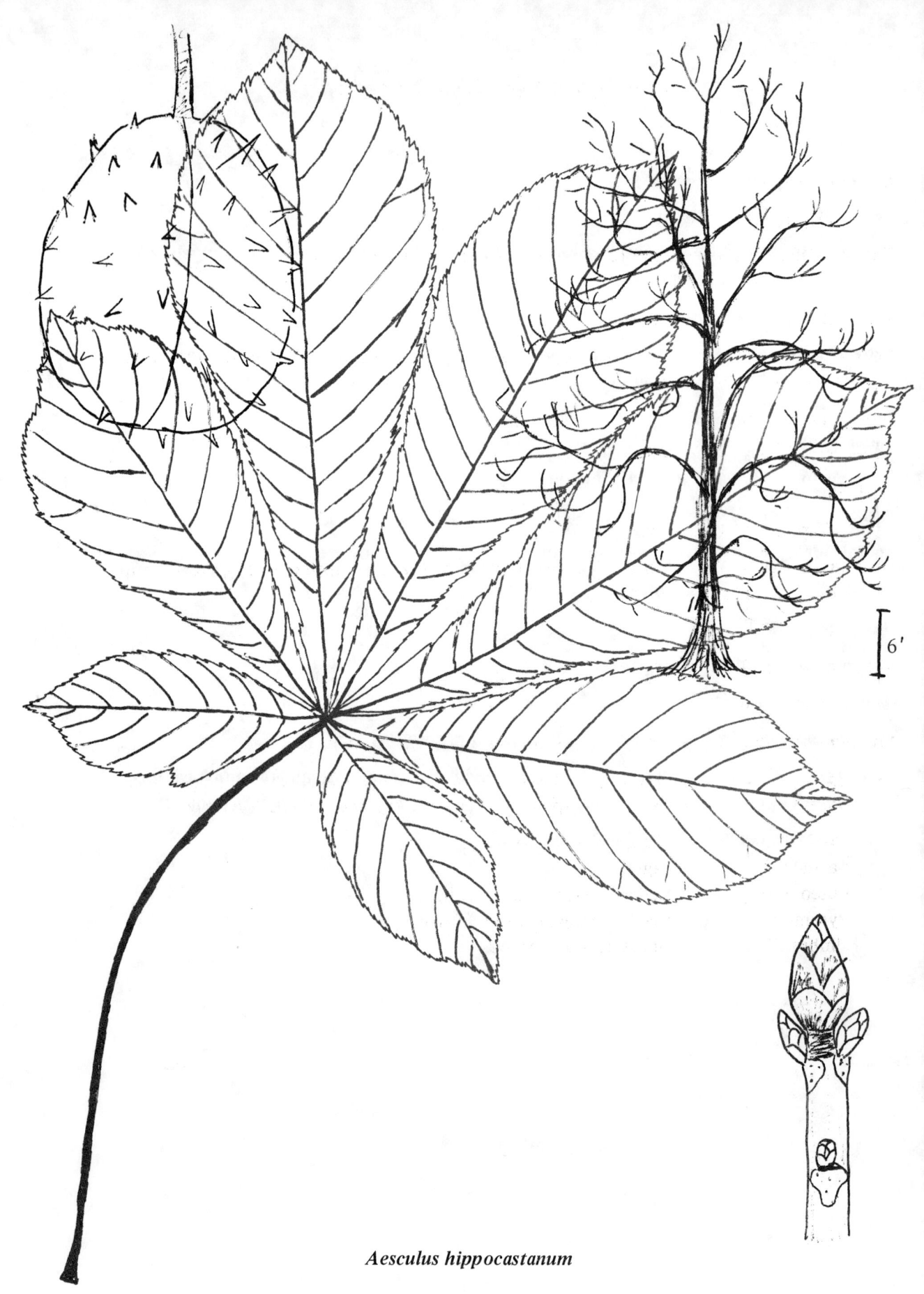

Aesculus hippocastanum

Aesculus hippocastanum

Common Name: Horse Chestnut

Family: Hippocastanaceae

Foliage: 7 leaflets; wider toward the apex; double teeth; no stalklets; rich, bright green; yellow-brown in autumn

Flowers: large, erect panicles; white tinged with yellow, red or purple; April-May

Fruit: approximately 2 inches in diameter; large spines on husk; yellowish brown when ripe; brown seed with a high gloss; ripens mid-September to early October

Buds: smooth; shiny; sticky; dark brown

Twigs: stout; smooth; reddish brown; no foul odor when broken

Bark: dark brown; scaly

Roots: fibrous; transplants well

Growth Habit: 30-65 feet in height; low branching; branches appear to have turned up ends; round top, pyramidal crown

Hardiness: zone 3

Site: moist, well-drained soil; sun

Growth Rate: slow

Maintenance: fruit can be messy; weak wood; tolerates light pruning

Propagation: seed—fall sow and protect from rodents, or stratify in sand or sand/peat mixture at 41°F for 120 days; root cuttings; graft on *A. hippocastanum* understock

Selections: 'Baumannii' — double white flowers; no fruit
'Laciniata' — cut foliage
'Luteo-variegata' — yellow variegations on foliage
'Pyramidalis' — compact, narrow, pyramidal crown
'Umbraculifera' — compact, round crown

Leaf: ½ actual size

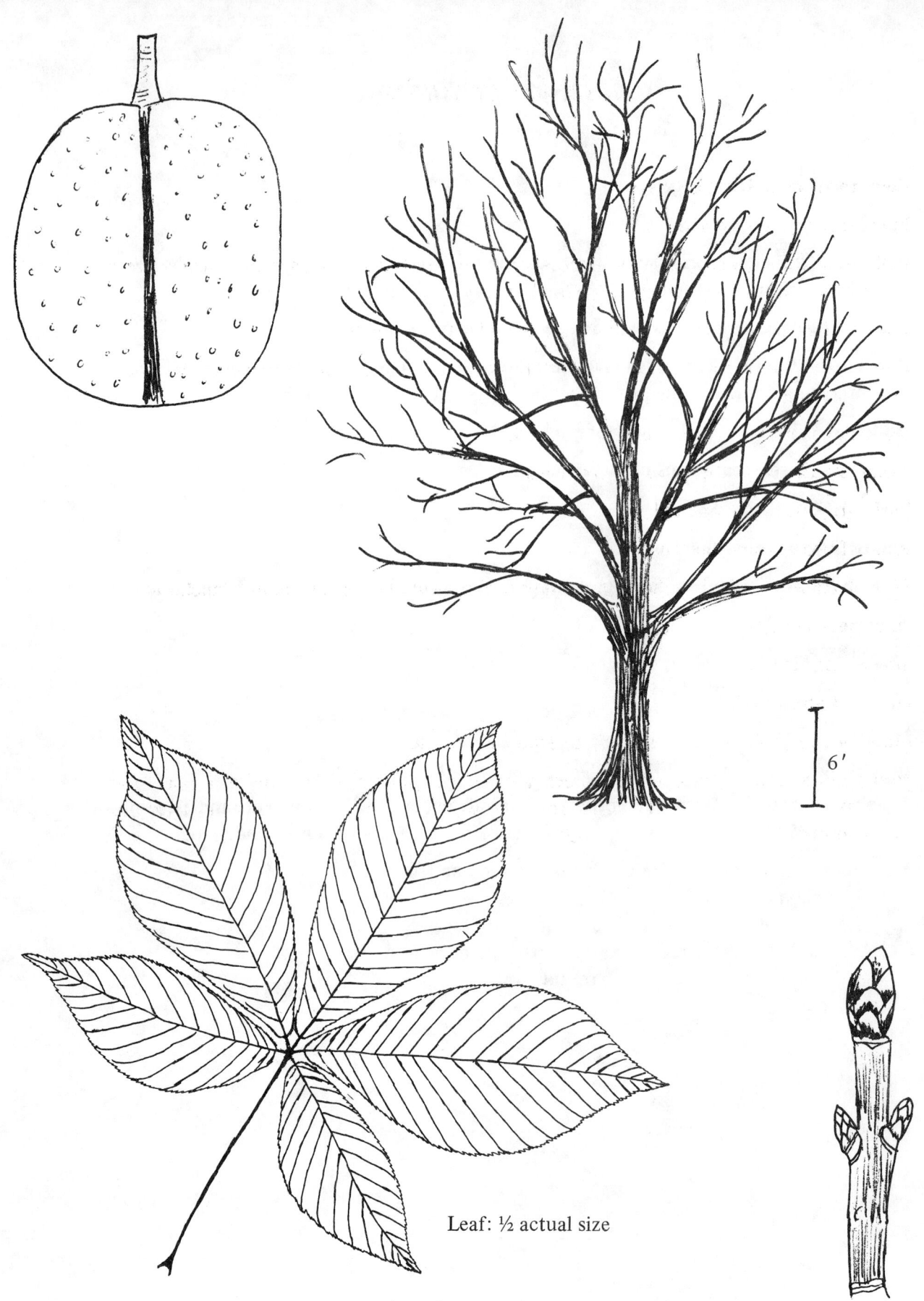

Aesculus octandra

32

Aesculus octandra

Common Name: Sweet Buckeye

Family: Hippocastanaceae

Foliage: 5 leaflets; each leaflet 4-6 inches long; fine teeth; dark green above; yellow-green below; hairy below when young; stalklets present; yellowish in autumn

Flowers: large, erect panicles; yellowish; unequal petals; May-June

Fruit: about 2 inches in diameter; smooth husks with warts; 2 reddish brown seeds; ripens September

Buds: large terminal; grayish brown; not sticky

Twigs: stout; smooth; no odor when crushed

Bark: gray; irregularly plated

Roots: fibrous; transplants well

Growth Habit: 50-60 feet in height; round to oval crown; upright, spreading branches

Hardiness: zone 3

Site: moist, rich soil; sun

Growth Rate: slow

Maintenance: fruit can be messy; will tolerate light pruning

Propagation: seed—fall sow and protect from rodents, or stratify in sand or a sand/peat mixture at 41° F for 120 days; root cuttings; graft on *A. octandra* or *A. glabra* understock

Leaf: ½ actual size

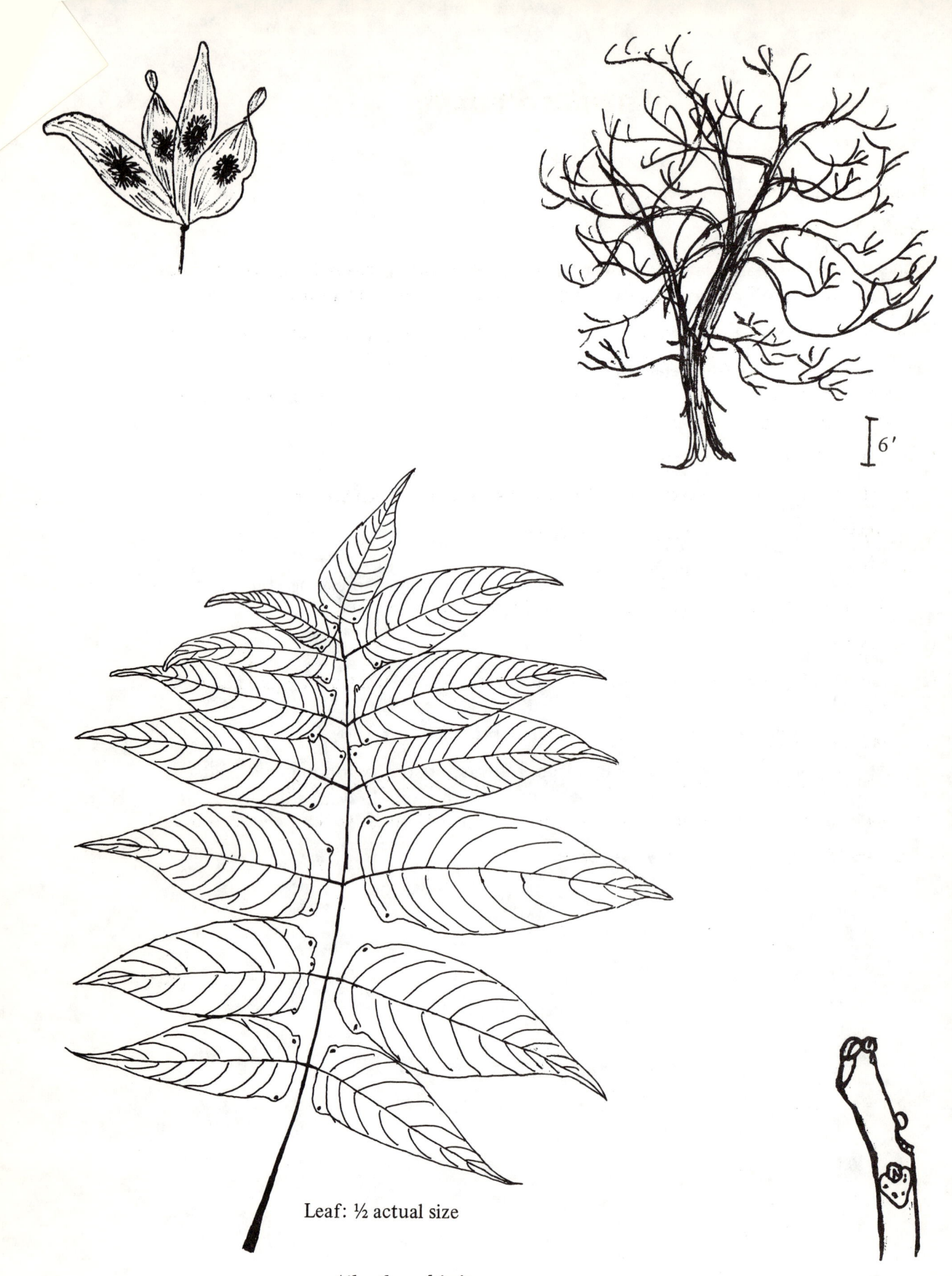

Ailanthus altissima

34

Ailanthus altissima

Common Name: Tree of Heaven

Family: Simaroubaceae

Foliage: 13-25 leaflets; each leaflet 2-5 inches long; entire margin except for 1-3 blunt, glandular teeth at leaflet base; odor when crushed; orange or green in autumn

Flowers: male and female separate on separate trees; male flowers have a foul odor; clusters up to 12 inches long; produced terminally; yellowish green; July

Fruit: 1-1 1/2 inch samara in spirally twisted clusters; red seed in center of oblong, green wing; ripens September-October

Buds: no terminal; small; brown

Twigs: stout; light brown; velvety; large leaf scars; strong odor when broken

Bark: gray; smooth becoming shallowly furrowed

Roots: fibrous; spreading; transplants well

Growth Habit: 40-70 feet in height; open, irregular crown; suckers freely

Hardiness: zone 4

Site: tolerant of many soils; sun or partial shade; extremely tolerant of city and industrial areas

Growth Rate: rapid

Maintenance: control suckers; abundant fruit production; tolerant to pruning

Propagation: seed—fall sow dry seed, or stratify in sand at 41°F for 60 days; root cuttings

Selections: 'Pendulifolia' — drooping leaves

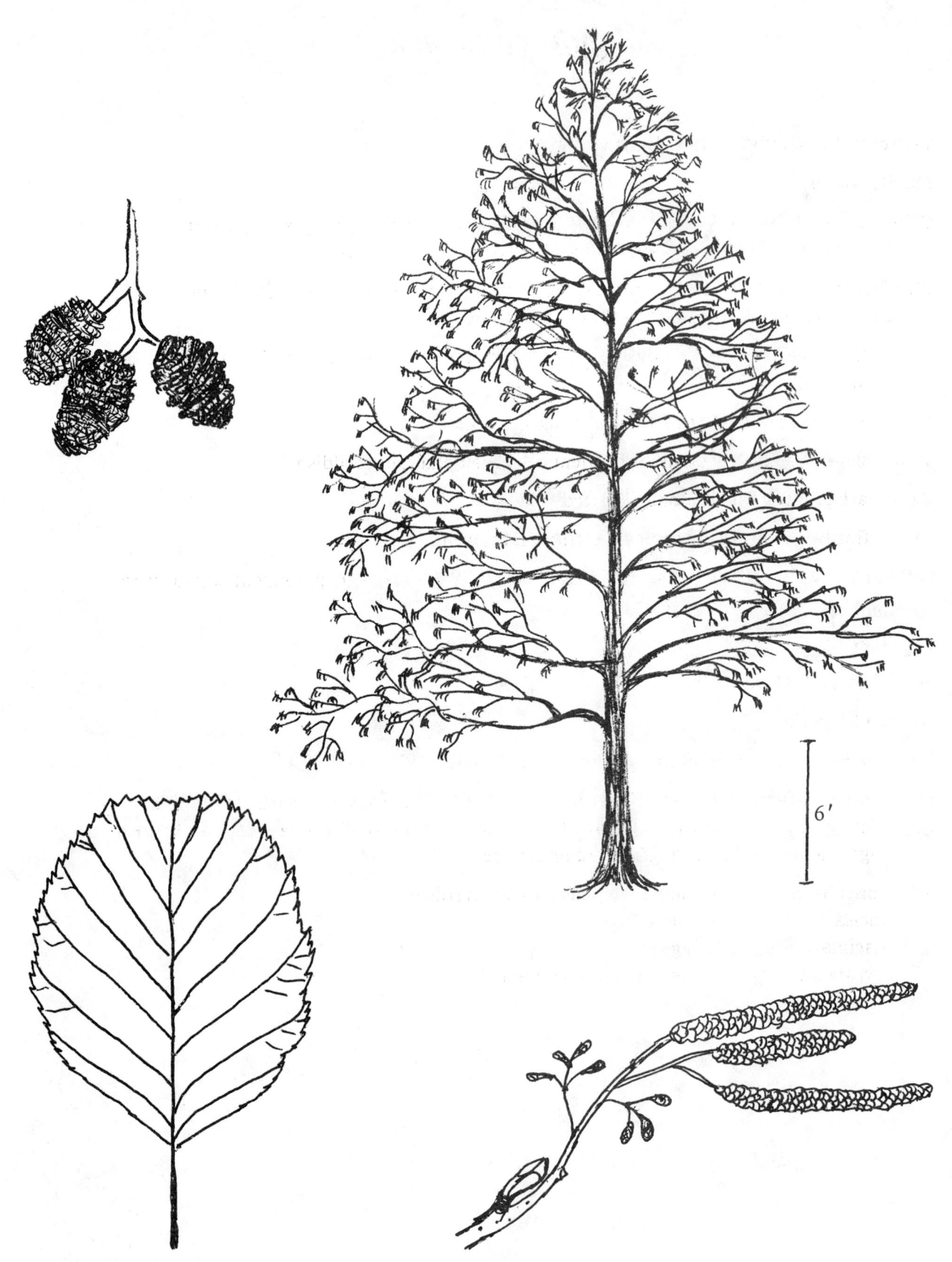

Alnus glutinosa

36

Alnus glutinosa

Common Name: Black Alder; European Alder

Family: Betulaceae

Foliage: 2-4 inches long; almost round; double, coarse teeth; slightly sticky when young; axillary tufts of hair beneath; dark green; drops while still green

Flowers: male and female separate on same tree; pendent; female: brown catkins in clusters of 3-5; male: red catkins in clusters of 3-7; March-May

Fruit: 1/2-3/4 inch woody cone; stalked; winged nutlets within; persistent; ripens in autumn

Buds: terminal absent; laterals stalked; oval; 2-3 scales; pinkish

Twigs: slender; slightly gummy; raised lenticels; triangular pith; reddish

Bark: dark gray; smooth becoming plated

Roots: fibrous; shallow and spreading; transplants well

Growth Habit: 30-45 feet in height; spreading branches; irregular, pyramidal crown; very dense; often with multiple trunks

Hardiness: zone 3

Site: wet soil; full sun

Growth Rate: rapid

Maintenance: clean; tolerant to pruning

Propagation: seed—fresh seed will germinate without a pretreatment; dried seed should be stratified in a moist medium at 41°F for 180 days followed by 3 days at −4°F; cuttings; suckers; graft on *A. glutinosa* understock

Selections: 'Imperialis' — small, very deep lobes on foliage
'Incisa' — deep lobes on foliage
'Laciniata' — cut foliage
'Pyramidalis' — narrow, pyramidal crown

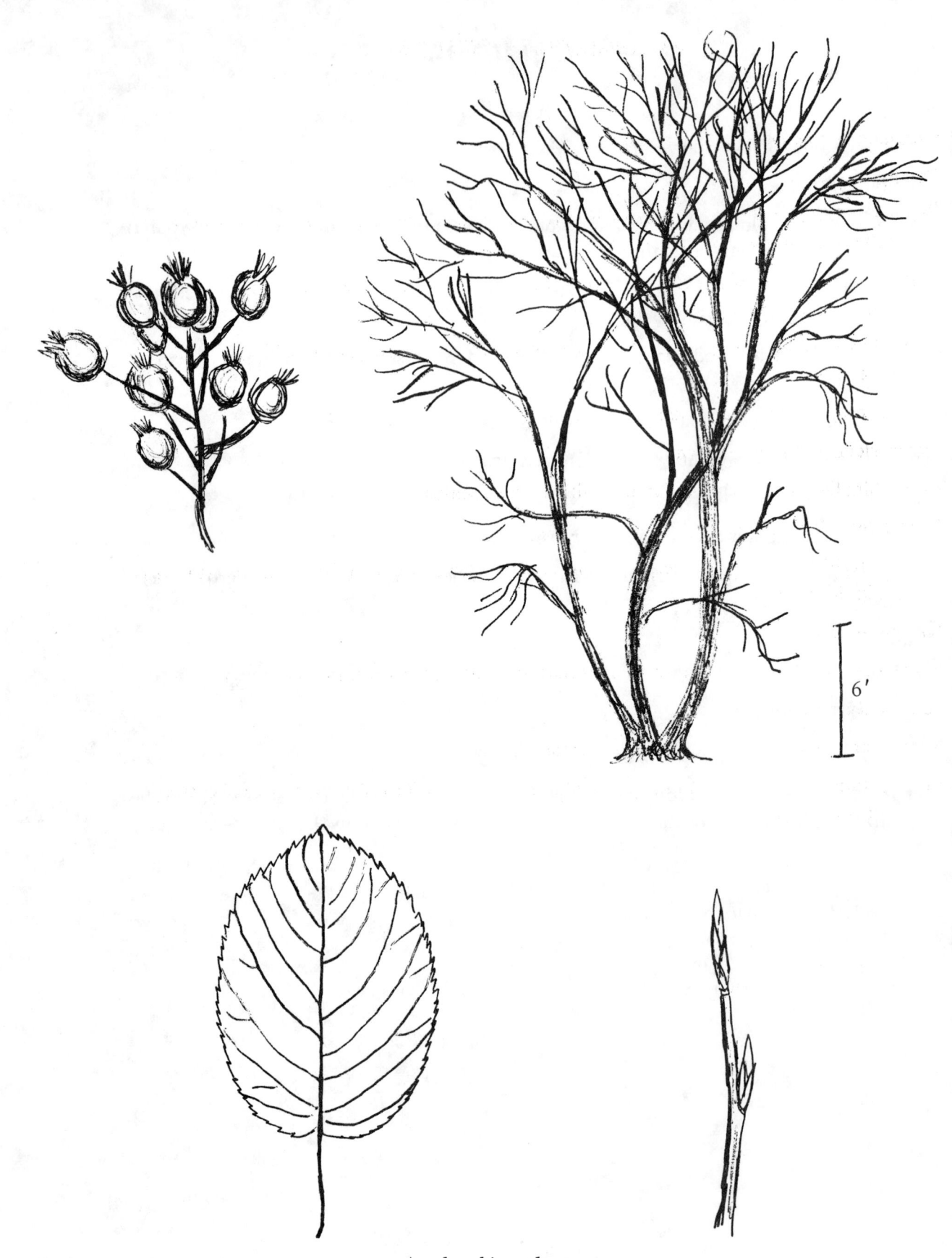

Amelanchier arborea

Amelanchier arborea

Common Name: Downy Serviceberry

Family: Rosaceae

Foliage: 2 1/2-3 inches long; sharp teeth; round or heart shape base; hairy veins beneath; dull green; orange or red in autumn

Flowers: 4-10 flowers per cluster; covered with silky down; white, sometimes with a pinkish cast; March-June

Fruit: 1/4-1/2 inch pome; reddish purple; bloomy; dry inside; hardly edible; ripens late June-August

Buds: chestnut-brown; long pointed

Twigs: slender; reddish brown

Bark: thin; light gray; shallow furrows with narrow, scaly ridges

Roots: deep fibrous

Growth Habit: 20-60 feet in height; open, round crown, ascending branches; usually with multiple trunks

Hardiness: zone 4

Site: moist, well-drained, rich soil; sun or partial shade; protect from strong winds

Growth Rate: moderate-rapid

Maintenance: clean; fairly tolerant to pruning

Propagation: seed—stratify in a moist medium at 41°F for 90-120 days; softwood cuttings; root cuttings

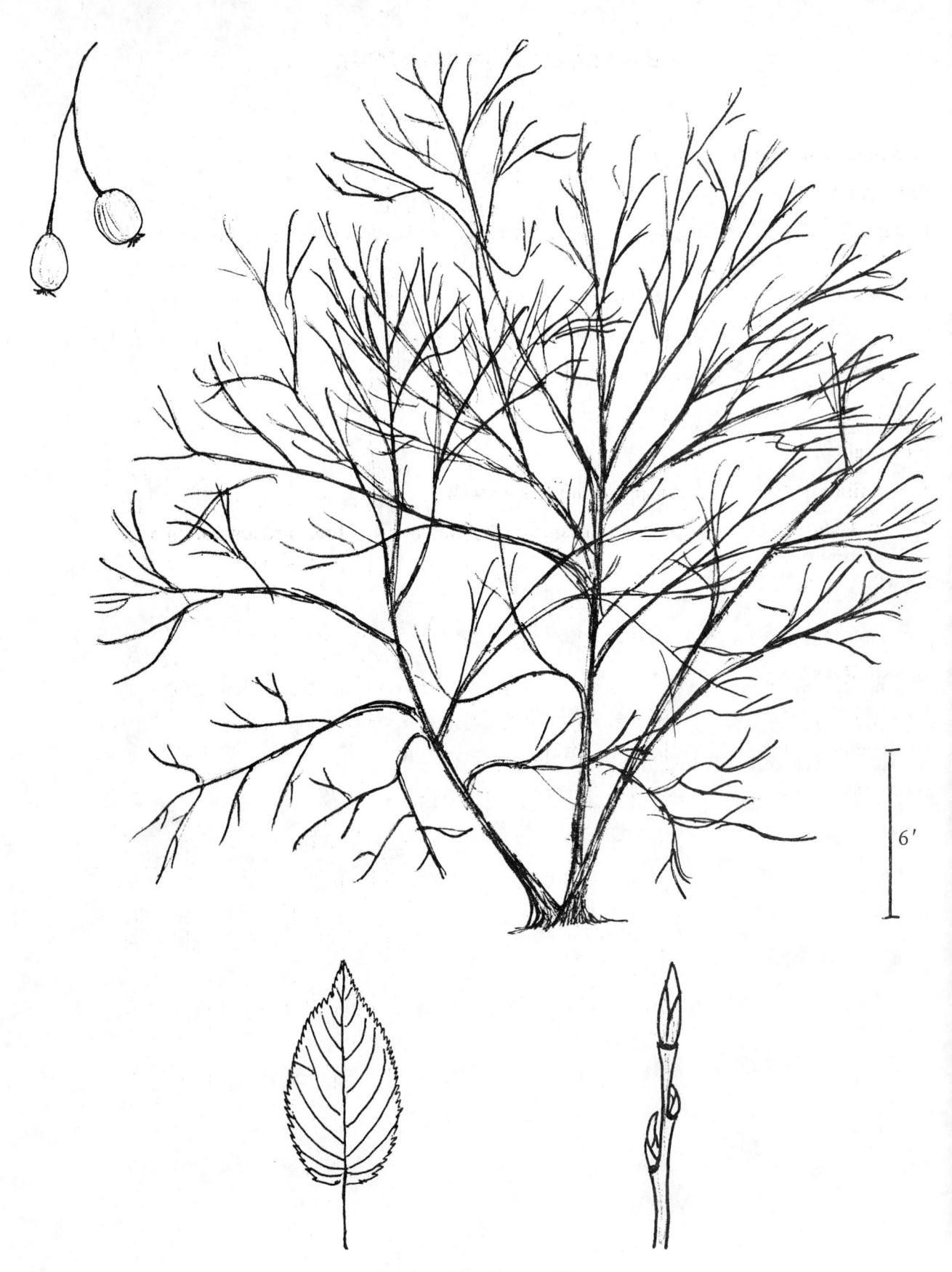

Amelanchier X *grandiflora*

40

Amelanchier X grandiflora

Common Name: Apple Serviceberry

Family: Rosaceae

Foliage: 1-1 1/2 inches long; small teeth; dense; young leaves reddish and fuzzy; shiny; yellow or orange in autumn

Flowers: in clusters; white; early May

Fruit: 1/4 inch pome; juicy and edible; red to black; ripens May-June

Buds: slender; sharply pointed; reddish brown; pink flower buds

Twigs: slender; reddish brown

Bark: light gray

Roots: fibrous; spreading; transplants moderately well

Growth Habit: 25-30 feet in height; widespreading, round crown; branched low; often with multiple trunks

Hardiness: zone 4

Site: poor soil; sun or partial shade; shelter from strong winds

Growth Rate: slow to moderate

Maintenance: clean; moderate tolerance to pruning

Propagation: softwood cuttings; root cuttings

Selections: 'Rubescens' — pinkish flowers when first open

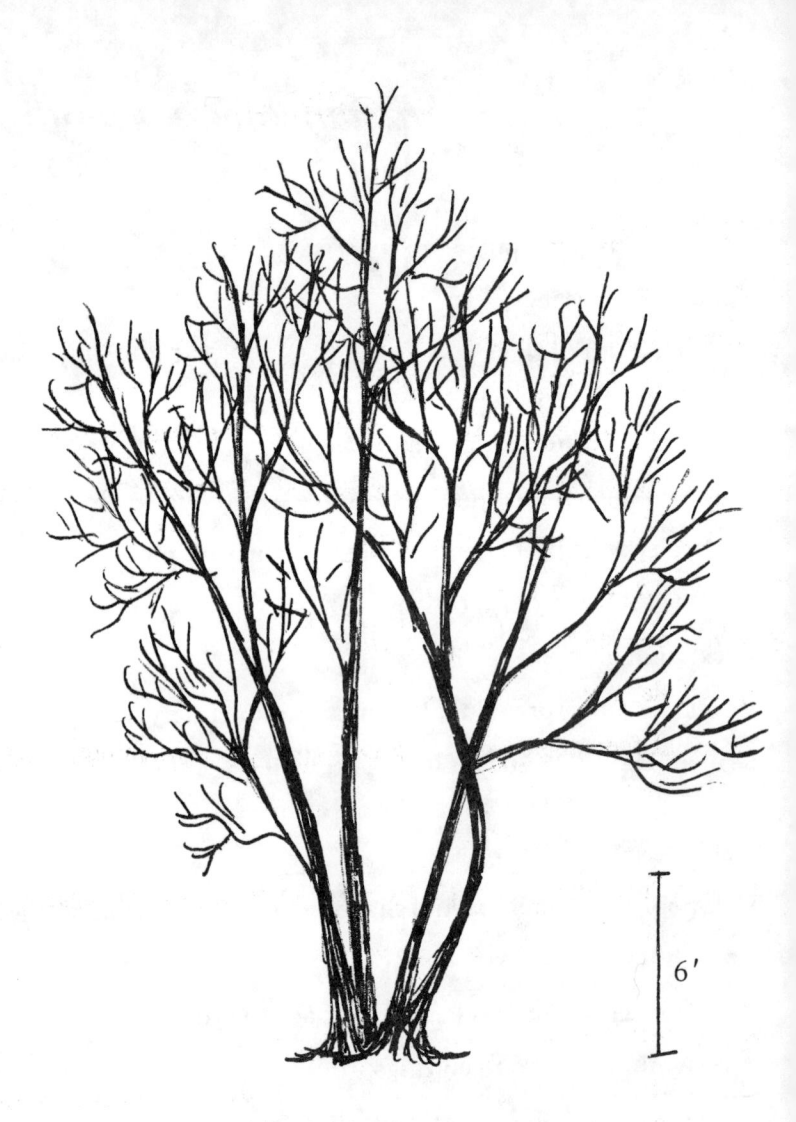

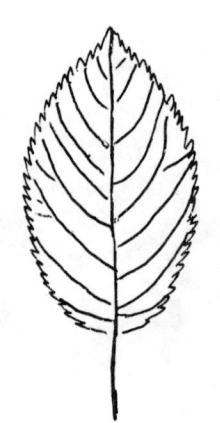

Amelanchier laevis

42

Amelanchier laevis

Common Name: Smooth Northern Shadbush; Allegheny Serviceberry

Family: Rosaceae

Foliage: 1 1/2-2 inches long; rounded base; fine teeth; smooth; young leaves purplish bronze; copper in autumn

Flowers: small; in clusters; white; May

Fruit: small, purple pome; sweet and edible; 1-2 inch stalk; ripens June-July

Buds: long pointed; tinged with red

Twigs: slender, purplish brown

Bark: light gray; smooth becoming darker and scaly

Roots: shallow; spreading; transplants well

Growth Habit: 15-40 feet in height; upright, spreading, irregular crown; sometimes with multiple trunks

Hardiness: zone 4

Site: deep, rich, moist soil preferred but will tolerate alkaline and acid soils; sun or shade; shelter from strong winds

Growth Rate: moderate-rapid

Maintenance: clean; intolerant to pruning

Propagation: seed—scarify in sulfuric acid then stratify in moist medium at 41° F for 90-120 days; softwood cuttings; root cuttings

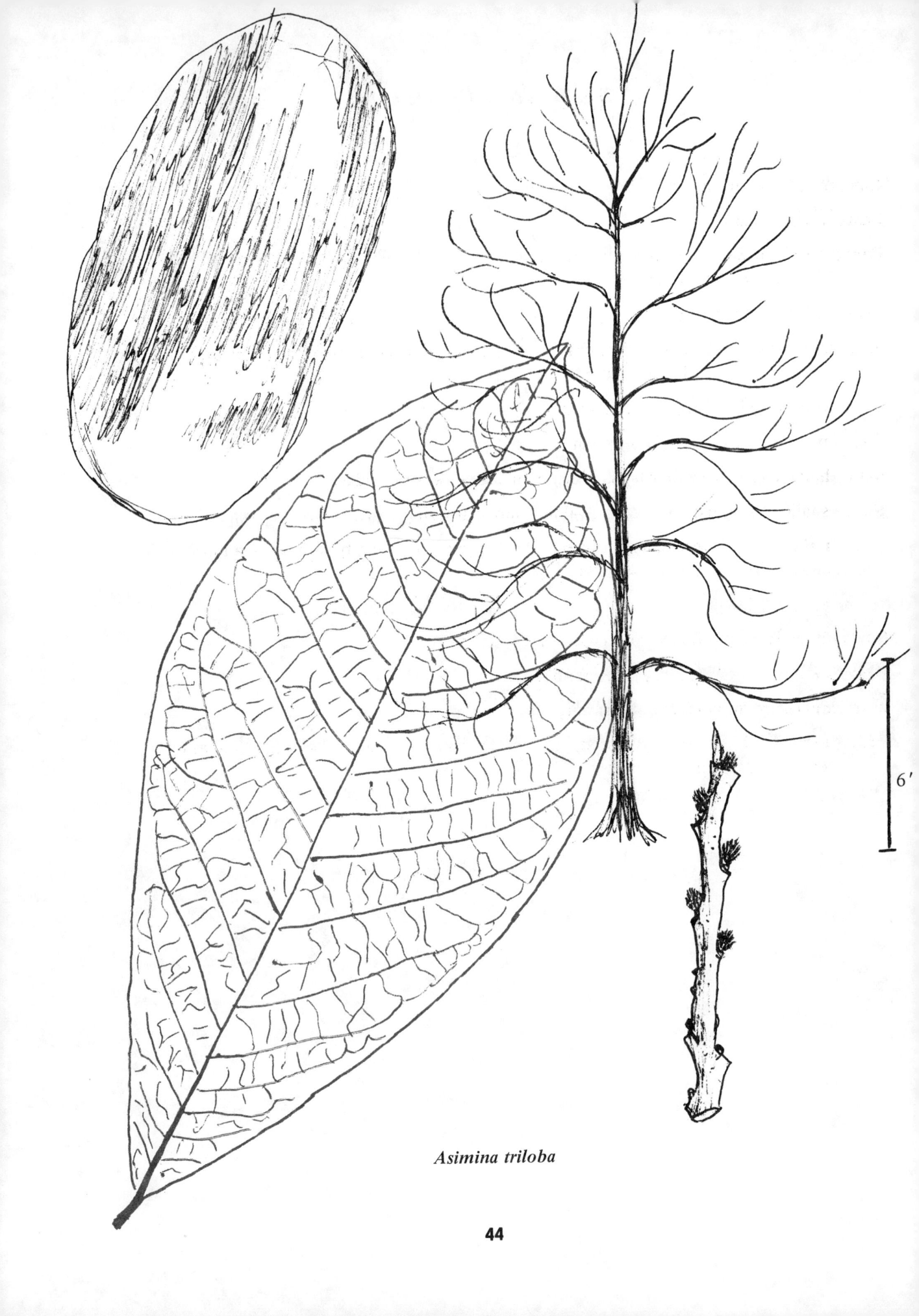

Asimina triloba

Asimina triloba

Common Name: Pawpaw

Family: Annonaceae

Foliage: 6-12 inches long; drooping; without teeth; smooth on both surfaces; rank odor when crushed; yellow in autumn

Flowers: 1 1/2-2 inches in diameter; maroon; cup shaped; March-May

Fruit: large, cylindrical berry; somewhat bean shaped; 2-4 inches long; bluish gray and edible; dark brown seeds; ripens September-October

Buds: without scales; long pointed terminal; round laterals; dark brown hairy

Twigs: moderate thickness; dark brown

Bark: thin; dark brown with whitish blotches and small wartlike ridges

Roots: shallow; fibrous; difficult to establish; move in spring only

Growth Habit: 10-40 feet in height; erect; short trunk; spreading branches; pyramidal or round crown; often multiple trunks

Hardiness: zone 5

Site: rich, moist, well-drained soil; shade tolerant; cool

Growth Rate: slow to moderate once established

Maintenance: clean; intolerant to pruning

Propagation: seed—fall sow fresh seed, or stratify in a moist medium at 41°F for 100 days; layers; root cuttings

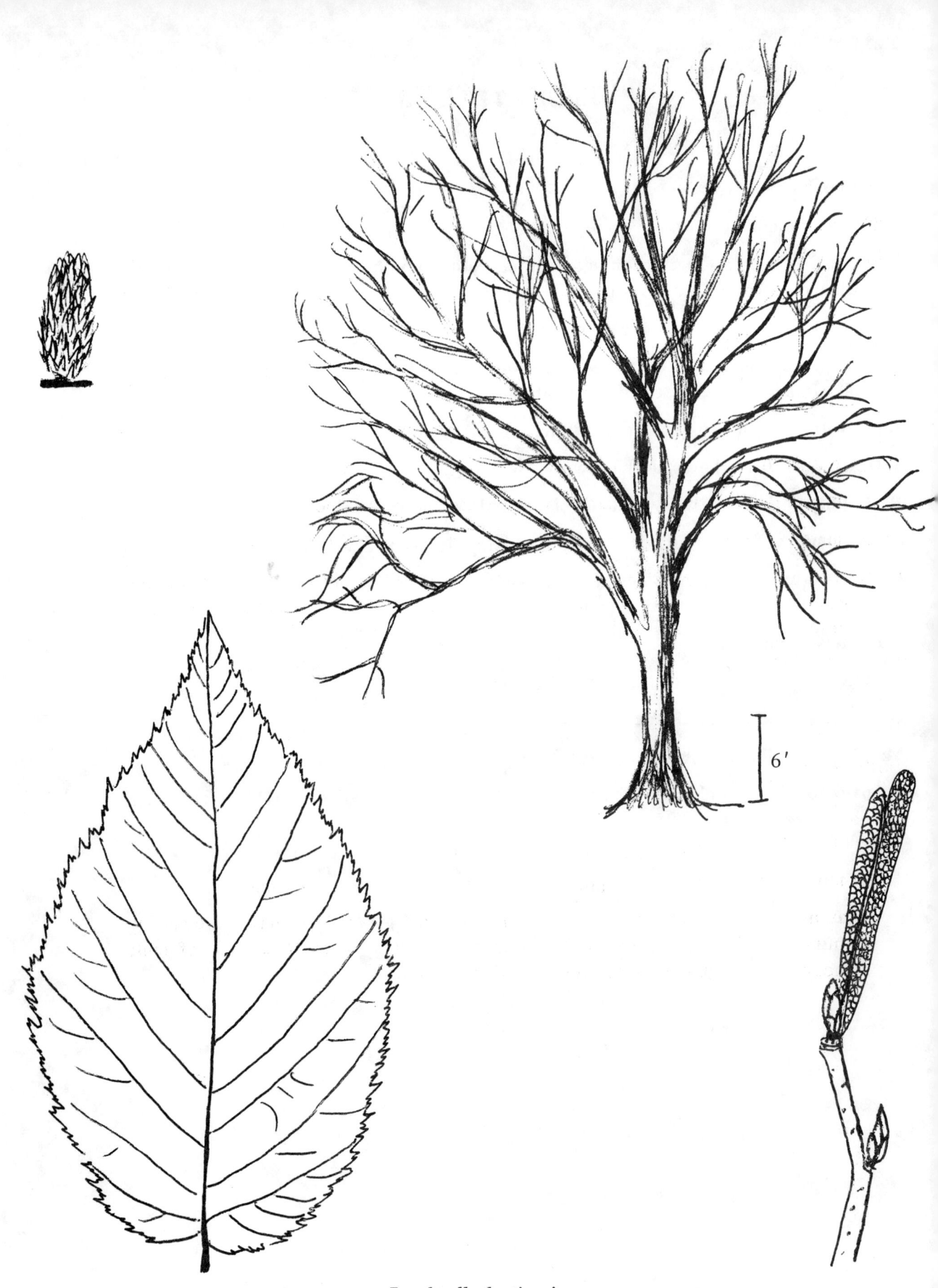

Betula alleghaniensis

Betula alleghaniensis (lutea)

Common Name: Yellow Birch

Family: Betulaceae

Foliage: 2-5 inches long; sharp, double teeth; rounded, unequal bases; slightly aromatic when crushed; dull, dark green and smooth above; paler and hairy below; yellow in autumn

Flowers: male and female separate but on the same tree; catkins; male: 2 inches, purplish yellow and present during winter in clusters at the ends of twigs; female: green and develop in April

Fruit: 1-1 1/2 inch, erect strobile; hairy scales; winged nutlets whose scales shed; ripens August-October

Buds: no terminal; chestnut-brown; hair on scale margins; sharply pointed

Twigs: slender; smooth; lustrous; wintergreen flavor; green-brown to yellow-brown

Bark: bronze to silvery yellow when young becoming reddish brown to black; peeling horizontally into thin, papery curls; breaking into dark plates on old trees; bitter to taste

Roots: fibrous; shallow; widespreading; transplants well when young; transplants best in spring

Growth Habit: 60-70 feet in height; broad, open, round crown; pendulous lower branches

Hardiness: zone 3

Site: moist, rich soils; cool; sun or partial shade

Growth Rate: rapid when young

Maintenance: clean; intolerant to pruning

Propagation: seed—fall sow, or stratify in sand or peat at 41°F for 30-60 days; seed may be germinated without pretreatment in glass covered container under 16-20 hours of light; do not cover deeply; keep surface moist until germination

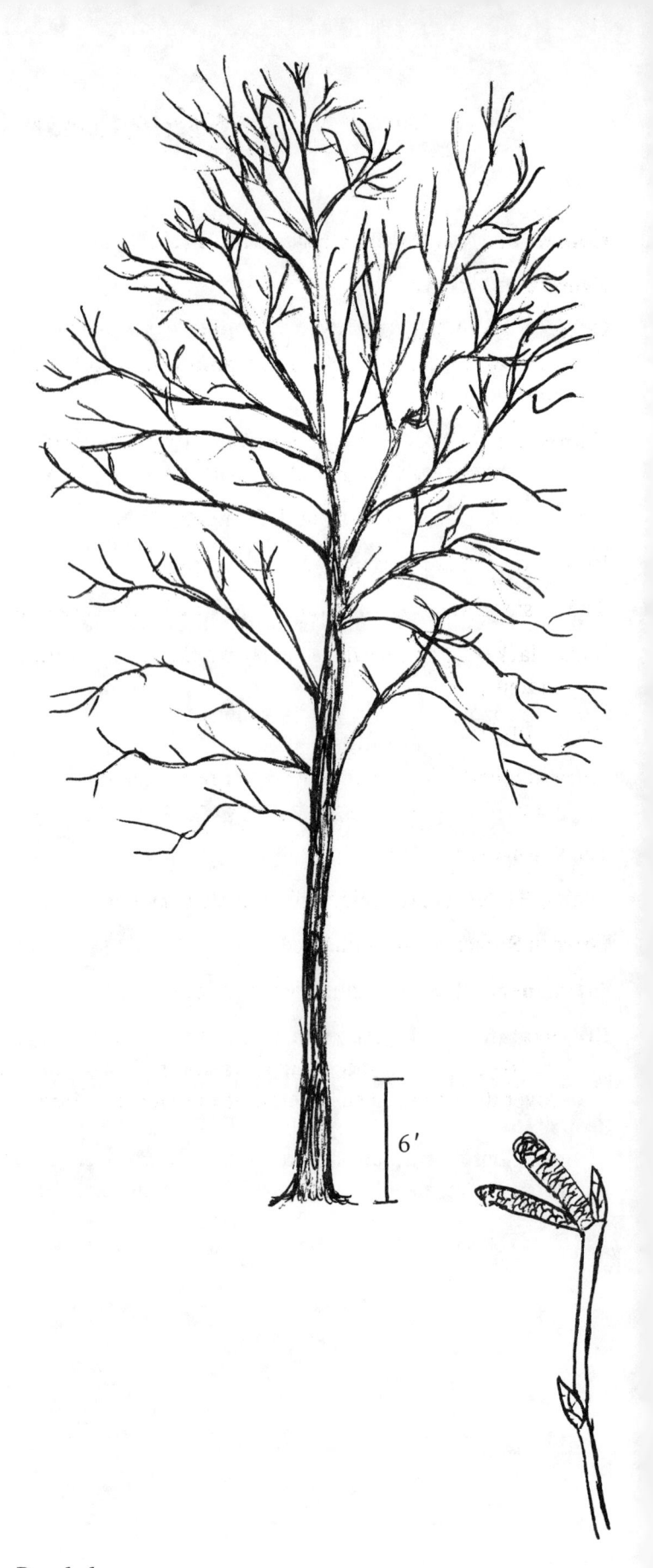

Betula lenta

Betula lenta

Common Name: Cherry Birch; Sweet Birch

Family: Betulaceae

Foliage: 2 1/2-5 inches long; teeth; dark green and smooth above; pale below; axillary tufts of hair on veins; strong aroma when crushed; deep groove on leaf stalk; yellow or orange in autumn

Flowers: male and female separate but on same tree; catkins; male: 1 inch, yellowish and present during winter in clusters at twig ends; female: greenish and appear in April

Fruit: 1-1 1/2 inch, erect strobile; winged nutlets; ripens August-September

Buds: no terminal; reddish brown; sharply pointed

Twigs: slender; smooth; reddish brown; wintergreen to taste; pale, raised lenticels

Bark: dark reddish brown to nearly black; smooth with horizontal lenticels; becoming scaly plated

Roots: fibrous; deep spreading; transplants well

Growth Habit: 50-60 feet in height; tapering trunk; narrow, oval to round crown; open with pendulous lower branches; upper branches ascending; fine texture

Hardiness: zone 3

Site: will tolerate poor, dry soils; sun or partial shade

Growth Rate: slow to moderate

Maintenance; fairly clean; little tolerance to pruning

Propagation: seed—germinate at high temperatures; stratify in sand or peat at 32-41°F for 40-70 days, or germinate in glass covered containers under 16-20 hours of light; do not cover deeply; keep surface moist until germination

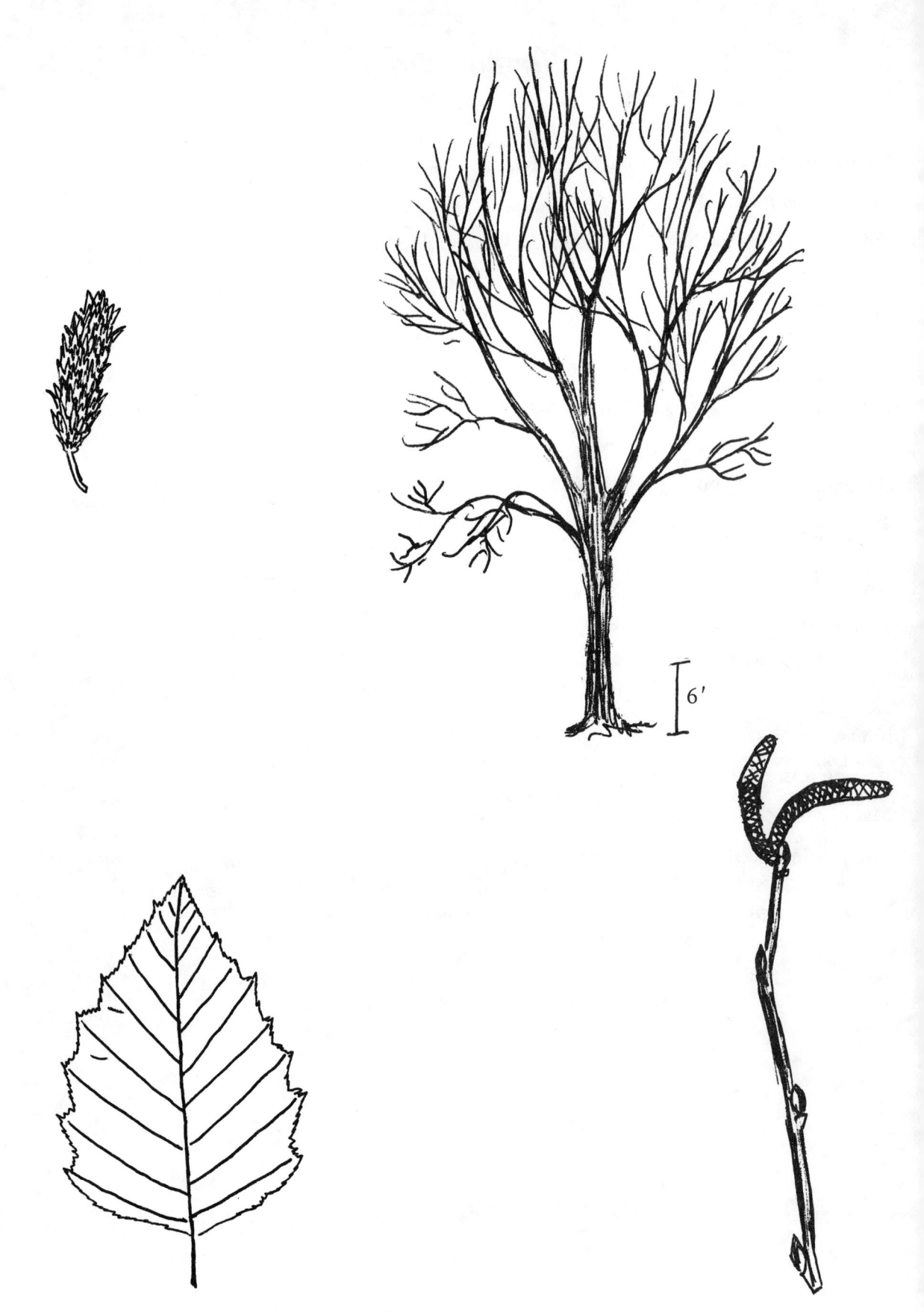

Betula nigra

Betula nigra

Common Name: River Birch

Family: Betulaceae

Foliage: 2-4 inches long; diamond shaped; double teeth; whitish and hairy below; hairy leaf stalk; yellow in autumn

Flowers: male and female separate but on the same tree; catkins; male: terminal, reddish brown, visible in winter; female; erect, yellowish green, April-May

Fruit: 1 inch, erect strobile; stout stalk; downy scales; ripens May-June

Buds: light chestnut-brown; hairy

Twigs: slender; reddish brown; many lenticels; hairy at first becoming shiny; nonaromatic

Bark: thin; reddish brown; peeling in thin, papery curls; furrowed and shaggy at trunk base

Roots: deep fibrous; transplants well

Growth Habit: 60-70 feet in height; ascending branches; open, irregularly rounded crown; often with multiple trunks

Hardiness: zone 4

Site: prefers rich, moist soil; sun

Growth Rate: moderate-rapid

Maintenance: clean; intolerant to pruning

Propagation: seed—plant immediately when mature; do not cover deeply; keep surface moist until germination

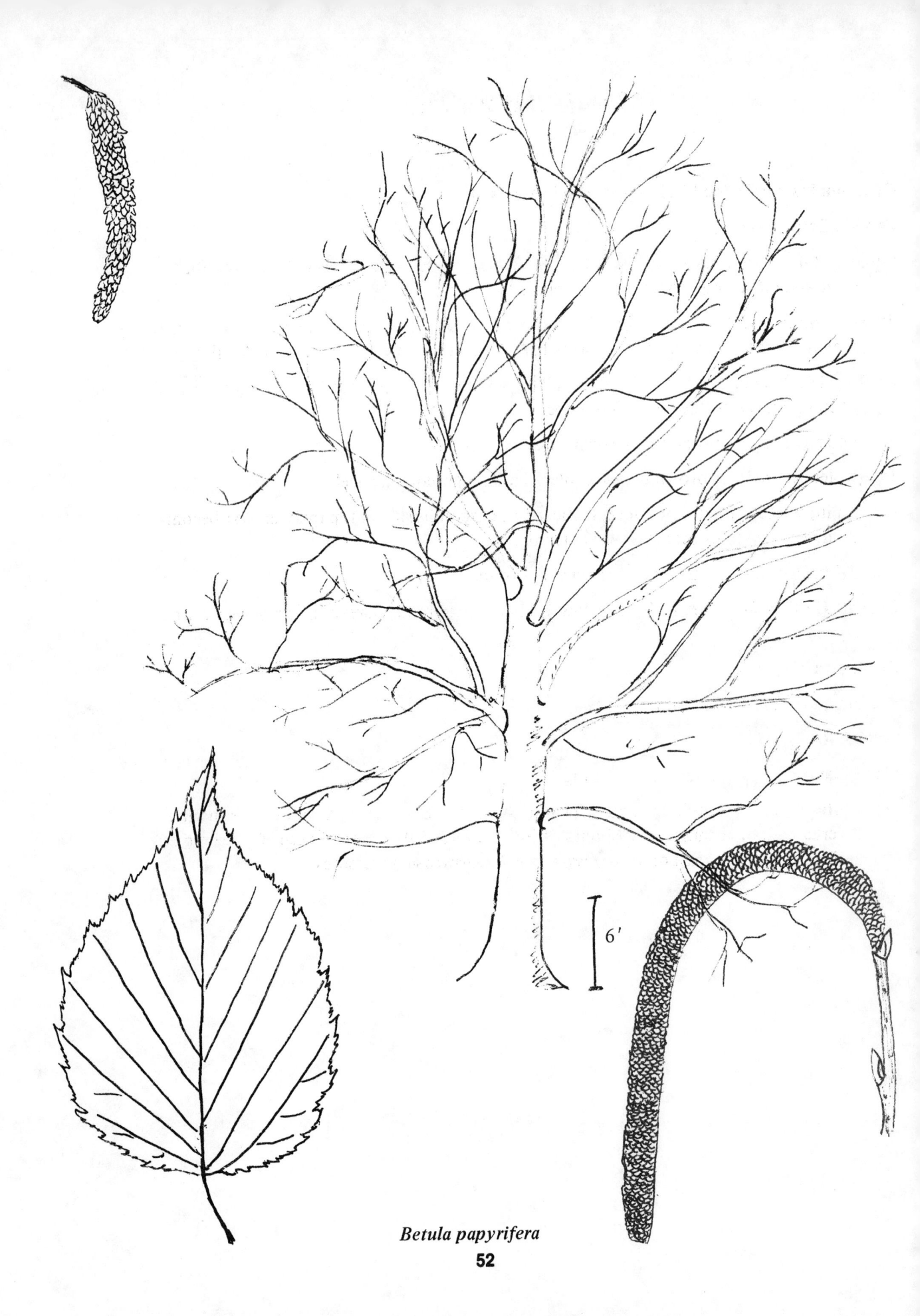

Betula papyrifera

52

Betula papyrifera

Common Name: Canoe Birch, Paper Birch; White Birch

Family: Betulaceae

Foliage: 2-4 inches long; double teeth; round base; dark, dull green and smooth above; paler and more or less hairy below; yellow in autumn

Flowers: male and female separate but on the same tree; catkins; male: 4 inches long, brown, terminal, present during the winter; female: red styles, produced in April-June

Fruit: 1 1/2-2 inch, pendent strobile; stalked; contains winged nutlets; hairy scales fall when mature; ripens August-September

Buds: no terminal; dark chestnut-brown; slightly resinous

Twigs: slender; reddish brown to nearly black; orange, oblong lenticels

Bark: thin; white; raised, horizontal lenticels; peeling in horizontal, papery layers; becoming irregularly thick scaled on lower trunk

Roots: fibrous; shallow; transplants well when young

Growth Habit: 40-70 feet in height; low branching; upright, spreading branches; round topped, oval crown

Hardiness: zone 2

Site: rich, moist soil; cool; sun

Growth Rate: rapid

Maintenance: claan; intolerant to pruning

Propagation: seed—stratify in sand or peat at 41°F for 60-75 days, or germinate in glass covered container under 16-20 hours of light; do not cover deeply; keep surface moist until germination; graft on *B. papyrifera* or *B. verrucosa* understock

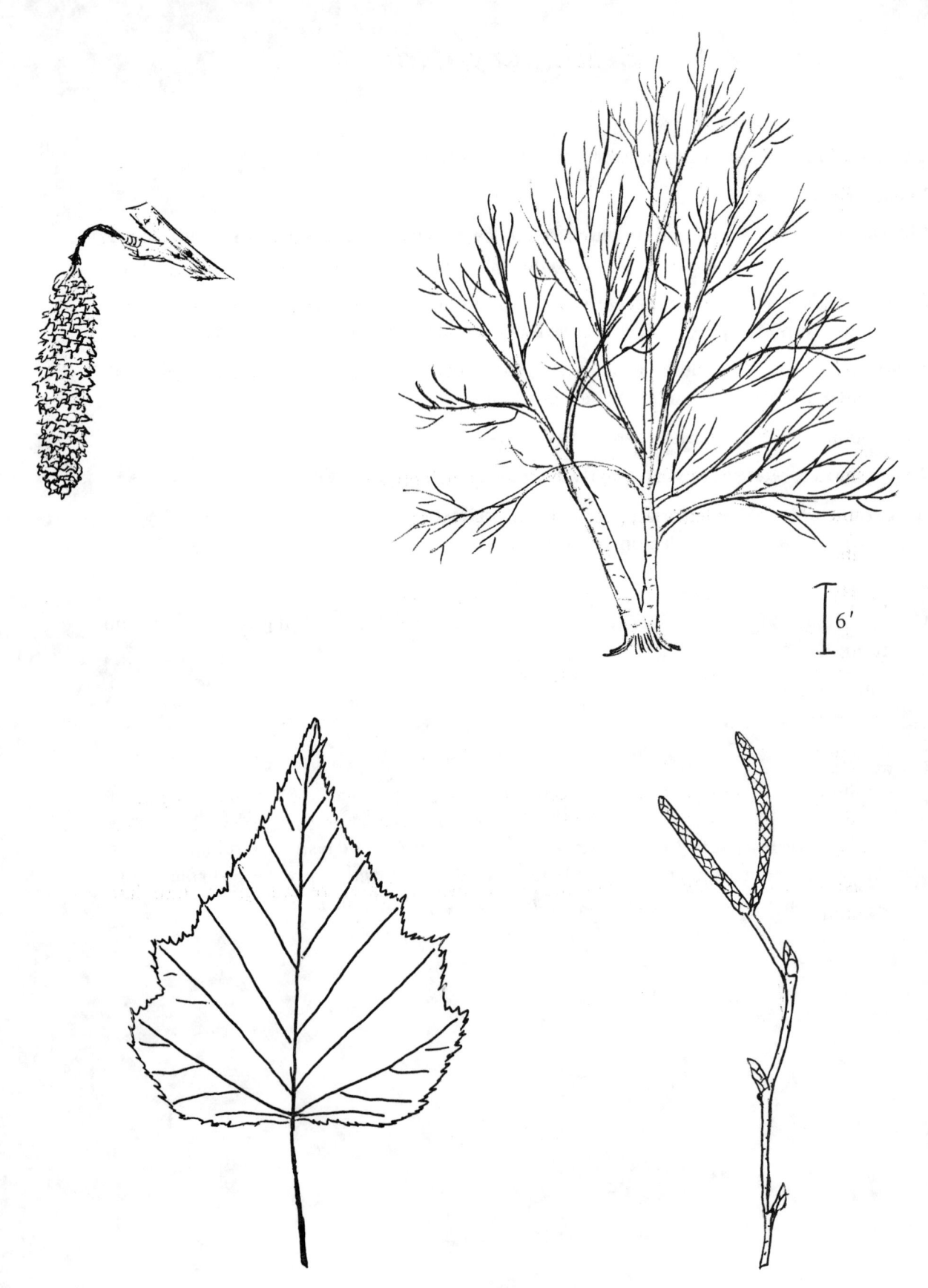

Betula platyphylla

Betula platyphylla

Common Name: Asian White Birch

Family: Betulaceae

Foliage: 1 1/2-2 1/2 inches long; taper pointed apex; base ends abruptly or in a broad wedge; irregular teeth; smooth or sparingly resin dotted; dark green above; paler below

Flowers: male and female separate but on the same tree; catkins; male: terminal, present in clusters in winter; female: on short shoots in spring

Fruits: 1-1 1/2 inch, pendulous strobile; middle lobe of scales short; wings as broad or slightly broader than nutlets; ripens in autumn

Buds: pointed; sticky; brown

Twigs: smooth; slender; reddish gray with many white lenticels

Bark: white with darker lenticels; peeling in papery flakes

Roots: fibrous

Growth Habit: 40-60 feet in height; oval, fairly open crown

Hardiness: zone 3

Site: moist to dry; will grow on poor soils; sun

Growth Rate: rapid

Maintenance: clean

Propagation: seed—germinate in glass covered containers under 16-20 hours of light, or stratify in sand or peat at 41°F for 30-60 days; do not cover deeply; keep moist surface until germination

Selections: var. *szehuanica* — widespreading branches; leaves remain green until late autumn

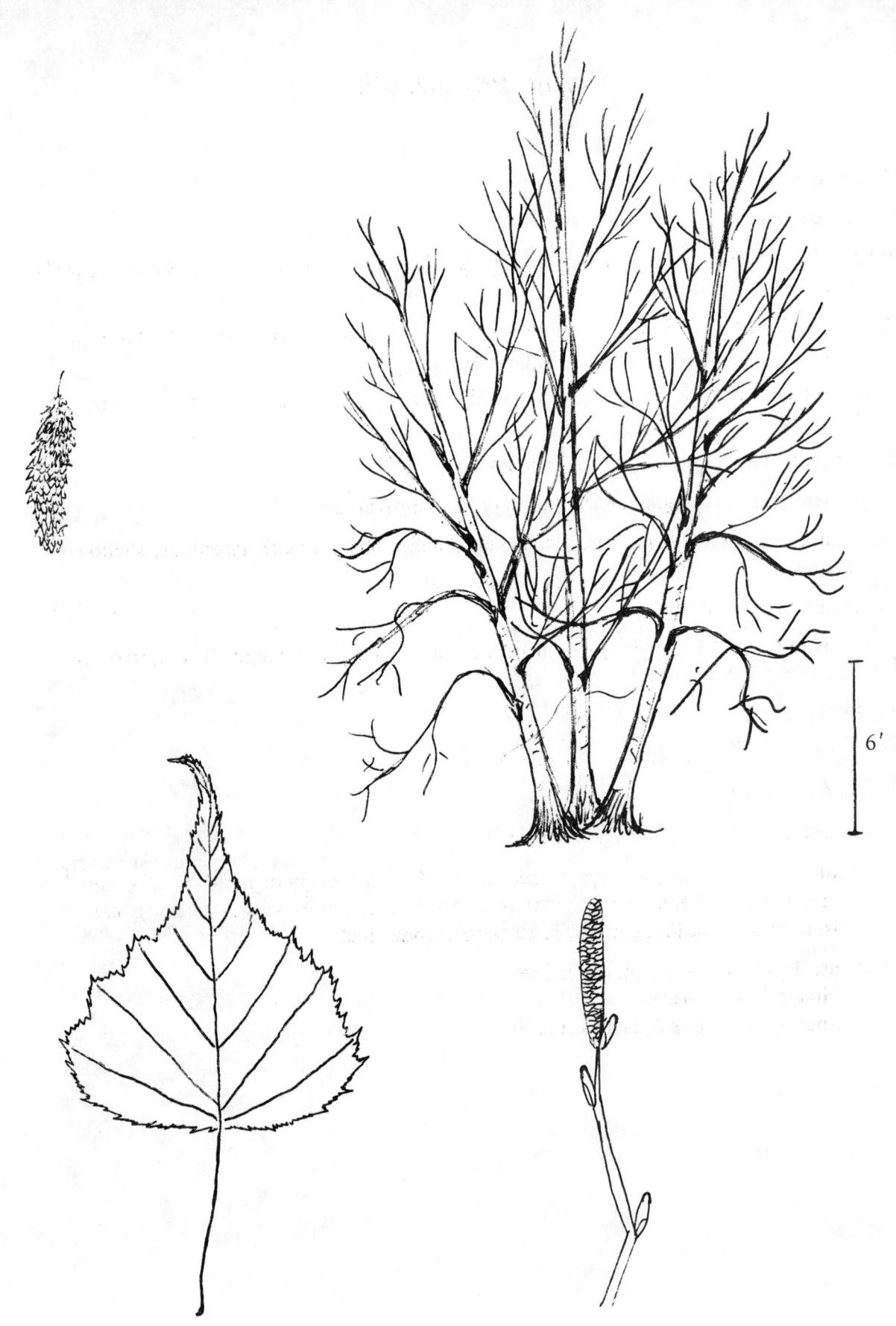

Betula populifolia

56

Betula populifolia

Common Name: Gray Birch

Family: Betulaceae

Foliage: 2-3 inches long; long, pointed apex; double teeth; shiny above; long, slender leaf stalk; yellow in autumn

Flowers: male and female separate on same tree; catkins; male is terminal, single and present in winter; female appears in April-May

Fruit: 3/4-1 inch strobile; pendent or semi-erect; stalked; fine, hairy scales; ripens September-October

Buds: no terminal; blunt; chestnut-brown; gummy

Twigs: slender; resinous; glandular; reddish yellow; nonaromatic

Bark: thin; gray-white; firm, black triangular patches below branch insertions; shallow fissures

Roots: fibrous; spreading

Growth Habit: 20-30 feet in height; contorted branches extend to ground; open, pyramidal crown; often with multiple trunks

Hardiness: zone 4

Site: dry or moist, poor soil; sun

Growth Rate: rapid

Maintenance: fairly clean; intolerant to pruning

Propagation: seed—stratify in sand or peat or 32-50° F for 60-90 or more days, or germinate in glass covered containers at 16-20 hours of light; do not cover deeply; keep moist until germination; graft on *B. papyrifera* understock

Selections: 'Pendula' — weeping branches
    'Laciniata' — cut leaves
    'Purpurea' — young foliage purple

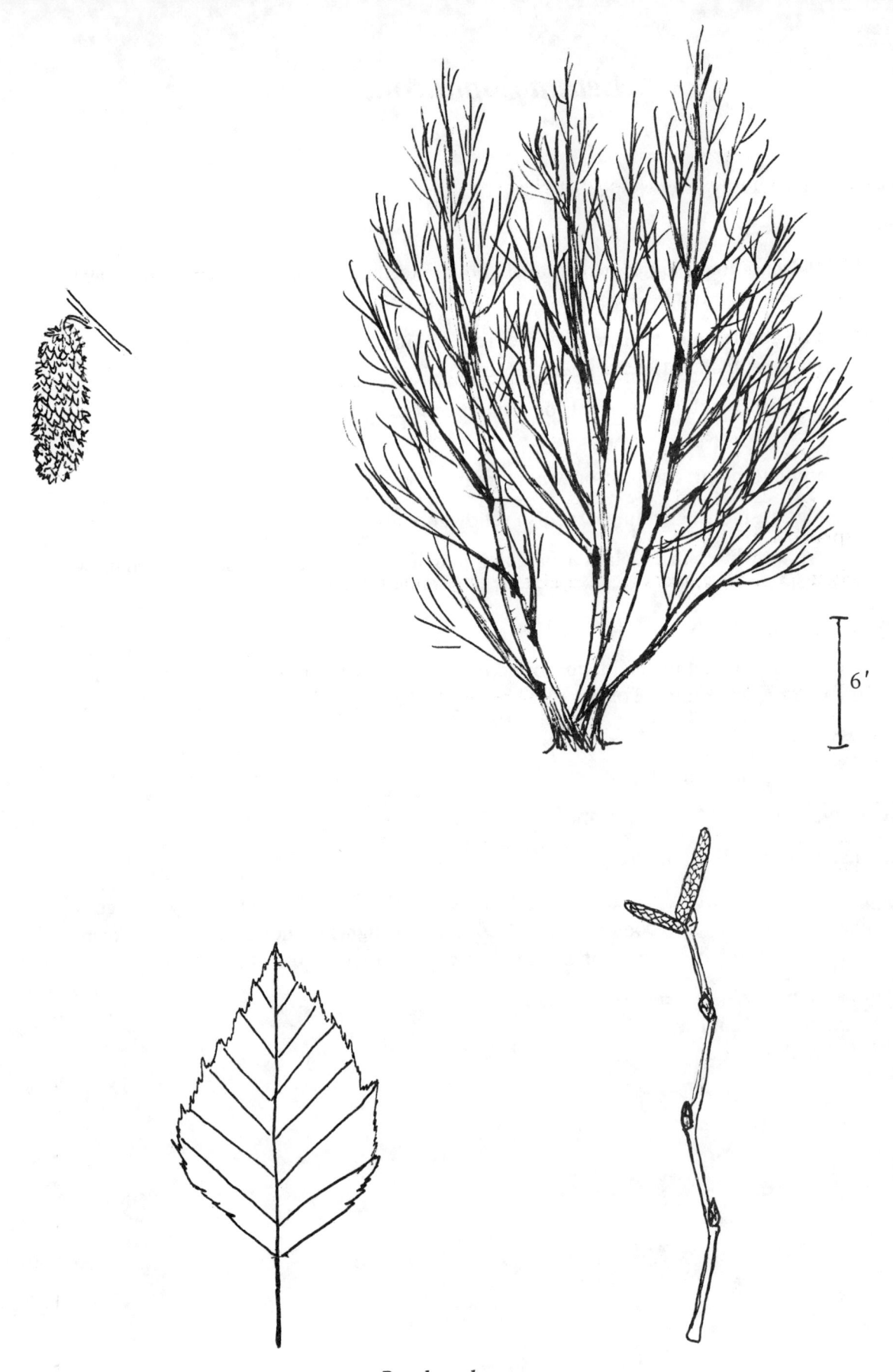

Betula pubescens

Betula pubescens

Common Name: Hairy Birch

Family: Betulaceae

Foliage: 1 1/2-2 inches long; base usually wedge shape; irregular, coarse teeth; shiny green above; pale and hairy beneath; yellow in autumn

Flowers: male and female separate but on the same tree; catkins; male: terminal, present in clusters in winter; female: single, on short shoots in May-June

Fruit: 1 inch, pendulous strobile; stalked; fine, hairy scales; ripens August-September

Buds: smooth scales with hairy edges; brown

Twigs: hairy; reddish brown

Bark: smooth; grayish white; peeling; black triangular markings below branch insertions; thick and deeply fissured at base of old trunks

Roots: fibrous; widespreading

Growth Habit: 30-50 feet in height; slender, conical crown; ascending branches

Hardiness: zone 2

Site: moist to wet, acid soil; sun

Growth Rate: moderate

Maintenance: clean

Propagation: seed—germinate in glass covered containers under 16-20 hours of light, or stratify in sand or peat at 41°F for 30-60 days; do not cover deeply; keep surface moist until germination; softwood cuttings; graft on *B. papyrifera*

Selections: 'Aurea' — young leaves yellow
   'Incisa' — leaves with 3 or 4 large lobes
   'Variegata' — white variegations on young leaves; ascending crown

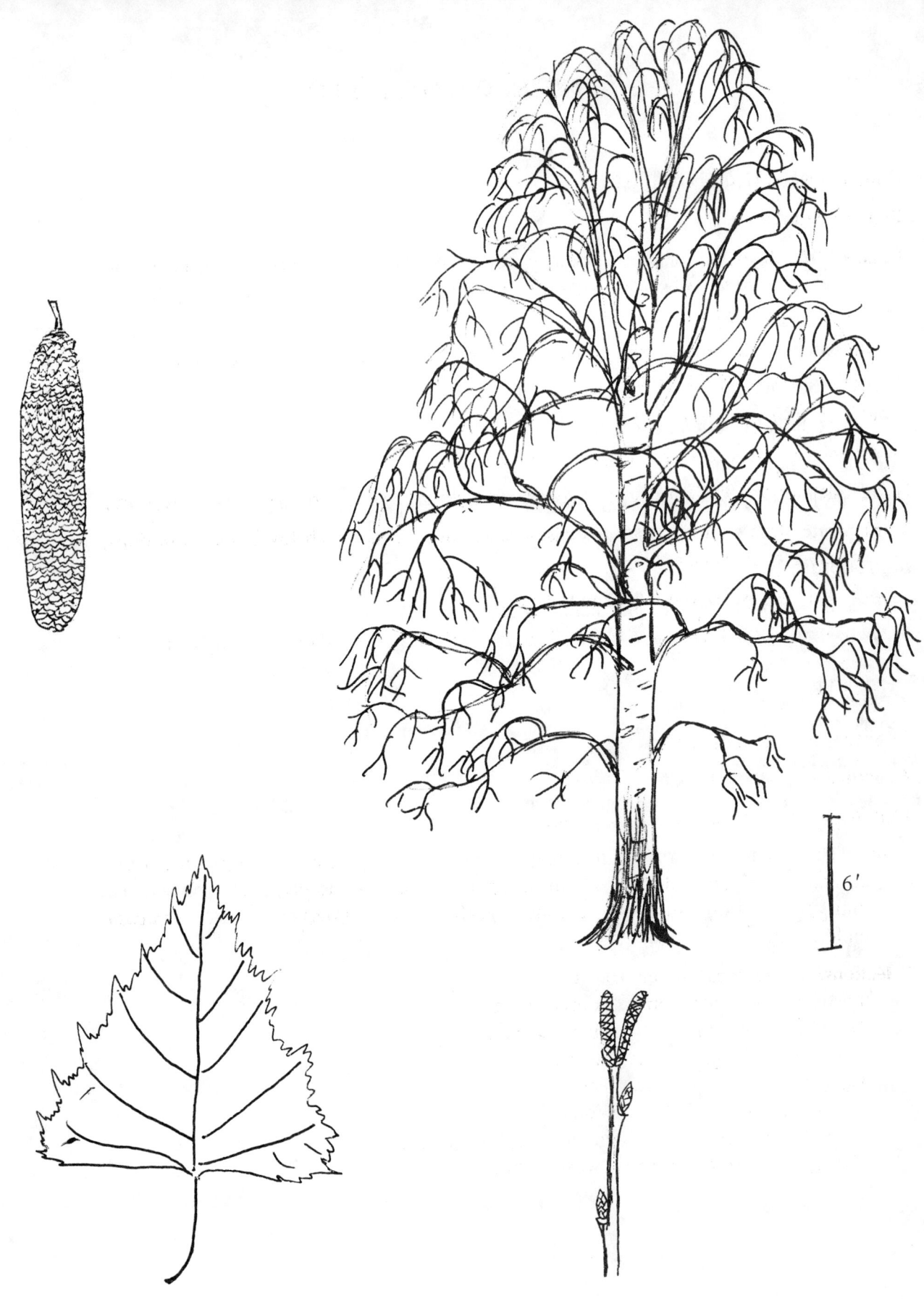

Betula verrucosa

Betula verrucosa (pendula)

Common Name: European Birch

Family: Betulaceae

Foliage: 1-2 1/2 inches long; triangular shape; wedge shape base; taper pointed apex; double teeth; dotted with glands; hairy; bright green above; whitish below; yellow in autumn

Flowers: male and female separate but on the same tree; catkins; male present in winter; female produced April-June

Fruit: 2 inch strobile; ripens July-August

Buds: pointed; dark reddish brown; hairy scales

Twigs: slender; black; light-colored lenticels; densely covered with resin glands when young

Bark: white; peeling; horizontal lenticels; black triangular patches below branch insertions; rough and furrowed at base

Roots: deep; widespreading; difficult to transplant

Growth Habit: 30-60 feet in height; upright, spreading, pyramidal crown; weeping branchlets

Hardiness: zone 2

Site: dry, average soil; cool; sun

Growth Rate: moderate

Maintenance: clean; intolerant to pruning

Propagation: seed—stratify in sand or peat at 32-50°F for 30-60 days, or germinate in glass covered containers under 16-20 hours of light; do not cover deeply; keep surface moist until germination; softwood cuttings; graft on *B. papyrifera* or *B. verrucosa* understock

Selections: 'Dalecarlica' — cut foliage
　'Fastigiata' — columnar; dark green foliage
　'Gracilis' — cut foliage; weeping branches
　'Laciniata' — leaves lobed and sharply pointed
　'Obelisk' — narrowly columnar
　'Purpurea' — purplish green foliage
　'Tristis' — round, irregular crown; weeping branches
　'Youngii' — irregular crown; weeping branches

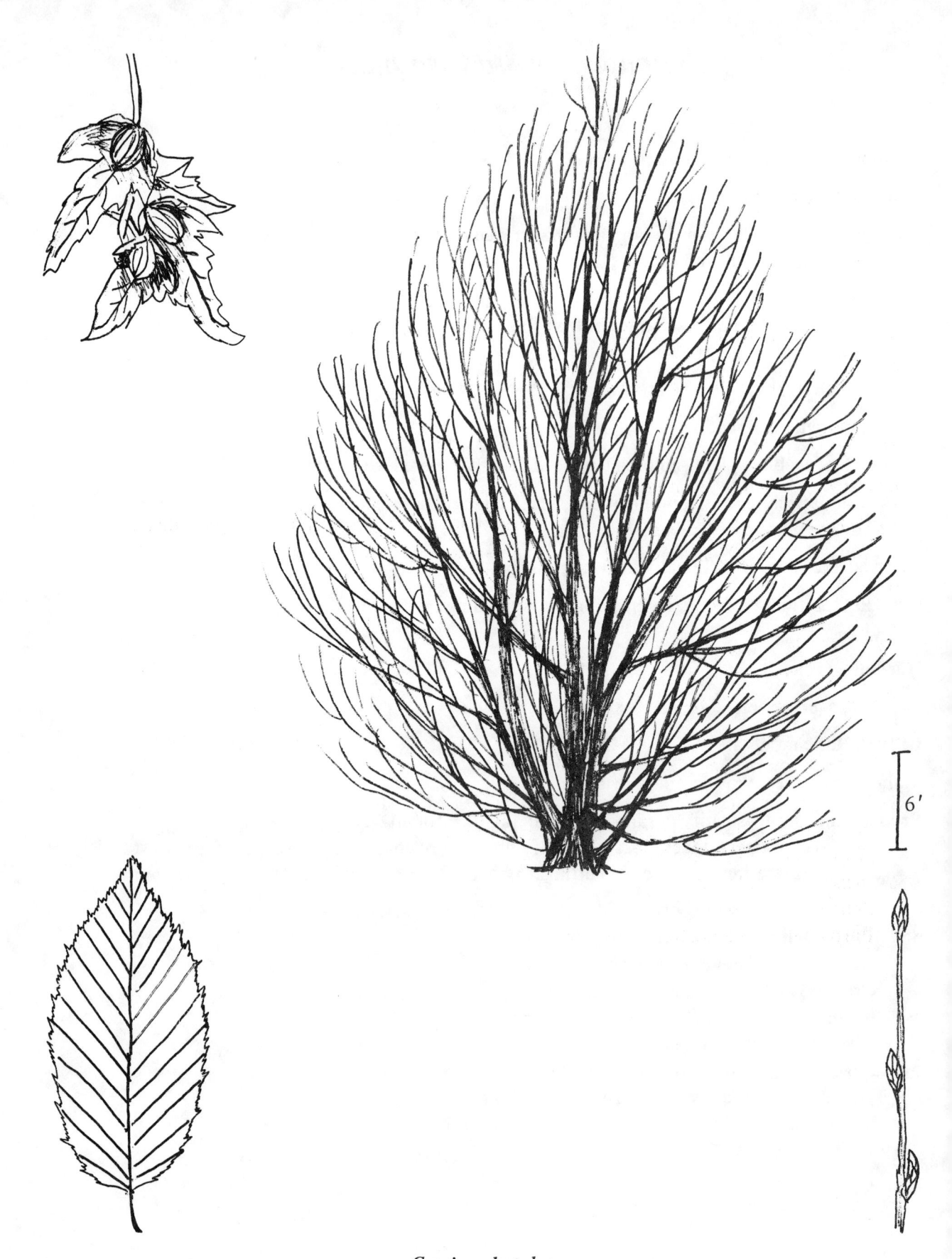

Carpinus betulus

62

Carpinus betulus

Common Name: European Hornbeam

Family: Betulaceae

Foliage: 2-2 1/2 inches long; fine, double teeth; light green turning darker through the summer; yellow in autumn; often persistent through winter

Flowers: male and female produced separate on the same tree; green catkins; April-May

Fruit: small nutlet in a leaflike bract; pendulous clusters; ripens August-November

Buds: long pointed; reddish brown

Twigs: slender; reddish brown

Bark: dark gray; smooth; firm

Roots: shallow; fibrous; transplant when young

Growth Habit: 30-50 feet in height; dense, pyramidal crown; sometimes multiple trunks; branches extend to ground

Hardiness: zone 5

Site: tolerant to many soils; sun or partial shade

Growth Rate: slow

Maintenance: clean; tolerant to pruning

Propagation: seed—stratify in sand/peat mixture at 68° F for 28 days then at 41° F for 87-98 days; graft on *C. betulus* or *C. caroliniana* understock

Selections: 'Columnaris' — upright, oval crown; central trunk
'Fastigiata' — narrow, upright crown which becomes vase shaped; no central trunk
'Horizontalis' — flat topped
'Incisa' — cut foliage
'Pendula' — weeping branches
'Purpurea' — young foliage purple

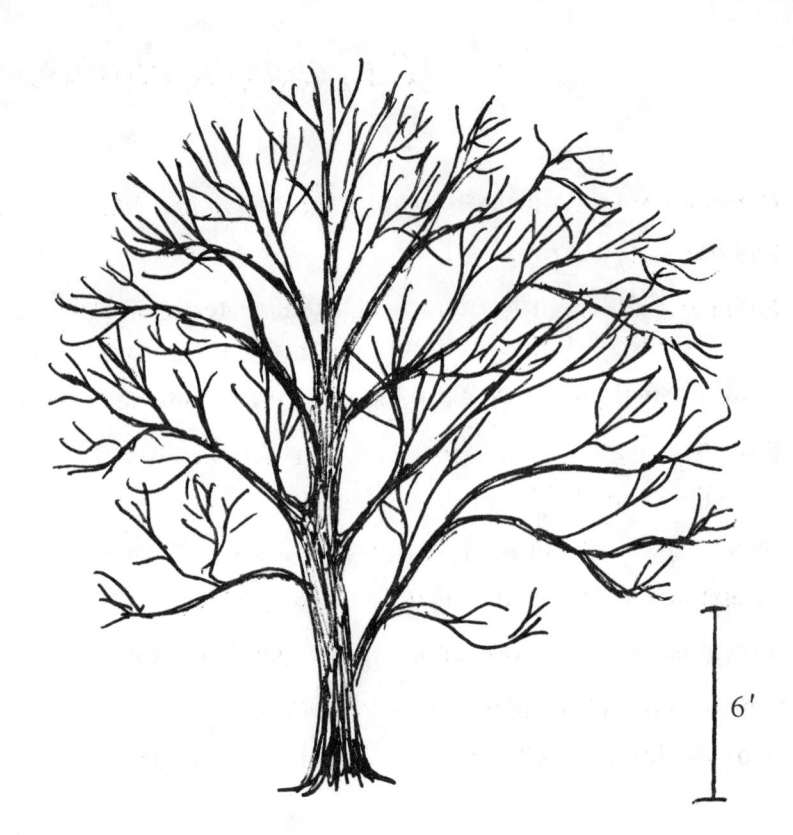

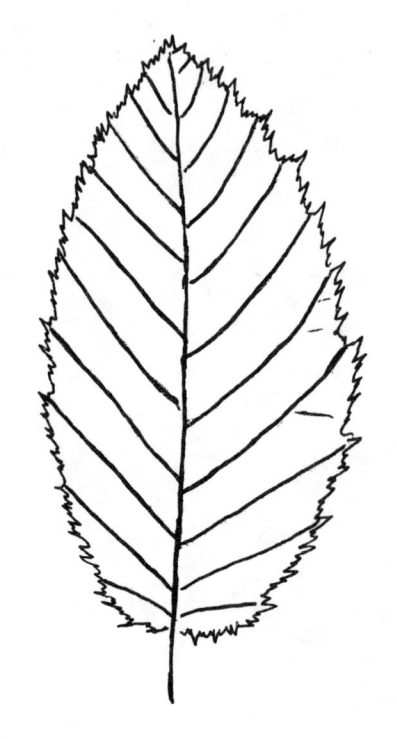

Carpinus caroliniana

Carpinus caroliniana

Common Name: American Hornbeam; Blue Beech; Water Beech

Family: Betulaceae

Foliage: 2-4 inches long; sharp, fine, double teeth; thin; smooth; dull, dark green above; paler below with axillary tufts of hair; yellow-orange in autumn

Flowers: male and female separate but on the same tree; catkins; April-May

Fruit: small, flat brown nut at base of a trilobed, leafy bract; in pendulous clusters; ripens August-September; persistent

Buds: rusty brown; blunt; scaly; 4 sided in cross section

Twigs: slender; shiny; dark reddish brown; smooth

Bark: thin; smooth; gray; appearing as "knotted muscles"

Roots: fibrous; transplant only when young

Growth Habit: 20-40 feet in height; dense, rounded, irregular crown; spreading, zigzag branches

Hardiness: zone 2

Site: rich, moist soil; tolerant of alkaline soils; very shade tolerant

Growth Rate: slow

Maintenance: clean; tolerant to pruning

Propagation: seed—stratify in sand/peat mixture at 68-86°F for 60 days then at 41°F for 60 days; graft on *C. caroliniana* understock

Selections: 'Ascendens' — upright crown
    'Fastigiata' — columnar crown

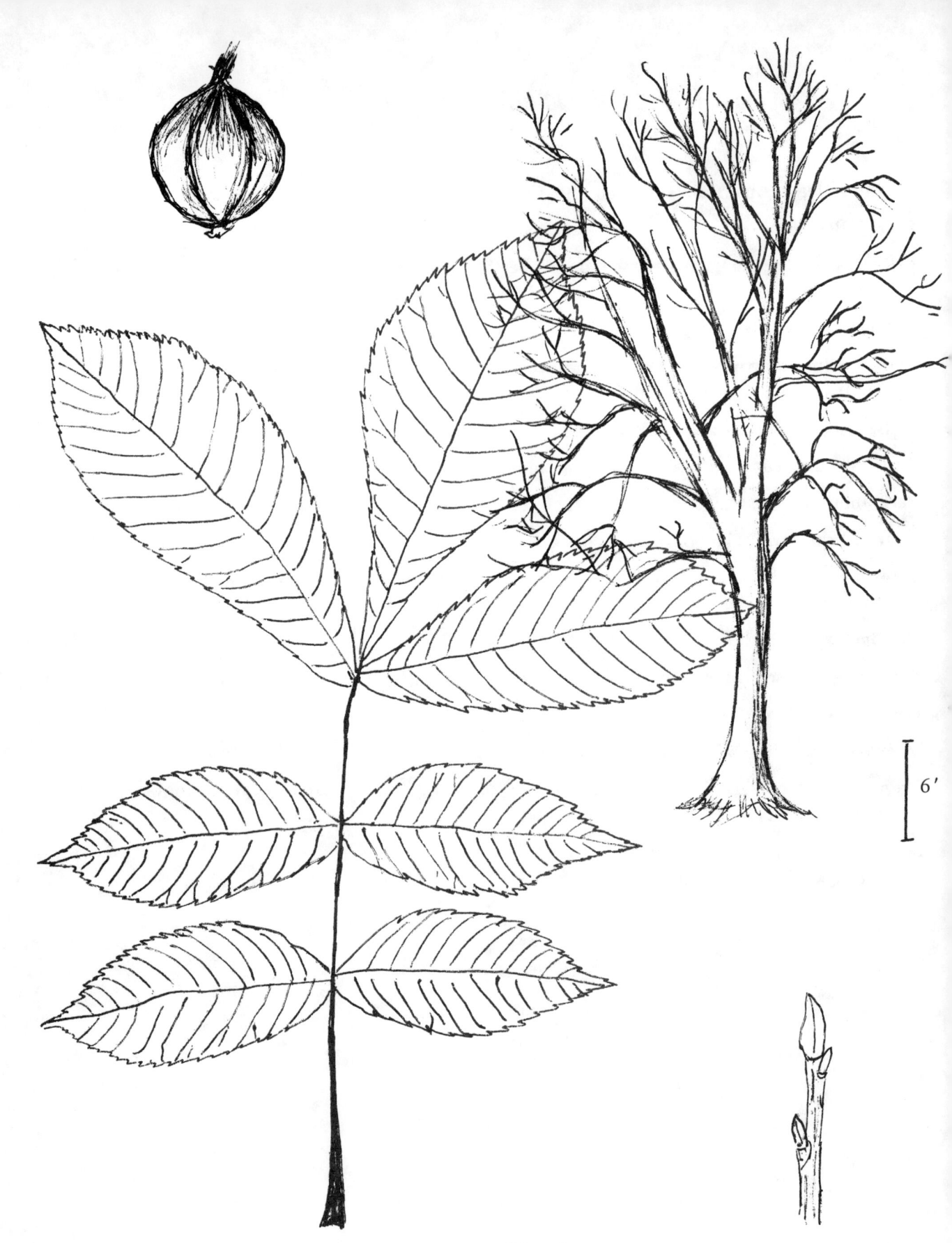

Carya cordiformis

Carya cordiformis

Common Name: Bitternut Hickory

Family: Juglandaceae

Foliage: 6-10 inches long; 7-11 leaflets; terminal slightly larger than laterals; teeth; bright green above; hairy below; yellow in autumn

Flowers: male and female separate but on the same tree; greenish; April-May

Fruit: 1 inch; subglobose; thin husks with yellow-green hairs; aromatic; husk splits half way to base; nut: 4 winged sutures, smooth, thin shelled and bitter; ripens September-October

Buds: bright yellow; flattened; long-pointed; paired scales; hairy; aromatic when crushed

Twigs: moderately stout; gray-brown

Bark: gray; finely ridged

Roots: long, thick taproot; difficult to transplant

Growth Habit: 50-60 feet in height; open, round crown; slender, ascending branches

Hardiness: zone 4

Site: moist, rich soil; sun or partial shade

Growth Rate: moderate

Maintenance: fruit can be messy; limited tolerance to pruning

Propagation: seed—fall sow, mulch and protect from rodents; or soak in water 2-4 days and stratify in a moist medium at 33-40° F for 90 days; if seed is stored for 1 year, stratify only 30-60 days

Carya glabra

Carya glabra

Common Name: Sweet Pignut Hickory

Family: Juglandaceae

Foliage: 6-12 inches long; 5 leaflets; terminal 3 leaflets approximately the same size; teeth; smooth above and beneath

Flowers: male and female separate but on the same tree; catkins; April-May

Fruit: 1-1 1/4 inches in diameter; thin husks; husk splits only part way to base; nut: thin shell, unribbed with a sweet kernel; ripens September-October

Buds: short; stout; overlapping scales; gray

Twigs: moderately stout; reddish brown

Bark: gray; furrowed with round ridges

Roots: taproot; difficult to transplant

Growth Habit: 50-75 feet in height; open, oblong crown with pendulous lower branches

Hardiness: zone 4

Site: rich, moist or dry soil; sun

Growth Rate: slow

Maintenance: fruit can be messy; limited tolerance to pruning

Propagation: seed—fall sow, mulch, and protect from rodents; or soak in water 2-4 days then stratify in a moist medium at 33-40° F for 90-120 days; if stored for 1 year, stratify 30-60 days

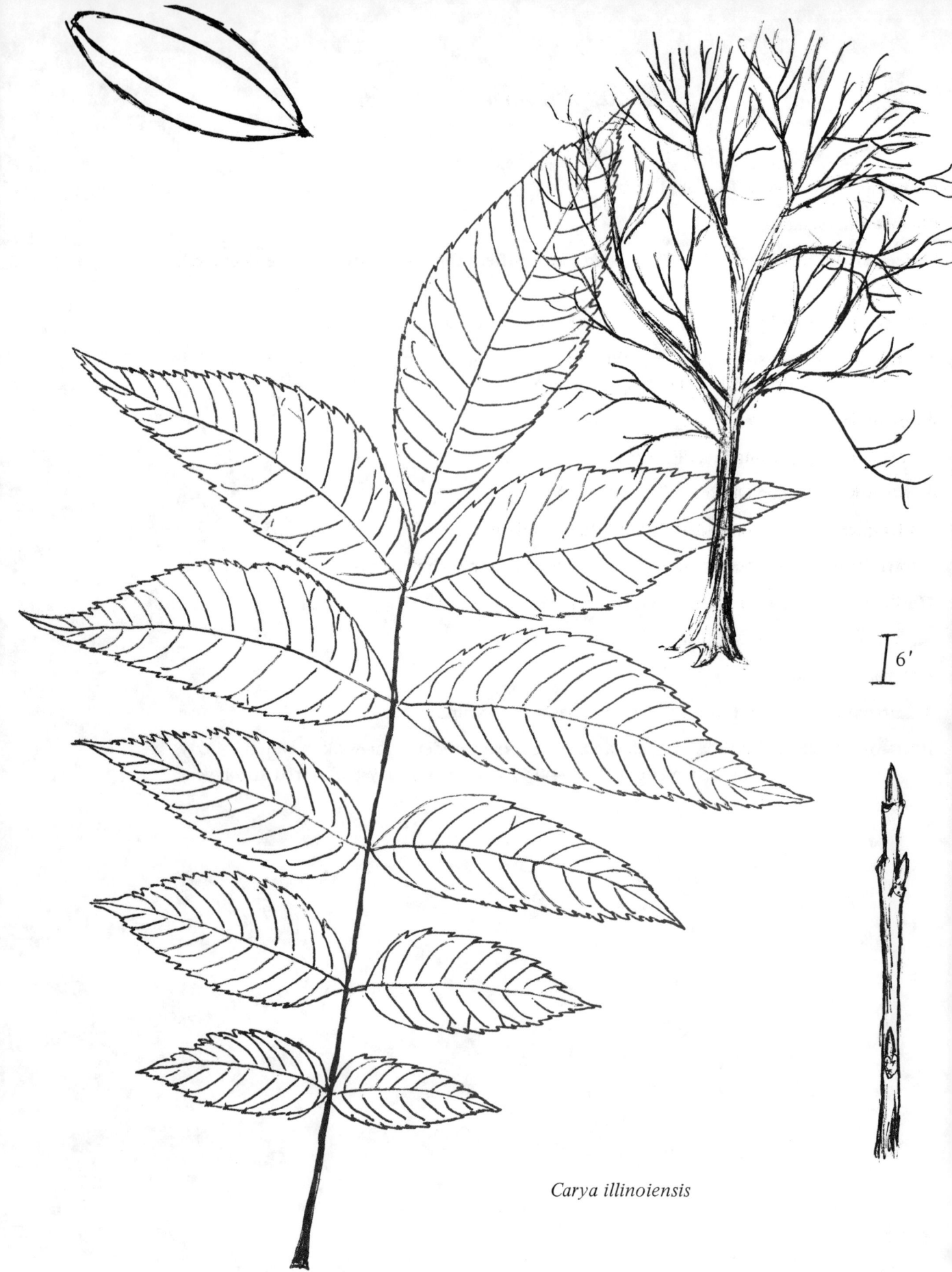

Carya illinoiensis

70

Carya illinoiensis

Common Name: Pecan

Family: Juglandaceae

Foliage: 10-20 inches long; 11-17 leaflets; yellow-green; double teeth; tapering apex; long, hairy petiole; yellow in autumn

Flowers: male and female separate but on the same tree; catkins; March-May

Fruit: 1-2 1/2 inches long; in elongated clusters; thin husk that splits almost to base; nut: smooth with thin shell and sweet kernel; ripens September-October

Buds: yellow; hairy; paired scales that do not overlap; pointed

Twigs: moderately stout; brown with orange lenticels

Bark: dark gray; rough plates

Roots: thick taproot; somewhat difficult to transplant

Growth Habit: 80-100 feet in height; broad, spreading, round crown

Hardiness: zone 5 (the tree itself is hardy in zone 4 but the fruit will not ripen)

Site: rich, moist soil; sun

Growth Rate: slow

Maintenance: fruit can be messy; moderate tolerance to pruning

Propagation: seed—fall sow fresh seed, mulch, and protect from rodents; or soak in water 2-4 days then stratify in a moist medium at 33-40° F for 30-90 days; if stored for 1 year, stratify 30-60 days

Leaf: ½ actual size

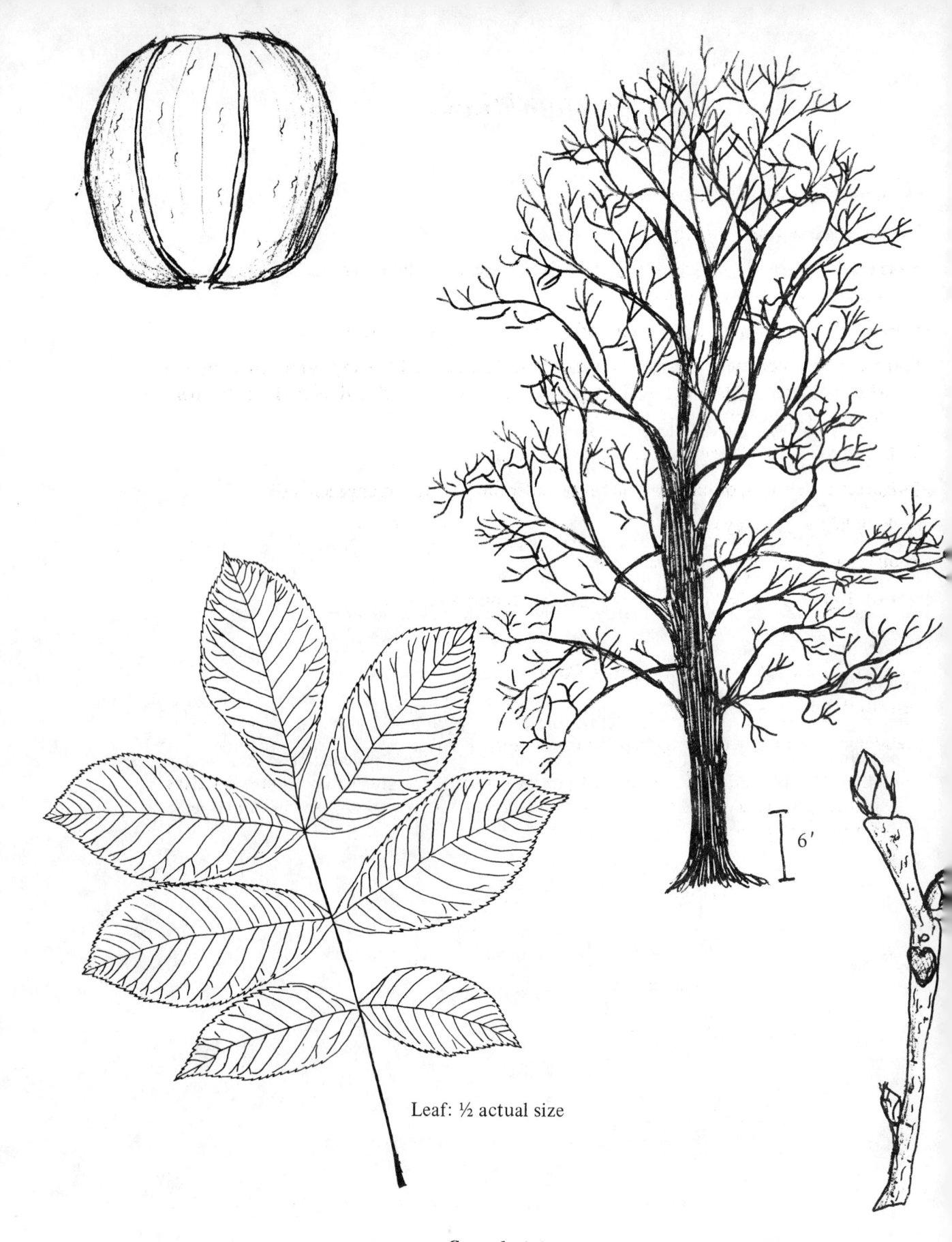

Carya laciniosa

Carya laciniosa

Common Name: Big Shellbark Hickory

Family: Juglandaceae

Foliage: 10-22 inches long; usually 7 leaflets; fine teeth; dark green; paler and hairy beneath; yellow in autumn

Flowers: male and female separate but on the same tree; catkins; April-June

Fruit: 2 inches in diameter; thick husk; husk splits in 4 parts all the way to the base; nut: 4-6 ribs with both ends pointed, light brown with a thick shell and sweet kernel; ripens September-November

Buds: large with overlapping scales; light brown; hairy

Twigs: stout; hairless; orange-brown; fuzzy under the leaf scar; orange lenticels

Bark: light gray; shaggy strips

Roots: taproot; difficult to transplant

Growth Habit: 60-80 feet in height; straight trunk; narrow crown

Hardiness: zone 4

Site: rich, moist soil; can tolerate limited flooding; sun

Growth Rate: very slow

Maintenance: fruit can be messy; moderate tolerance to pruning

Propagation: seed—fall sow, mulch and protect from rodents; or soak in water 2-4 days then stratify in a moist medium at 33-40° F for 90-120 days; if stored for 1 year, stratify 30-60 days

Leaf: ½ actual size

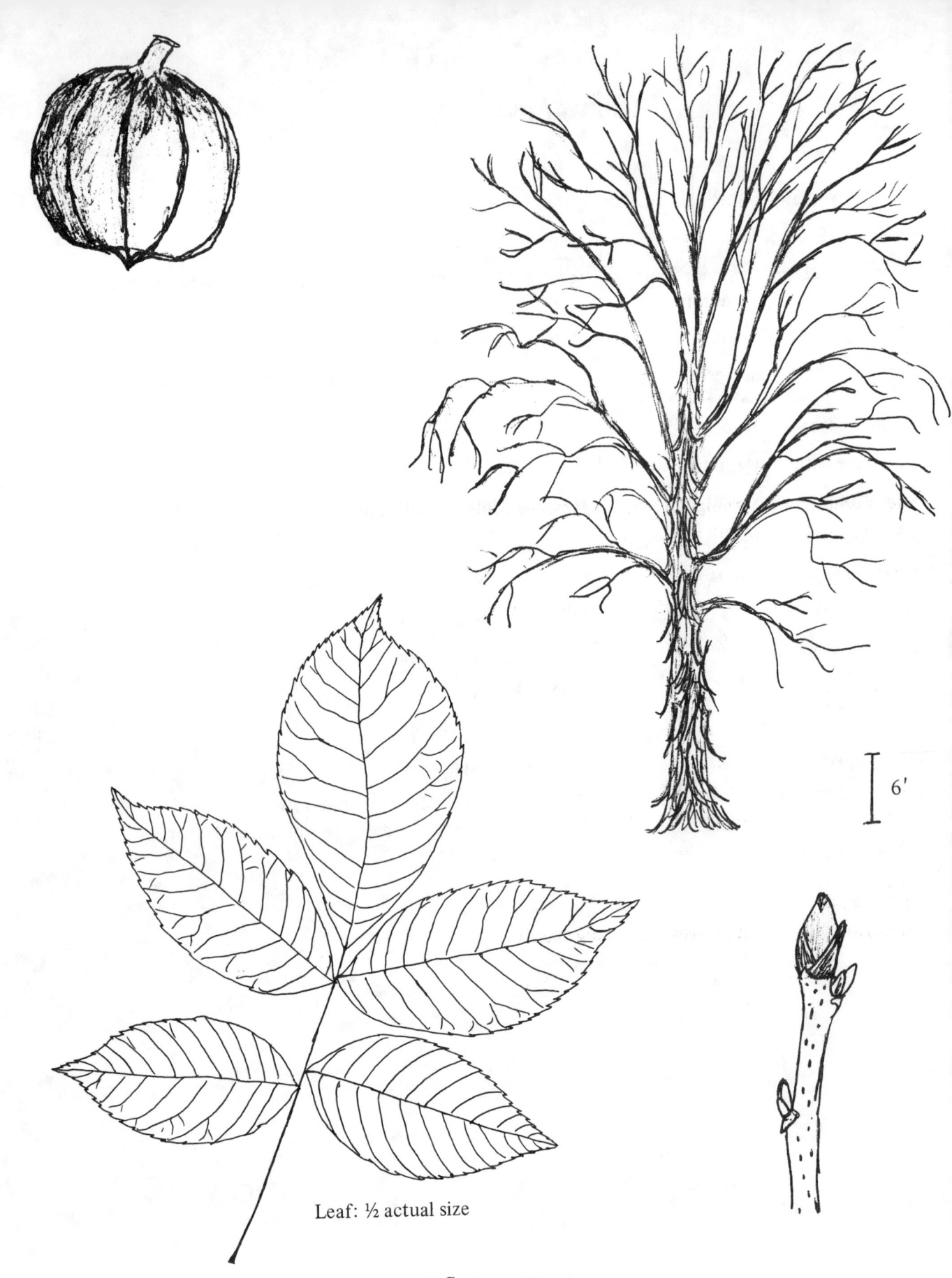

Carya ovata

Carya ovata

Common Name: Shagbark Hickory

Family: Juglandaceae

Foliage: 8-12 inches long; usually 5 leaflets; fine teeth; thick; dark green above; paler beneath; golden brown in autumn

Flowers: male and female separate but on the same tree; catkins; April-June

Fruit: 1-2 1/2 inches in diameter; thick husk that splits completely; nut: 4 ribs with a thick shell, sweet kernel; ripens September-October

Buds: 3-4, loose fitting, overlapping scales; hairy; gray

Twigs: stout; gray; somewhat hairy

Bark: dark gray; long, loose shaggy plates

Roots: taproot; difficult to transplant

Growth Habit: 60-100 feet in height; open, oblong crown; large, rather pendulous lower branches

Hardiness: zone 4

Site: rich, well-drained soil; sun or shade

Growth Rate: very slow

Maintenance: fruit can be messy; limited tolerance to pruning

Propagation: seed—fall sow, mulch and protect from rodents; or soak in water 2-4 days then stratify in a moist medium at 33-40° F for 60-150 days; if stored for 1 year, stratify 30-60 days

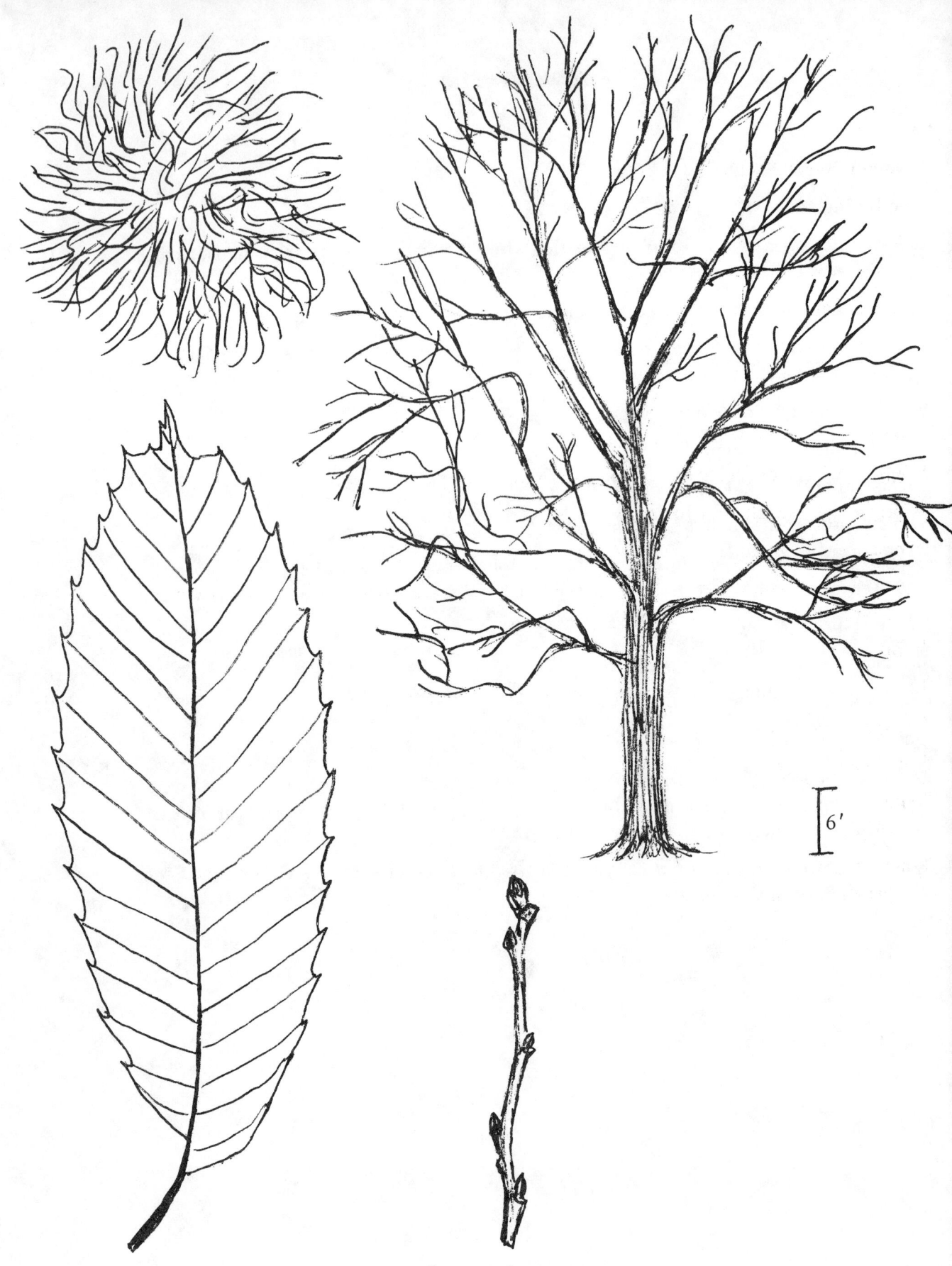

Castanea dentata

Castanea dentata

Common Name: American Chestnut

Family: Fagaceae

Foliage: 5-8 inches long; coarse, incurved, glandular teeth with a vein extending to each tooth; smooth; apex pointed; stout leaf stalk

Flowers: male and female separate but on the same tree; greenish spikes; June

Fruit: 2-3 inches in diameter; globose; thick branched burs on husk; hairy inside husk; opened by 4 valves; usually contains 2 or 3 nuts; nuts: dark brown with white downy apex, sweet, edible kernel; ripens September-October

Buds: no terminal; small; blunt; brown

Twigs: slender; reddish brown; smooth; star shaped pith

Bark: dark brown; shallow furrows

Roots: deep; transplants well

Growth Habit: 70-100 feet in height; straight trunk; broad, round, widespreading crown; symmetrical

Hardiness: zone 4

Site: deep, well-drained soil; tolerant to acidic soil; shade tolerant

Growth Rate: rapid

Maintenance: clean; tolerant to pruning

Propagation: seed—fall sow fresh seed and protect from rodents; or stratify in a moist medium in cold conditions until ready to plant

Note: because of the Chestnut Blight persistence, this species is not recommended for general planting at this time

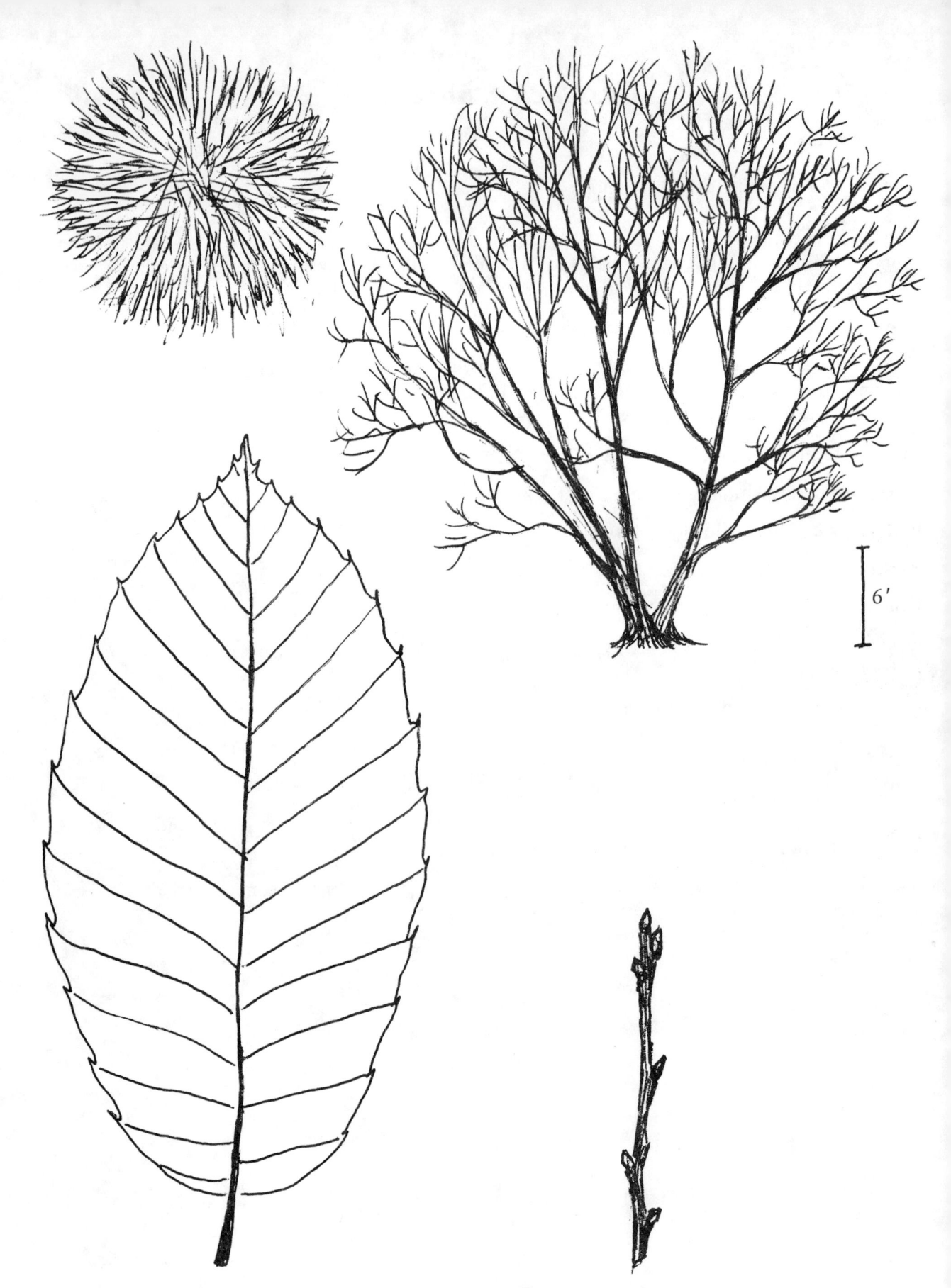

Castanea mollissima

Castanea mollissima

Common Name: Chinese Chestnut

Family: Fagaceae

Foliage: 3-6 inches long; thick; sharp, jagged teeth with a vein extending to each tooth; younger leaves hairy below; glossy; yellow to bronze in autumn; persists late into winter

Flowers: male and female separate but on the same tree; pale yellow catkins; male: ill scented, 4-5 inches long; June

Fruit: 2 inches in diameter; prickly bur; contains 1-3 nuts; nut: downy with a small scar at place of attachment, edible; ripens September-October

Buds: fuzzy; dark reddish brown

Twigs: slender, hairy; reddish brown

Bark: dark gray; firm; rather smooth

Roots: taproot

Growth Habit: 30-40 feet in height; round crown; spreading branches; branched low

Hardiness: zone 4

Site: rich, well-drained soil; sun

Growth Rate: moderately rapid

Maintenance: clean; not very tolerant to pruning

Propagation: seed—fall sow fresh seed and protect from rodents, or stratify in a moist medium under cold conditions until ready to plant

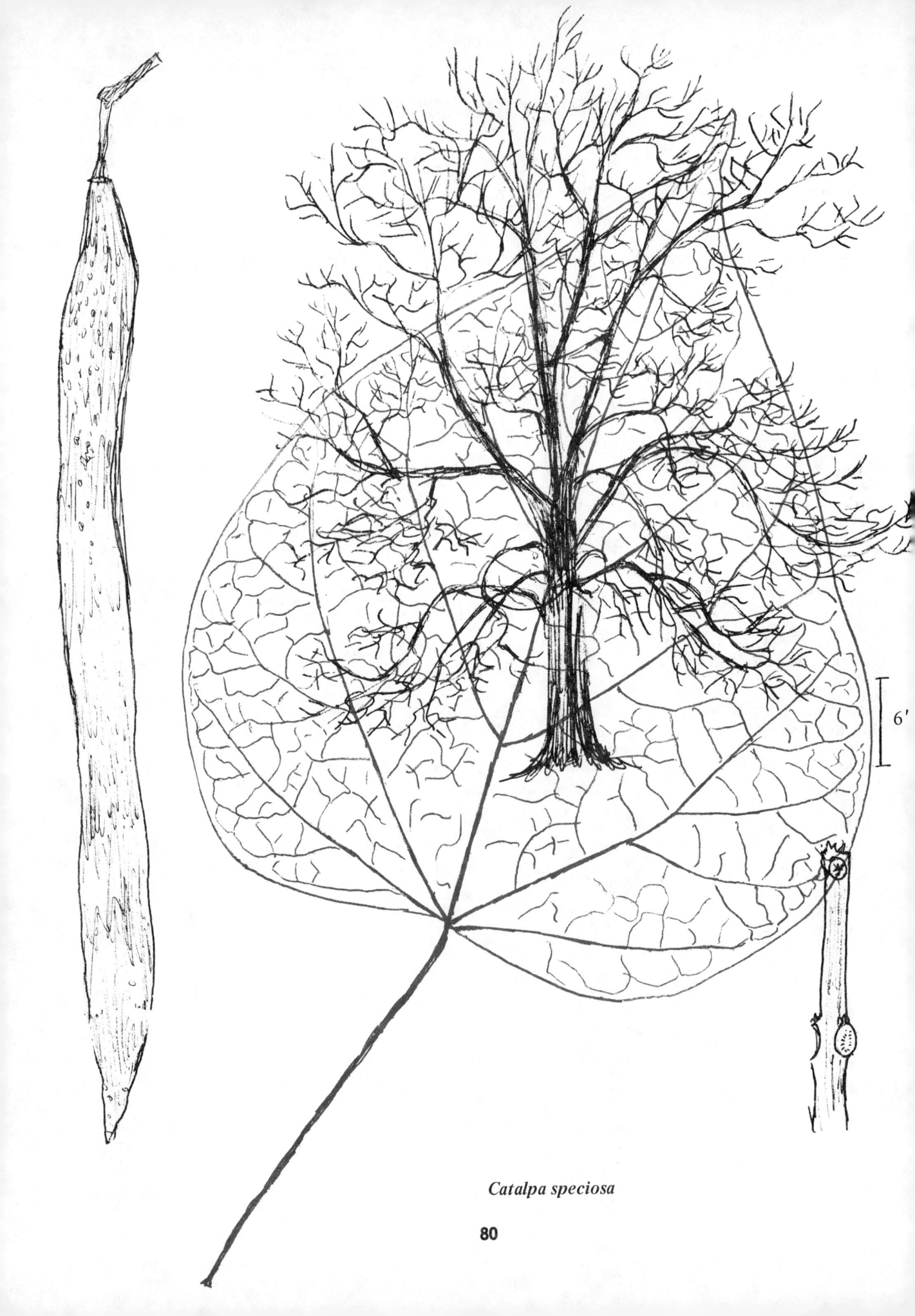

Catalpa speciosa

Catalpa speciosa

Common Name: Western Catalpa; Cigar-tree

Family: Bignoniaceae

Foliage: 6-12 inches long; light smell when broken; hairy beneath; yellow-green long petiole; yellow-green or brown in autumn

Flowers: 2 1/2 inches long; born in loose panicles about 6 inches long; white with 2 rows of yellow blotches and purple spots inside; May-June

Fruit: capsule to 18 inches long; thick walls; many seeds with papery fringed edges; ripens in October

Buds: no terminal; laterals small; embedded in bark

Twigs: very stout; brown

Bark: brown; deep furrows with thick scales

Roots: coarsely fibrous with a main taproot; transplants moderately well

Growth Habit: 50-60 feet in height; broad, round or pyramidal crown

Hardiness: zone 4

Site: moist, rich, well-drained soil; sun; tolerant to drought and heat

Growth Rate: rapid; slower with age

Maintenance: messy flowers and fruit; tolerant to pruning

Propagation: seed—no pretreatment; sow in late spring

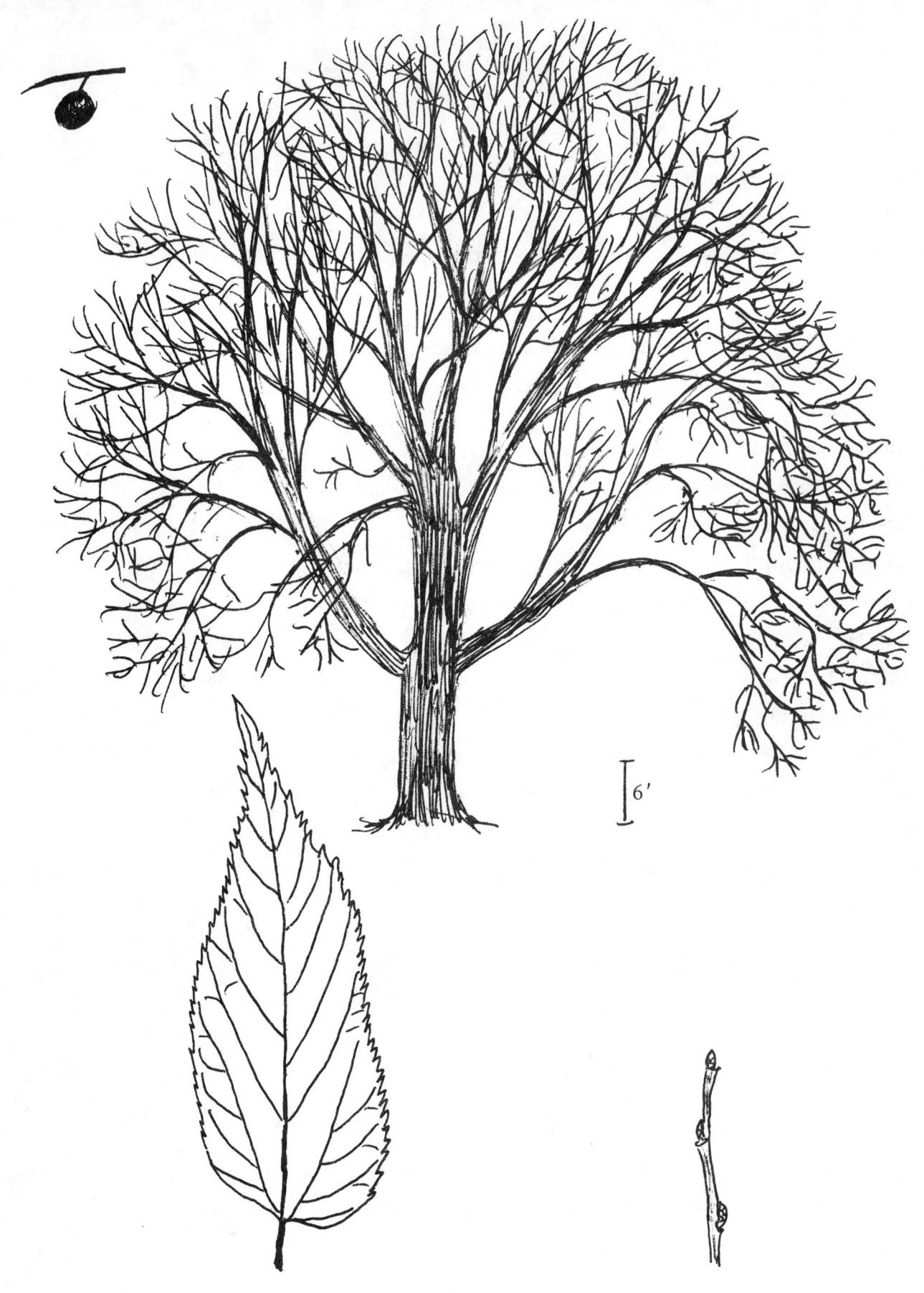

Celtis occidentalis

82

Celtis occidentalis

Common Name: Hackberry

Family: Ulmaceae

Foliage: 2-4 inches long; narrow, curved tip; round, uneven base; coarse teeth; teeth absent from lower margin; thin, light green and rough above; pale and hairy along veins beneath; yellow in autumn

Flowers: male and female separate on the same tree; drooping stalk; greenish; April-May

Fruit: 1/3 inch in diameter; fleshy with pit; orange turning deep purple; ripens September-October

Buds: brown; no terminal; pointed; hairy; appressed

Twigs: slender; light brown; smooth; pith chambered only at nodes

Bark: thick; gray; corky warts and ridges

Roots: fibrous; shallow; spreading; transplants well

Growth Habit: 80-100 feet in height; symmetrical; round top, vase shaped crown; spreading branches; lower branches often drooping; often infested with Witches' Broom

Hardiness: zone 2

Site: rich, moist, well-drained soil; tolerant of dry conditions; sun or partial shade

Growth Rate: moderate-rapid

Maintenance: clean; tolerant to pruning

Propagation: seed—fall sow dry seed and mulch, or stratify in a moist medium at 41°F for 60-90 days; softwood cuttings

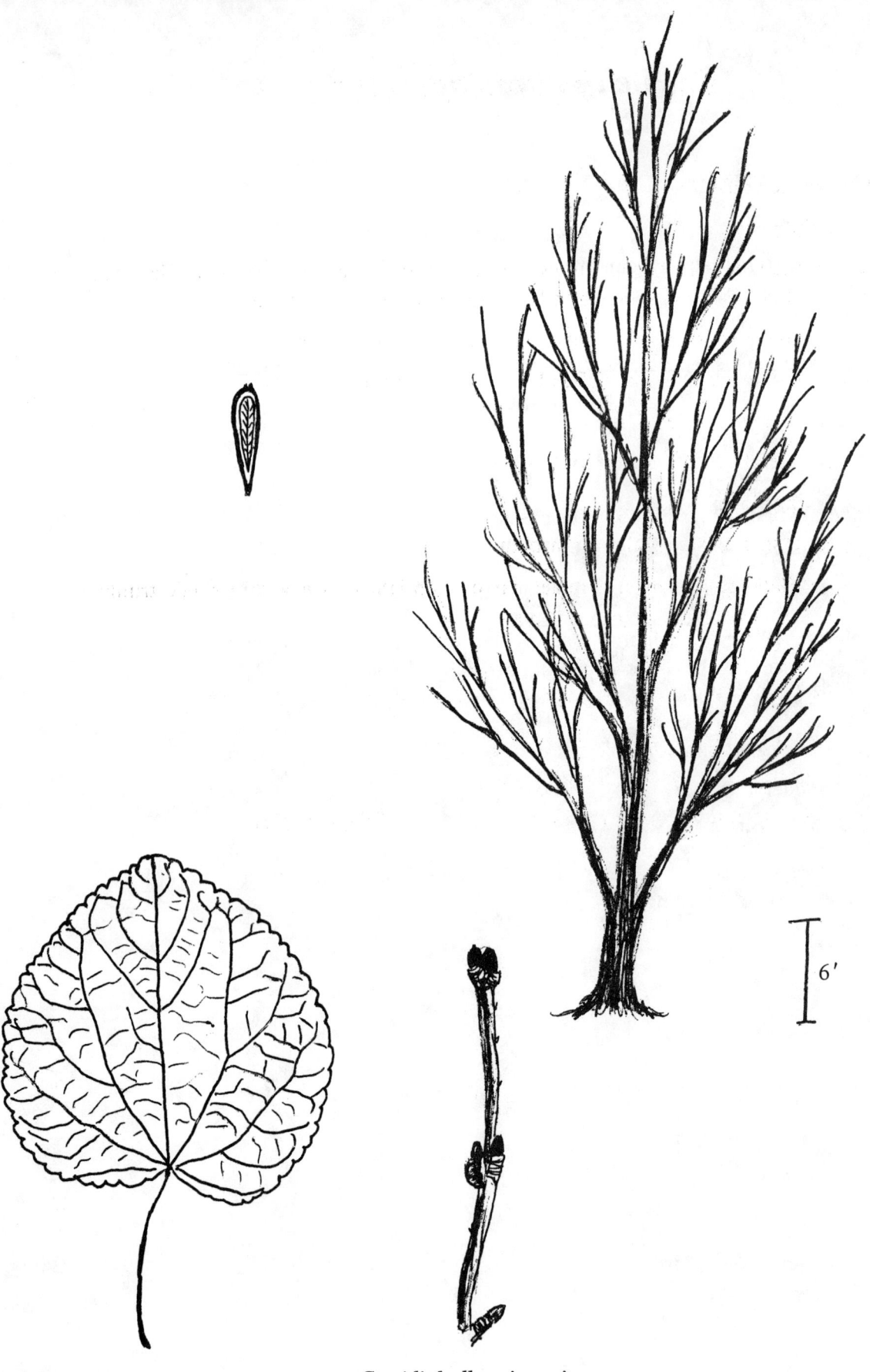

Cercidiphyllum japonicum

Cercidiphyllum japonicum

Common Name: Katsura Tree

Family: Cercidiphyllaceae

Foliage: 2-4 inches long; heart shape; bluish green; scalloped margins with glandular tips; paler beneath; leaf stalks and veins and sometimes red; yellow in autumn

Flowers: male and female separate on separate trees; red; axillary; May

Fruit: 3/4 inch pod; in clusters; ripens October; persists most of winter

Buds: no terminal; red; 3 scales

Twigs: slender; lateral spurs; gray-brown

Bark: gray; shaggy plates

Roots: spreading; shallow; difficult to transplant

Growth Habit: 50-60 feet in height; male: narrow, upright crown with a single trunk; female: widespreading with multiple trunks

Hardiness: zone 4

Site: rich, moist, well-drained soil; sun to partial shade

Growth Rate: rapid

Maintenance: clean; intolerant to pruning

Propagation: seed—fall sow or stratify in sand at 41°F for 90 days; cuttings

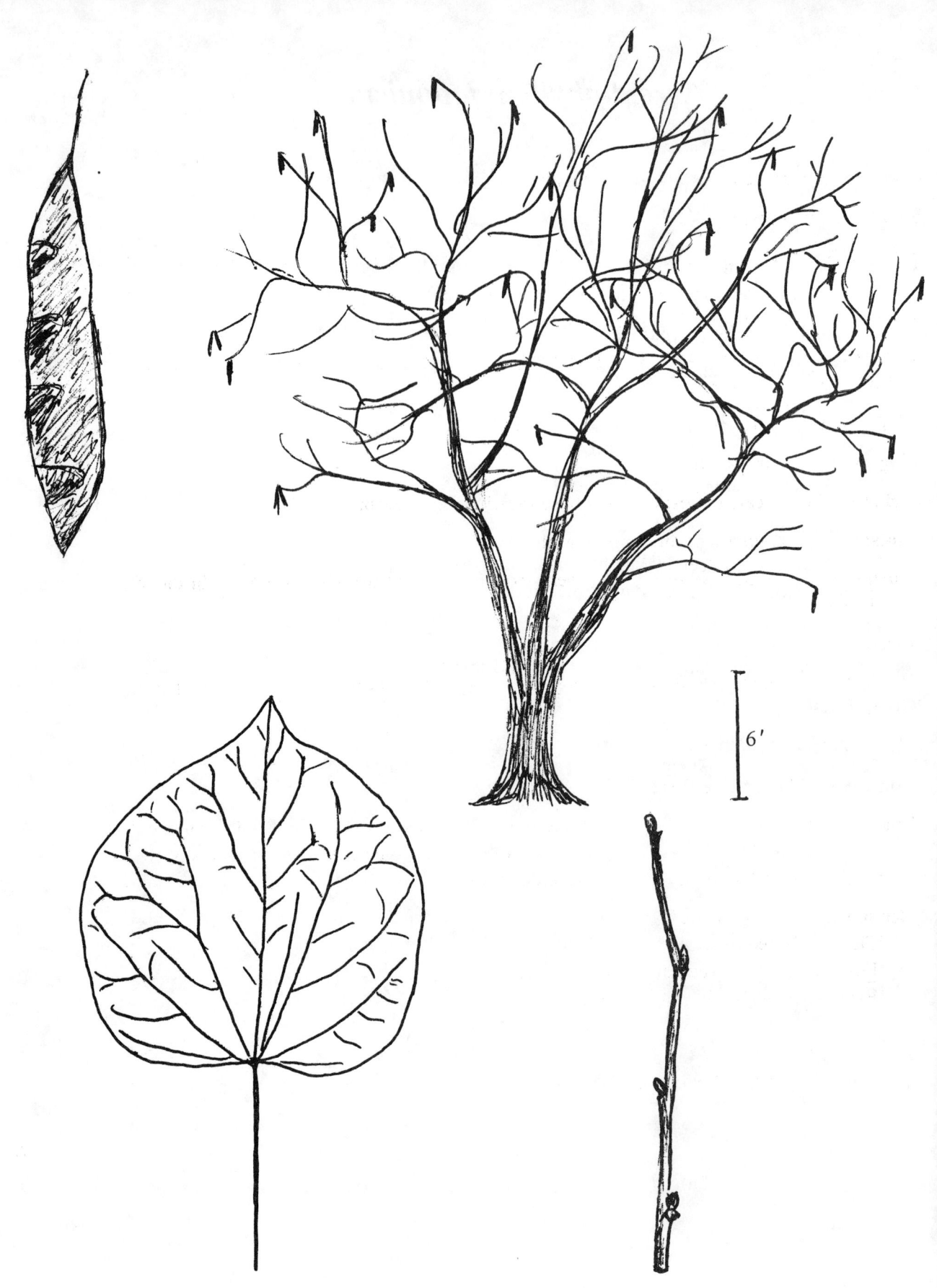

Cercis canadensis

86

Cercis canadensis

Common Name: Eastern Redbud; Judas Tree

Family: Leguminosae

Foliage: 3-5 inches across; heart shaped; without teeth; 5-9 prominent, radiating veins; long, slender leaf stalks; yellow in autumn

Flowers: stalkless clusters; rosy-pink to purplish; March to mid-May

Fruit: 2-4 inch, thin, flat, brown pod; stalked; sharp apex; reddish brown seed; ripens July-August; persists through winter

Buds: small; no terminal; scaly; chestnut-brown

Twigs: slender; dark reddish brown

Bark: thin; gray; scaly plates; flakes at base showing red underbark

Roots: fibrous; transplants moderately well

Growth Habit: 20-35 feet in height; open, irregular crown; upright, spreading branches; flat top

Hardiness: zone 4

Site: light, rich, moist, well-drained soil; tolerant to acid and alkaline conditions; sun or partial shade

Growth Rate: slow-moderate

Maintenance: clean; tolerant to moderate pruning

Propagation: seed—scarify in concentrated sulfuric acid, or boil in water for 1 minute then stratify in sand at 35-41° F for 37-60 days (treatment time depends on hardness of seed coat); graft or bud on *C. canadensis* understock

Selections: 'Alba' — white flowers
    'Flame' — red flowers
    'Forest Pansy' — reddish foliage
    'Pink Bud' — bright pink flowers
    'Royal White' — white flowers
    'White bud' — white flowers
    'Withers Pink Charm' — pink flowers

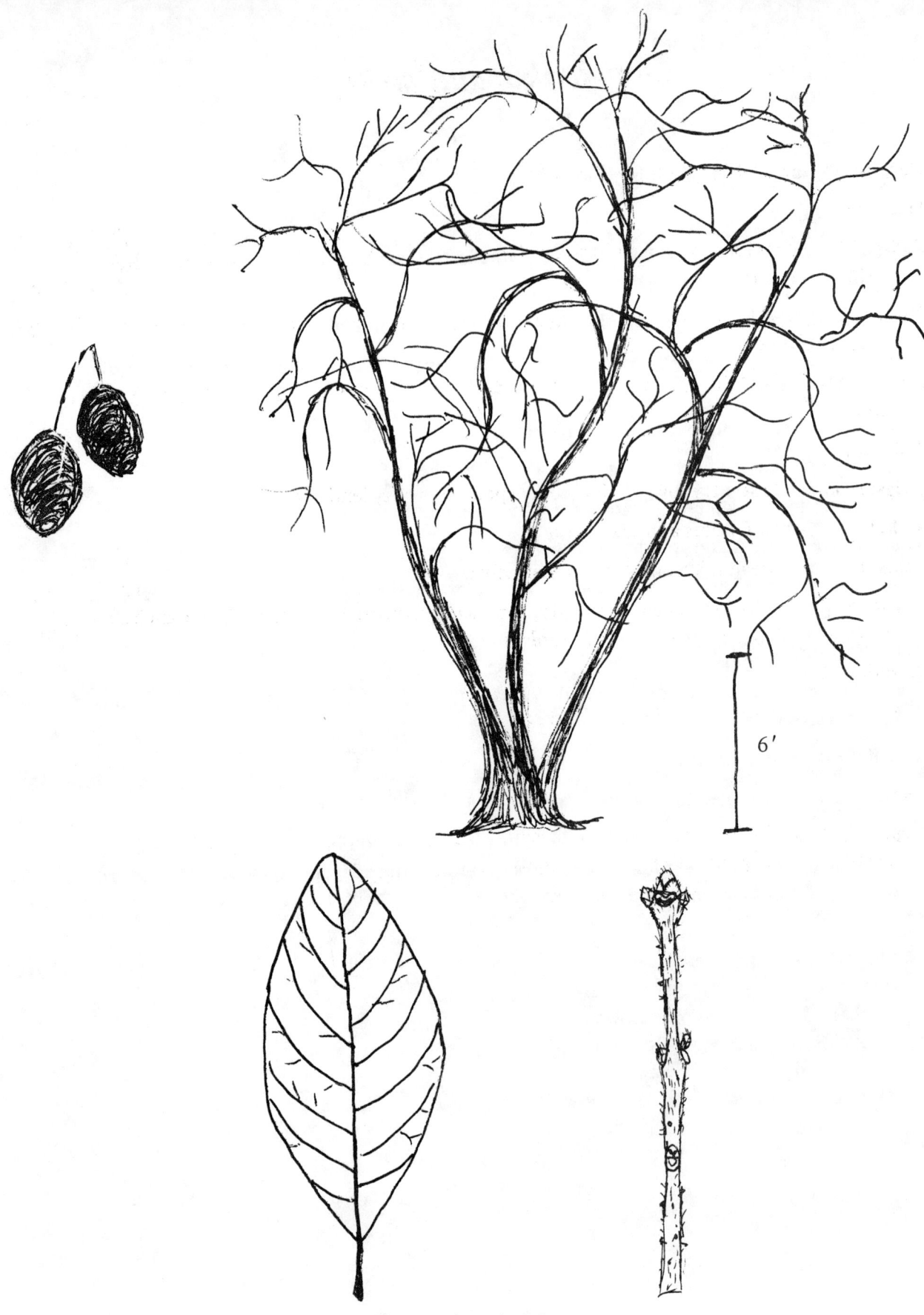

Chionanthus virginicus

Chionanthus virginicus

Common Name: Old-Mans-Beard; White Fringe Tree

Family: Oleaceae

Foliage: 3-8 inches long; without teeth; dark green above; paler below; downy veins; bright yellow in autumn

Flowers: male and female separate on separate trees; 4-6 inch, drooping panicles; white and feathery; June

Fruit: 3/4 inch, oval drupe; thin flesh; in clusters; dark blue-black; large stone; ripens October

Buds: scaly; white

Twigs: moderately stout; brown; hairy; corky spots and warty lenticels

Bark: thin; shallow fissures and scaly; gray

Roots: fibrous; spreading; transplants moderately well

Growth Habit: 15-30 feet in height; upright, somewhat contorted, widespreading branches; rounded crown; sometimes with multiple trunks

Hardiness: zone 4

Site: moist, well-drained soil; full sun or light shade

Growth Rate: slow

Maintenance: clean

Propagation: seed—fall sow and mulch, or provide both warm and cold stratification periods; layers; graft on *Fraxinus* sp. understock

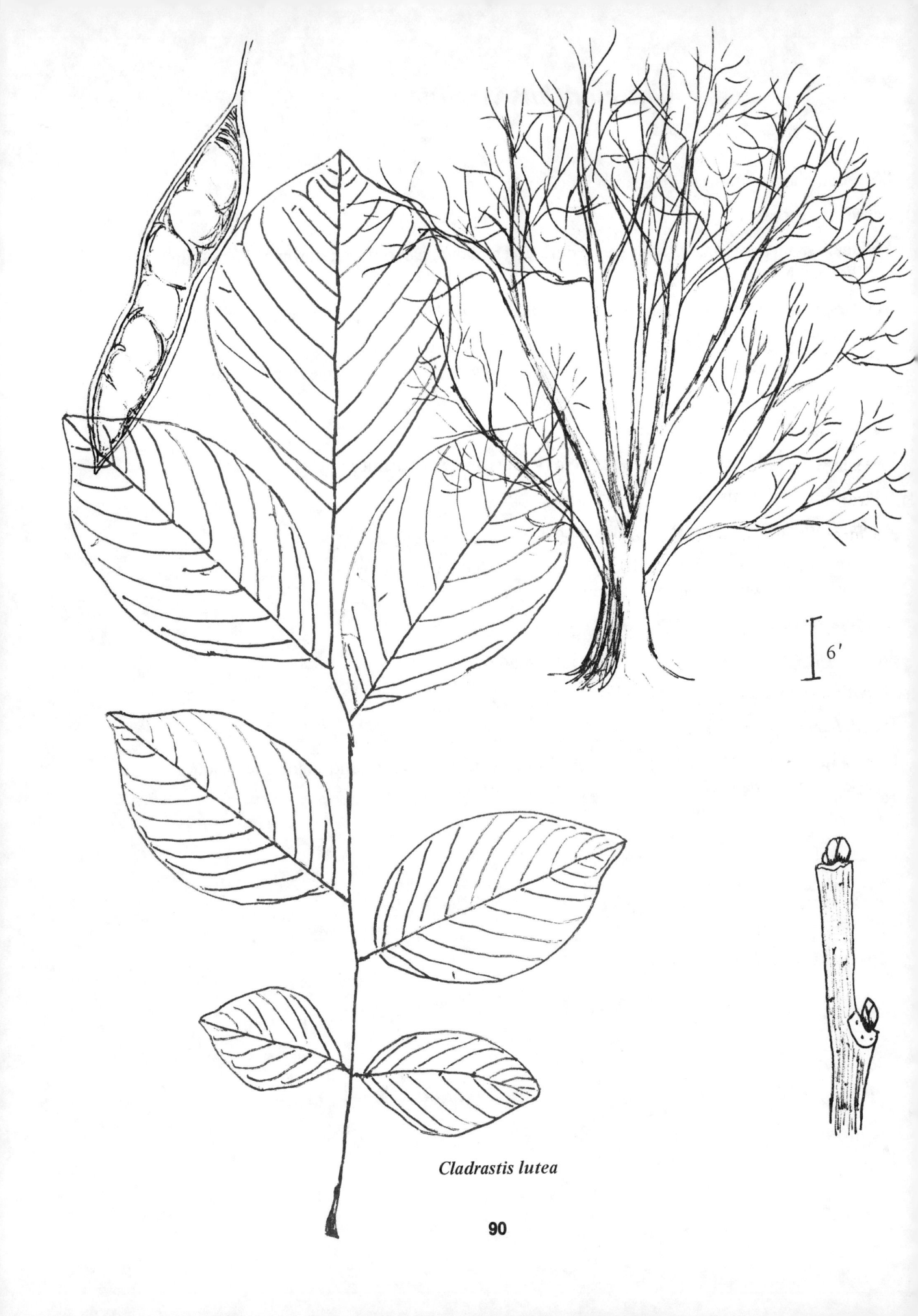

Cladrastis lutea

90

Cladrastis lutea

Common Name: Yellowwood

Family: Leguminosae

Foliage: 8-12 inches long; 7-11, stalked leaflets; without teeth; yellow-green; leaf stalk with enlarged base that covers buds; bright yellow in autumn

Flowers: white; terminal, pendulous panicles; fragrant; late May-June

Fruit: 3-4 inch, dark brown pod; flat; ripens August-September; persists through winter

Buds: small; in clusters but appear as one; conical; brown; hairy

Twigs: gray; somewhat zigzag; scars nearly encircling bud

Bark: thin; gray; smooth

Roots: deep; transplants well when young

Growth Habit: 50-60 feet in height; low branching; open, round crown

Hardiness: zone 3

Site: moist, rich, well-drained soil; drought resistant; tolerant to slightly alkaline soil; sun or partial shade

Growth Rate: moderate

Maintenance: clean; moderate tolerance to pruning

Propagation: seed—fall sow and mulch, or stratify in sand or sand/peat mixture at 41°F for 90 days, or scarify in concentrated sulfuric acid for 30-60 minutes and store for 30 days; graft on *C. lutea* understock

Selections: 'Rosea' — light pink flowers

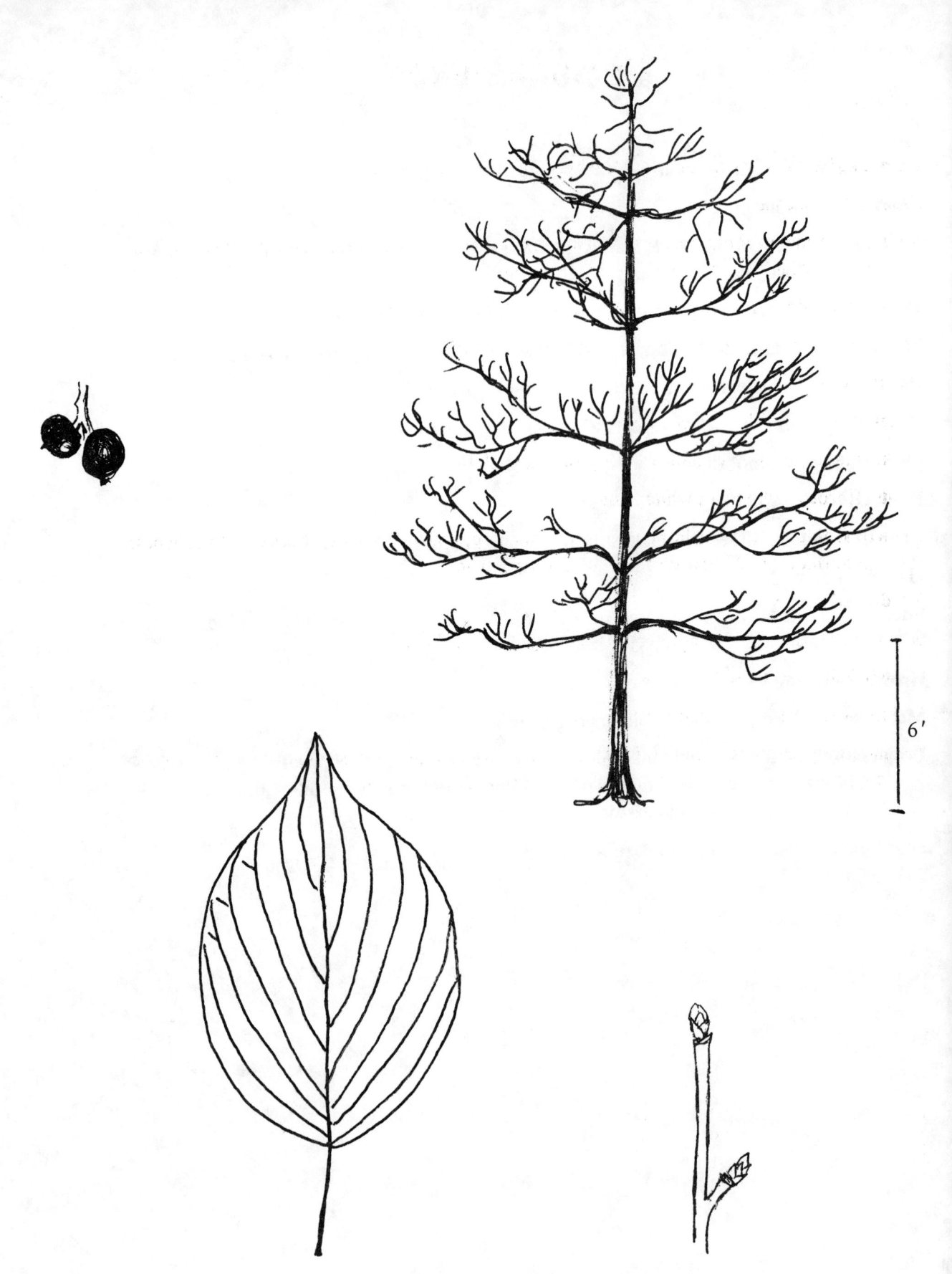

Cornus alternifolia

Cornus alternifolia

Common Name: Pagoda Dogwood; Alternate-leaved Dogwood

Family: Cornaceae

Foliage: 3-5 inches long; clustered at twig ends; alternately arranged on branches; without teeth; prominent parallel veins; hairy beneath; purplish red in autumn

Flowers: terminal, flat top clusters; 4, cream color, petallike bracts; May-June

Fruit: 1/8-1/4 inch, bluish black drupe; bitter; red stalks; ripens August-September

Buds: smooth

Twigs: slender; reddish green; shiny; smooth

Bark: smooth becoming shallowly fissured; grayish brown

Roots: fibrous; transplant while young

Growth Habit: 15-25 feet in height; low branching; whorled tiers of horizontal branches; open, flat topped crown; often with multiple trunks

Hardiness: zone 3

Site: rich, moist, well-drained soil; cool; sun or partial shade

Growth Rate: moderate

Maintenance: clean; tolerant to pruning

Propagation: seed—fall sow and mulch, or stratify in a moist medium at 68-86°F for 60 days then at 41°F for 60 days; softwood or hardwood cuttings

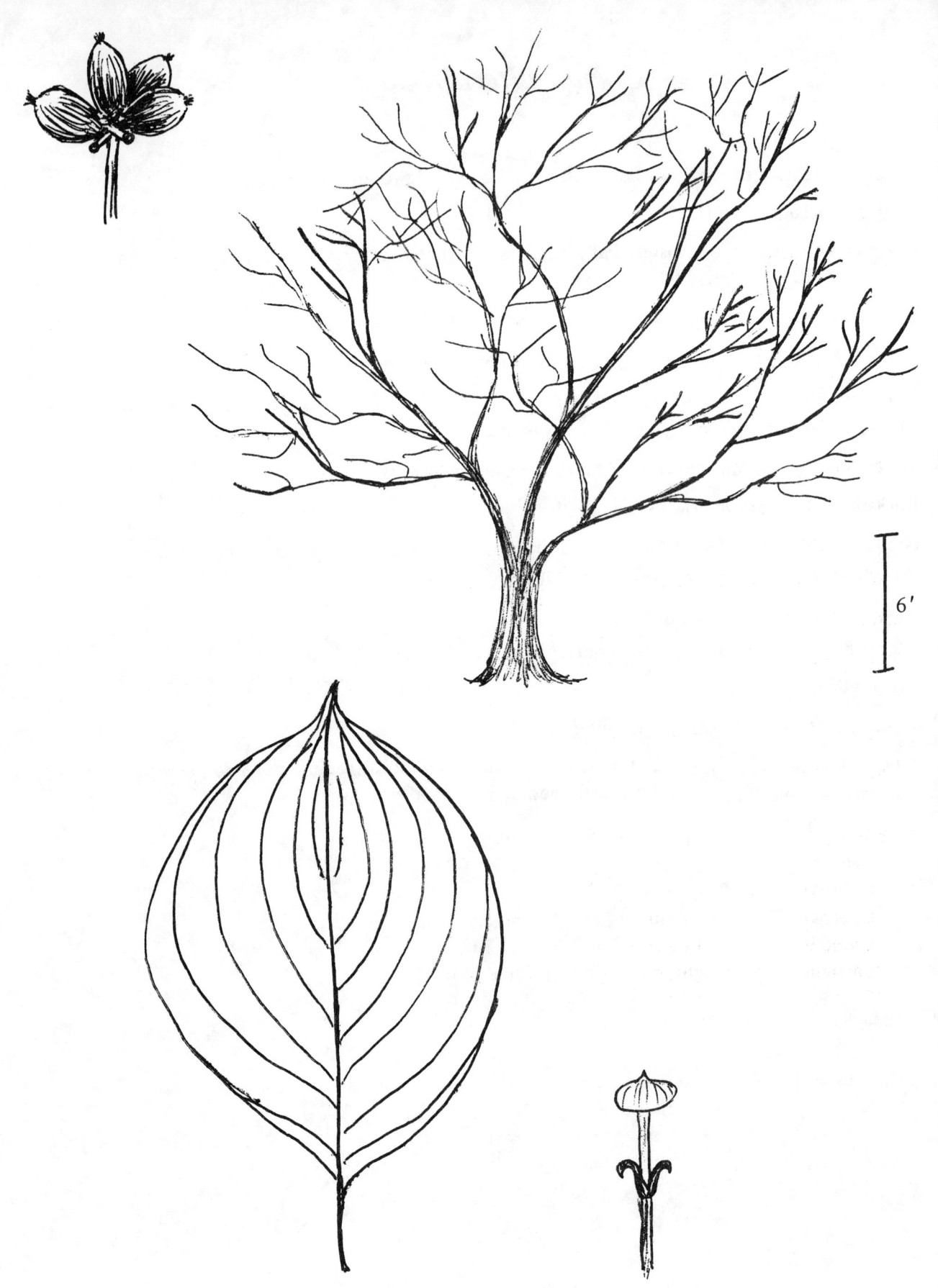

Cornus florida

94

Cornus florida

Common Name: Flowering Dogwood

Family: Cornaceae

Foliage: 3-6 inches long; oval; without teeth; parallel veins; bright green above; paler and hairy below; scarlet in autumn

Flowers: 4, notched, white or pinkish petallike bracts; large; May

Fruit: 1/8-1/2 inch, red drupe; in clusters of 3-4; bitter flesh; ripens September

Buds: terminal flower buds stalked and appear as "lamp posts"; grayish; 2 scales; oppositely arranged on twig

Twigs: slender; angled or diamond shape; dark purple; whitish bloom

Bark: thin; dark red-brown; checkered plates

Roots: fibrous; difficult to transplant

Growth Habit: 15-40 feet in height; flat topped crown; spreading

Hardiness: zone 4

Site: rich, moist, well-drained, acidic soil; sun or shade

Growth Rate: slow

Maintenance: clean; tolerant to pruning

Propagation: seed—stratify in sand at 41° F for 120 days; cuttings; graft or bud on *C. florida* understock

Selections, 'Apple blossom' — bracts light pink with white center
    'Belmont Pink' — pink bracts
    'Cherokee Chief' — red bracts
    'Cherokee Princess' — improved white bracts
    'Cloud 9' — larger bracts
    'Fastigiata' — upright, narrow crown while young
    'First Lady' — white variegated foliage
    'Gigantea' — very large bracts
    'Magnifica' — large bracts
    'Prosser' — dark red bracts
    'Rainbow' — yellow, green, pink variegated foliage
    'Sweetwater Red' — deep red bracts; reddish foliage
    'Welchii' — green, white, pink variegated foliage; pink in autumn
    'White Cloud' — large, white bracts

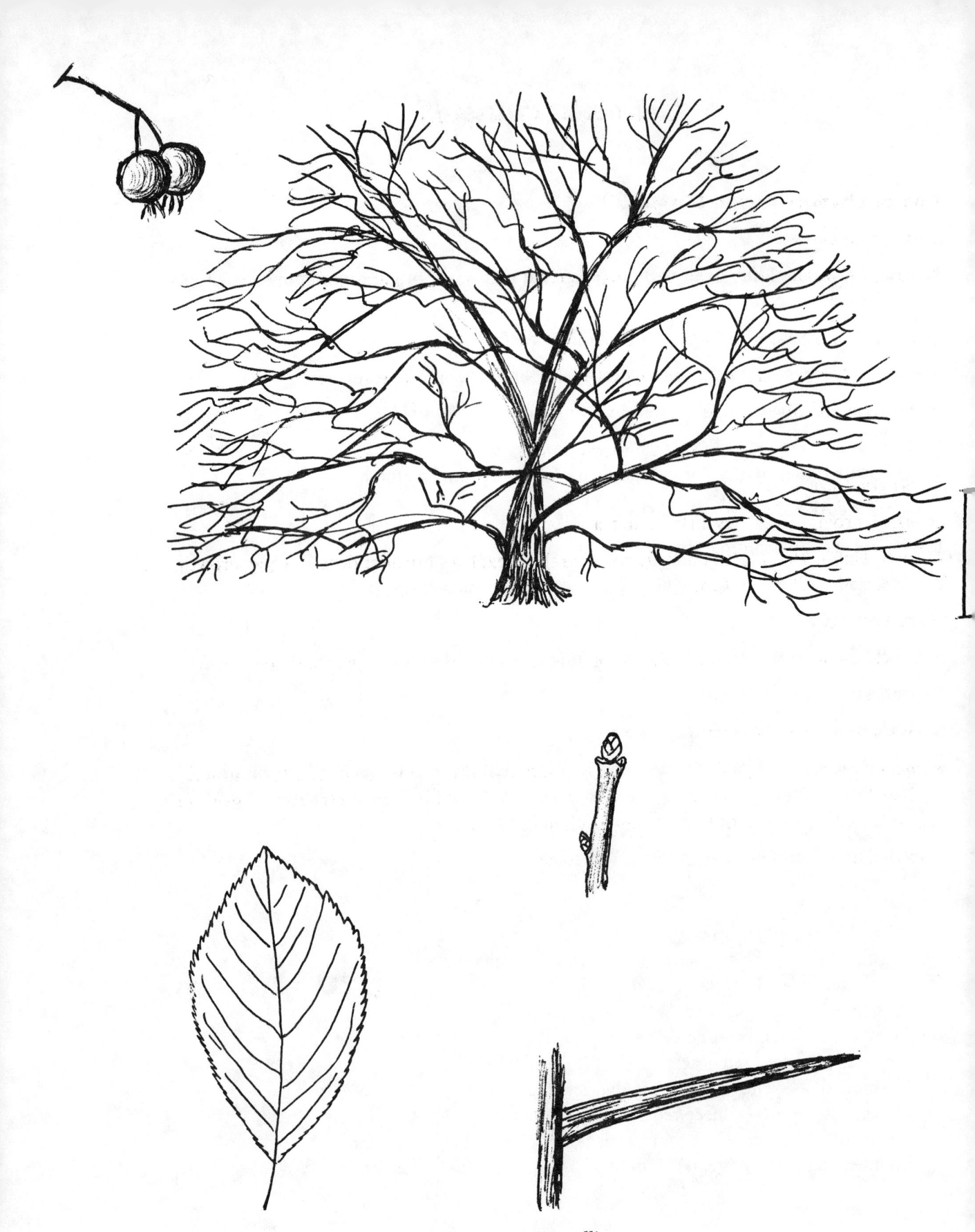

Crataegus crus-galli

Crataegus crus-galli

Common Name: Cockspur Thorn

Family: Rosaceae

Foliage 1-3 inches long; small teeth; dark green; glossy; short leaf stalk; orange-scarlet in autumn

Flowers: white; ill scented; May-June

Fruit: 1/3-1/2 inch, dull, red pome; long stalks; ripens October; persistent

Buds: shiny; reddish brown; blunt

Twigs: slender; light brown; 3-4 inch thorns; glossy

Bark: gray; scaly

Roots: taproot; sometimes difficult to transplant

Growth Habit: 20-30 feet in height; horizontal, spreading branches; dense, twiggy growth; gnarled trunk; round crown

Hardiness: zone 3

Site: prefers rich, well-drained soil but tolerant to other types; sun or partial shade

Growth Rate: slow-moderate

Maintenance: clean; tolerant to pruning

Propagation: seed—scarify dried seed 2-3 hours in sulfuric acid then stratify in a moist medium at 70-80°F for 30-90 days then at 36-41°F for 90-180 days; cuttings; graft or bud on *C. punctata* or *C. phaenopyrum* understock

Selections: var. *splendens* — very shiny foliage

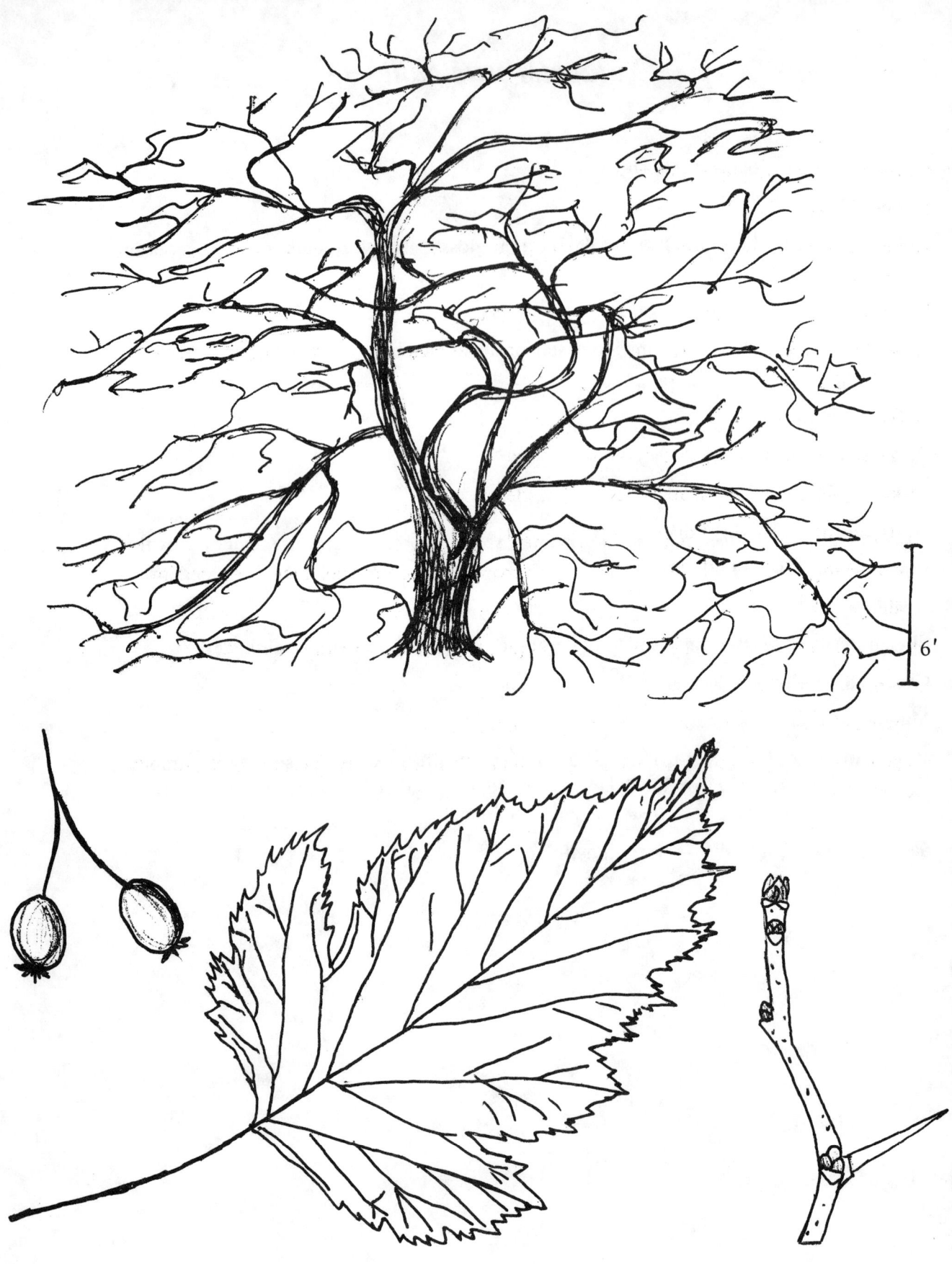

Crataegus mollis

Crataegus mollis

Common Name: Downy Hawthorn

Family: Rosaceae

Foliage: 2-4 inches long; 4-5 pairs of lobes; sharp, double teeth; hairy on veins; yellow in autumn

Flowers: white; April-May

Fruit: 1/2-1 inch, scarlet pome; hairy; sweet, mealy flesh; ripens August-October; falls when ripe

Buds: shiny; brown

Twigs: slender; brown; occasional 1-2 inch thorn

Bark: gray-black; shaggy strips with brown underbark

Roots: taproot; sometimes difficult to transplant

Growth Habit: 25-35 feet in height; half round crown; horizontal branching; branched low

Hardiness: zone 3

Site: moist, well-drained soil preferred but tolerant to dry; sun or partial shade

Growth Rate: moderate

Maintenance: fruit can be messy; tolerant to pruning

Propagation: seed—stratify in a moist medium at 86°F for 21 days then at 50°F for 180 days; cuttings

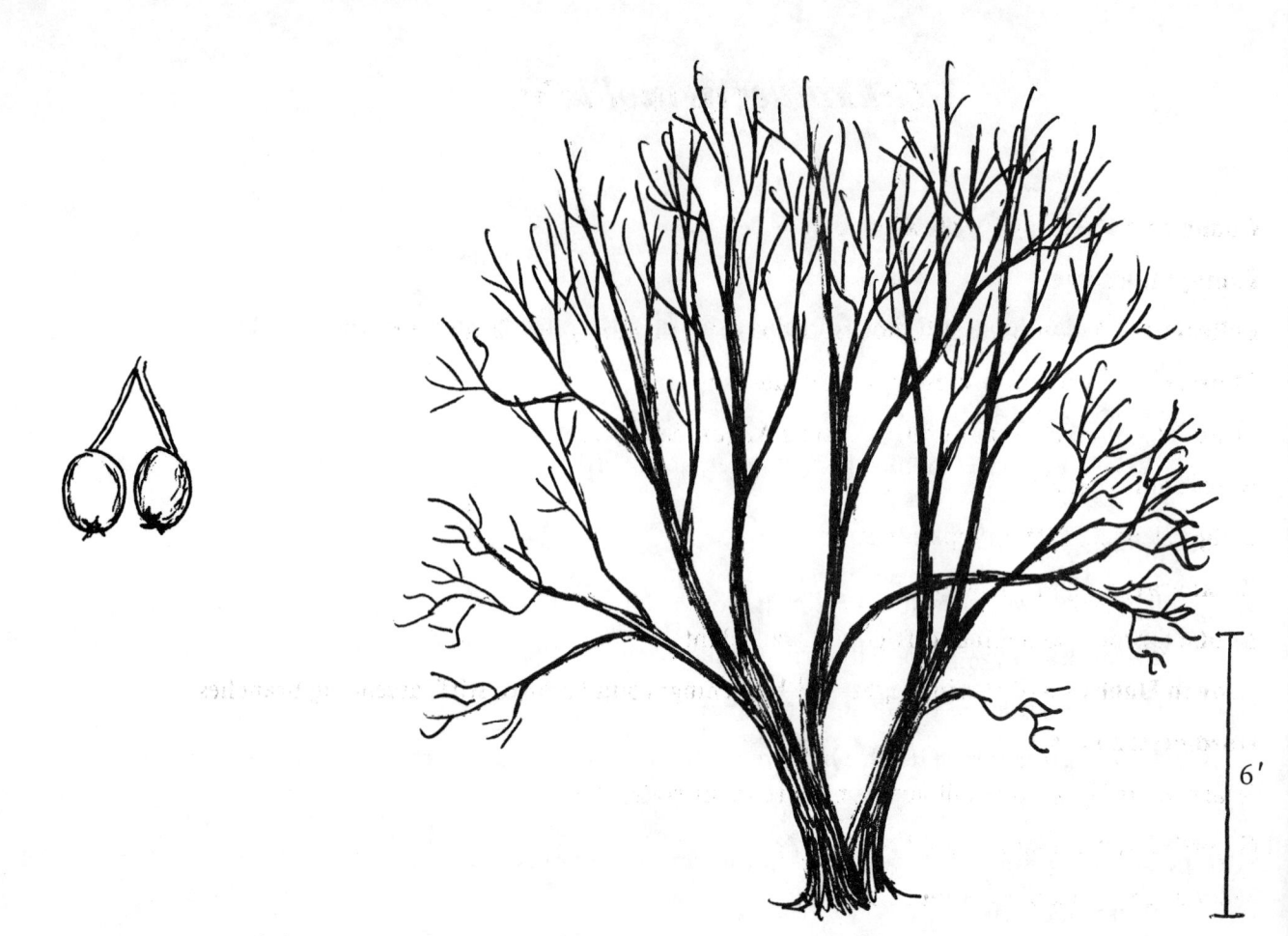

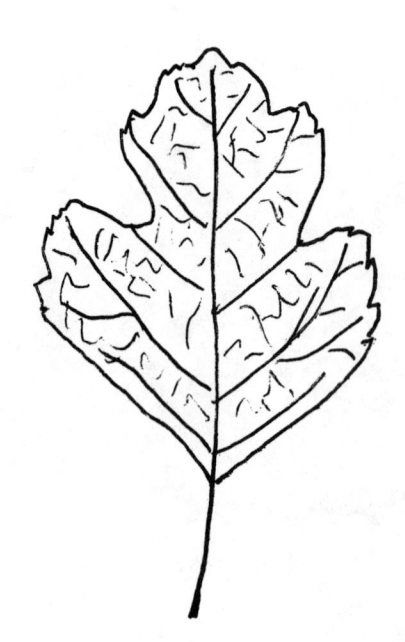

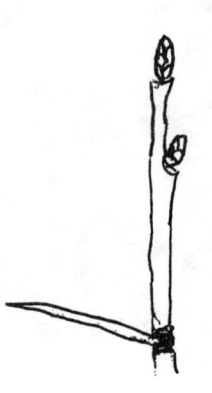

Crataegus oxycantha

Crataegus oxyacantha

Common Name: English Hawthorn

Family: Rosaceae

Foliage: 1/2-5 inches long; 3-5 lobes; deep green; remains green in autumn

Flowers: 5-12 flowers in cluster; white; late May

Fruit: 1/8-1/4 inch, scarlet pome; ripens August-September

Buds: shiny; brown

Twigs: slender; stiff, sharp thorns

Bark: gray; scaly; furrowed

Roots: taproot; sometimes difficult to transplant

Growth Habit: 15-20 feet in height; low branching; round crown; stiff, ascending branches

Hardiness: zone 4

Site: prefers heavy, dry soil but tolerant to many soils; sun

Growth Rate: moderate-rapid

Maintenance: clean; tolerant to pruning

Propagation: seed—stratify in a moist medium at 86° F. for 21 days then at 50° F. for 180 days; cuttings; graft or bud on *C. punctata* or *C. phaenopyrum* understock.

Selections: 'Paul's Scarlet' — double, scarlet flowers; few fruits
    'Punicea' — dark red flowers
    'Plena' — double, white flowers; few fruits
    'Rosea' — light rose flowers
    'Rosea Plena' — double, rose flowers

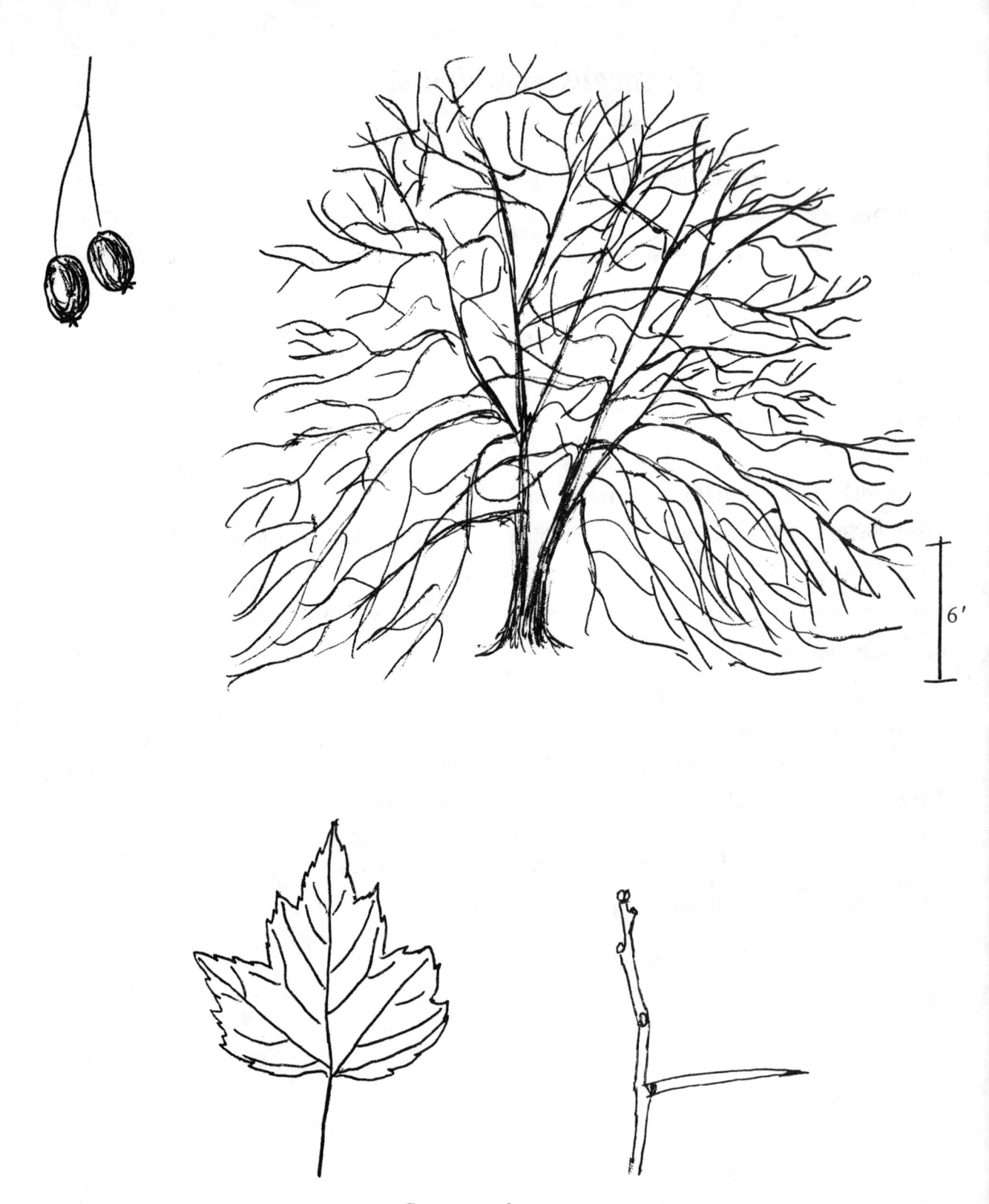

Crataegus phaenopyrum

Crataegus phaenopyrum

Common Name: Washington Thorn

Family: Rosaceae

Foliage: 1-2 inches long; 3 main lobes; deep green; sharp teeth; glossy; red to bronze in autumn

Flowers: white; ill scented; late May-June

Fruit: 1/4-1/2 inch, red pome; in clusters; very showy; ripens October-November; persistent

Buds: shiny; small; reddish brown

Twigs: slender; reddish brown with a grayish bloom; stiff, sharp thorns which are 1-3 inches long and dark purple-brown

Bark: dark gray; flaky

Roots: taproot; less difficult to transplant than many Hawthorns

Growth Habit: 25-30 feet in height; often with multiple trunks; low branching; open, round, spreading crown

Hardiness: zone 4

Site: tolerant to many soils; sun

Growth Rate: rapid

Maintenance: clean; tolerant to pruning

Propagation: seed—fall sow or stratify in a moist medium at 41-50° F for 135 days; cuttings; graft or bud on *C. punctata* or *C. phaenopyrum* understock

Selections: 'Fastigiata' — upright habit

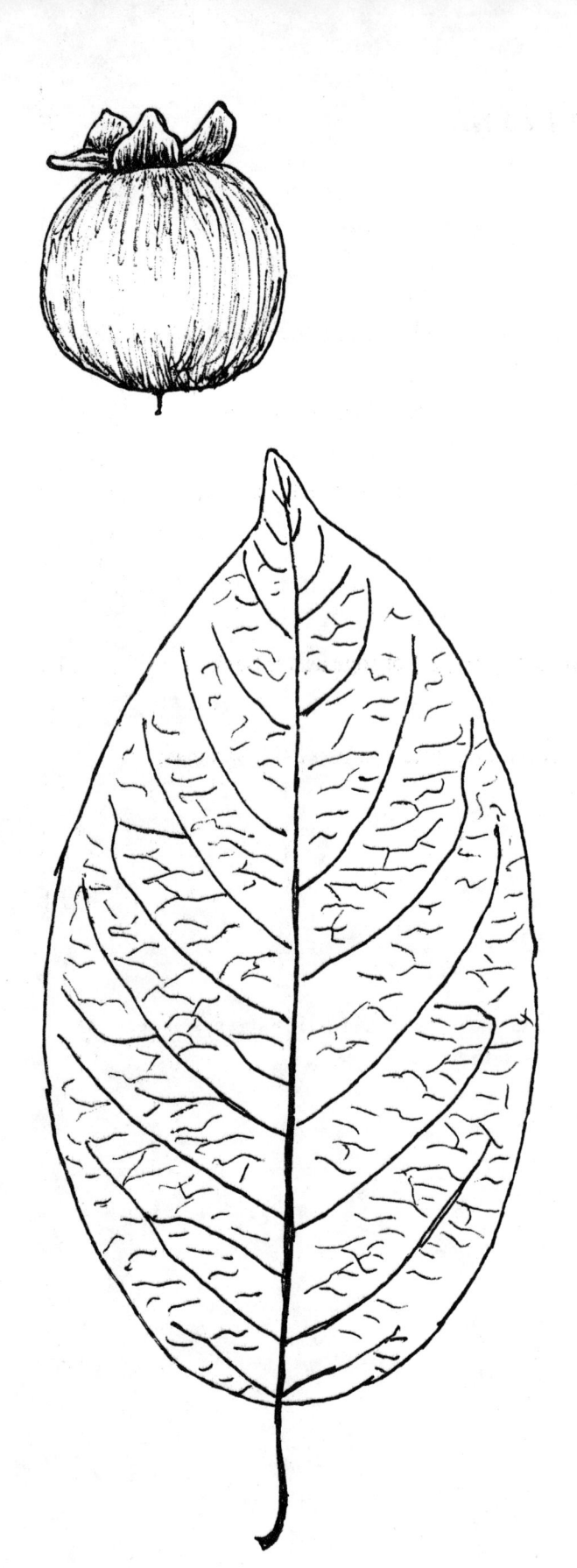

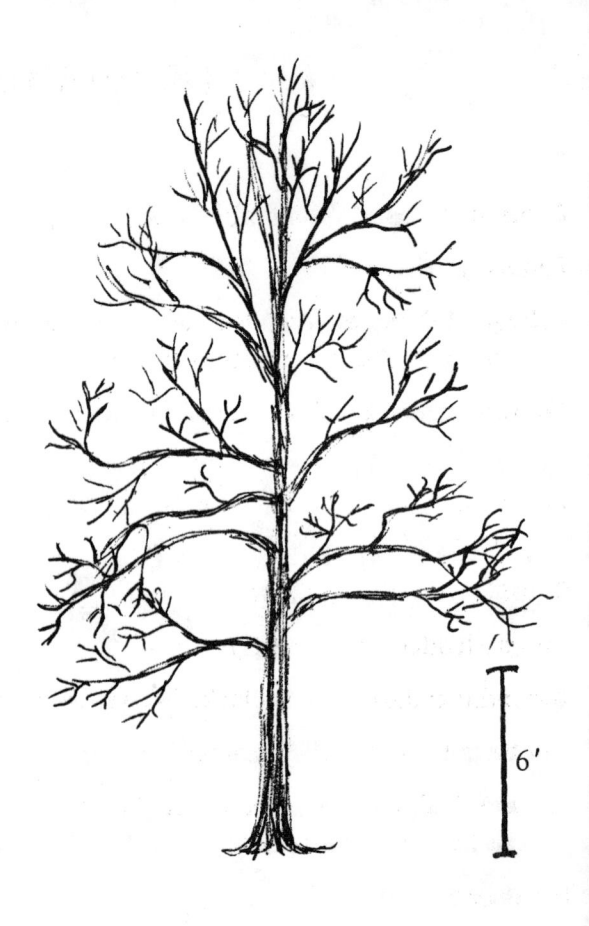

Diospyros virginiana

104

Diospyros virginiana

Common Name: Common Persimmon

Family: Ebenaceae

Foliage: 2-6 inches long; leathery; without teeth; dark green and shiny above; paler and sometimes hairy beneath; stout leaf stalk; orange in autumn

Flowers: male and female separate on separate trees; yellow-green; bell shaped; May to mid-June

Fruit: 1-1 1/2 inch, orange berry; astingent until frost then edible; flattened seed; ripens September-October

Buds: conical; reddish black; 2 scales

Twigs: slender; gray; velvety

Bark: thick; dark gray to black; fissures with irregular corky ridges; orange under bark

Roots: rather easily transplanted

Growth Habit: 35-50 feet in height; oval crown; spreading often contorted branches; suckers freely; often forming thickets or groves

Hardiness: zone 4

Site: rich or sandy, well drained soil; light sun

Growth Rate: slow-moderate

Maintenance: clean; limited tolerance to pruning

Propagation: seed—fall sow clean seed and mulch, or stratify in sand or peat at 37-50° F for 60-90 days

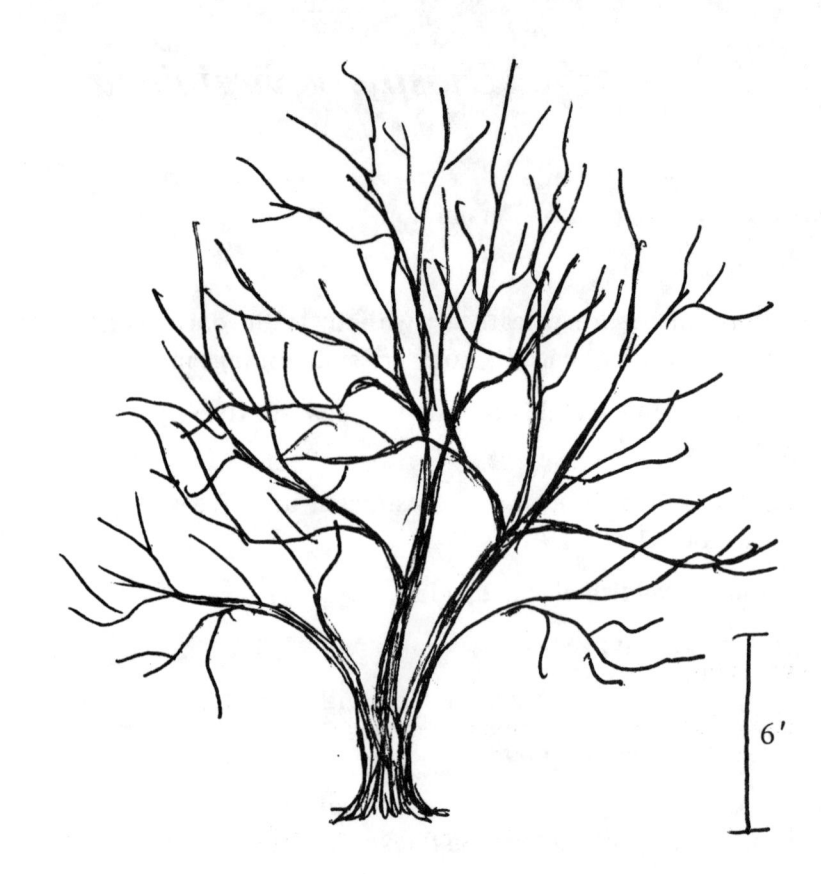

Elaeagnus angustifolia

Elaeagnus angustifolia

Common Name: Russian Olive; Oleaster

Family: Elaeagnaceae

Foliage: 2-4 inches long; without teeth; blunt apex; green or silvery above; silver and scaly below

Flowers: tubular bell shaped; 1-3 per cluster; axillary; silvery outside with yellow inside; fragrant; June

Fruit: 1/2 inch, fleshy drupe; silvery gray flesh; yellow inside; sweet but not palatable; scaly; ripens August-October

Buds: scaly; yellow with gray hairs; small

Twigs: slender; gray with white bloom; spiny

Bark: dark gray; shaggy plates

Roots: very fibrous; transplants well

Growth Habit: 20-30 feet in height; dense, broad, round crown; low branching; trunk often crooked; often as wide as it is high

Hardiness: zone 2

Site: rich, moist, well-drained soil; sun

Growth Rate: rapid

Maintenance: weak wood; tolerant to pruning

Propagation: seed—fall sow dry seed and mulch, or stratify in a moist medium at 34-50°F for 10-90 days; hardwood cuttings; root cuttings; layers

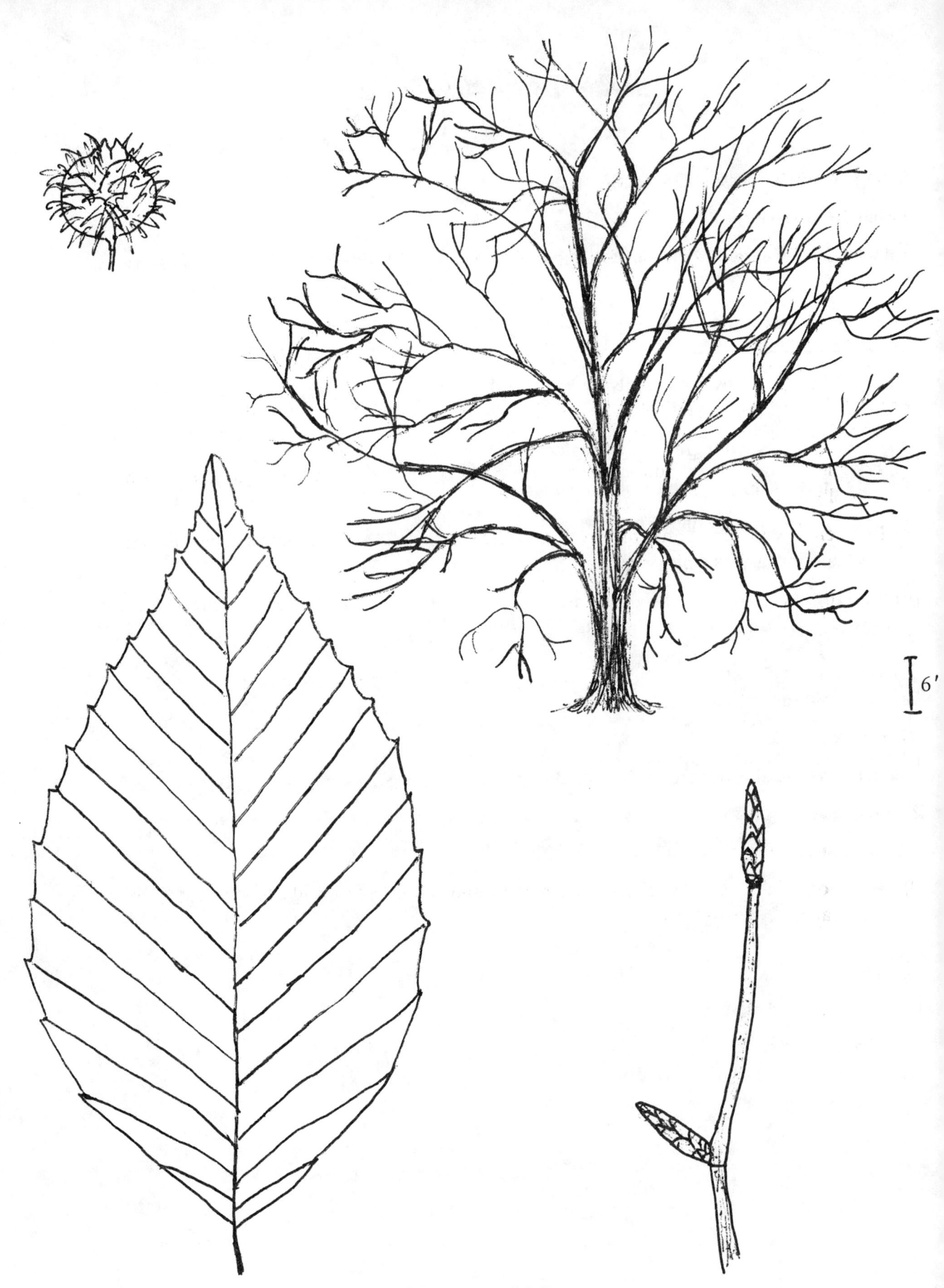

Fagus grandifolia

Fagus grandifolia

Common Name: American Beech

Family: Fagaceae

Foliage: 3-6 inches long; narrowed at base; coarse teeth; a vein ending at each tooth; deep green and smooth above; paler with hairy veins beneath; hairy, short leaf stalk; yellow to orange in autumn

Flowers: male and female separate but on the same tree; male: globose heads on 1 inch stems; female: short spikes; March-May

Fruit: 3/4 inch, stalked bur; densely downy; recurved, unbranched spines; usually in pairs; 4 valves; 2-3 triangular nuts which are sweet and edible; ripens September-November

Buds: long, slender; sharp pointed; brown; all buds equal in size; scale margins hairy with woolly patch at scale tip

Twigs: slender; smooth; shiny; brown; somewhat zigzag; stipule scars almost encircle twig; orange-gray lenticels

Bark: thin; smooth; gray

Roots: very fibrous; matted; frequently difficult to transplant

Growth Habit: 70-100 feet in height; straight trunk; round crown; broader near base with drooping branches; compact

Hardiness: zone 3

Site: rich, well-drained, sandy soil; does not adapt readily to heavy clay soil; shade tolerant

Growth Rate: slow-moderate

Maintenance: clean; very tolerant to pruning

Propagation: seed—fall sow clean seed, mulch, and protect from rodents; or stratify in sand at 41°F for 90 days

Fagus sylvatica

Fagus sylvatica

Common Name: European Beech

Family: Fagaceae

Foliage: 2-4 inches long; dark green; blunt teeth; 5-9 pairs of veins each ending in a tooth; glossy; gold or bronze in autumn

Flowers: male and female separate but on the same tree; brownish; April-May

Fruit: nut enclosed in prickly bur; ripens September-October

Buds: long, slender; pointed apex; all buds are equal in size; stalked

Twigs: smooth; reddish brown

Bark: dark gray; smooth; musclelike

Roots: very fibrous; frequently difficult to transplant

Growth Habit: 60-90 feet in height; widespreading crown; low, horizontal branching

Hardiness: zone 4

Site: light, moist, well-drained soil; sun

Growth Rate: slow

Maintenance: clean; very tolerant to pruning

Propagation: seed—fall sow clean seed, mulch and protect from rodents; or stratify in moist sand at 37-41°F for 40 days then at 68°F for 28 days; graft on *F grandifolia* or *F. sylvatica* understock

Selections: 'Asplenifolia' — cut foliage
'Atropunicea' — purple foliage
'Cuprea' — reddish bronze foliage
'Dawyckii' — fastigiate habit
'Laciniata' — cut foliage
'Pendula' — weeping branches
'Purpurea Pendula' — weeping habit with purple foliage
'Riversii' — compact; deep purple foliage
'Rohanii' — purple, cut foliage
'Roseomarginata' — purple foliage with light pink margins
'Rotundifolia' — round foliage; pyramidal crown
'Spaethiana' — purple foliage
'Tortuosa' — contorted branches
'Tricolor' — green, white and pink foliage
'Zlatia' — young leaves gold

Leaf: ½ actual size

Fraxinus americana

112

Fraxinus americana

Common Name: White Ash

Family: Oleaceae

Foliage: 8-12 inches long; 5-9 stalked leaflets; few if any irregular, blunt teeth; dark green above; pale and silvery below; yellow or purple in autumn

Flowers: male and female separate on separate trees; in loose panicles; April-May

Fruit: 1-2 inch samara; narrow, terminal wing; hangs in clusters; ripens October; persists into winter

Buds: small; rounded; broader than long

Twigs: stout; gray shiny; U shape leaf scars; scars with a notch

Bark: thick; gray; fissures and ridges; diamond shape pattern

Roots: shallow; fibrous; transplants well

Growth Habit: 50-100 feet in height; broad, oval crown; straight trunk

Hardiness: zone 3

Site: moist, rich soil; sun; prefers cold climates

Growth Rate: rapid

Maintenance: abundant seed production; moderate tolerance to pruning

Propagation: seed—fall sow fresh seed and mulch, or stratify in sand at 68-86°F for 30 days then at 41°F for 60 days; graft or bud on *F. americana* or *F. pensylvanica* ssp. *pensylvanica* understock

Selections: 'Autumn Purple' — seedless; deep purple foliage in autumn
'Rosehill' — very hardy; purplish red fall color

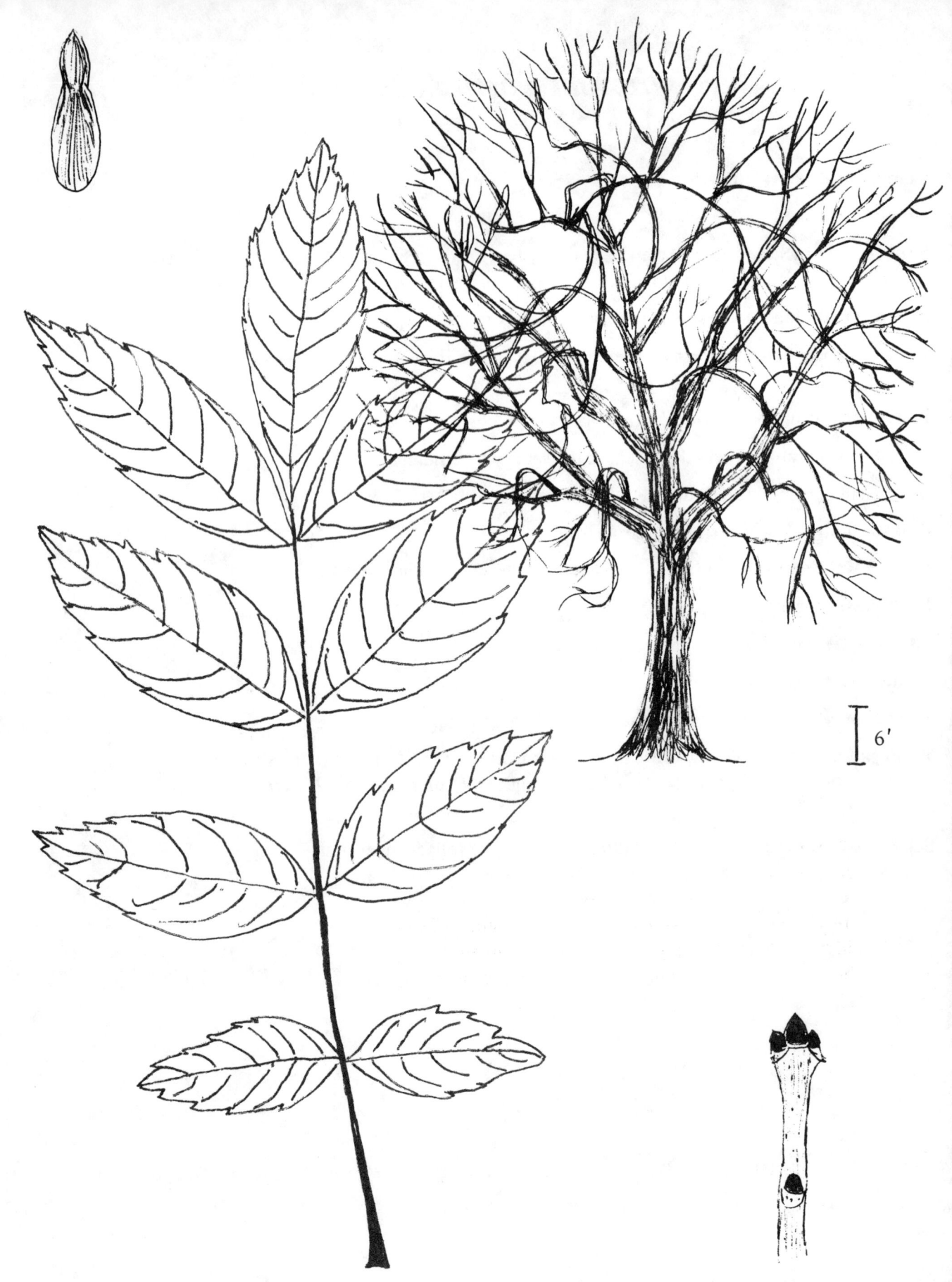

Fraxinus excelsior

Fraxinus excelsior

Common Name: European Ash

Family: Oleaceae

Foliage: 7-11 leaflets; small teeth; stalkless; dark green above; lighter below; yellow in autumn

Flowers: male and female may be in one flower or produced separate flowers; greenish yellow; April-May

Fruit: 1-1 1/2 inch samara; produced in a cluster; ripens August-September

Buds: black; prominent; fuzzy

Twigs: stout; greenish gray

Bark: dark gray; smooth becoming ridged

Roots: very fibrous; shallow; transplants well

Growth Habit: 80-95 feet in height; broad, widespreading, round crown

Hardiness: zone 3

Site: rich, moist, alkaline soil; sun

Growth Rate: moderate-rapid

Maintenance: clean; tolerant to pruning

Propagation: seed—stratify in sand or peat at 68°F for 60-90 days then at 41°F for 60-90 days; graft or bud on *F. pensylvanica* ssp. *pensylvanica* understock

Selections: 'Aurea' — gold twigs; seedless
    'Aurea Pendula' — yellow foliage; weeping branches
    'Aureovariegata' — yellow variegated foliage
    'Hessei' — simple leaves; seedless
    'Heterophylla Pendula' — larger leaves; weeping branches
    'Jaspidea' — young bark yellow; often with green stripes
    'Kimberly' — seedless; compact, symmetrical crown
    'Nana' — globular habit
    'Pendula' — round crown with weeping branches

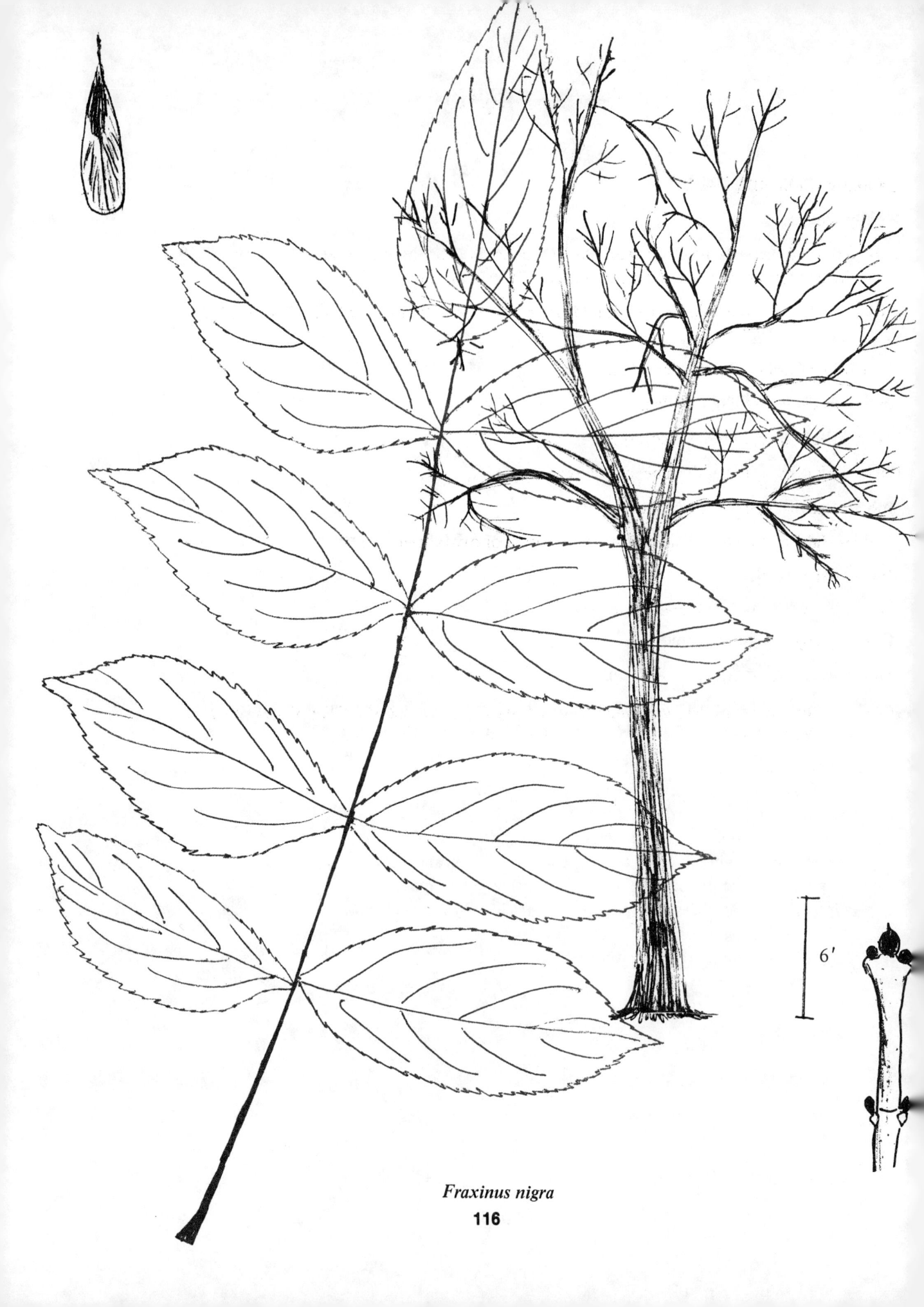

Fraxinus nigra
116

Fraxinus nigra

Common Name: Black Ash

Family: Oleaceae

Foliage: 10-16 inches long; 7-11 leaflets; fine teeth; without stalks on leaflets; dark green above; paler below; brown hair on veins; yellow in autumn

Flowers: male and female may be in one flower or in separate flowers; loose panicles; May-June

Fruit: 1 inch samara; ripens September

Buds: conical; stout; almost black

Twigs: stout; gray; dull; light colored lenticels

Bark: dark gray; thin; smooth becoming scaly

Roots: shallow; fibrous; transplants well

Growth Habit: 50-80 feet in height; narrow, round or oval crown

Hardiness: zone 2

Site: wet or very moist soil; shade tolerant

Growth Rate: rapid

Maintenance: clean; tolerant to pruning

Propagation: seed—fall sow and mulch, or stratify in sand at 68-86°F for 60 days then at 41°F for 90 days

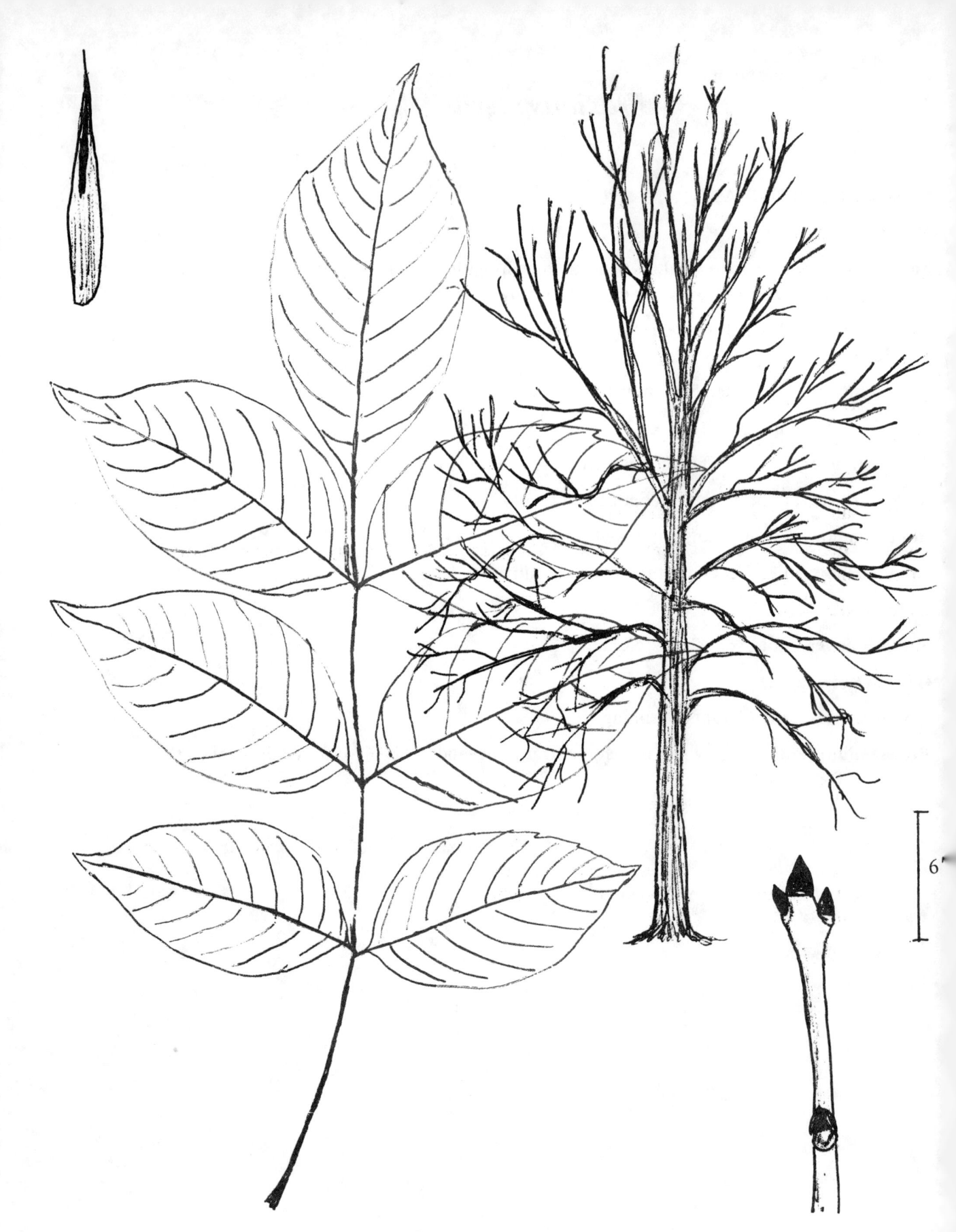

Fraxinus pensylvanica

118

Fraxinus pensylvanica

Common Name: Red Ash

Family: Oleaceae

Foliage: 9-12 inches long; 7-9 leaflets with stalks; with or without fine teeth; yellow-green above; paler and hairy beneath; hairy leaf stalk; yellow in autumn

Flowers: male and female separate on separate trees; in dense clusters; May

Fruit: 1-2 inch samara; in clusters; ripens September-October; persists through winter

Buds: dark brown; hairy

Twigs: stout; gray; downy; leaf scar straight on upper edge

Bark: gray; shallow fissures with scaly ridges

Roots: shallow; fibrous; transplants well

Growth Habit: 30-60 feet in height; low branching; irregular, narrowly pyramidal crown; stiff branching

Hardiness: zone 3

Site: moist or dry soil; sun

Growth Rate: rapid

Maintenance: clean; tolerant to pruning

Propagation: seed—fall sow and mulch, or stratify in a moist medium at 68°F for 60 days then at 32-41°F for 210 days (or stratify in a plastic bag at 35°F for 150 days); graft or bud on *F. pensylvanica* ssp. *pensylvanica* understock

Selections: ssp. *pensylvanica* (var. *subintegerrima*) Green Ash; twigs without hair; leaves green on both sides and have more teeth; hardy to zone 2
   F. p. p. 'Marshall Seedless' — seedless; upright
   F. p. p. 'Summit' — upright

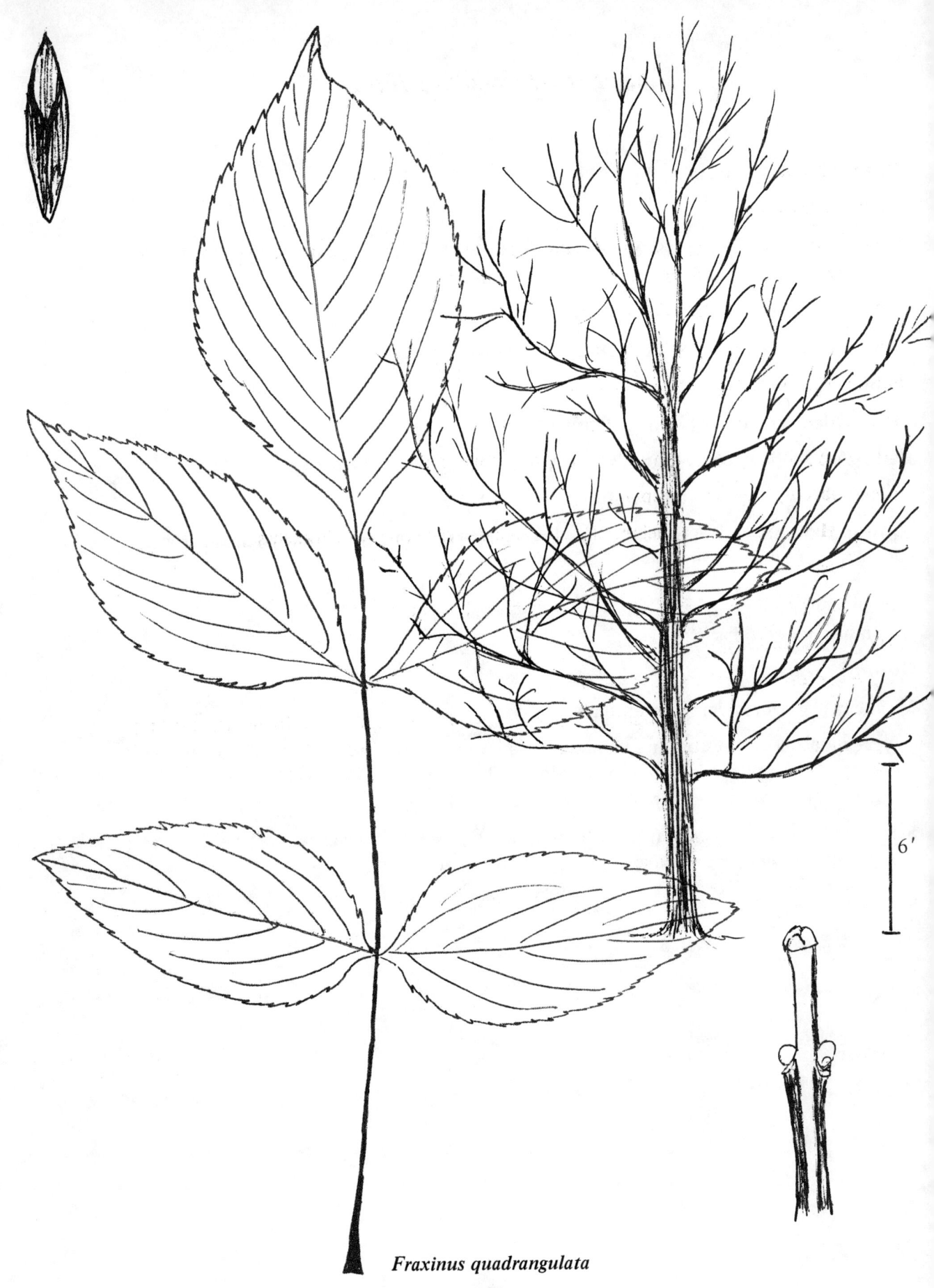

Fraxinus quadrangulata

120

Fraxinus quadrangulata

Common Name: Blue Ash

Family: Oleaceae

Foliage: 8-12 inches long; usually 7 leaflets; coarse teeth; thick; yellow-green above; paler below; pale yellow in autumn

Flowers: in loose panicles; March-April

Fruit: 1-2 inch samara; broad; ripens September-early October

Buds: small; round; somewhat hairy; dark brown

Twigs: stout; square with 4 corky ridges; orange-brown

Bark: gray; deep fissures with scales; inner bark turns blue on exposure

Roots: fibrous; shallow; transplants well

Growth Habit: 30-40 feet in height; narrow, rounded crown; coarse branches

Hardiness: zone 3

Site: rich, moist, well-drained soil; does well in alkaline soil; sun

Growth Rate: moderate

Maintenance: clean; tolerant to pruning

Propagation: seed—stratify in sand at 68-86°F for 60 days and at 41°F for 90 days; spring sow only

Leaf: ½ actual size

Fraxinus tomentosa

Fraxinus tomentosa (profunda)

Common Name: Pumpkin Ash

Family: Oleaceae

Foliage: 10-12 inches long; 7-9 stalked leaflets; usually without teeth; yellow-green above; pale and hairy below; leaf stalk hairy; yellow in autumn

Flowers: male and female separate on separate trees; in clusters; small; April-May

Fruit: 2-3 inch samara with a terminal wing; ripens September-October

Buds: brown; hairy

Twigs: stout; gray; hairy

Bark: gray; fissured and scaly

Roots: shallow; fibrous; transplants well

Growth Habit: 80-100 feet in height; upright, spreading branches; broad, oblong, round top crown

Hardiness: zone 5

Site: moist or wet soil; sun or partial shade

Growth Rate: rapid

Maintenance: clean; tolerant to pruning

Propagation: seed—stratify on moist paper at 40° F for 60 days; graft or bud on *F pensylvanica* ssp. *pensylvanica* understock using only buds or twigs from the terminal portion of the tree

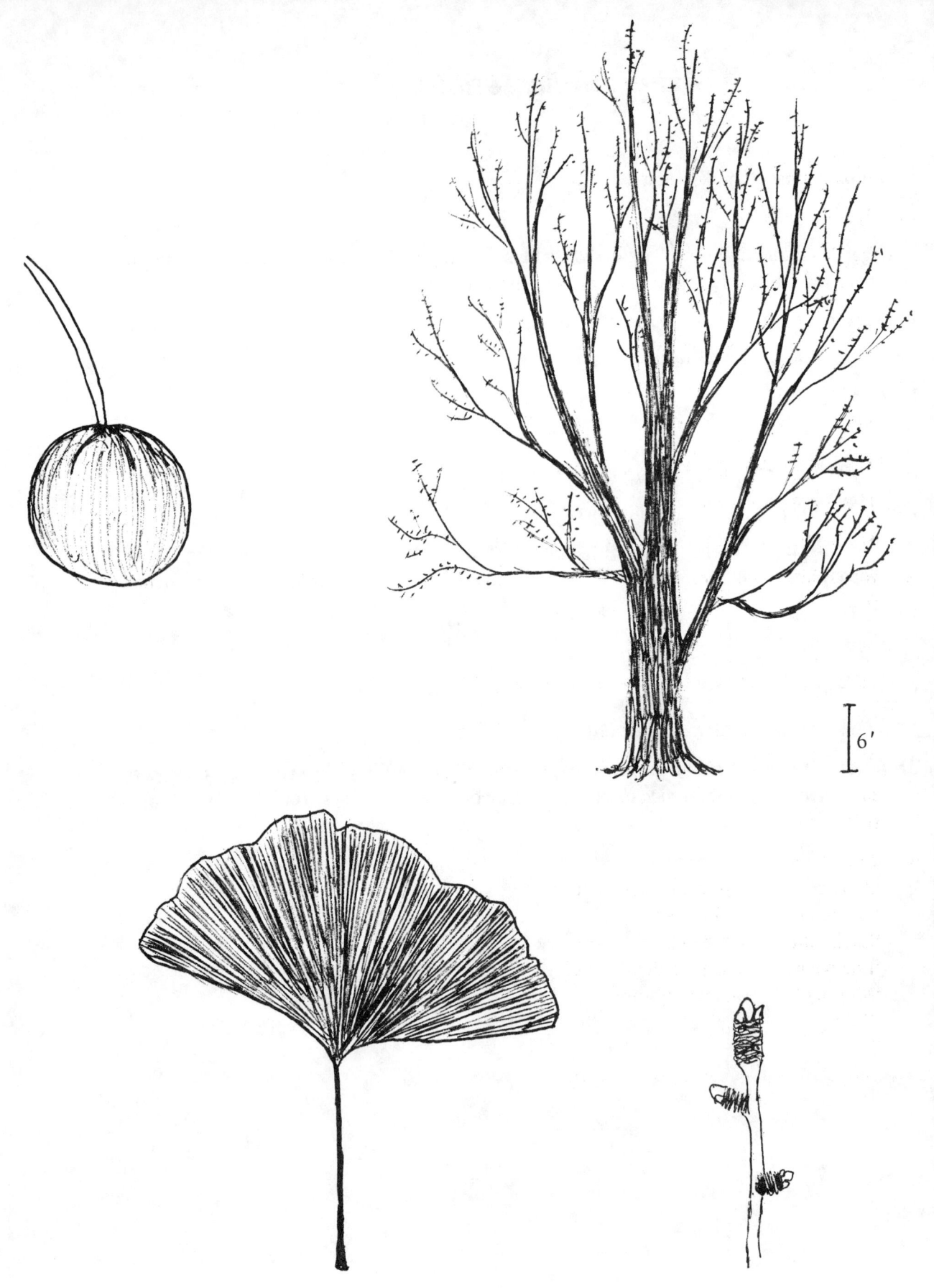

Gingko biloba

Ginkgo biloba

Common Name: Ginkgo; Maidenhair Tree

Family: Ginkgoaceae

Foliage: 2-5 inches long; fan shape; often notched into 2 lobes; wavy margin; veins radiate from the base; on thick spurs; yellow in autumn

Flowers: male and female separate on separate trees; male: greenish catkins; female: small, paired pollen sacs on slender spikes; March-April

Fruit: 1 inch drupe; foul smelling; edible kernel; ripens to an orange-yellow in October

Buds: light brown; short; conical

Twigs: gray; stubby spurs

Bark: light gray; irregular ridges

Roots: fibrous; sometimes difficult to transplant

Growth Habit: 60-90 feet in height; irregular, pyramidal crown; stiff ascending branches; few twigs; female is less erect and more open than the male

Hardiness: zone 4

Site: adaptable to many soil types; sun or partial shade

Growth Rate: slow

Maintenance: female produces heavy fruit crops; tolerant to pruning

Propagation: seed—fall sow and mulch, or stratify in moist sand at 41° F for 30-60 days; softwood cuttings; graft on *G. biloba* understock

Selections: 'Aurea' — yellow foliage
    'Autumn Gold' — male; compact
    'Fastigiata' — columnar
    'Laciniata' — cut foliage
    'Lakeview' — male; conical crown
    'Mayfield' — male; more upright
    'Palo Alto' — male; more upright
    'Pendula' — weeping branches
    'Santa Cruz' — male; more upright
    'Variegata' — yellow variegated foliage

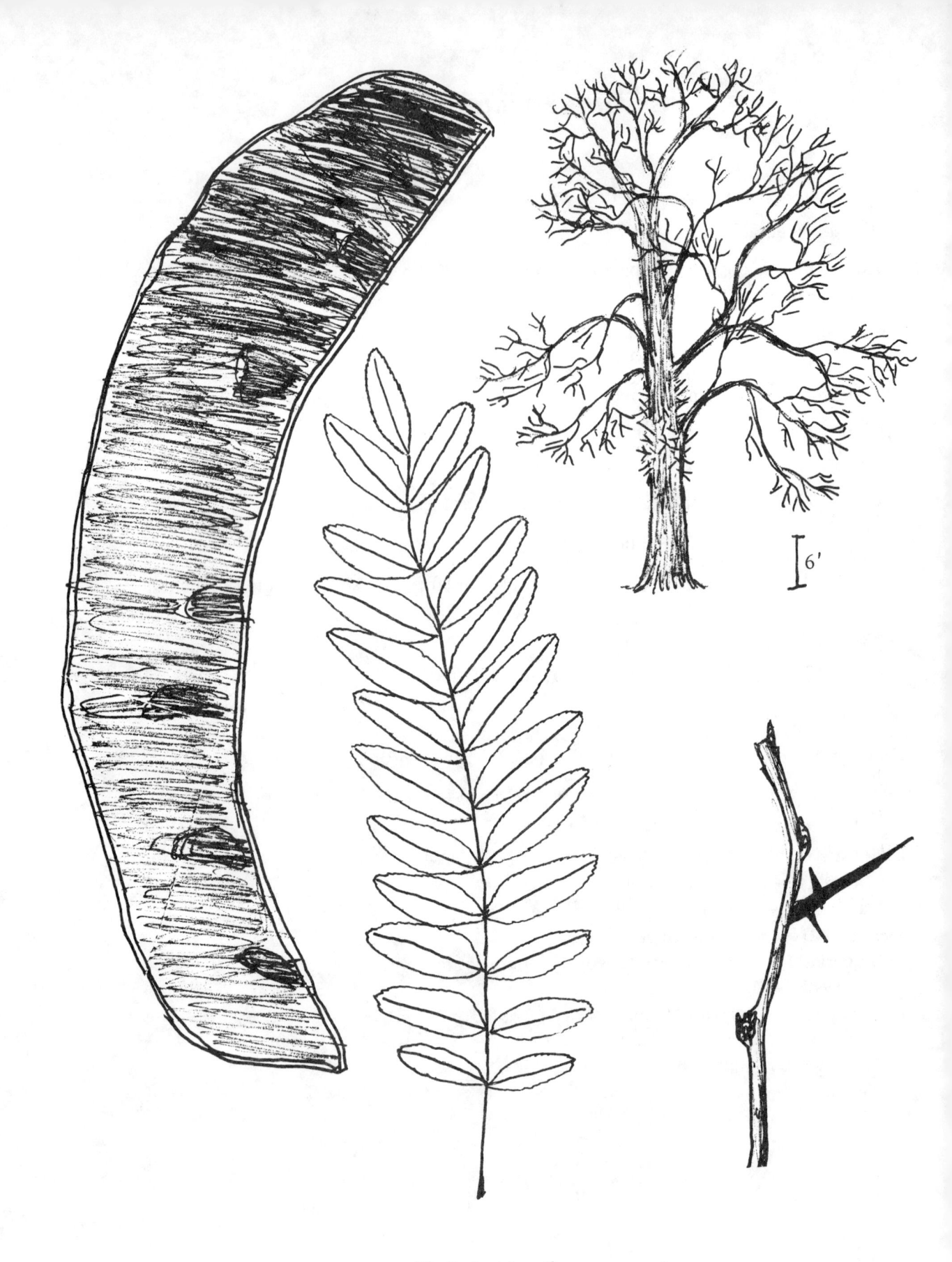

Gleditsia tricanthos

Gleditsia triacanthos

Common Name: Honey Locust

Family: Leguminosae

Foliage: 6-12 inches long; 18 or more leaflets; tiny teeth; lustrous, dark green above; lighter below; hairy leaf stalk that is grooved and has a swollen base; yellow in autumn

Flowers: male and female in one flower or separate; clusters; greenish white; fragrant; May-June

Fruit: flattened, often twisted pod; may be up to 12 inches in length; curved with wavy edges; dark brown; shiny; ripens September-October

Buds: no terminal; hidden by leaf stalk base; brown; 3 or more superimposed

Twigs: thin; shiny; reddish brown to gray; 2 or 3, branched thorns which may be 2-3 inches in length

Bark: dark brown; long vertical plates; thorns may be up to 8 inches

Roots: few fibrous; difficult to transplant in larger sizes

Growth Habit: 50-70 feet in height; open, spreading crown; light, airy appearance; large thorns on trunk and branches

Hardiness: zone 4

Site: prefers moist, well-drained soil but is tolerant to dry, sandy soil; sun or partial shade

Growth Rate: rapid

Maintenance: fruit can be messy; tolerant to pruning

Propagation: seed—scarify in concentrated sulfuric acid 1-2 hours or soak in water until swollen, spring sow only; root cuttings; hardwood cuttings; graft or bud on *G. tricanthos* understock

Selections: 'Bryotti' — pendulous branches
  'Imperial' — compact; central leader; more symmetrical than 'Skyline'; thornless; seedless
  'Majestic' — thornless; seedless; more upright; dark foliage
  'Moraine' — widespreading crown; thornless; seedless
  'Rubylace' — seedless; thornless; young leaflets tips are ruby-red
  'Shademaster' — thornless; seedless; more open, globular crown
  'Skyline' — thornless; seedless; central leader; symmetrical crown; bright green foliage
  'Sunburst' — seedless; thornless; young leaflets yellow

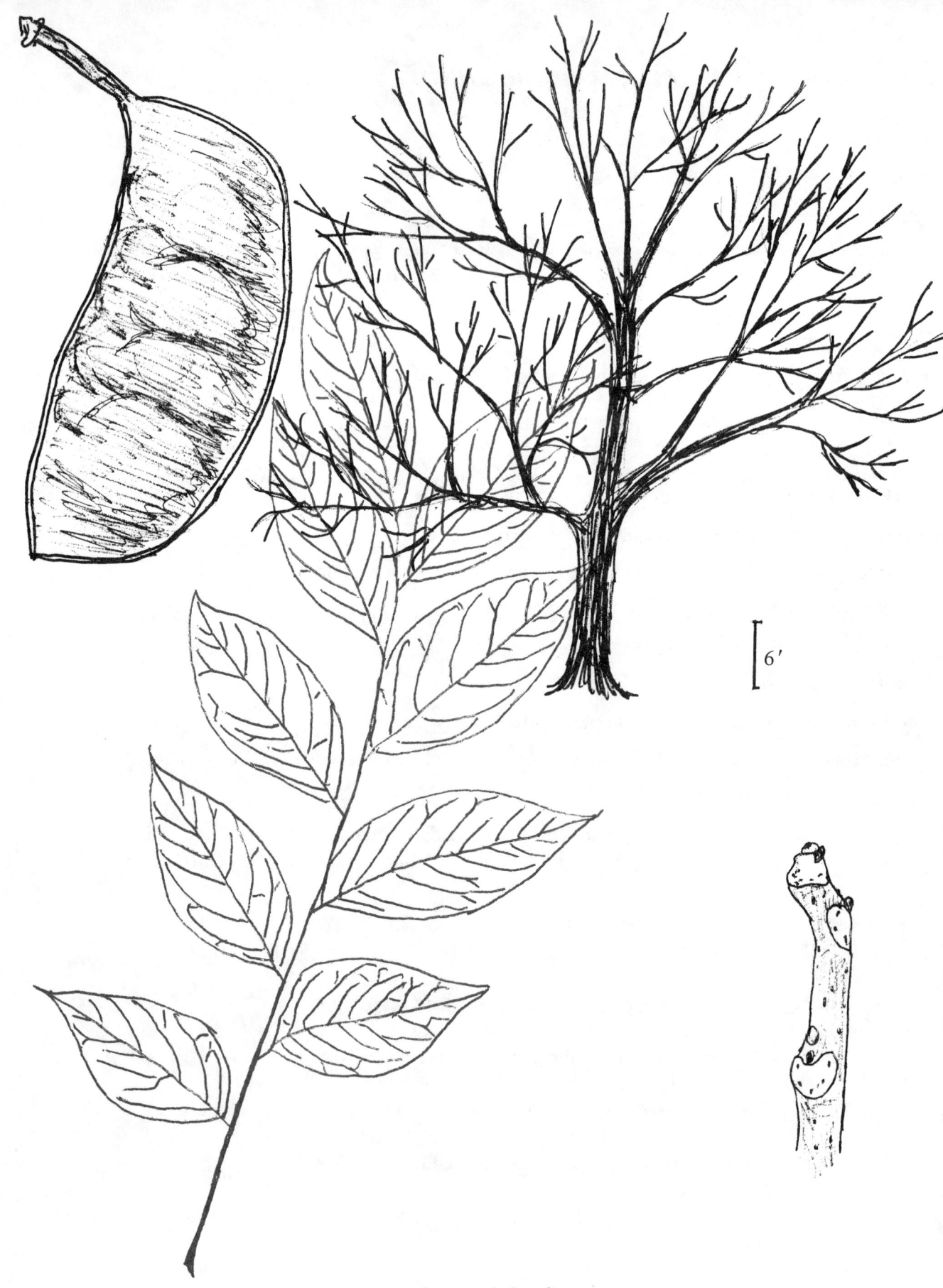

Gymnocladus dioecus

Gymnocladus dioecus

Common Name: Kentucky Coffee-tree

Family: Leguminosae

Foliage: 1-3 feet long; 40 or more leaflets; singly or double compound; without teeth; short stalked; dark green above; pale below; yellow in autumn

Flowers: male and female separate on separate trees; terminal, drooping clusters; greenish white; May-June

Fruit: 4-10 inch, woody pod; short stalk; often in cluster; brown; ripens September-October

Buds: no terminal; 2 in each leaf axil; small; depressed; brown with silky hair

Twigs: stout; large leaf scars; dark orange pith

Bark: thick; gray; deep fissures with shaggy scales

Roots: few, thick, fibrous; transplants fairly well

Growth Habit: 60-100 feet in height; round crown with coarse, stiff branches

Hardiness: zone 4

Site: rich, moist, well drained soil; will not tolerate wet sites; tolerant of dry sites; sun

Growth Rate: slow

Maintenance: clean; limited tolerance to pruning

Propagation: seed—soak in water at room temperature for 24 hours then scarify in concentrated sulfuric acid 2 hours, rinse in water, spring sow only; root cuttings

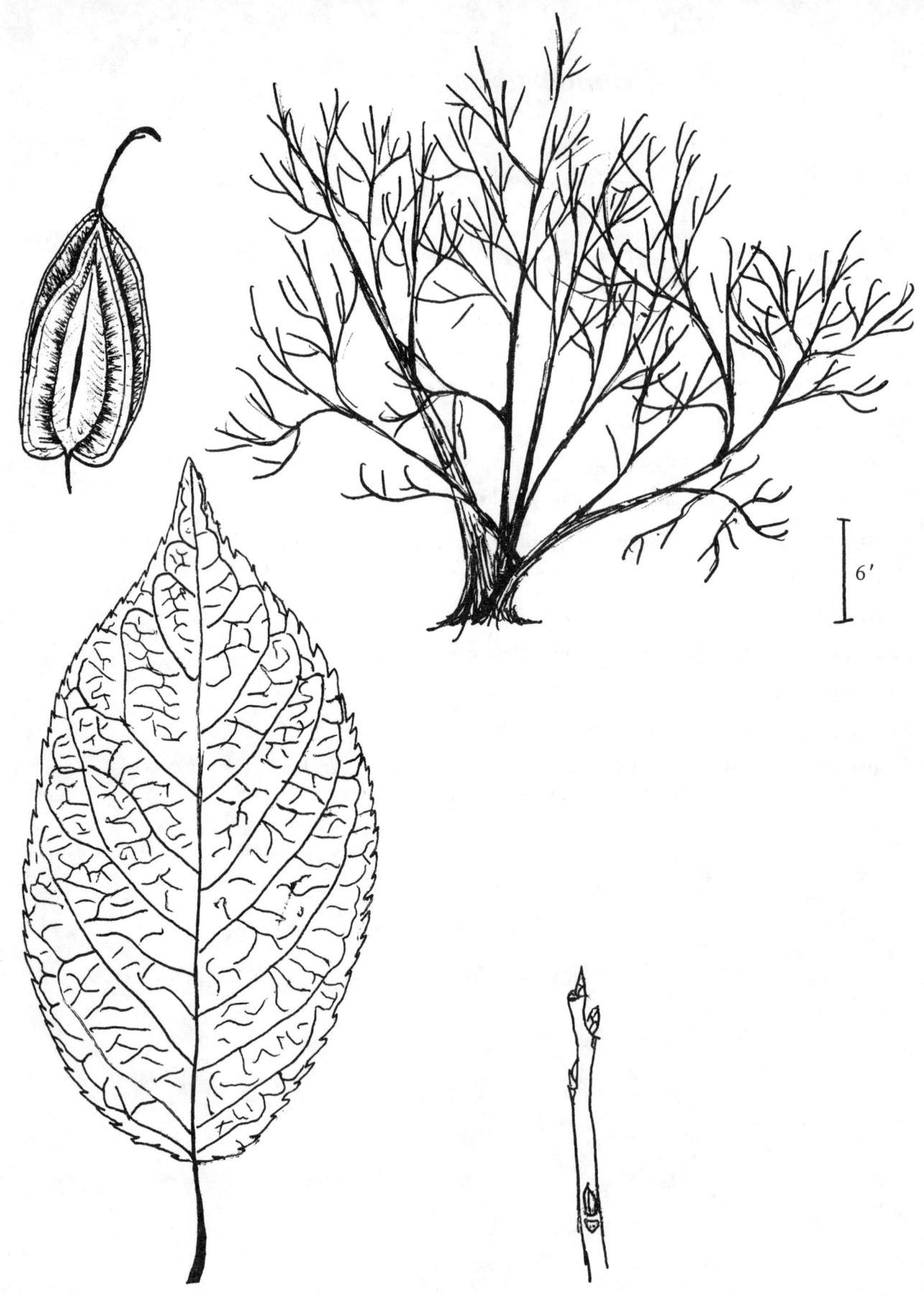

Halesia carolina
130

Halesia carolina

Common Name: Carolina Silverbell

Family: Styracaceae

Foliage: 2-5 inches long; fine teeth; yellow-green above; pale and hairy below; yellow in autumn

Flowers: bell shaped; drooping clusters of 2-5; white; axillary; April-May

Fruit: 1-1 1/2 inch, dry, 4 winged drupe; ripens late autumn; persists through winter

Buds: no terminal; reddish brown; pointed

Twigs: slender; light brown; diaphragmed pith

Bark: thin; brown; striped on young branches; fissures with flat ridges

Roots: fibrous; transplants well

Growth Habit: 30-35 feet in height; broad, round crown; often with multiple trunks

Hardiness: zone 4

Site: rich, well-drained soil; tolerant to alkaline conditions; sun or partial shade

Growth Rate: slow-moderate

Maintenance: clean; fairly tolerant to pruning

Propagation: seed—stratify in a moist medium at 56-86°F for 60-120 days then at 33-41°F for 60-90 days; layers; root cuttings; softwood cuttings

Leaf: ½ actual size

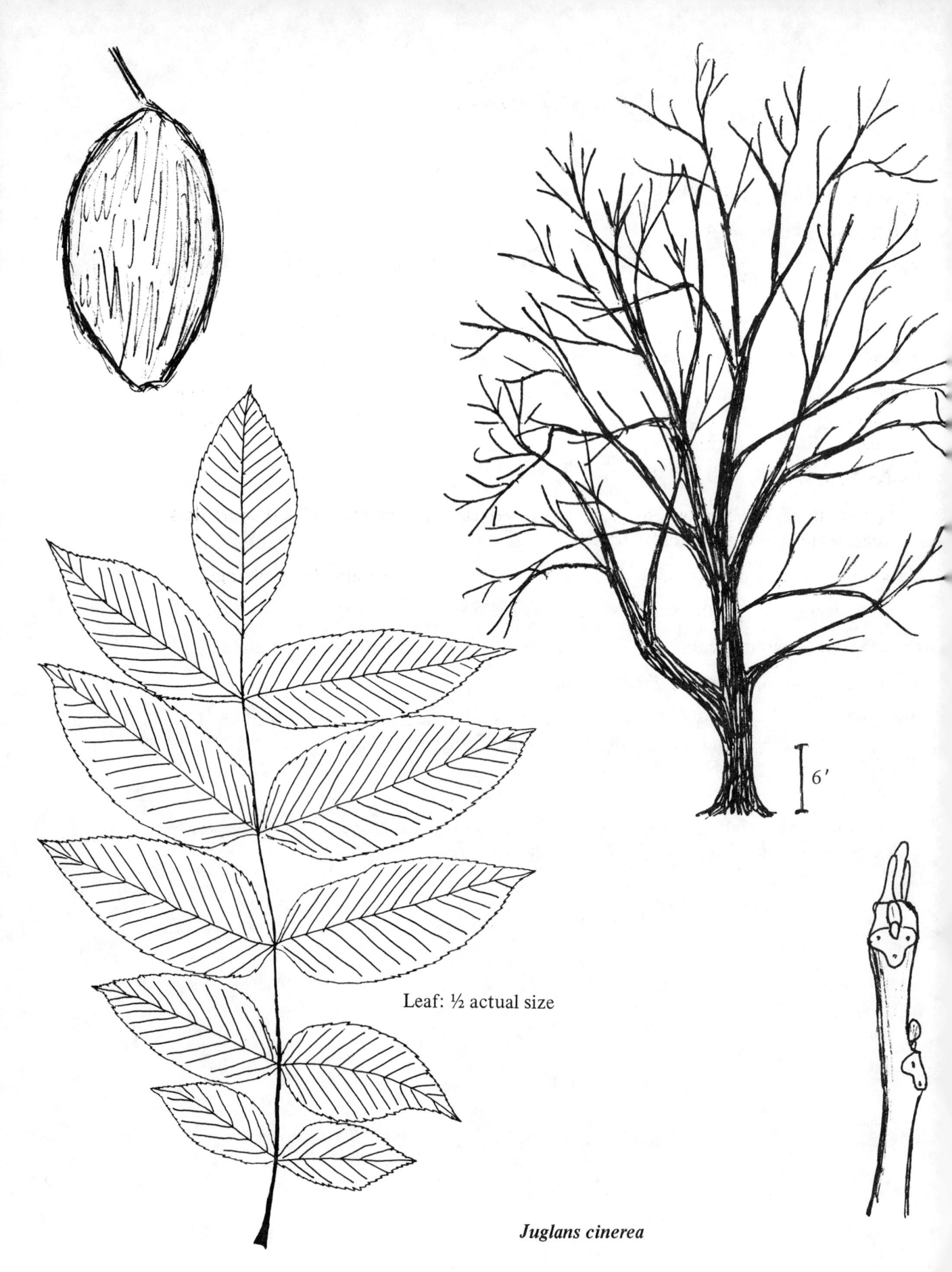

Juglans cinerea

Juglans cinerea

Common Name: Butternut

Family: Juglandaceae

Foliage: 1-2 feet long; 11-17 leaflets; fine teeth; yellow-green; hairy below; yellow in autumn

Flowers: male and female separate but on the same tree; male: green catkins; female: short spikes; April-June

Fruit: 1 1/2-1 1/2 inches in diameter; oblong; 2-5 per cluster; tapered at both ends; sticky; hairy; thick, greenish brown husk; deeply corrugated nut shell with a sweet, edible kernel; ripens September-October

Buds: blunt; hairy; yellow

Twigs: stout; greenish brown to gray; hairy; velvety ridge above leaf leaf scar; dark chocolate, chambered pith

Bark: thick; somewhat gray; smooth becoming furrowed with vertically flattened ridges

Roots: taproot; difficult to transplant

Growth Habit: 70-100 feet in height; oval to round crown; upright, spreading branches

Hardiness: zone 3

Site: prefers deep, rich, moist, well drained soil but will tolerate some dryness; sun

Growth Rate: moderate-rapid

Maintenance: clean except for fruit; limited tolerance to pruning

Propagation: seed—fall sow (with or without husk), mulch, and protect from rodents; or stratify in a moist media at 34-41°F for 90-120 days

Leaf: ½ actual size

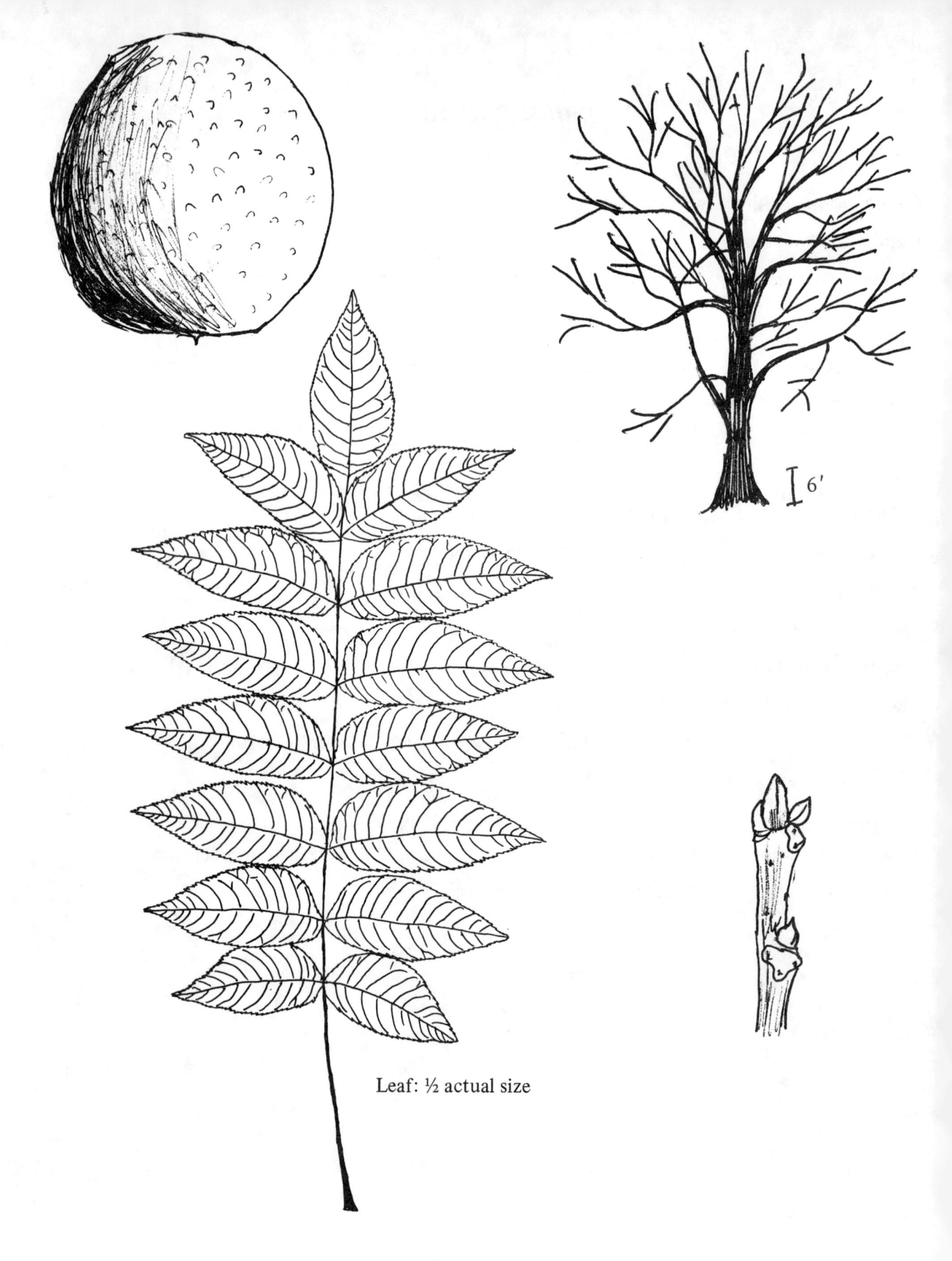

Juglans nigra

Juglans nigra

Common Name: Black Walnut

Family: Juglandaceae

Foliage: 1-2 feet long; 15-23 leaflets; long pointed apex; fine teeth; yellow-green; yellow in autumn; drops early

Fruit: 1 1/2-2 inches in diameter; round; in clusters of 2-3; thick, light green husk; dark brown, corrugated nut shell; kernel sweet and edible; ripens September-October

Buds: blunt; hairy; gray

Twigs: stout; light brown; bitter taste; buff colored, chambered pith

Bark: thick; black; deep, narrow furrows form a diamond like pattern

Roots: long, large taproot; difficult to transplant

Growth Habit: 70-150 feet in height; broad, open, round crown

Hardiness: zone 4

Site: rich, moist soil; sun

Growth Rate: moderate-rapid

Maintenance: abundant fruit production; limited tolerance to pruning

Propagation: seed—fall sow, mulch and protect from rodents; or stratify in a moist medium at 34-41°F for 90-120 days; graft on *J. nigra* understock

Selections: 'Laciniata' — cut foliage; low nut production
'Demming's Purple' — young foliage purplish becoming greenish purple in the summer; low nut production

Note: many selections with superior fruiting are available

Juniperus chinensis

136

Juniperus chinensis

Common Name: Chinese Juniper

Family: Pinaceae

Foliage: scalelike, evergreen needles; light green; sharp; stiff

Flowers: male and female separate on separate trees; male: yellow, tufted; female: yellowish; March-April

Fruit: 3/8 inch berry; brown with thick, mealy bloom; matures second year

Twigs: dark gray

Bark: dark gray; splitting and peeling

Roots: taproot; transplants well if root pruned

Growth Habit: 20-60 feet in height; pyramidal crown; upright, spreading branches

Hardiness: zone 4

Site: adaptable; prefers dry, well-drained soil; sun or partial shade

Growth Rate: rapid

Maintenance: clean; tolerant to pruning

Propagation: seed—fall sow and mulch, or remove flesh and stratify in sand or peat at 41°F for 30-90 days; cuttings; graft on *J. chinensis* or *J. virginiana* understock

Selections: 'Ames' — bluish foliage
    'Columnaris' — narrowly columnar; deep green
    'Fairview' — narrowly pyramidal; bright green
    'Iowa' — blue-green foliage
    'Kaizuka' — narrow, conical habit; contorted tips
    'Ketelleeri' — narrowly pyramidal; dense; green
    'Leeana' — slender; male
    'Mas' — columnar; male; light colored foliage
    'Mountbatten' — pyramidal; gray-green foliage
    'Obelisk' — narrowly columnar; bluish foliage
    'Olympia' — columnar, bluish
    'Pendula' — weeping branches
    'Pyramidalis' — compact, pyramidal crown; male
    'Story' — male; columnar; dark green foliage

Note: immune to Cedar Apple Rust; therefore an excellent substitute for *J. virginiana*

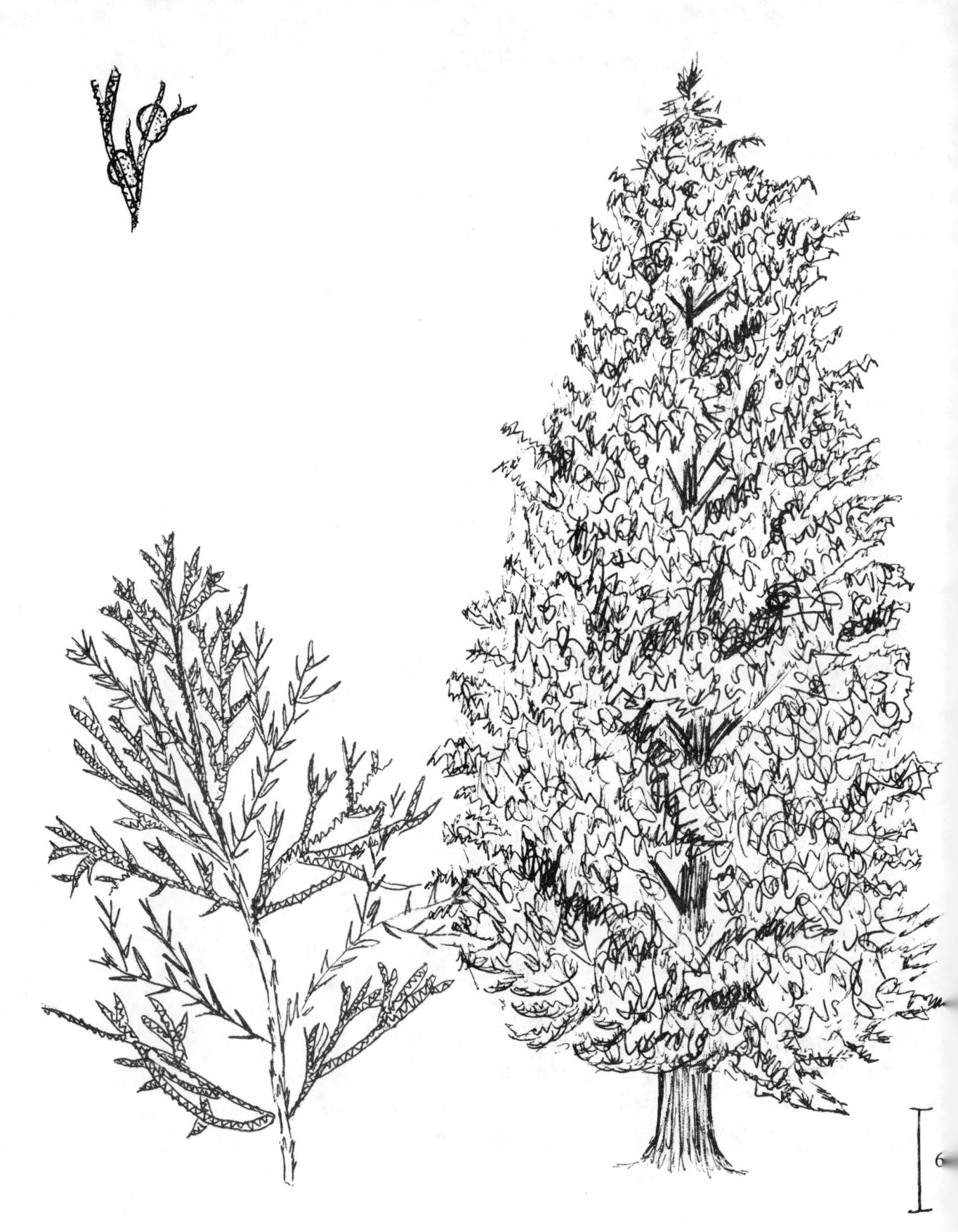

Juniperus virginiana

Juniperus virginiana

Common Name: Red Cedar

Family: Pinaceae

Foliage: evergreen; scalelike and needlelike; glandular; aromatic; dark bluish green becoming bronze in winter

Flowers: male and female separate on separate trees; male: yellow; female: green; mid-March to mid-May

Fruit: 1/4-3/4 inch berry; blue with whitish bloom; fleshy; ripens in one season; ripens September-November

Twigs: slender; 4 angled; brown

Bark: thin; reddish brown becoming gray; shedding long, narrow strips

Growth Habit: 40-90 feet in height; dense, pyramidal crown

Hardiness: zone 2

Site: poor, dry alkaline soil; sun

Growth Rate: moderate

Maintenance: clean; very tolerant to pruning

Propagation: seed—fall sow and mulch, or soak in a 1 percent citric acid solution for 4 days then stratify in sand or peat at 41°F for 30-120 days; cuttings; graft on *J. virginiana* or *J. chinensis* understock

Selections: 'Burkii' — compact, narrowly pyramidal crown; sivler-blue foliage
'Canaertii' — dark green foliage; abundant fruit production
'Chamberlaynii' — male; weeping branchlets; grayish foliage
var. *crebra* — columnar
'Cupressifolia' — bright green, cypresslike foliage
'Deforest Green' — deep green foliage
'Elegantissima' — yellow leaf tips
'Filifera' — divided branchlets; grayish foliage
'Hillspire' — male; bright green
'Glauca' — columnar; silvery-blue foliage
'Pendula' — weeping branchlets
'Pseudocupressus' — columnar; blue-green foliage
'Schottii' — narrowly pyramidal; dense
'Skyrocket' — very narrow crown; bluish green
'Triomphe d'Angers' — white spots on foliage

Leaf: ½ actual size

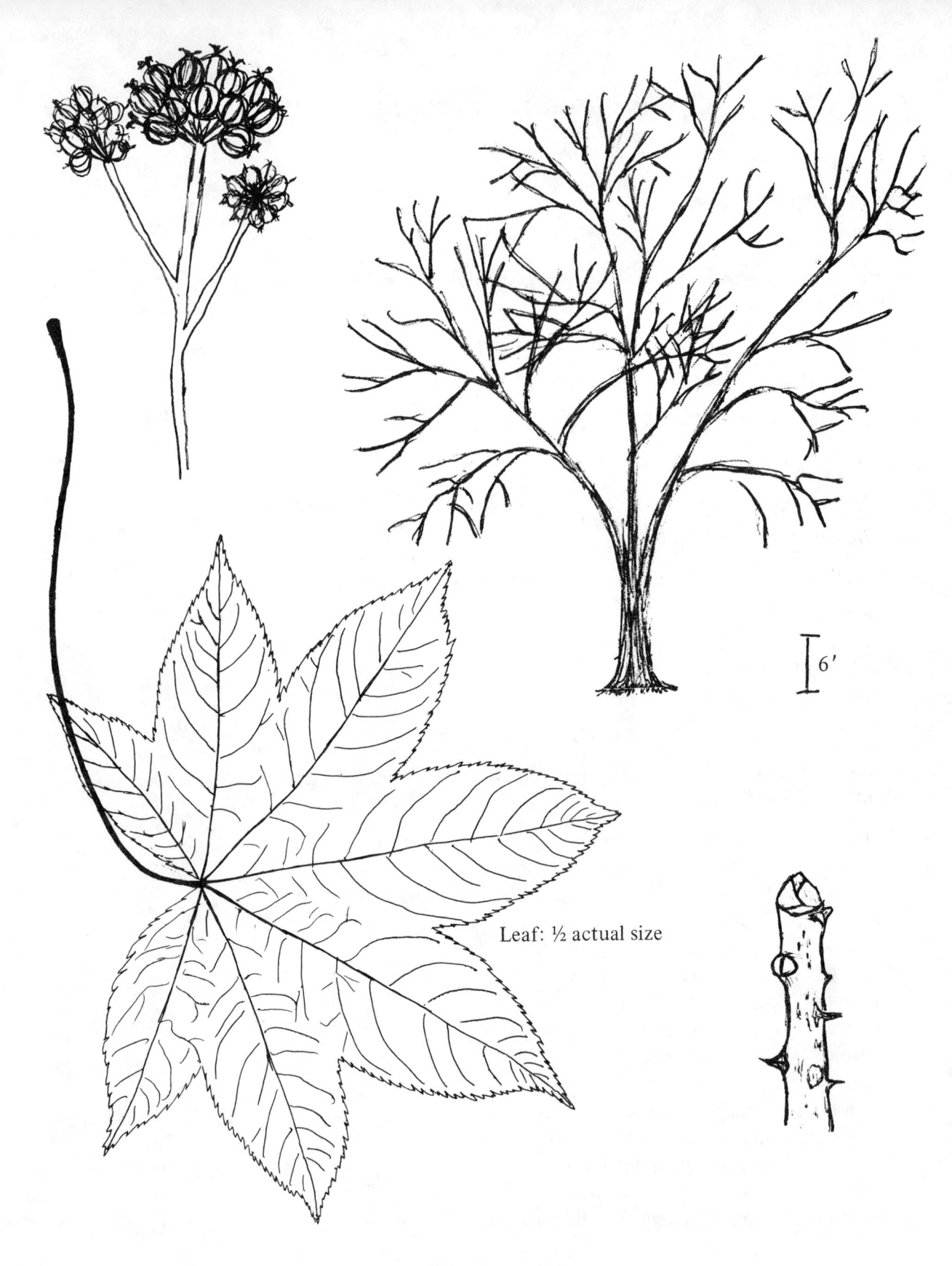

Kalopanax pictus

Kalopanax pictus

Common Name: Castor-aralia

Family: Araliaceae

Foliage: 5-9 lobes; teeth; maplelike in appearance; deep green and shiny above; pale with brownish hair below while young; leaf stalks up to 20 inches long; reddish in autumn

Flowers: 1 inch, ball-like clusters in a 6-8 inch umbel; small; greenish white; July-August

Fruit: small, bluish black drupe; ripens September-October

Buds: large terminal; conical; several scales; reddish brown

Twigs: stout; spiny; greenish gray; prominent lenticels

Bark: ashy gray; vertical fissures with ridges; stout spines on young branches

Roots: fibrous; transplant while young

Growth Habit: 90-100 feet in height; open, round crown; stout branches

Hardiness: zone 4

Site: rich, moist soil; sun

Growth Rate: rapid

Maintenance: clean; intolerant to pruning

Propagation: seed—fall sow fresh seed, or soak in sulfuric acid 30 minutes then stratify in sand at 41°F for 90 days; root cuttings

Selections: var. *maximowiczii* — more deeply lobed foliage

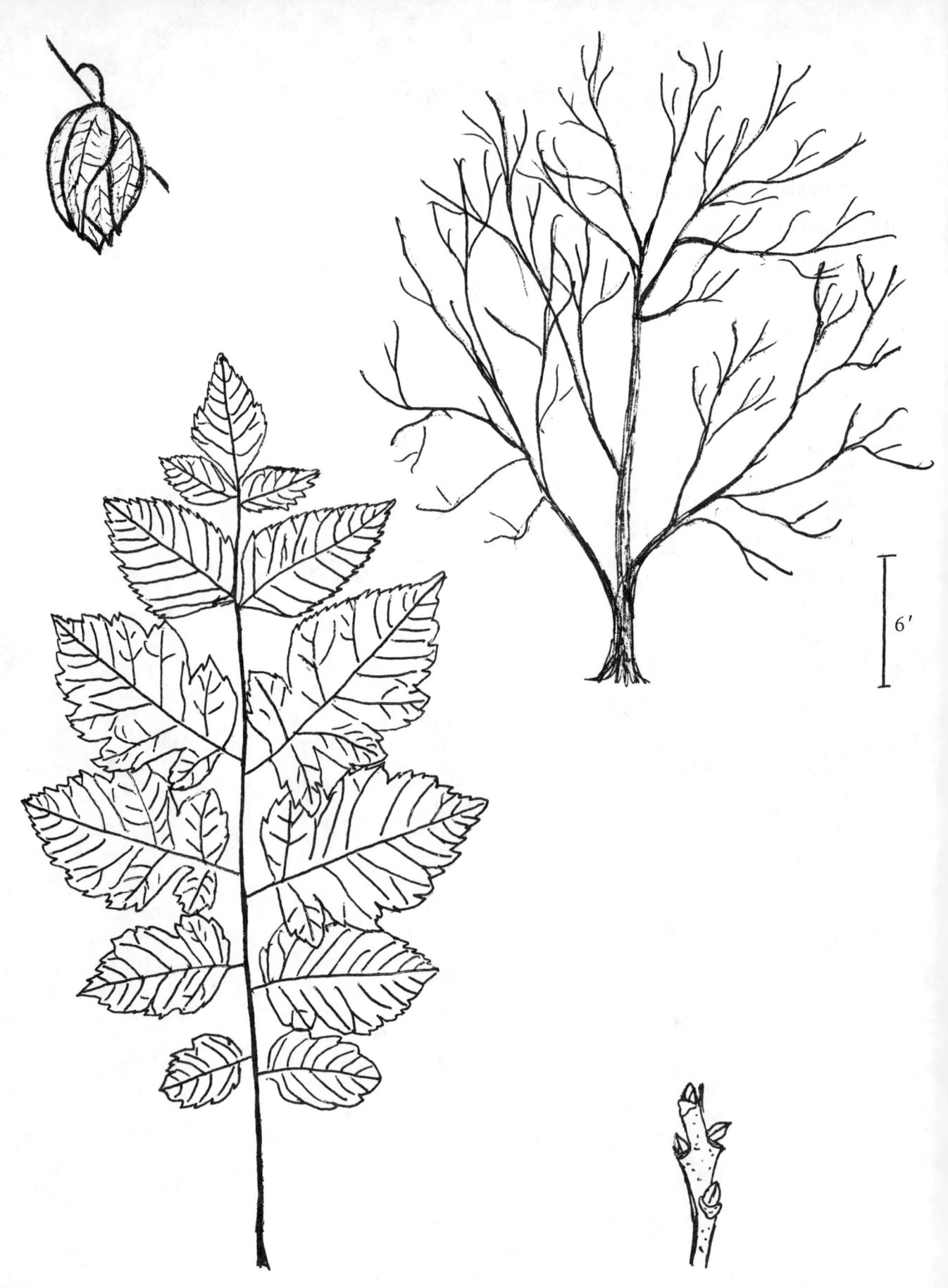

Koelreuteria paniculata

Koelreuteria paniculata

Common Name: Golden Rain Tree; China-tree

Family: Sapindaceae

Foliage: up to 14 inches long; 7-15 leaflets; coarse teeth; deep, bright green; yellow in autumn

Flowers: irregular, upright panicles to 12 inches long; yellow; July-September

Fruit: 1 1/2-2 inch capsule; triangular; inflated sac with papery walls; red to brown; 3 black seeds; ripens September-October

Buds: fat; pointed; 2 scales

Twigs: brown; raised, reddish lenticels

Bark: brown to gray; rough

Roots: fibrous; transplants well

Growth Habit: 20-30 feet in height; often wider than tall; round or irregular crown; sparingly branched

Hardiness: zone 5

Site: tolerant to many soils; drought and heat tolerant; sun or partial shade

Growth Rate: slow

Maintenance: clean; limited tolerance to pruning

Propagation: seed—fall sow clean seed, or scarify in concentrated sulfuric acid for 1 hour then stratify in moist sand at 41°F for 90 days; root cuttings; softwood cuttings; layers

Larix decidua

Larix decidua

Common Name: European Larch

Family: Pinaceae

Foliage: 1 inch, deciduous needles; green; clustered on short spurs; gold in autumn

Flowers: male and female separate but on the same tree; male: yellow; female: short stalked, red; March-May

Fruit: 1-2 inch cone; stalked; bracts turn out; brown; erect; hairy scales; ripens September-December; persists several years

Buds: dark red; shiny

Twigs: moderately stout; gray spurs

Bark: gray; longitudinally fissured and flaky

Roots: deep fibrous; transplants well when root pruned

Growth Habit: 30-110 feet in height; conical to pyramidal when young; irregular at maturity; weeping branchlets

Hardiness: zone 2

Site: adaptable; prefers moist, well drained soil; full sun

Growth Rate: moderate-rapid

Maintenance: clean; tolerant to pruning

Propagation: seed—no pretreatment

Selections: 'Pendula' — weeping branches

Larix laricina

Larix laricina

Common Name: American Larch; Tamarack

Family: Pinaceae

Foliage: 1/2-1 inch, deciduous needles; whorled on spurs; soft; light green; yellow in autumn

Flowers: male and female separate but on the same tree; male: yellow; female: bright red; April-May

Fruit: 1/2-3/4 inch cone; short stalk; erect; brown; ripens August-September; persists on tree 2 years

Buds: small; shiny; dark reddish brown

Twigs: slender; spurs; orange-brown

Bark: thin, reddish brown; small scales

Roots: fibrous; transplants well

Growth Habit: 40-65 feet in height; open, pyramidal crown when young becoming irregular at maturity; branched to ground

Hardiness: zone 1

Site: wet soil; sun

Growth Rate: moderate

Maintenance: breaks with wind; intolerant to pruning

Propagation: seed—no pretreatment

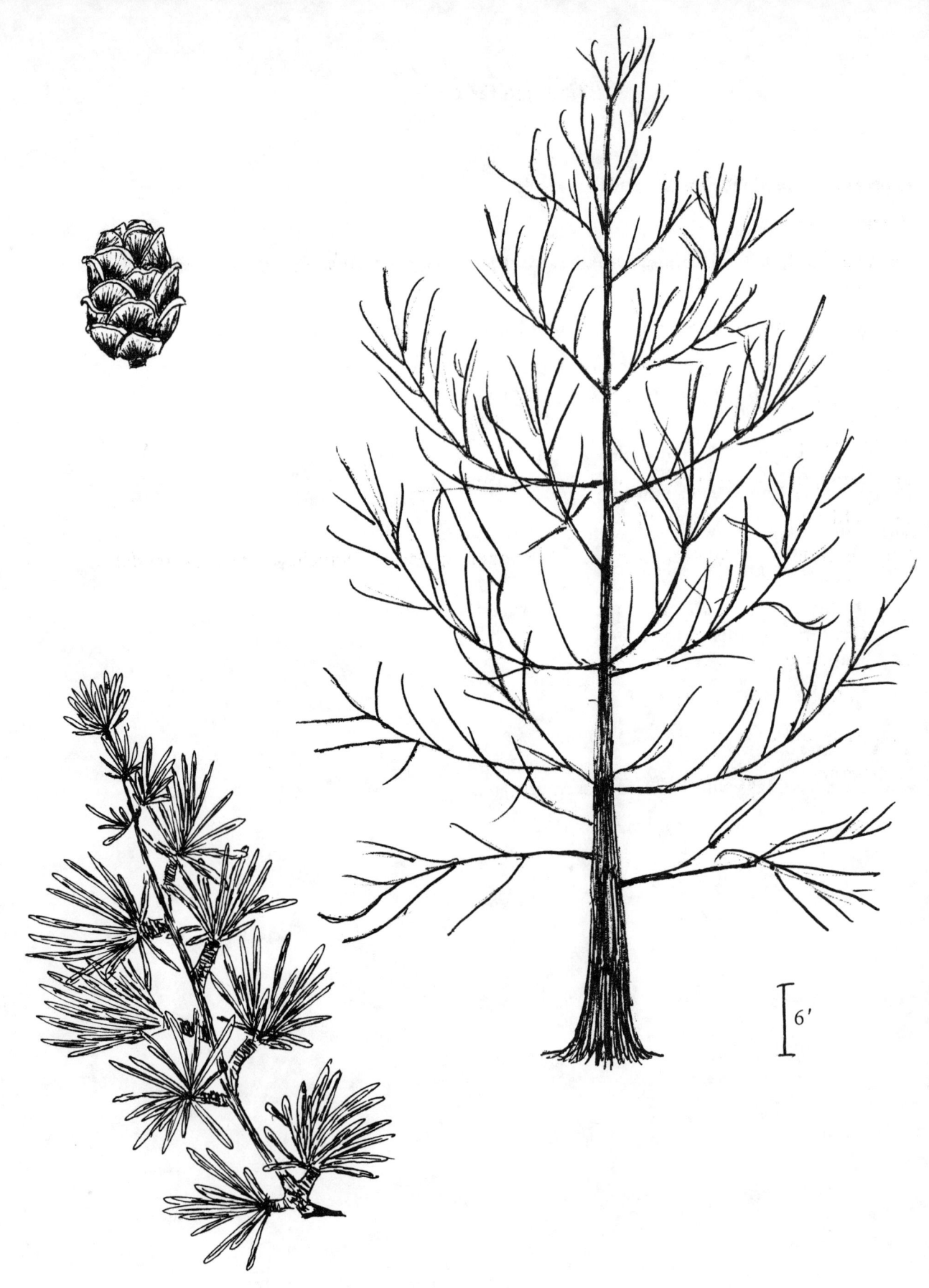

Larix leptolepis

148

Larix leptolepis

Common Name: Japanese Larch

Family: Pinaceae

Foliage: 1/2-1 inch, deciduous needles; whorled on spurs; white bands beneath; yellow in autumn

Flowers: male and female separate but on the same tree; April-May

Fruit: 3/4-1 1/4 inch cone; short stalked; brown; ripens September

Buds: conical; dark brown

Twigs: brown; bloomy

Bark: gray; flaky plates peeling in strips; brown under bark

Roots: fibrous; transplants well

Growth Habit: 90-100 feet in height; horizontal spreading branches; open, pyramidal crown

Hardiness: zone 4

Site: adaptable; sun or partial shade

Growth Rate: moderate-rapid

Maintenance: clean; intolerant to pruning

Propagation: seed—no pretreatment

Liquidambar styraciflua
150

Liquidambar styraciflua

Common Name: Sweet Gum

Family: Hamamelidaceae

Foliage: 4-7 inches long; 5-7 deep lobes; star shaped; teeth; bright, shiny, green above; paler below with tufts of hair in vein axils; fragrant when crushed; yellow to red in autumn

Flowers: male and female separate but on the same tree; round heads; yellow-green; March-May

Fruit: 1-1 1/2 inches; made of beaked capsules; globular; long stalk; ripens September-November; persists through winter

Buds: pointed; large; shiny; scaly; orange-brown

Twigs: stout; greenish-brown; stubby spur branches; corky wings develop on second year's growth; star shaped pith

Bark: thick; dark gray; furrowed into ridges

Roots: taproot; difficult to transplant

Growth Habit: 80-100 feet in height; long, tapering trunk; broad, pyramidal or oblong crown; symmetrical

Hardiness: zone 4

Site: rich, moist, well-drained soil; sun or partial shade

Growth Rate: slow-moderate

Maintenance: fruit can be messy; tolerant to pruning

Propagation: seed—stratify in moist sand at 41° F for 15-90 days, or soak 14-20 days in water at 35-41° F; softwood cuttings; graft on *L. styraciflua* understock

Selections: 'Aurea' — yellow foliage
'Burgundy' — purplish foliage
'Festival' — narrowly upright; red, yellow and green in autumn
'Palo Alto' — red in autumn
'Variegata' — yellow variegated foliage

Liriodendron tulipifera

152

Liriodendron tulipifera

Common Name: Tulip Tree; Yellow Poplar

Family: Magnoliaceae

Foliage: 4-8 inches long; 4 lobed; without teeth; smooth; spicy aroma when crushed; 2 stipules; long, slender leaf stalk; yellow in autumn

Flowers: up to 2 inches long; yellow, green and orange; tulip like; May-June

Fruit: a group of spirally arranged samaras; light brown; each samara 1 1/2 inches long; terminal wing; ripens August; central stalk persistent

Buds: large terminal; 2 outer scales; flattened; dark red

Twigs: moderately stout; shiny; bitter; reddish brown; purplish bloom; diaphragmed pith

Bark: thick; light gray; furrows with rounded ridges

Roots: widespreading; deep; frequently difficult to transplant with age

Growth Habit: 100-150 feet in height; massive branches; broad, oblong or pyramidal crown; straight trunk

Hardiness: zone 4

Site: rich, moist, well-drained soil; sun

Growth Rate: moderate-rapid

Maintenance: clean; intolerant to pruning

Propagation: seed—fall sow, or stratify in moist peat or peat/sand mixture at 35-36°F for 60-90 days (or store cold and naked in a plastic bag for 140-168 days); graft or bud on *L. tulipifera* understock

Selections: 'Aureomarginatum' — yellow margins on foliage
'Fastigiatum' — narrow, upright crown

Maclura pomifera

Maclura pomifera

Common Name: Osage Orange

Family: Moraceae

Foliage: 3-5 inches long; long pointed apex; without teeth; thick; dark green and shiny above; paler and sometimes hairy below; milky juice when crushed; yellow in autumn

Flowers: male and female separate on separate trees; minute; green; April-June

Fruit: small druplets clustered into a multiple fruit; 3-4 inches in diameter; pale green; milky juice; ripens September-October

Buds: no terminal; round; reddish-brown; partially embedded into twig

Twigs: stout; orange-brown; sharp, 1/2-1 inch spines

Bark: dark orange-brown; furrows with shaggy ridges

Roots: fibrous; transplants well

Growth Habit: 30-40 feet in height; low branching; open, irregular, round crown; often contorted branches; very twiggy

Hardiness: zone 4

Site: tolerant to many soil types; withstands drought; sun

Growth Rate: rapid

Maintenance: clean; tolerant to pruning

Propagation: seed—fall sow and mulch, or soak in water 48 hours, or stratify in sand or peat at 41°F for 30 days

Selections: 'Inermis' — thornless

Magnolia acuminata

156

Magnolia acuminata

Common Name: Cucumber-tree

Family: Magnoliaceae

Foliage: 1-7 inches long; thin; wavy margin; bright yellow-green and smooth above; pale and smooth or hairy below; yellow to bronze in autumn

Flowers: irregular bell-shaped; not especially showy; greenish yellow; April

Fruit: 2-3 inch, irregular, conelike pod; each segment releases a bright red seed on a slender thread; ripens August-September

Buds: large terminal; green with silvery hairs

Twigs: moderately stout; shiny; reddish brown; aromatic

Bark: thin; gray; furrowed with squarish flaky ridges

Roots: fleshy; frequently difficult to transplant, particularly with age

Growth Habit: 40-90 feet in height; pyramidal crown with branches extending near the ground; upper branches ascending

Hardiness: zone 4

Site: rich, moist, well-drained soil; sun

Growth Rate: moderate-rapid

Maintenance: intolerant to pruning

Propagation: seed stratify in sand at 32-41° F for 90-180 days, spring sow; softwood cuttings

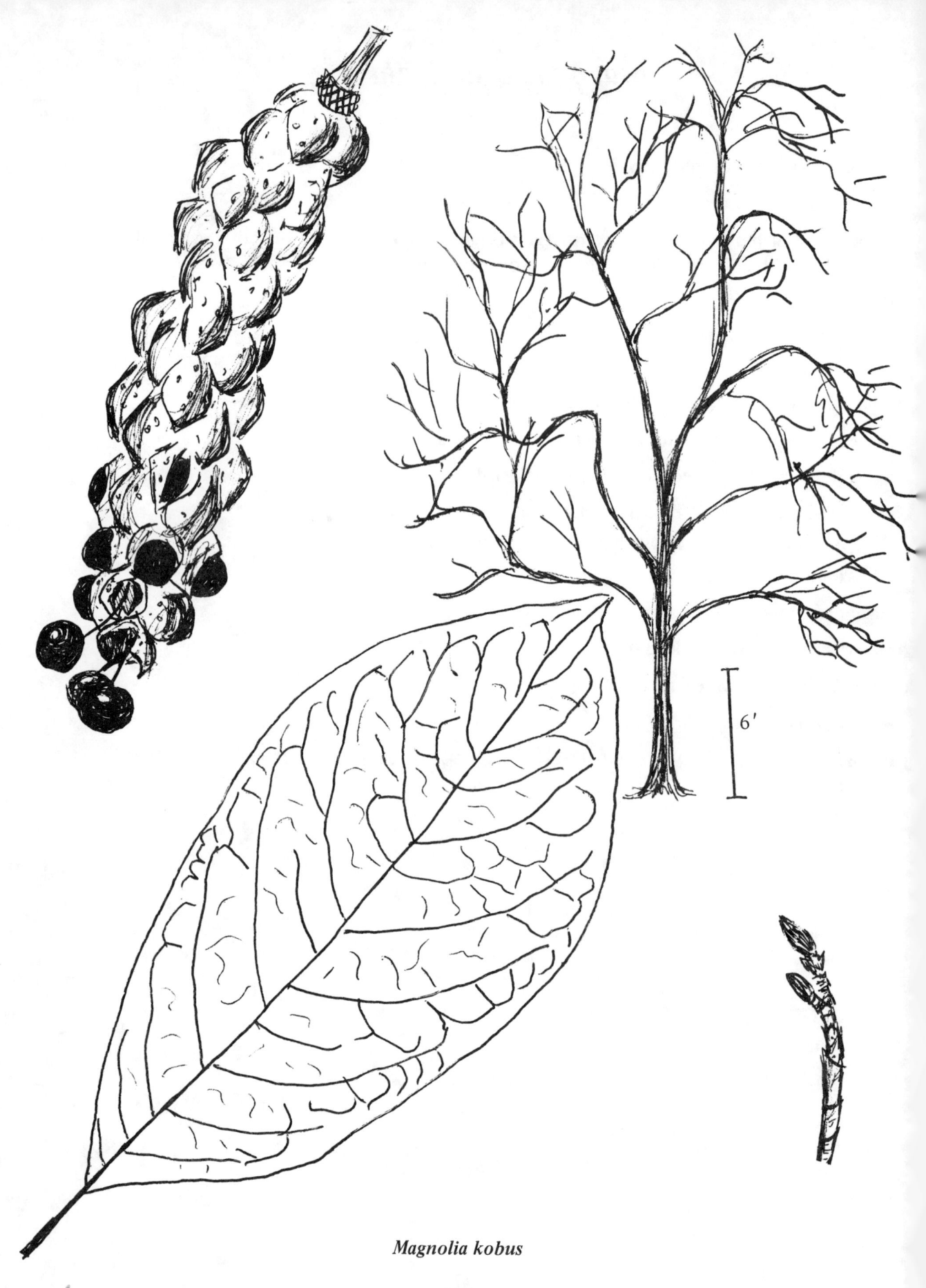

Magnolia kobus

Magnolia kobus

Common Name: Thurber's Magnolia; Kobus Magnolia

Family: Magnoliaceae

Foliage: 4-6 inches long; dark green above; lighter beneath with hair on veins

Flowers: 4-5 inches across; white with red toward the base; March-April

Fruit: oblong, usually incurved, cucumberlike pod; red with white spots; ripens September-October

Buds: green; terminal has a small subsidiary bud; hairy; foliage buds gray

Twigs: slightly zigzag; dark brown with prominent lenticels

Bark: smooth; gray

Roots: fibrous; somewhat difficult to transplant

Growth Habit: 30-35 feet in height; upright; oval crown

Hardiness: zone 4

Site: rich, moist, well-drained soil; sun

Growth Rate: slow

Maintenance: clean; moderate tolerance to pruning

Propagation: seed—stratify in sand at 32-41°F for 90-180 days, spring sow; softwood cuttings; graft on *M. kobus* or *M. acuminata* understock

Selections: var. *borealis* — larger flowers which are pure white
'Wada's Memory' — blooms while young

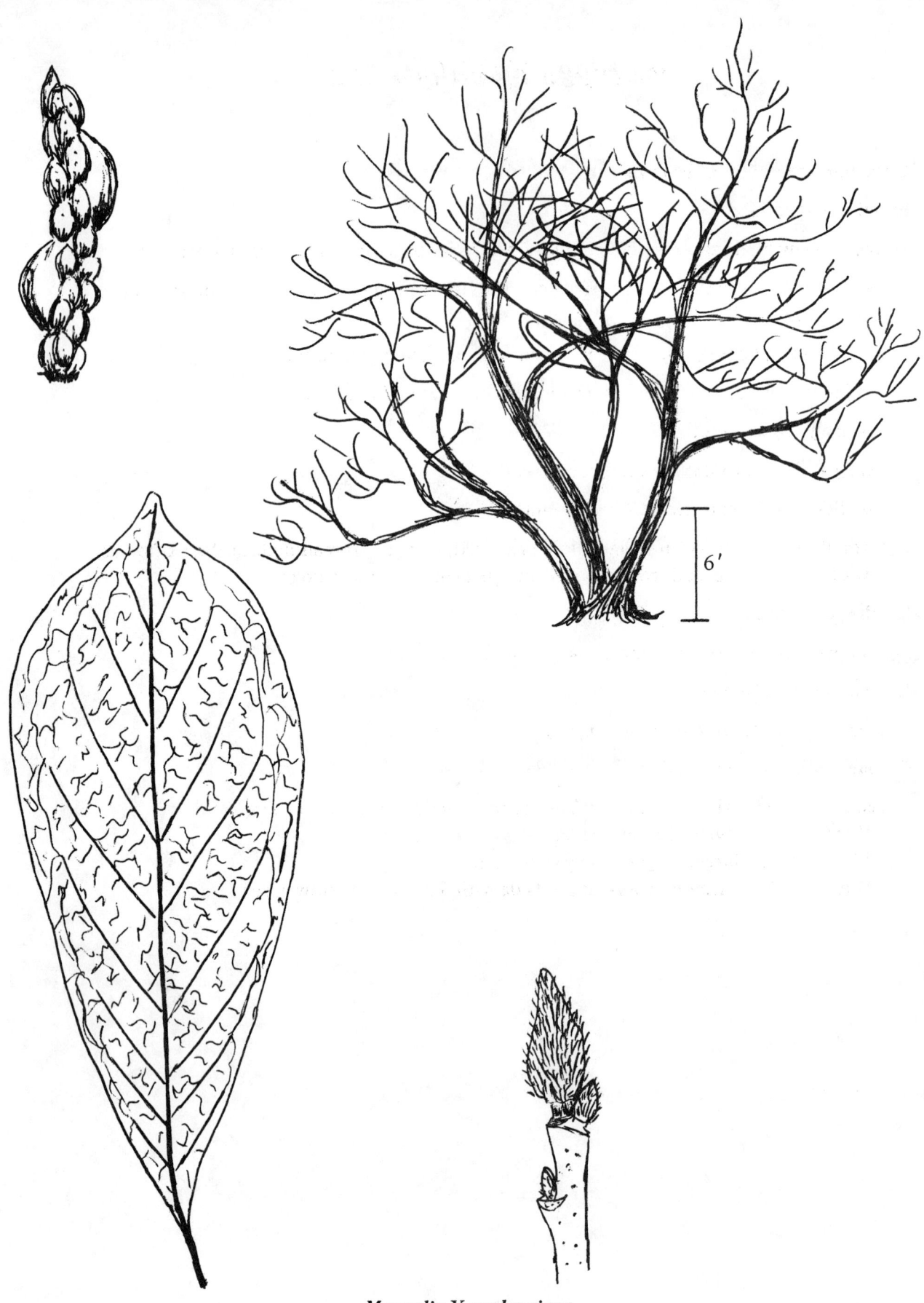

Magnolia X *soulangiana*

Magnolia X soulangiana

Common Name: Saucer Magnolia

Family: Magnoliaceae

Foliage: 4-8 inches long; without teeth; leathery; hairy beneath; yellow-brown in autumn

Flowers: 5-6 inches in diameter; cupshaped; white tips; purple toward base; with or without scent; late April

Fruit: oblong, conelike pod; distorted; reddish seeds; ripens in autumn

Buds: flower buds are hairy and green; foliage buds are hairy and gray

Twigs: gray; dark lenticels

Bark: light gray; smooth; dark horizontal lenticels

Roots: fleshy; brittle; difficult to transplant

Growth Habit: 20-30 feet in height; low branched; upright, spreading branches; often as wide as it is tall; broad, rounded crown; often with multiple trunks

Hardiness: zone 5

Site: moist, well drained soil; sun or partial shade

Growth Rate: moderate

Maintenance: clean; intolerant to pruning

Propagation: softwood cuttings

Selections: 'Alexandrina' — flowers rose-purple outside with white inside
    'Lennei' — flowers dark purple outside; white inside
    'San Jose' — large, fragrant purple flowers
    'Verbanica' — flowers rosy-pink outside with white inside; slow growth rate

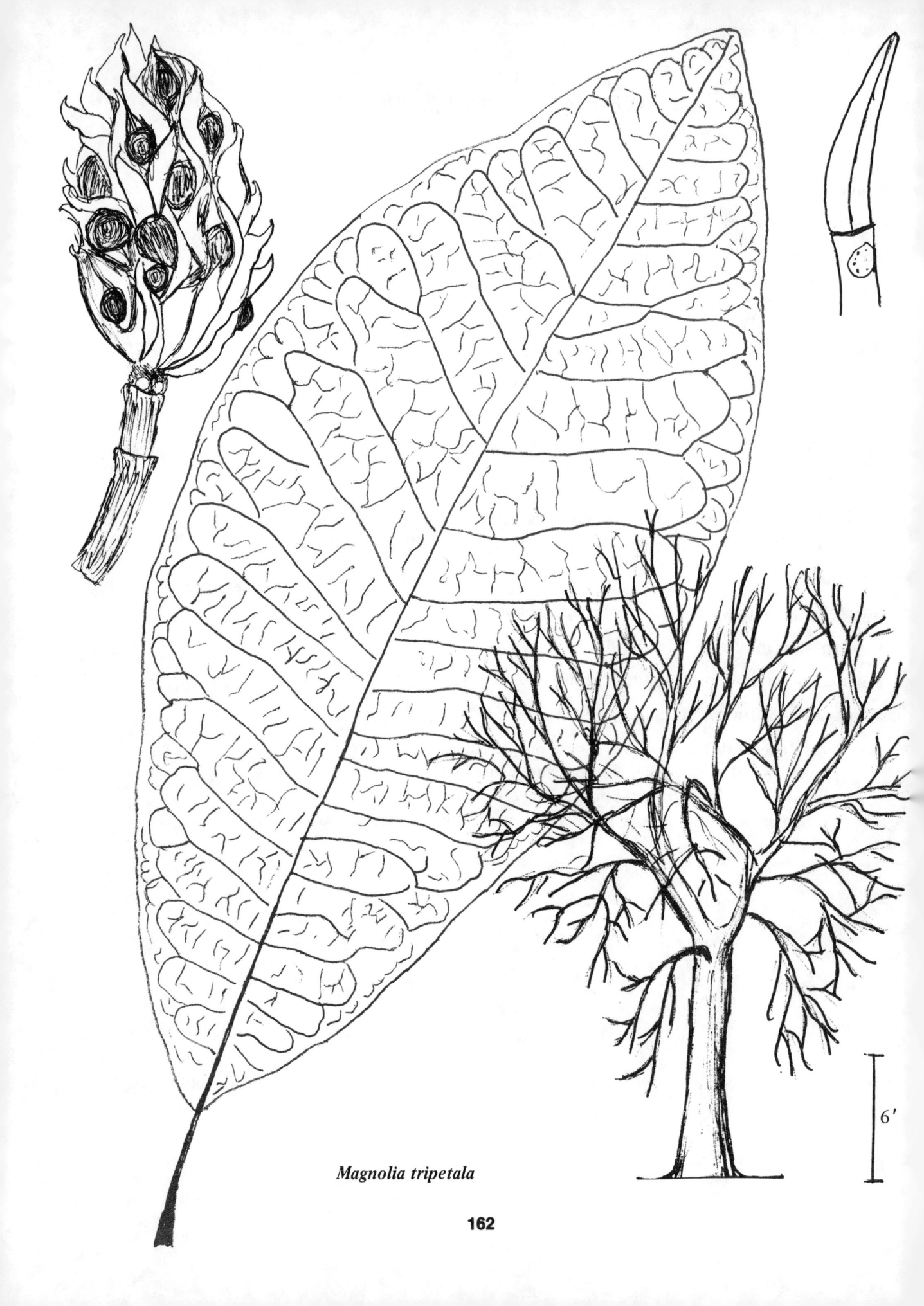

Magnolia tripetala

6'

Magnolia tripetala

Common Name: Umbrella Magnolia

Family: Magnoliaceae

Foliage: 10-24 inches long; without teeth; long tapering point; deep, bright green above; pale and hairy below; grow in clusters at ends of twigs; bronze-yellow in autumn

Flowers: 7-10 inches across; cup-shaped; creamy white; ill scented; May-June

Fruit: 2-4 inch conelike pod; knobby; rosy red with scarlet seeds on slender threads; ripens in autumn

Buds: large, hooked terminal; hairless; reddish brown

Twigs: stout, coarse; brown with white lenticels

Bark: light gray; smooth

Roots: fleshy; brittle; frequently difficult to establish

Growth Habit: 20-30 feet in height; loose, open round crown; tropical appearance

Hardiness: zone 4

Site: rich, moist soil; partial shade

Growth Rate: moderate

Maintenance: clean; intolerant to pruning

Propagation: seed—fall sow and mulch, or stratify in sand at 32-41 °F for 90-180 days

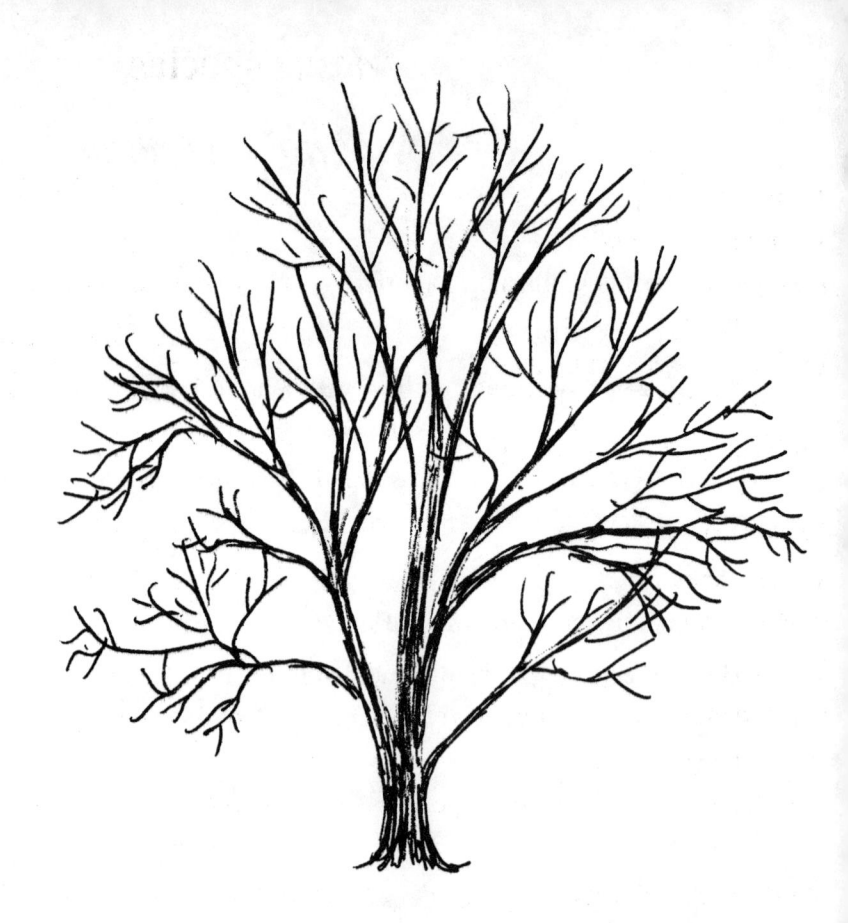

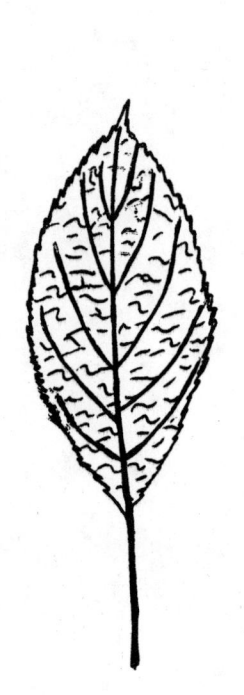

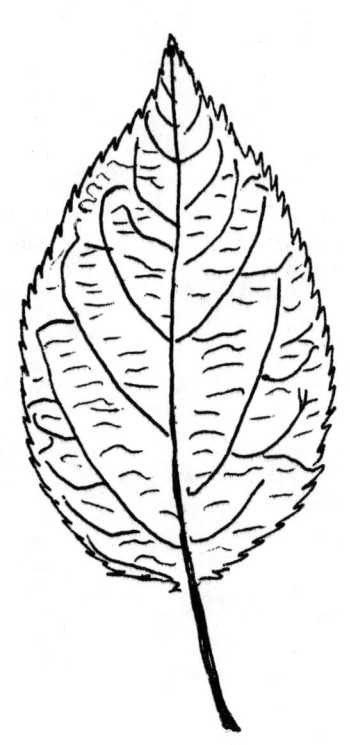

Malus species

Malus species

Common Name: Apple; Flowering Crabapple

Family: Rosaceae

Foliage: 1-5 inches long; most are green; small teeth; with or without lobes; yellowish in autumn

Flowers: white, pink, purple, or red; single, semi-double or double; some are fragrant; April-May

Fruit: up to 2 inch pome; yellow, green, red or purple; some are edible; ripens August-October

Buds: variable

Twigs: slender; many are hairy; produce spurs

Bark: variable

Roots: fibrous; spreading; transplants well

Growth Habit: 8-35 feet in height; often with a round crown

Hardiness: zone 4

Site: general, well-drained soil; sun or partial shade

Growth Rate: variable

Maintenance: usually clean; fruit can be messy; tolerant to pruning

Propagation: graft or bud on *M.* species understock

Note: there are many crab varieties available; those presented in this list were selected on the basis of disease resistance

Selections	Flowers	Fruit	Other
'Adams'	magenta	red	
baccata 'Jackii'	white	tiny; dark red	upright habit
'Baskatong'	purplish red fading to pink	purplish red	
'Beverly'	pink fading to white	red; persistent	
'Coralburst'	double pink		dwarf
'Dolgo'	large; white	large; red	edible fruit
'Gibbs' Golden Cage'	white	yellow	
'Golden Hornet'	pink fading to white	yellow	
'Henry Kohankie'	white and pink	shiny; red	
'Kibele'	red	dark red	
moerlandsii 'Liset'	dark red	shiny; dark red	columnar
'Mary Potter'	white	red	picturesque form
'Ormiston Roy'	pink	tiny; yellow; persistent	
'Pattie'	pink	large; green to yellow	
'Pink Spires'	pink	deep red	upright, copper in autumn
'Professor Sprenger'	white	orange	
purpurea 'Lemoinei'	red	purple	
'Red Jade'	white	red	weeping habit
'Red Jewel'	white	red	
rocki	white	red	
sargentii	white	dark red	
'Selkirk'	rosy pink	shiny; red	bronze foliage
'White Angel'	white	shiny; large, red	shiny foliage

Morus alba

166

Morus alba

Common Name: White Mulberry

Family: Moraceae

Foliage: 2 1/2-7 inches long; shiny; smooth; often with several irregular lobes; dull, coarse teeth; light, bright green; yellowish in autumn

Flowers: male and female separate on sane or different trees; May

Fruit: 1 inch, fleshy achene; white becoming pink or purple; edible; ripens July-August

Buds: no terminal; light brown

Twigs: slender; yellowish brown; smooth oblong, white lenticels

Bark: yellow-brown to light gray; narrow ridges

Roots: fibrous; spreading; shallow; transplants well

Growth Habit: 35-45 feet in height; low branching; broad, spreading, round crown

Hardiness: zone 4

Site: rich, dry soil; sun or partial shade

Growth Rate: rapid

Maintenance: weedy; abundant fruit; tolerant to pruning

Propagation: seed—stratify in moist sand at 33-41 °F for 30-90 days, spring sow only; softwood cuttings; graft on *M. alba* understock

Selections: 'Pendula' — weeping branches
    var. *tatarica* — very hardy

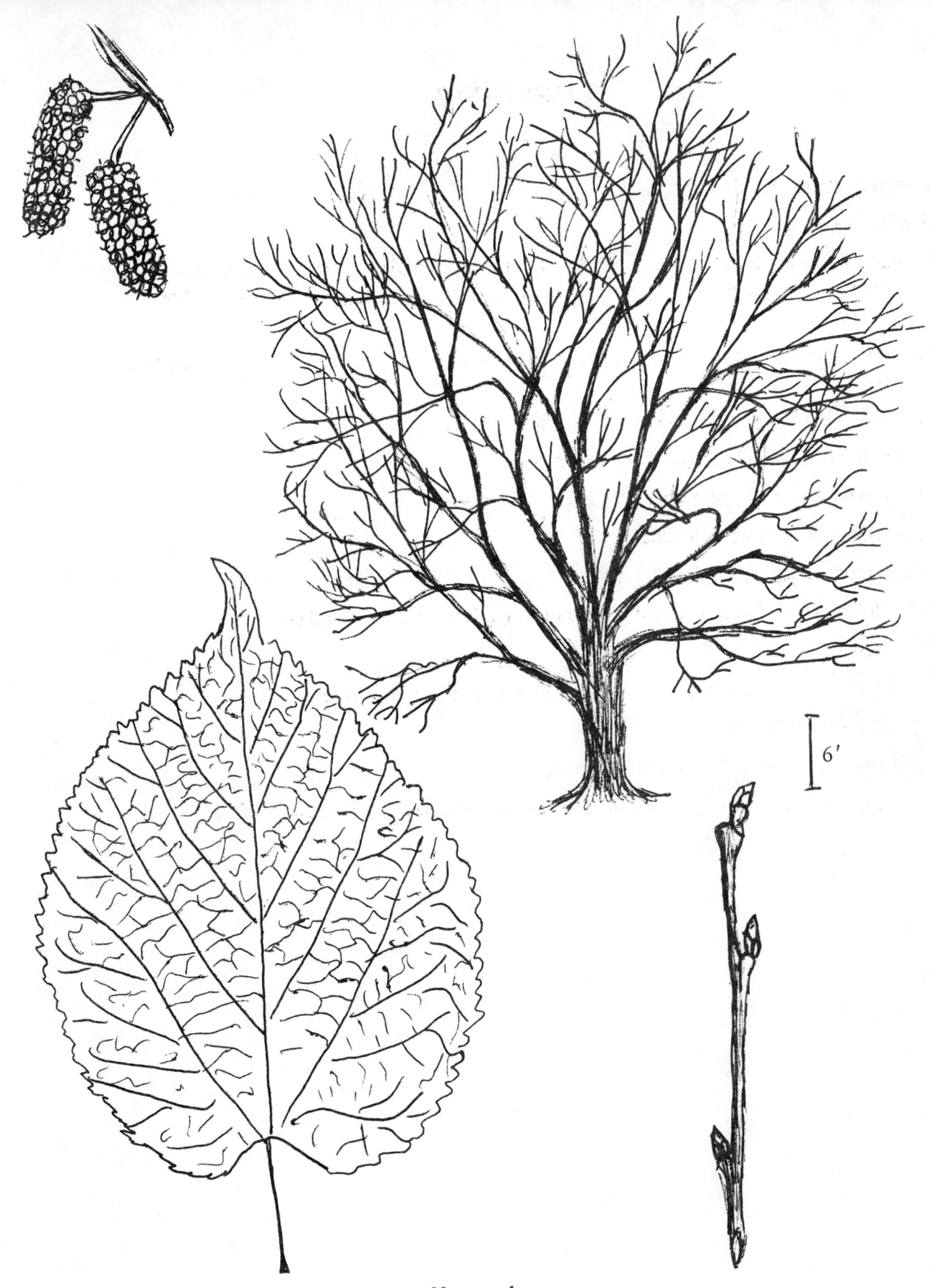

Morus rubra

Morus rubra

Common Name: Red Mulberry

Family: Moraceae

Foliage: 3-7 inches long; abruptly pointed; often with irregular lobes; dull, dark green and rough above; paler and hairy below; rounded teeth; milky juice in leaf stalk; yellow in autumn

Flowers: male and female separate on same or different trees; male: green clusters; female: dense spikes; May

Fruit: 1-1 1/2 inch, purple achene; edible; ripens June-July

Buds: no terminal; shiny; light brown; pointed

Twigs: slender; brown; smooth; milky sap

Bark: thin; dark brown with scales

Roots: taproot; transplants well

Growth Habit: 40-70 feet in height; low branching; dense; broad, round crown

Hardiness: zone 4

Site: prefers rich, moist soil; will tolerate drought; sun or partial shade

Growth Rate: moderate

Maintenance: messy fruit; tolerant to pruning

Propagation: seed—stratify in sand at 33-41 °F for 30-90 days, spring sow only

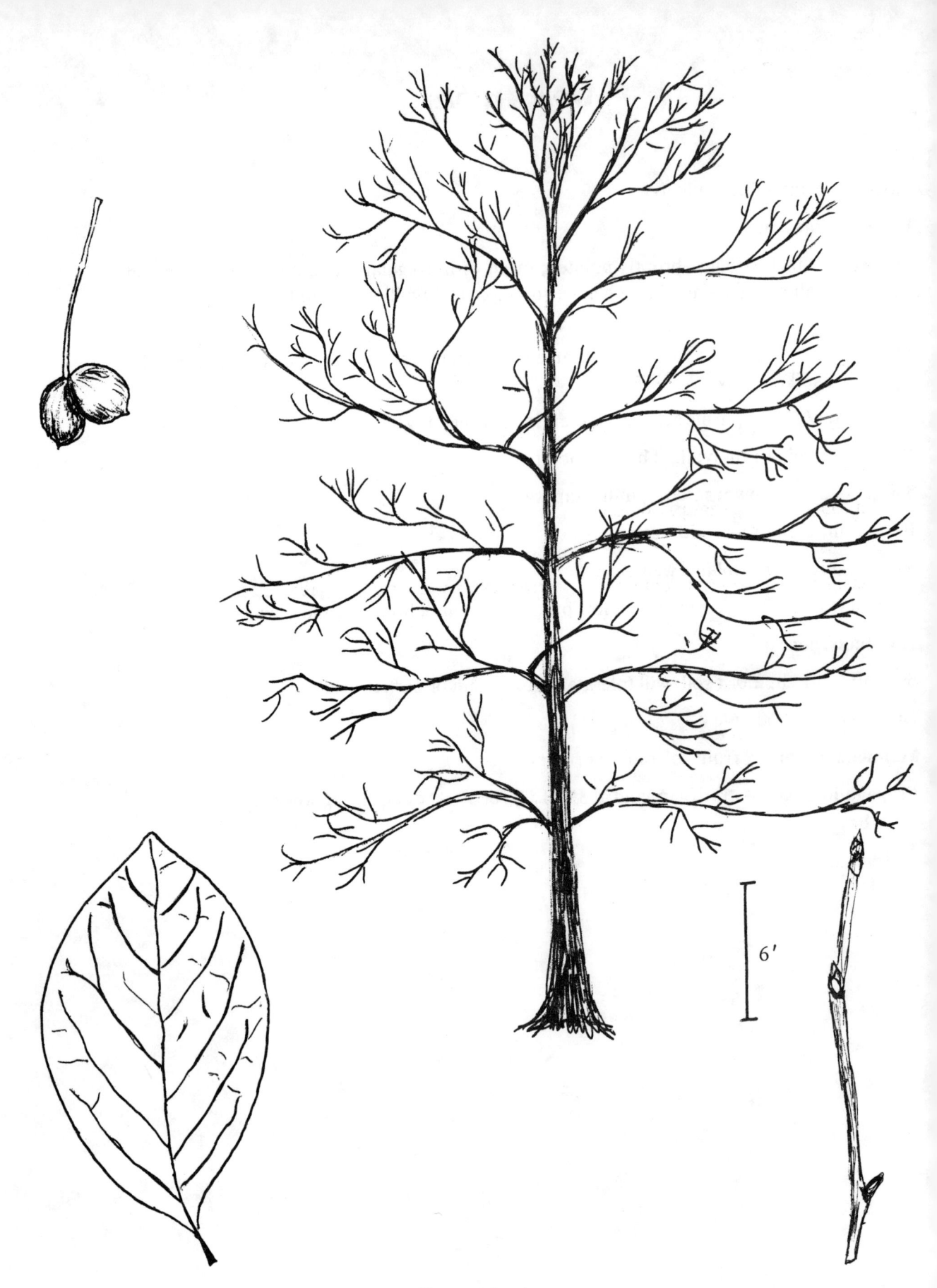

Nyssa sylvatica

Nyssa sylvatica

Common Name: Black Gum; Sour Gum; Tupelo

Family: Nyssaceae

Foliage: 2-5 inches long; entire or wavy margins; wider toward the tip; bright green and shiny above; paler below; leathery; crowded at ends of lateral branches; scarlet to orange-red in autumn

Flowers: male and female separate on same or different trees; clusters; small; greenish white; May-June

Fruit: 1/4-1/2 inch, fleshy, blue-black drupe; 2-3 per stem; bitter; ridged pit; long, slender stalk; ripens September-October

Buds: red

Twigs: slender; green to reddish brown; smooth; diaphragmed pith

Bark: thick; dark gray; deeply fissured into irregular blocks

Roots: very long; sometimes taproot; difficult to transplant

Growth Habit: 40-50 feet in height; flat topped crown; open, horizontal branches

Hardiness: zone 4

Site: average or wet, acid soil; sun or partial shade

Growth Rate: slow-moderate

Maintenance: clean; limited tolerance to pruning

Propagation: seed—fall sow and mulch, or stratify in moist sand (or naked in plastic bags) at 30-41°F for 30-120 days; layers; suckers

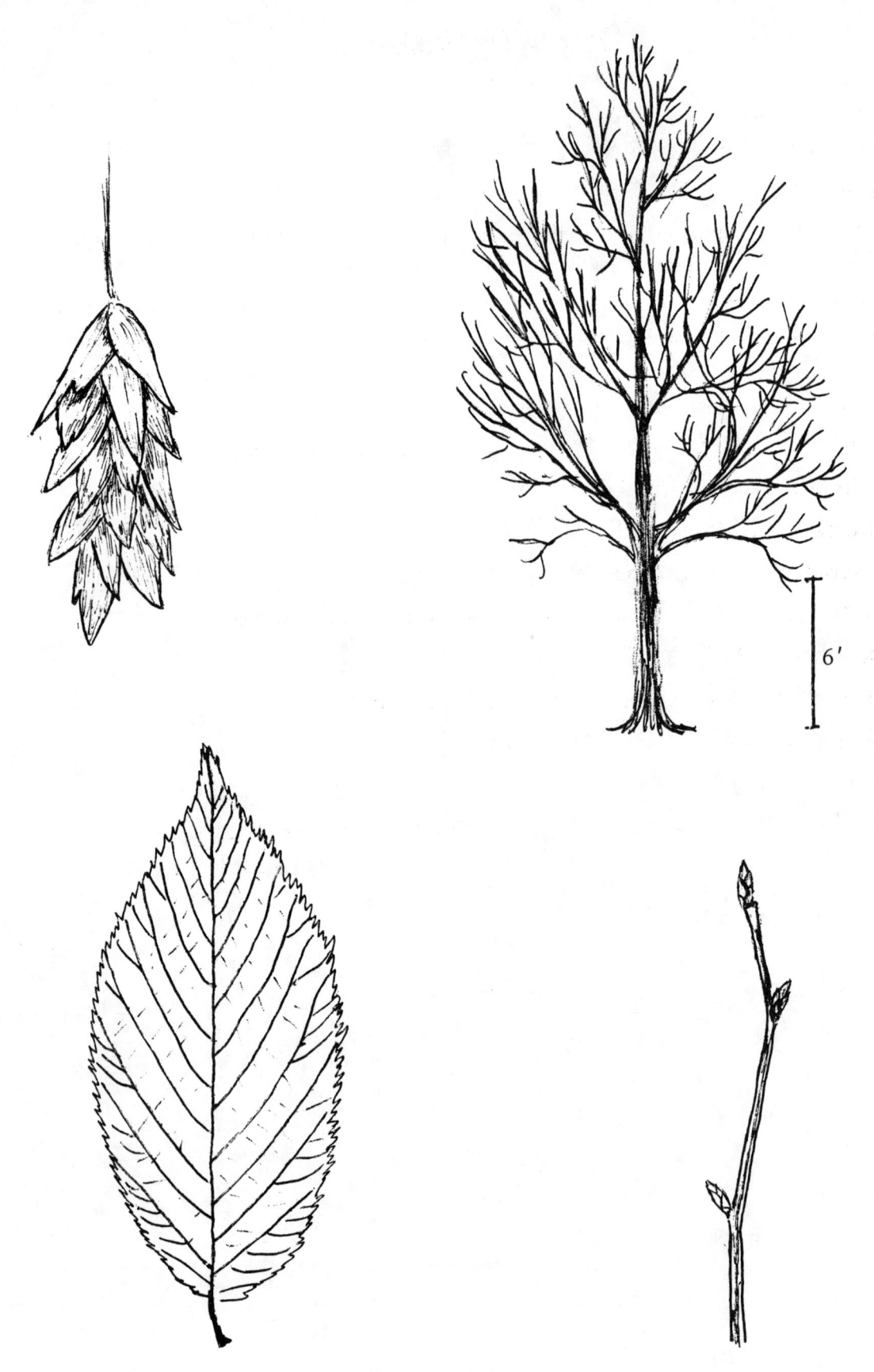

Ostrya virginiana

Ostrya virginiana

Common Name: American Hop Hornbeam; Ironwood

Family: Betulaceae

Foliage: 2-5 inches long; fine, double teeth; bright green and smooth above; paler below with tufts of hair in vein axils; yellow to rusty-brown in autumn

Flowers: male and female separate but on the same tree; male: yellow-green catkins formed the preceding year; female: reddish cluster; April-May

Fruit: ribbed nutlet in a sac formed in loose, conelike clusters that look like hops; green becoming tan; ripens August-September

Buds: no terminal; longitudinal striations on scales; chestnut brown; conical

Twigs: slender; reddish brown; zigzag

Bark: gray; small flakes; shaggy

Roots: spreading; difficult to transplant

Growth Habit: 25-60 feet in height; round to oval crown; slender branches

Hardiness: zone 3

Site: adaptable; drought and moisture tolerant; shade tolerant

Growth Rate: very slow

Maintenance: clean; very tolerant to pruning

Propagation: seed—fall sow and mulch for winter, or stratify for spring sowing

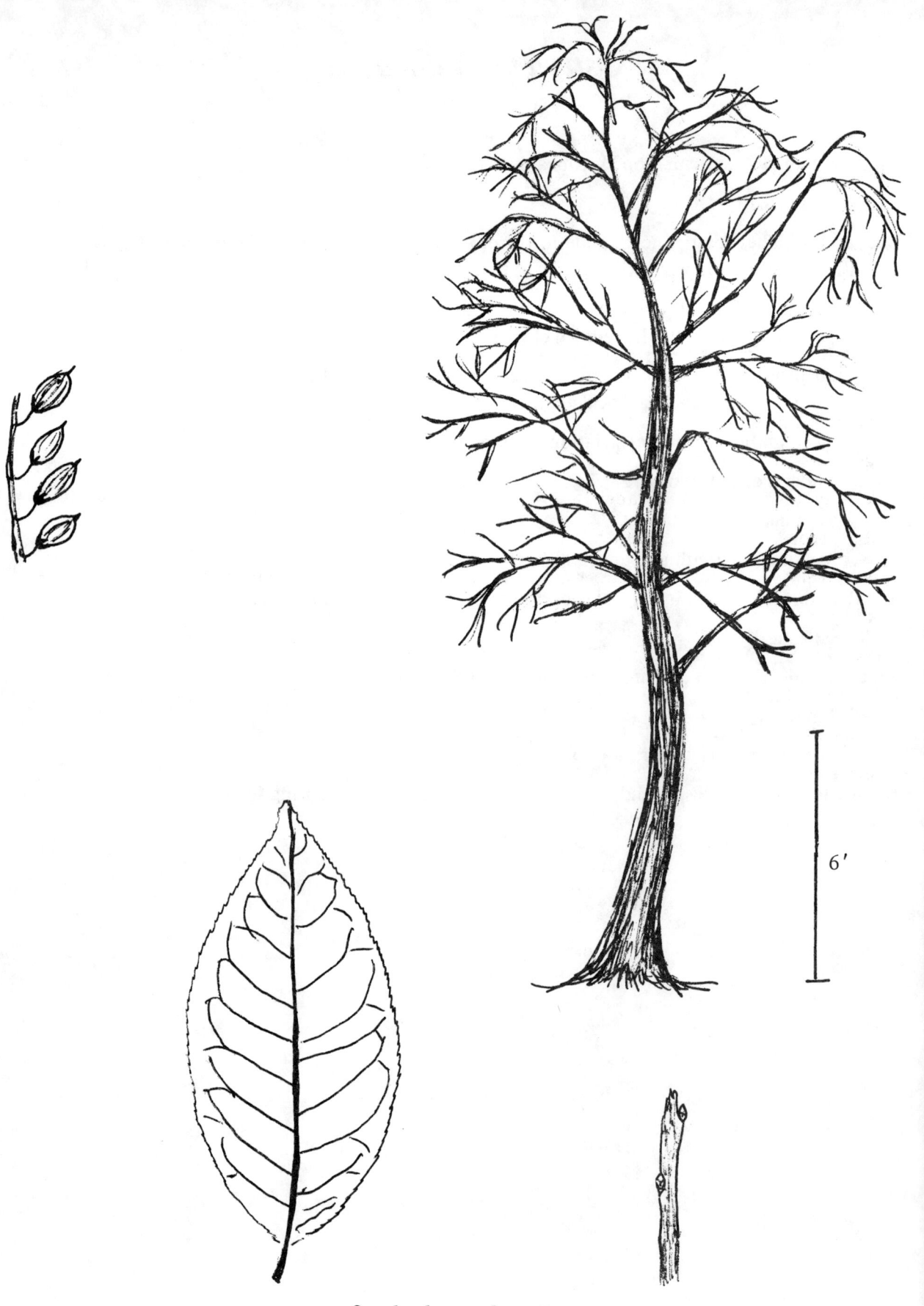

Oxydendrum arboreum

Oxydendrum arboreum

Common Name: Sorrel-tree; Sourwood

Family: Ericaceae

Foliage: 3-8 inches long; very fine teeth; thin; sour taste; dark green and shiny above; paler with hairy veins below; red in autumn

Flowers: 6-8 inch clusters; bell-shaped; white; July-August

Fruit: 5 lobed, dry capsule; gray; many slender seeds; ripens September-October; persists through winter

Buds: no terminal; embedded in the bark; very small; red scaly

Twigs: slender; reddish brown

Bark: gray tinged with deep orange furrows

Roots: fibrous; transplants well when young

Growth Habit: 20-25 feet in height; oblong to rounded crown; drooping branches

Hardiness: zone 4

Site: acidic, well-drained soil; sun or shade; prefers shelter from strong winds

Growth Rate: slow

Maintenance: clean; fairly tolerant to pruning

Propagation: seed—no pretreatment; softwood cuttings

Phellodendron amurense

Phellodendron amurense

Common Name: Amur Cork-tree

Family: Rutaceae

Foliage: 8-15 inches long; 5-13 leaflets; without teeth; young are hairy fringed; older leaves have only a hairy midrib; dark green and shiny above; stalk with enlarged bases; yellow in autumn

Flowers: male and female separate on separate trees; loose panicles; yellow-green; May-June

Fruit: 3/8 inch, bluish black drupe; in clusters; aromatic when crushed; ripens September-October; may persist through winter

Buds: no terminal; small; brown; triangular

Twigs: stout; stiff; brown; lenticels prominent

Bark: dark gray; deep corky ridges

Roots: shallow; fibrous; transplants well

Growth Habit: 25-50 feet in height; massive branches; widespreading, open, round crown

Hardiness: zone 3

Site: very tolerant to many soils; withstands drought and heat; sun

Growth Rate: moderate-rapid

Maintenance: can become weedy; limited tolerance to pruning

Propagation: seed—fall sow or stratify in a moist medium at 41 °F for 30 days; cuttings

Picea abies

178

Picea abies

Common Name: Norway Spruce

Family: Pinaceae

Foliage: 1/2-1 inch, evergreen needles; dark green; balsam odor when crushed; 4 sided; radial on twigs; sharp pointed; persists 7-10 years

Flowers: male and female separate but on the same tree; male: red, stalked, on lower portion of the tree; female: red, on upper 1/3 of tree

Fruit: 4-6 inch cone; thin, entire to ragged scale margin; pendent; scale bracts fall off; brown; ripens September-November

Buds: small; slender; light brown; conical; loose scales

Twigs: leaf scars raised; hazel

Bark: thin; gray; flaky scales

Roots: fibrous; spreading; transplants well when root pruned

Growth Habit: 100-200 feet in height; conical crown; branches often in tiers with weeping branchlets

Hardiness: zone 3 (young trees subject to winter damage and late spring frost damage)

Site: moist, well-drained soil; prefers full sun but tolerant

Growth Rate: rapid

Maintenance: clean; tolerant to pruning

Propagation: seed—no pretreatment; graft on *P. abies* or *P. glauca* understock

Selections: 'Acrocona' — cones born on primary branches; shoot tips with cone scales between the needles
'Argenteospica' — white tips on young twigs
'Aurea' — yellow foliage
'Cincinnata' — weeping branches
'Cupressina' — columnar
'Finedonensis' — pyramidal; young foliage yellowish
'Inversa' — very droopy branches
'Pyramidata' — narrowly pyramidal
'Virgata' — few branches; long and whorled

Picea engelmannii

180

Picea engelmannii

Common Name: Engelmann Spruce

Family: Pinaceae

Foliage: 1 inch, evergreen needles; point forward; 4 sided; deep bluish green; bloomy; sharp pointed; flexible; disagreeable odor when crushed; persists 7-10 years

Flowers: male and female separate but on the same tree; male: dark purple, on lower portion of the tree; female: bright red, on upper 1/3 of tree; June-July

Fruit: 1-3 inch cone; pendent; straw colored; ripens August-September

Buds: light brown; blunt

Twigs: yellowish brown; hairy

Bark: thin; russet-brown; resinous; loose scales

Roots: shallow; spreading; not easily established

Growth Habit: 60-150 feet in height; dense; narrowly pyramidal crown; short, whorled branches; lower branches often extend to ground

Hardiness: zone 4

Site: adaptable; very tolerant of shade

Growth Rate: slow-moderate

Maintenance: clean; tolerant to pruning

Propagation: seed—soak in water 24 hours then store in a plastic bag at 34° F for 21-42 days, spring sow only; graft on *P. abies* or *P. glauca* understock

Selections: 'Argentea' — silvery foliage
'Glauca' — bluish foliage

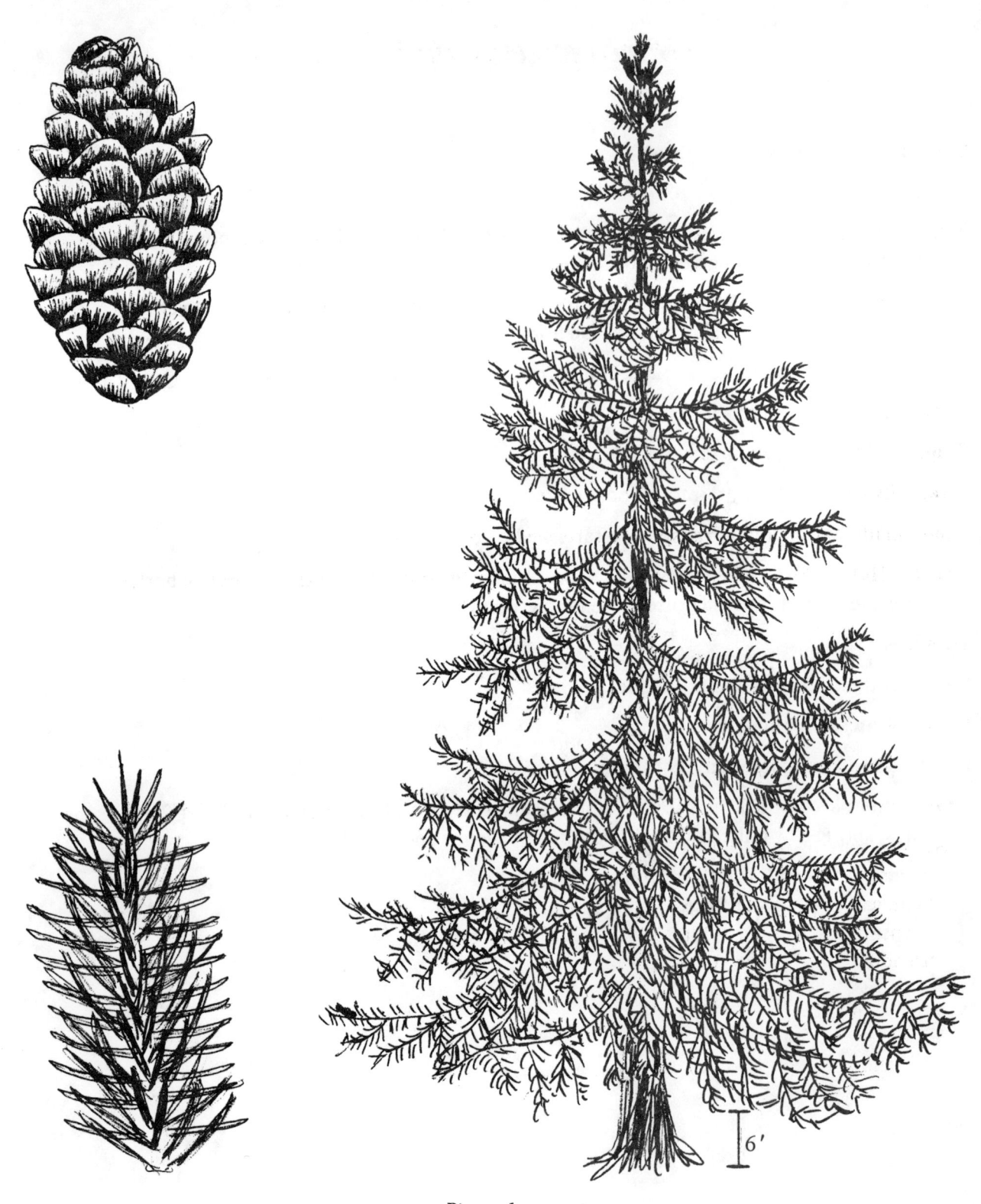

Picea glauca

182

Picea glauca

Common Name: White Spruce

Family: Pinaceae

Foliage: 1/3-3/4 inch, evergreen needles; blue-green; 4 sided; radial on twig; odor when broken; sharply pointed; persists 7-10 years

Flowers: male and female separate but on the same tree; male: red, on lower portion of tree; female: red to green; on upper 1/3 of tree; May

Fruit: 1-2 1/2 inch cone; glossy; stiff scales; brown; pendent; ripens mid-August

Buds: chestnut-brown; blunt; loose scales

Twigs: slender; grayish white; stink when bruised

Bark: ashy gray; scaly

Roots: shallow; spreading; transplants fairly well if root pruned

Growth Habit: 100-150 feet in height; long, straight trunk; conical crown; compact; branches often extend to ground

Hardiness: zone 2

Site: moist, well-drained soil; heat and drought tolerant; sun

Growth Rate: slow-moderate

Maintenance: clean; moderate tolerance to pruning

Propagation: seed—no pretreatment; graft on *P. abies* or *P. glauca* understock; cuttings

Selections: 'Aurea' — yellowish foliage on top
   'Coerulea' — bluish foliage
   'Conica' — dwarf; dense, conical crown
   'Densata' — compact; blue-green; slow growth rate
   'Pendula' — weeping branches

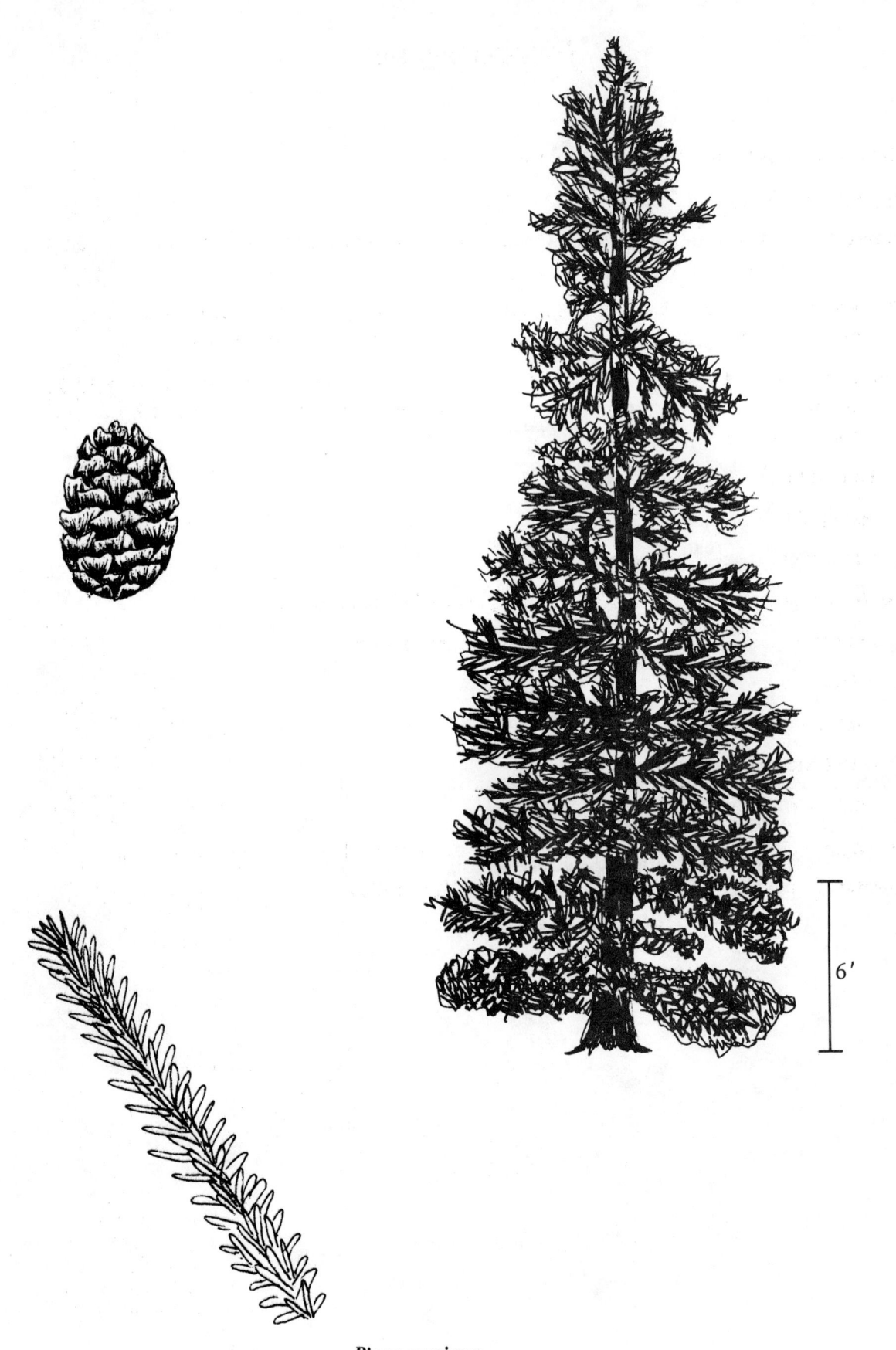

Picea mariana

184

Picea mariana

Common Name: Black Spruce; Bog Spruce

Family: Pinaceae

Foliage: 1/4 inch, evergreen needles; radial on twigs; bluish green with whitish bloom; 4 sided; persists 7-10 years

Flowers: male and female separate but on the same tree; male: dark red, on lower portion of tree; female: greenish red to purple, on upper 1/3 of tree; May-June

Fruit: 1/2-3/4 inch cone; pendent; scales with ragged margins; on short stalks; brittle; purple first winter becoming rich, purplish brown; incurved; often serotinous and will not open for many years; persist on tree many years

Buds: pointed; reddish brown

Twigs: light brown; hairy

Bark: thin; gray; scaly, underbark olive green

Roots: taproot with fibrous laterals; transplants well if root pruned

Growth Habit: 30-90 feet in height; narrow, pyramidal crown

Hardiness: zone 2

Site: rich, moist soil; sun or partial shade

Growth Rate: slow-moderate

Maintenance: clean; tolerant to pruning

Propagation: seed—no pretreatment; layering; graft on *P. abies* or *P. glauca* understock

Selections: 'Doumetii' — dwarf; dense; bluish green foliage

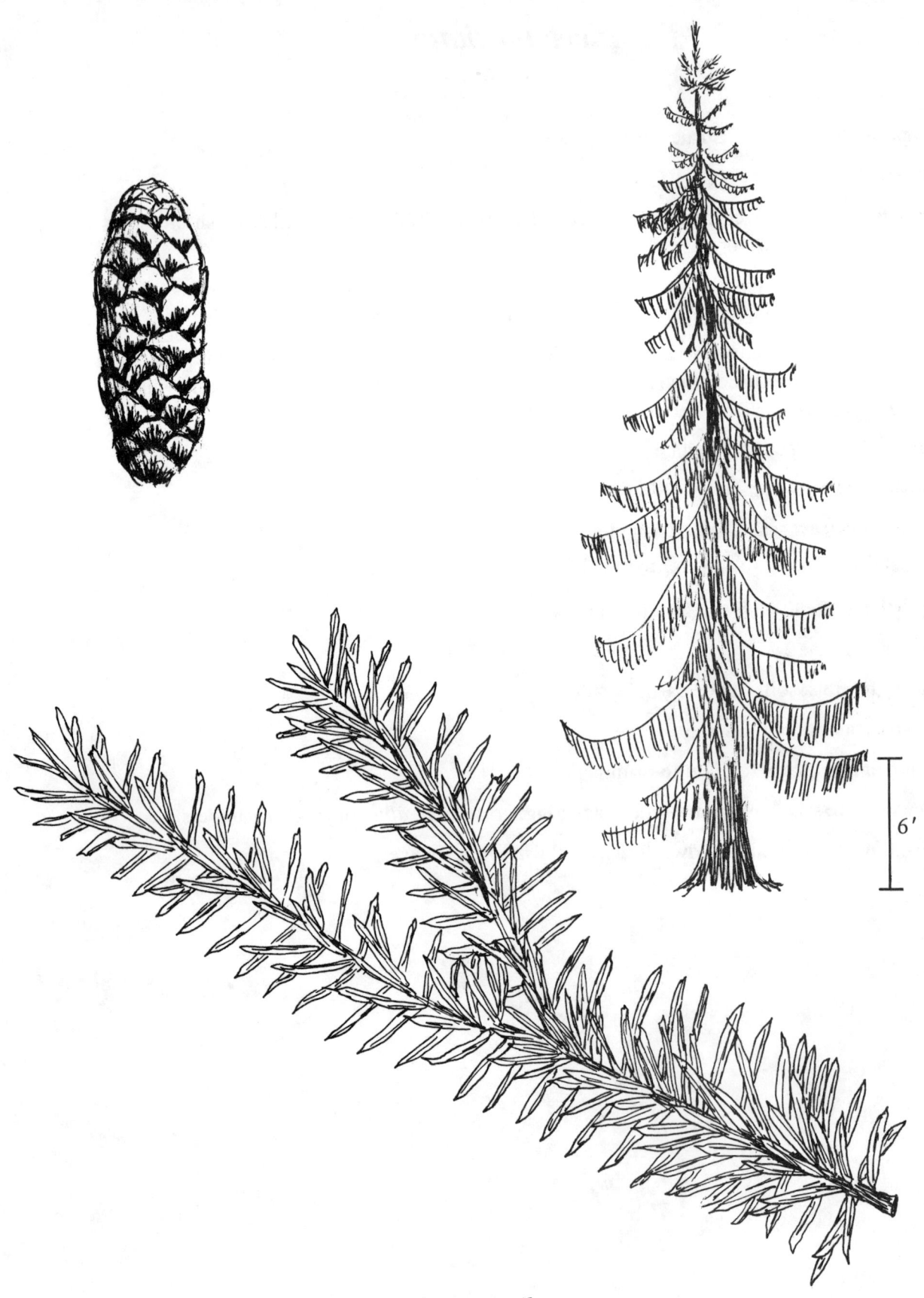

Picea omorika

Picea omorika

Common Name: Serbian Spruce

Family: Pinaceae

Foliage: 1/2-3/4 inch, evergreen needles; flat in cross section; blunt tips; flexible; midrib on upper side; pointed forward; glossy, dark green above; 2 whitish lines below; persists 7-10 years

Flowers: male and female separate but on the same tree; both are red; male on lower portion of tree; female on upper 1/4-1/3 of tree; late May-June

Fruit: 1 1/2-2 inch cone; pendent; dark purplish brown; ripens August; persists many years

Buds: dark brown; pointed

Twigs: brown; hairy

Bark: brown; scaly

Roots: taproot with shallow, fibrous laterals; transplant young

Growth Habit: 60 feet in height; slender, pyramidal crown; short, pendulous branches with upturned tips; often with pendulous branchlets

Hardiness: zone 4

Site: light, moist, slightly alkaline soil

Growth Rate: slow

Maintenance: clean; tolerant to pruning

Propagation: seed—no pretreatment; graft on *P. abies* or *P. glauca* understock

Selections: 'Pendula' — weeping branches

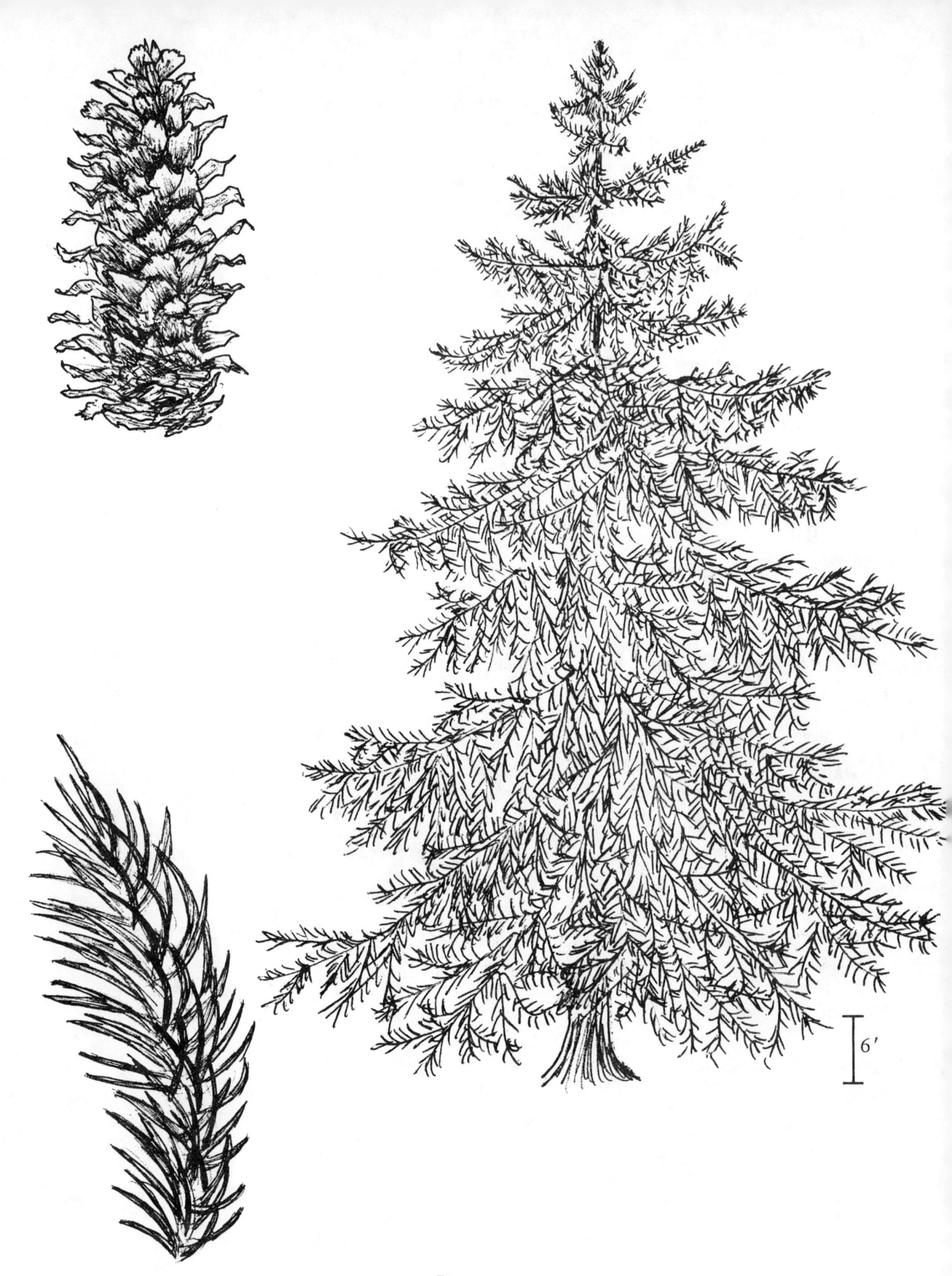

Picea pungens

188

Picea pungens

Common Name: Colorado Blue Spruce; Colorado Spruce

Family: Pinaceae

Foliage: 1-1 1/2 inch, evergreen needles; radial on twigs; green or blue-green; stiff; sharp odor when crushed; sharply pointed; 4 sided; dense; often with a silvery bloom; persists 7-10 years

Flowers: male and female separate but on the same tree; male: yellowish, on lower portion of tree; female: pale green, on upper 1/4-1/3 of tree; April-May

Fruit: 2-4 inch cone; shiny; pendent; fringed scales; straw colored; persists many years

Buds: light brown; pointed; loose scales

Twigs: orange-brown; leaf scars raised

Bark: gray; flaky

Roots: taproot; sometimes difficult to transplant on own roots

Growth Habit: 60-80 feet in height; conical crown; stiff; symmetrical

Hardiness: zone 2

Site: moist, rich, soil; tolerant to alkaline conditions; sun

Growth Rate: slow

Maintenance: clean; tolerant to pruning

Propagation: seed—stratify in moist vermiculite at 41°F for 40 days; graft on *P. abies, P. glauca,* or *P. pungens* understock

Selections: 'Aurea' — yellowish foliage
    'Bakeri' — deep blue foliage
    'Glauca' — silvery blue foliage
    'Glauca Pendula' — drooping branchlets with upturned tips; silvery
    'Hoopsii' — silvery blue foliage
    'Koster' — silvery blue foliage
    'Moerheim' — dense; blue foliage
    'Montgomery' — dwarf; silvery blue foliage
    'Spek' — open; dull, blue foliage
    'Thomsen' — whitish blue foliage

Pinus banksiana

Pinus banksiana

Common Name: Jack Pine

Family: Pinaceae

Foliage: 1 inch, evergreen needles; 2 per fascicle; bright green; twisted and curved; persists on tree 2-3 years; persistent sheath

Flowers: male and female separate but on the same tree; male: yellow; female: green to dark purple; May-June

Fruit: 1-2 inch cone; thickened scales; sessile; often recurved; assymmetrical; yellowish brown; matures in 2 or 3 years; persists for many years

Buds: reddish brown; resinous

Twigs: slender; flexible; reddish brown

Bark: reddish brown; scaly and rough

Roots: taproot; transplants moderately well if root pruned

Growth Habit: 50-60 feet in height; loose, open, irregular crown; flat top at maturity

Hardiness: zone 2

Site: poor, dry soil; sun

Growth Rate: slow-moderate

Maintenance: clean; tolerant to pruning

Propagation: seed—fall sow or sow fresh; for stored seed soak in water 1-2 days then stratify in a moist medium or a plastic bag at 33-41°F up to 7 days

Pinus densiflora

192

Pinus densiflora

Common Name: Japanese Red Pine

Family: Pinaceae

Foliage: 2-5 inch, evergreen needles; 2 per fasicicle; bright green; pale in winter; persists 2 years

Flowers: male and female separate but on same tree; dense clusters; spring

Fruit: 2 inch cone; short stalk; dull crown; ripens in autumn

Buds: red

Twigs: brown; bloomy

Bark: thin; orange branches with gray scales; flaky

Roots: taproot; transplants moderately well when root pruned

Growth Habit: 70-100 feet in height; broad, irregular crown; asymmetrical; often with a flat top

Hardiness: zone 4

Site: poor soil; sun

Growth Rate: rapid

Maintenance: clean; tolerant to pruning

Propagation: seed—sow fresh; for stored seed, soak in water 1-2 days then stratify in a moist medium or plastic bag at 33-41°F up to 20 days; graft on *P. densiflora* or *P. sylvestris* understock

Selections: 'Aurea' — yellowish foliage
'Globosa' — dwarf; round crown
'Oculus-draconis' — 2 yellow lines on foliage
'Pendula' — weeping branches
'Umbraculifera' — dwarf; umbrellalike habit

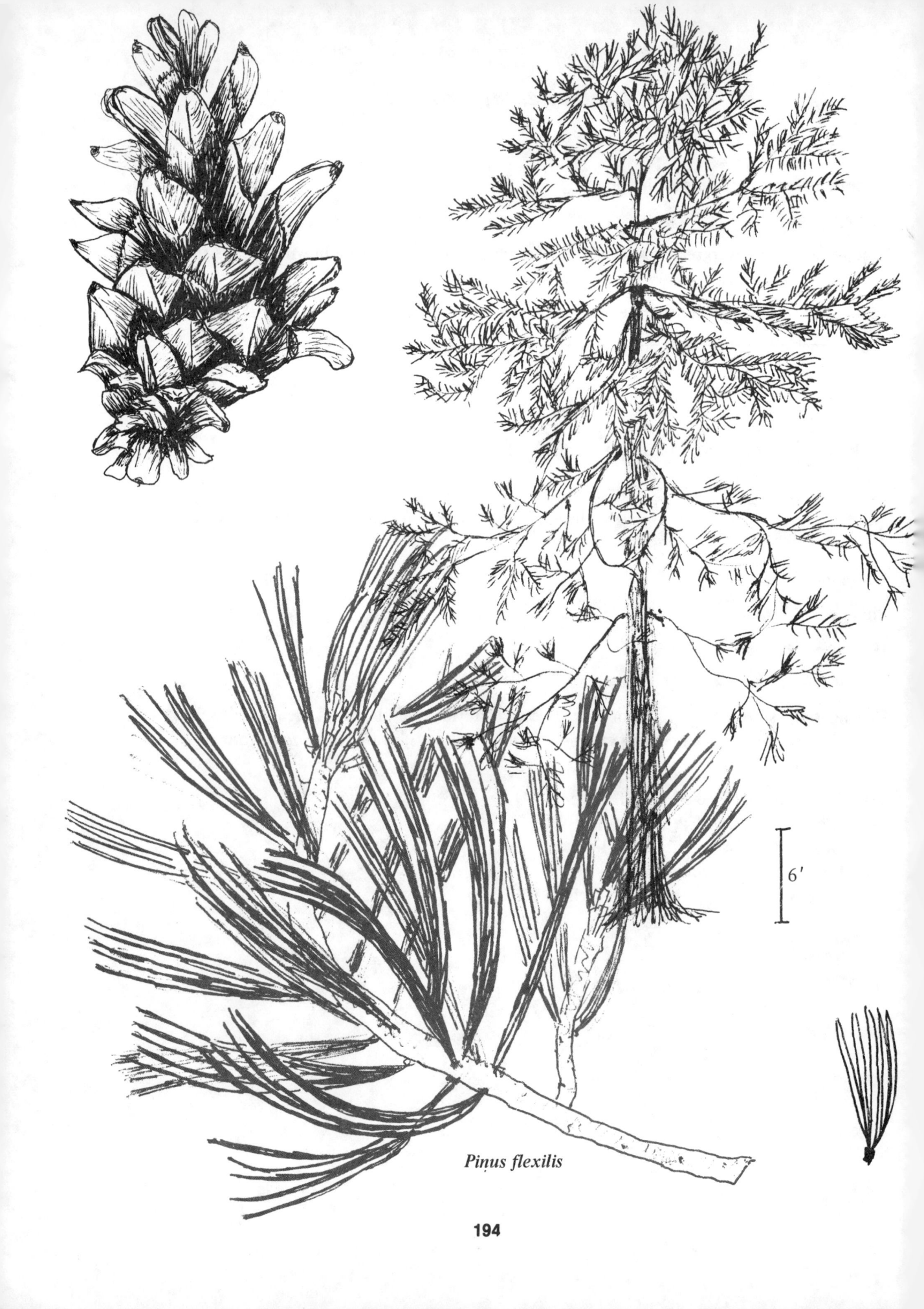

Pinus flexilis

194

Pinus flexilis

Common Name: Limber Pine

Family: Pinaceae

Foliage: 1-3 inch, evergreen needles; 5 per fascicle; points forward; white lines on all sides; persists 4-6 years; deciduous sheaths

Flowers: male and female separate but on the same tree; male: red spikes; female: reddish purple clusters; late spring

Fruit: 5-7 inch cone; short stalk; rigid; thick, dense scales; pendent; very resinous; yellowish brown; ripens in autumn

Buds: broad; pointed; brown

Twigs: stout; smooth; gray

Bark: thin; smooth; light gray; fissured

Roots: taproot; transplants well when root pruned

Growth Habit: 45-75 feet in height; broad, open crown; large, drooping branches

Hardiness: zone 4

Site: poor, dry soil; sun

Growth Rate: slow

Maintenance: clean; tolerant to pruning

Propagation: seed—soak in water 1-2 days then stratify in a moist medium or a plastic bag at 33-41°F for 21-90 days; graft on *P. flexilis* or *P. strobus* understock

Selections: 'Glenmore' — long, silvery foliage

Pinus jeffreyi

Pinus jeffreyi

Common Name: Jeffrey Pine

Family: Pinaceae

Foliage: 4-9 inch, evergreen needles; 2 or 3 per fascicle; sharp pointed; stiff but flexible; teeth on margin; blue-green; persists 6-9 years

Flowers: male and female separate but on the same tree; male: yellowish green; female: purplish clusters; late spring

Fruit: 5-10 inch cone; long, incurved prickles; light brown; short stalk; ripens in autumn

Buds: non resinous; reddish

Twigs: stout; purple-brown; pineapple odor when bruised; white bloom

Bark: dark gray; large, irregular, scaly plates

Roots: taproot; difficult to transplant

Growth Habit: 80-120 feet in height; open; upright, ascending branches; oval crown

Hardiness: zone 5

Site: poor, dry or well drained soil; sun

Growth Rate: moderate

Maintenance: clean; tolerant to pruning

Propagation: seed—no pretreatment; for stored seed, soak in water 1-2 days then stratify in a moist medium or plastic bag at 33-41° F up to 60 days; graft on *P. ponderosa* or *P. resinosa* understock

Leaf: ½ actual size

Pinus nigra

Pinus nigra

Common Name: Austrian Pine

Family: Pinaceae

Foliage: 4-6 inch, evergreen needles; dark green; 2 per fascicle; flexible; thick; persists 3 years; sheath is black and persistent

Flowers: male and female separate but the same tree; male: yellow clusters; female: yellowish green; spring

Fruit: 2-3 inch cone; conical; thickened scales; pendent; deciduously spine tipped; light brown; ripens in autumn

Buds: silvery

Twigs: green-yellow; shiny

Bark: gray; scaly

Roots: taproot; sometimes difficult to transplant

Growth Habit: 60-100 feet in height; widespreading; round top; dense foliage; low branching

Hardiness: zone 4

Site: adaptable; will tolerate moist soil, but prefers well drained; sun

Growth Rate: moderate-rapid

Maintenance: clean; tolerant to pruning

Propagation: seed—fall sow, or soak in water 1-2 days then stratify in a moist medium or plastic bag at 33-41 °F for 35-45 days; graft on *P. nigra* or *P. sylvestris* understock

Selections: 'Monstrosa' — dwarf; monstrous in appearance
'Pyramidalis' — narrowly pyramidal crown

Pinus parviflora

Pinus parviflora

Common Name: Japanese White Pine

Family: Pinaceae

Foliage: 3/4-2 inch, evergreen needles; 5 per fascicle; dark green outside; whitened toward the center; soft; slightly twisted; blunt apex; crowded into tufts at branch ends; persists 2 years; sheath deciduous

Flowers: male and female separate but on the same tree; male: purplish red; spring

Fruit: 2-3 inch cone; almost sessile; reddish brown; matures in one year; ripens in autumn; persists on tree 6-7 years

Buds: yellow-brown; slightly resinous

Twigs: greenish brown; becoming light gray; short

Bark: gray; thin; flaky plates

Roots: taproot with many laterals; transplants well if root pruned

Growth Habit: up to 100 feet in height; widespreading, horizontal branches; pyramidal crown

Hardiness: zone 5

Site: poor, well-drained soil; sun

Growth Rate: slow

Maintenance: clean; tolerant to pruning

Propagation: seed—stratify in a moist medium at 70-80°F for 60 days then at 33-41°F for 90 days; graft on *P. flexilis* or *P. strobus* understock

Selections: 'Glauca' — bluish foliage

Leaf: ½ actual size

Pinus ponderosa

Pinus ponderosa

Common Name: Ponderosa Pine; Western Yellow Pine

Family: Pinaceae

Foliage: 4-7 inch, evergreen needles; 2 or 3 per fascicle; dark green; persistent sheath; foliage persists 3-7 years

Flowers: male and female separate but on the same tree; male: yellow; female: red clusters; spring

Fruit: 3-6 inch cone; pendent; brown; scales with sharp tips; ripens autumn

Buds: resinous

Twigs: stout; orange; turpentine odor when crushed

Bark: thick; gray-red; large, flat plates

Roots: taproot; difficult to transplant

Growth Habit: 60-80 feet in height; open, oval crown

Hardiness: zone 4

Site: dry, poor or well drained soil; sun

Growth Rate: moderate

Maintenance: clean; fairly tolerant to pruning

Propagation: seed—no pretreatment

Leaf: ½ actual size

Pinus resinosa

Pinus resinosa

Common Name: Norway Pine; Red Pine

Family: Pinaceae

Foliage: 4-6 inch, evergreen needles; 2 per fascicle; straight; stiff, will break when bent; dark green; persists 4-5 years

Flowers: male and female separate but on the same tree; male: purple; female: scarlet; April-June

Fruit: 1 1/2-2 1/2 inch cone; sessile; pendent; basal scales brittle; chestnut-brown; attached at right angles to the branch; ripens August-October

Buds: red-brown with white, fringed edges

Twigs: stout; reddish brown

Bark: reddish brown; irregular, scaly plates

Roots: taproot with widespreading laterals

Growth Habit: 70-150 feet in height; open, broad crown

Hardiness: zone 2

Site: light, sandy soil; sun

Growth Rate: moderate

Maintenance: clean; tolerant to pruning

Propagation: seed—no pretreatment; for stored seed, soak in water 1-2 days then stratify in a moist medium or plastic bag at 33-41 °F for 60 days

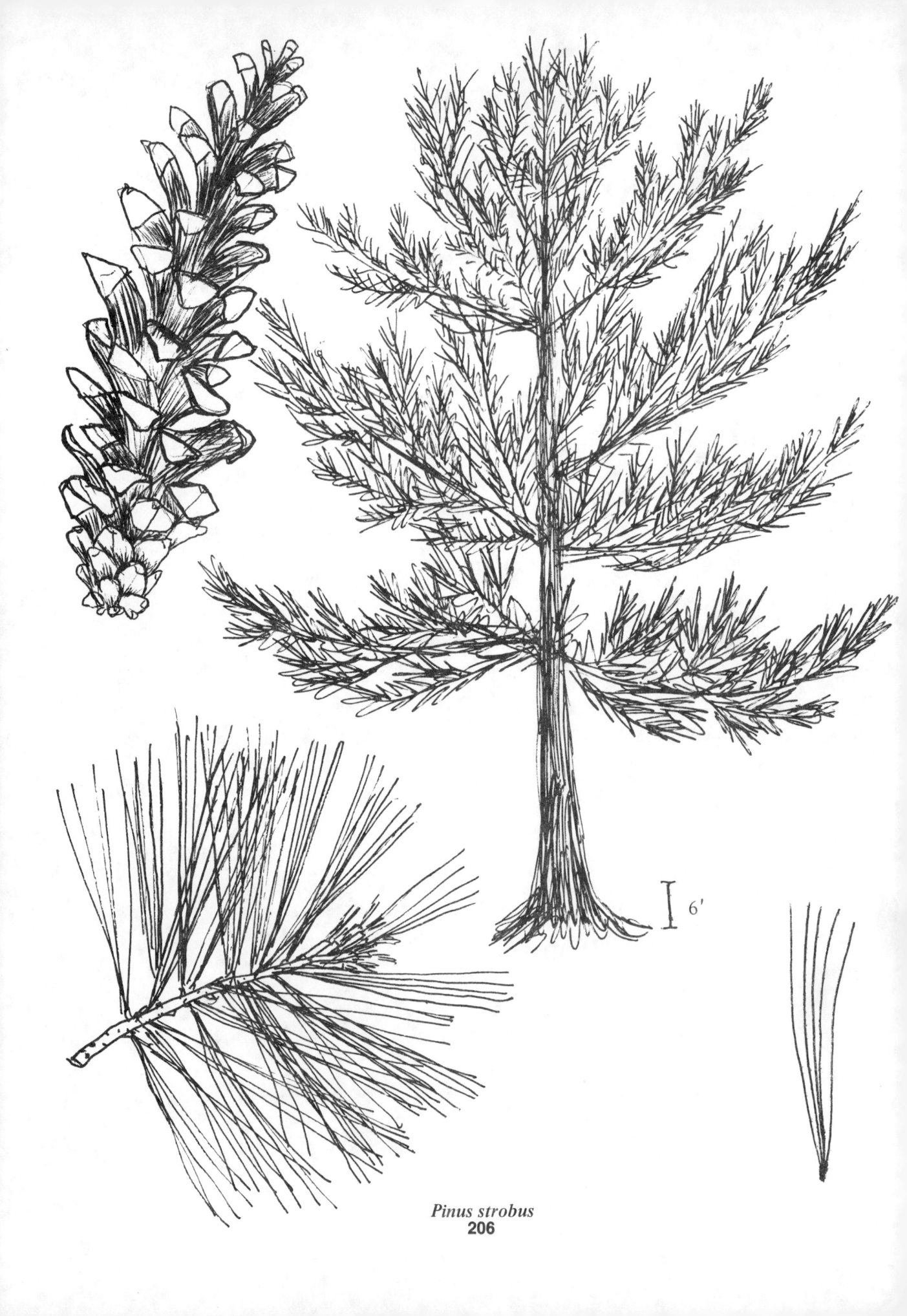

Pinus strobus
206

Pinus strobus

Common Name: Eastern White Pine

Family: Pinaceae

Foliage: 2-4 inch, evergreen needles; 5 per fascicle; soft and flexible; bluish green; small teeth; persists at least 2 years; deciduous sheath

Flowers: male and female separate but on the same tree; male: yellow; female: pinkish purple; May-June

Fruit: 4-6 inch cone; curved; tapering toward tip; narrow; rounded, resinous scales; pendent; light brown; ripens August-September

Buds: sharply pointed; brown; slightly resinous

Twigs: slender; smooth; reddish brown

Bark: dark gray; shallow fissures with plates

Roots: taproot with many laterals; transplants well if root pruned

Growth Habit: 100-150 feet in height; horizontal branching; open, pyramidal crown

Hardiness: zone 3

Site: moist, well drained, sandy soil; tolerates alkaline soil; sun

Growth Rate: moderate

Maintenance: clean; fairly tolerant to pruning

Propagation: seed—stratify in a moist medium or plastic bag at 33-41°F for 60 days; graft on *P. flexilis* or *P. strobus* understock

Selections: 'Fastigiata' — columnar habit
'Pendula' — weeping branches

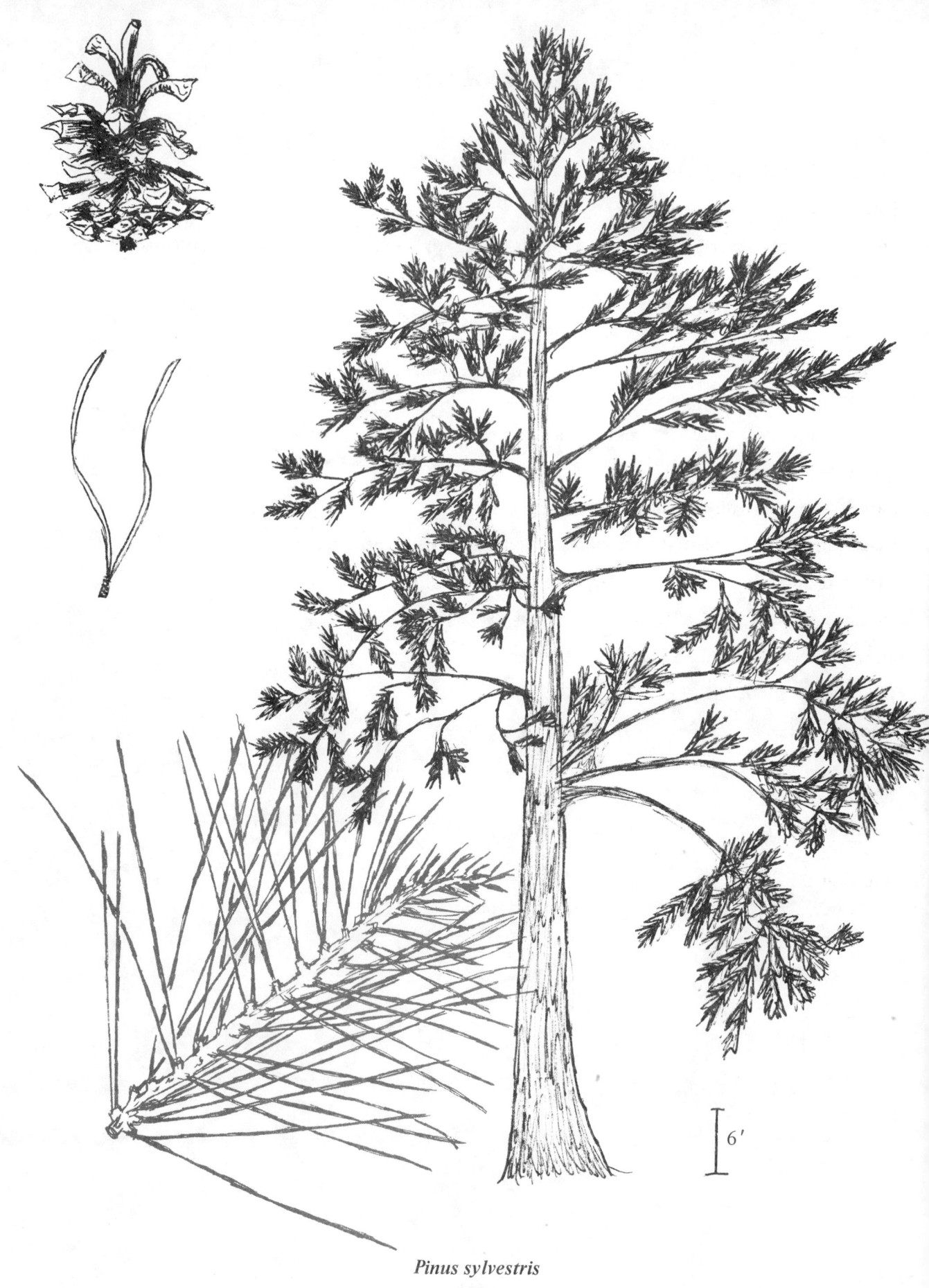

Pinus sylvestris

208

Pinus sylvestris

Common Name: Scotch Pine

Family: Pinaceae

Foliage: 1-3 inch, evergreen needles; 2 per cluster; stiff; twisted; sharply pointed tips; blue-green

Flowers: male and female separate but on the same tree; male: yellow; female: scarlet; spring

Fruit: 1 1/2-2 1/2 inch cone; pendent; stalked; recurved; thickened scales; dull brown; ripens autumn

Buds: long; red; resinous

Twigs: slender; dull brown

Bark: scaly; orange underbark

Roots: taproot with spreading laterals; transplants well if root pruned

Growth Habit: 60-100 feet in height; open, pyramidal crown; round topped and irregular at maturity

Hardiness: zone 2

Site: adaptable; well drained soil; sun

Growth Rate: rapid

Maintenance: clean; fairly tolerant to pruning

Propagation: seed—no pretreatment; for stored seed, soak in water 1-2 days then stratify in a moist medium or plastic bag at 33-41° F for 15-90 days; graft on *P. sylvestris* or *P. nigra* understock

Selections: 'Fastigiata' — columnar habit
    var. *rigensis* — very red bark; contorted foliage

Pinus virginiana

Pinus virginiana

Common Name: Jersey Pine; Scrub Pine

Family: Pinaceae

Foliage: 1 1/2-3 inch, evergreen needles; 2 per fascicle; twisted; dull; stiff; grayish green; persists 3-4 years; sheath persistent

Flowers: male and female separate but on the same tree; male: orange-brown; female: pale purplish; March-May

Fruit: 2-3 inch cone; stalkless; right angle to twigs; dark tips with sharp spines; cones produced in clusters; brown; ripens September-November; persists several years

Buds: dark brown; sharply pointed; resinous

Twigs: slender; whitish; waxy bloom

Bark: gray; resinous; fissures with scaly flakes

Roots: taproot with fibrous laterals; transplants well if root pruned

Growth Habit: 30-90 feet in height; open, flat top crown; branching sparse

Hardiness: zone 4

Site: poor, dry soil; sun

Growth Rate: slow

Maintenance: clean; fairly tolerant to pruning

Propagation: seed—no pretreatment; if stored, soak in water 1-2 days then stratify in a moist medium or plastic bag at 33-41°F up to 30 days

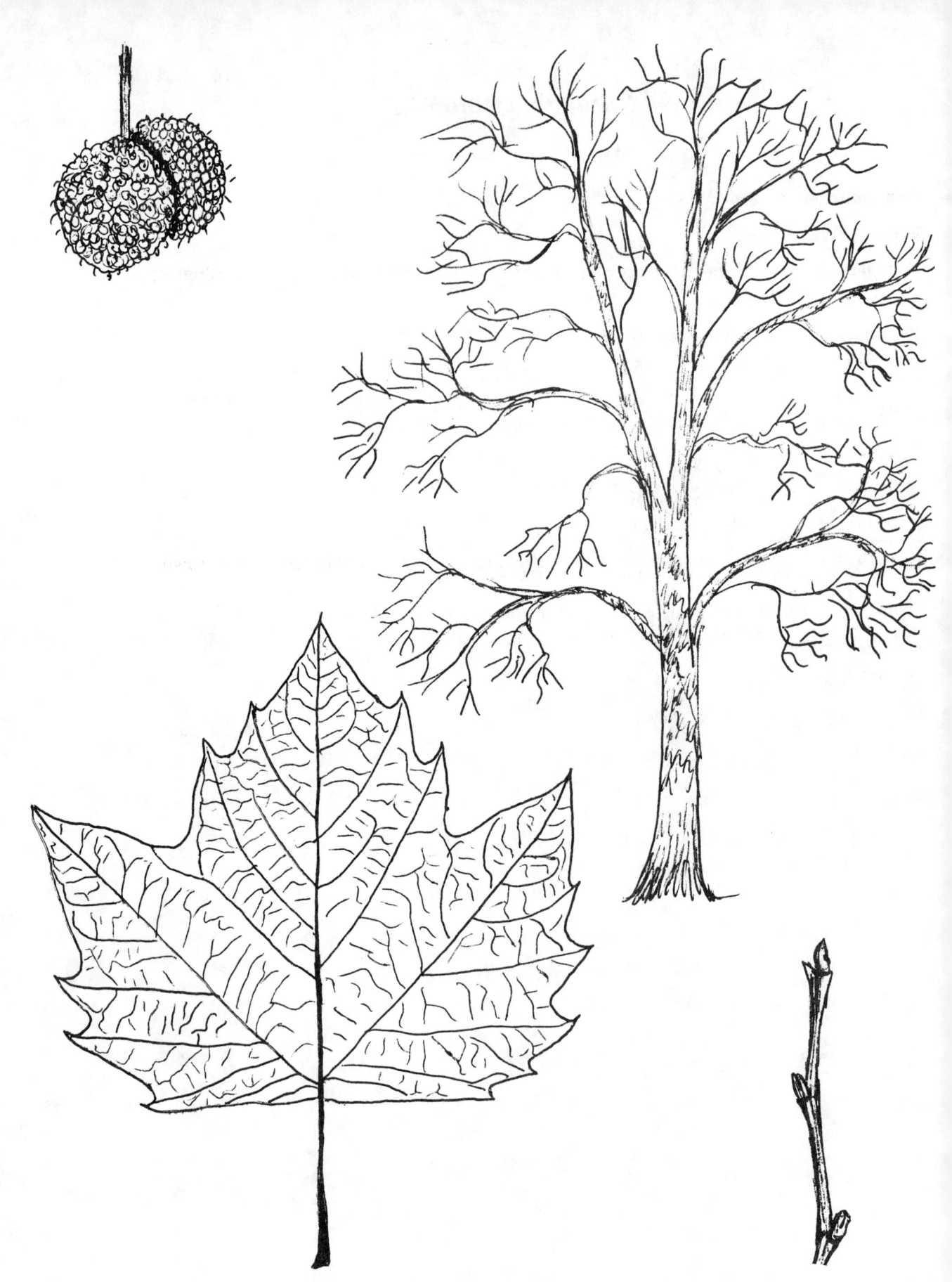

Platanus X *acerifolia*

Platanus X *acerifolia*

Common Name: London Plane

Family: Platanaceae

Foliage: 4-5 inches long; 3-5 lobes; sinuses 1/3 depth of blade; deep, yellow-green; light brown in autumn

Flowers: male and female separate but on the same tree; small; April-May

Fruit: 1 inch in diameter; 2 per cluster; made of achenes; pendulous; bristly surface

Buds: no terminal; conical; brown; single scale; hidden by leaf stalk

Twigs: moderately stout; orange-brown; young twigs are hairy

Bark: olive green to cream; exfoliating patches

Roots: fibrous; spreading; transplants well

Growth Habit: 50-100 feet in height; erect; drooping lower branches; broad, round crown

Hardiness: zone 5

Site: rich, moist soil preferred but adaptable; sun or partial shade

Growth Rate: rapid

Maintenance: clean; tolerant to pruning

Propagation: cuttings

Selections: 'Bloodgood Strain' — resistant to anthracnose
  'Kelseyana' — yellow variegated foliage
  'Suttneri' — white blotches on foliage
  'Pyramidalis' — upright, pyramidal crown

Platanus occidentalis

Platanus occidentalis

Common Name: American Plane Tree; Buttonwood; Sycamore

Family: Platanaceae

Foliage: 4-7 inches long; 3-5 lobes; lobes wider then long; coarse teeth; bright green and smooth above; paler and hairy along veins below; leaf stalk with enlarged base; brown in autumn

Flowers: male and female separate but on the same tree; round heads; May

Fruit: 1-1 1/4 inch in diameter; brown; single on a 3-6 inch stalk; made up of hairy achenes; ripens October; persistent

Buds: no terminal; conical; brown; 1 scale visible; hidden by leaf stalk

Twigs: moderately stout; light brown; shiny; zigzag

Bark: thin; large, mottled patches exfoliating; white outer bark; green, gray and brown inner bark

Roots: fibrous; spreading; transplants well

Growth Habit: 100-150 feet in height; widespreading, open, oblong crown

Hardiness: zone 4

Site: rich, moist soil; will adapt to drier sites; sun or partial shade

Growth Rate: rapid

Maintenance: clean; tolerant to pruning

Propagation: seed—no pretreatment, spring sow; cuttings

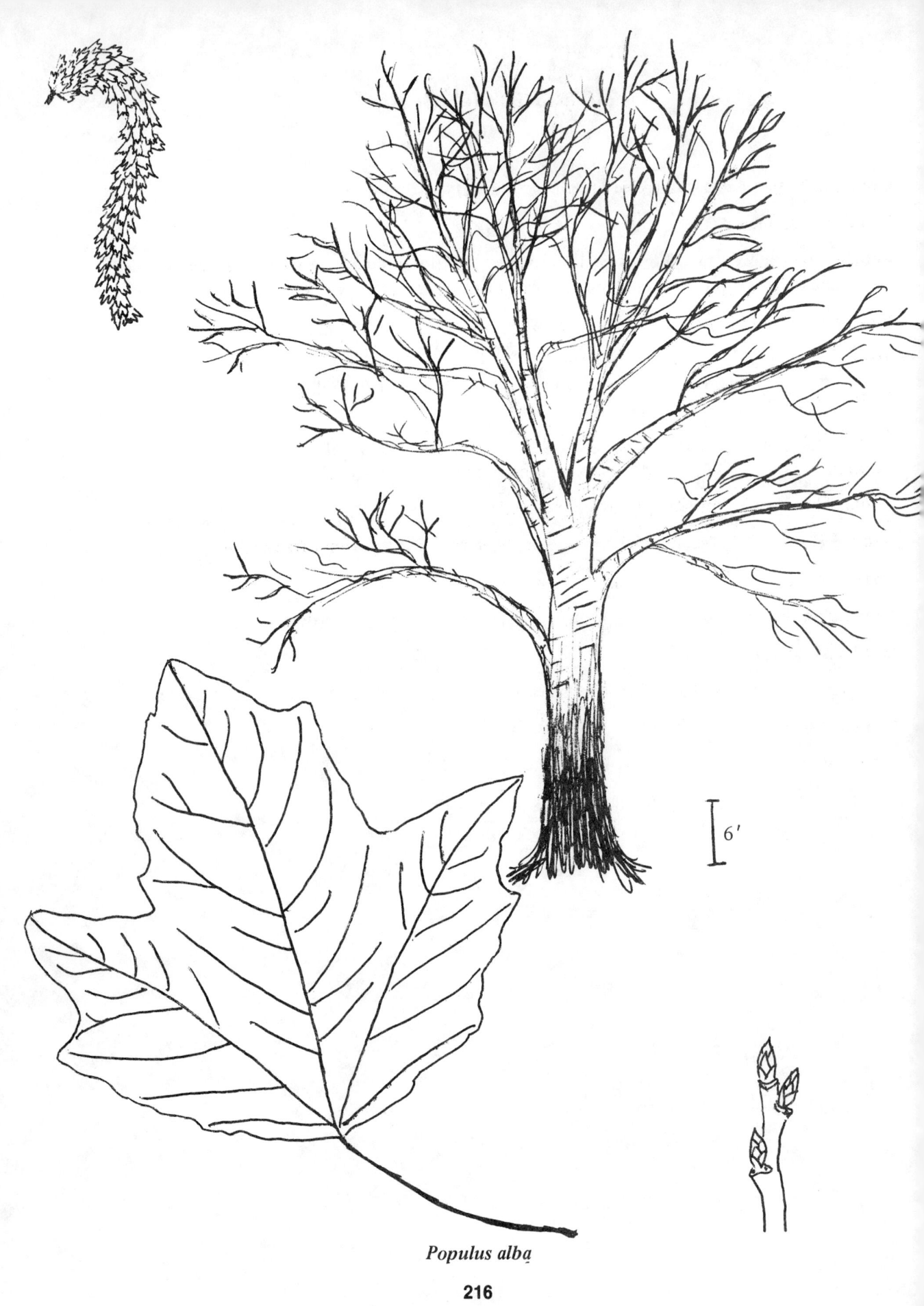

Populus alba

216

Populus alba

Common Name: Silver-leaved Poplar; White Poplar

Family: Salicaceae

Foliage: 2-5 inches long; often with 3-5 shallow lobes; deep, glossy green above; white and woolly beneath; white, flattened petiole; gold in autumn

Flowers: male and female separate on separate trees; drooping catkins; April-May

Fruit: small; gray capsule with tufted seeds

Buds: woolly

Twigs: woolly; greenish white; star shaped pith

Bark: dark gray to white; deeply fissured at base; horizontal lenticels

Roots: fibrous; widespreading; transplants well

Growth Habit: 70-90 feet in height; irregular, open round top crown; often suckers

Hardiness: zone 3

Site: moist; sun

Growth Rate: rapid

Maintenance: messy and brittle; suckers freely; intolerant to pruning

Propagation: seed—sow fresh; softwood and hardwood cuttings

Selections: 'Pendula' — weeping branches
    'Pyramidalis' — pyramidal crown
    'Richardii' — dull, yellow foliage

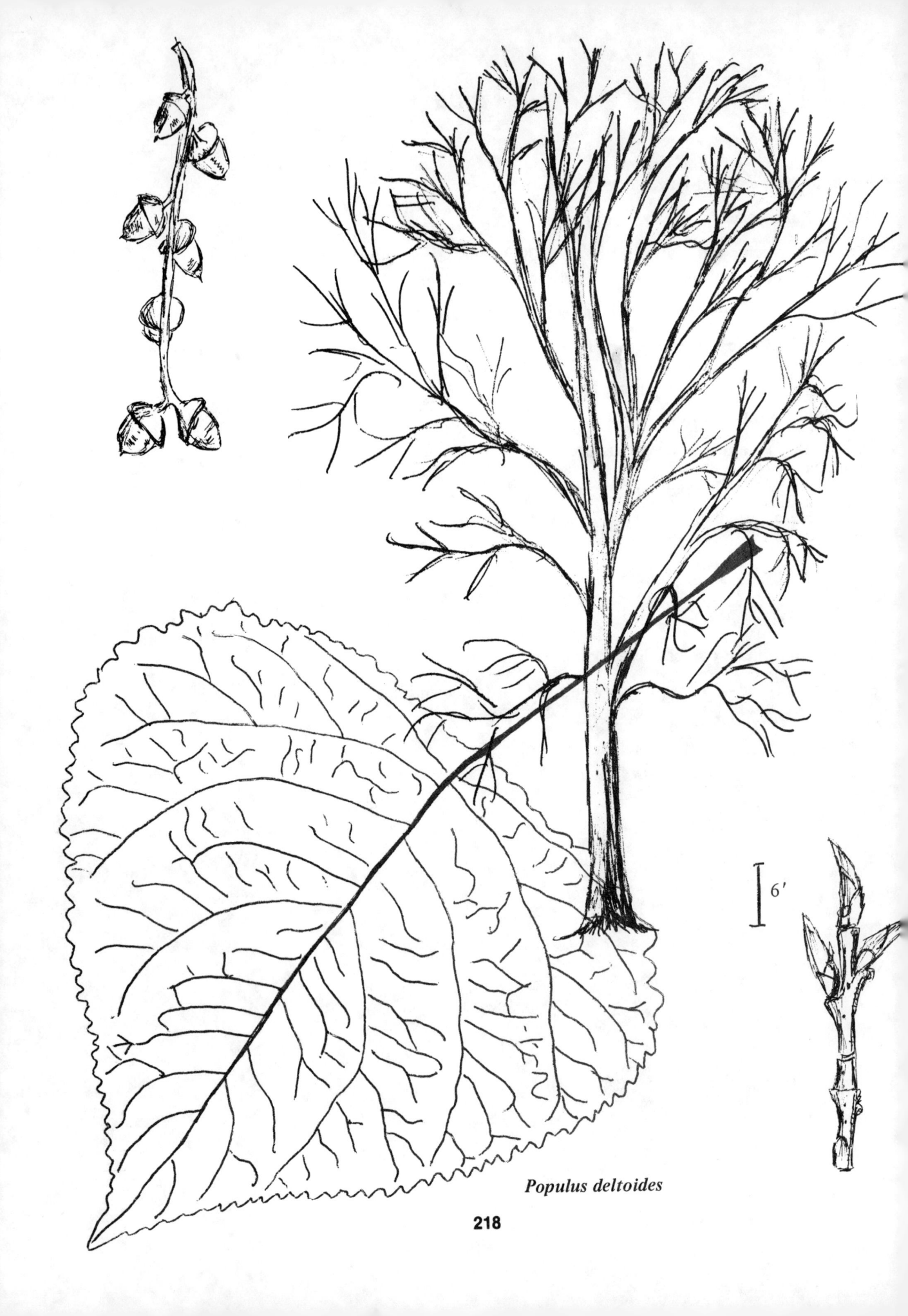

Populus deltoides

218

Populus deltoides

Common Name: Cottonwood

Family: Salicaceae

Foliage: 3-6 inches long; triangular shape; round, glandular teeth; smooth yellow-green and shiny above; paler below; leaf stalk flattened; yellow in autumn

Flowers: male and female separate on separate trees; catkins; April-May

Fruit: small capsules in an 8-12 inch cluster; light brown; cottony seed; ripens May-June

Buds: chestnut-brown; shiny; long pointed; resinous

Twigs: stout; yellowish brown; smooth; star shaped pith

Bark: gray with deep furrows

Roots: fibrous; shallow; transplants well

Growth Habit: 80-100 feet in height; large, spreading branches; open, upright, irregular crown

Hardiness: zone 2

Site: moist; tolerates many soils; sun

Growth Rate: rapid

Maintenance: messy seed; intolerant to pruning

Propagation: seed—no pretreatment, sow fresh; root cuttings; hardwood and softwood cuttings

Selections: 'Robusta' — cottonless; narrow habit
'Siouxland' — cottonless; more rust resistant

Populus tremuloides

Populus tremuloides

Common Name: Quaking Aspen; Trembling Aspen

Family: Salicaceae

Foliage: 1 1/2-3 inches long; thin; blunt, glandular teeth; pale yellow-green; flattened petiole as long or longer than leaf blade; yellow in autumn

Flowers: male and female separate on separate trees; 1-3 inch catkins; April-May

Fruit: thin walled, conical capsule; in clusters; ripens May-June

Buds: conical; sharp pointed; many scales; glossy; reddish brown

Twigs: chestnut-brown; slender; glossy; star shaped pith

Bark: smooth; yellowish gray

Roots: fibrous; shallow; transplants well

Growth Habit: 40-60 feet in height; slender branches; narrowly pyramidal crown; suckers freely

Hardiness: zone 1

Site: any moist soil; sun or partial shade

Growth Rate: rapid

Maintenance: suckering; intolerant to pruning

Propagation: seed—no pretreatment, spring sow; suckers; root cuttings; softwood cuttings

Selections: 'Pendula' — weeping branches

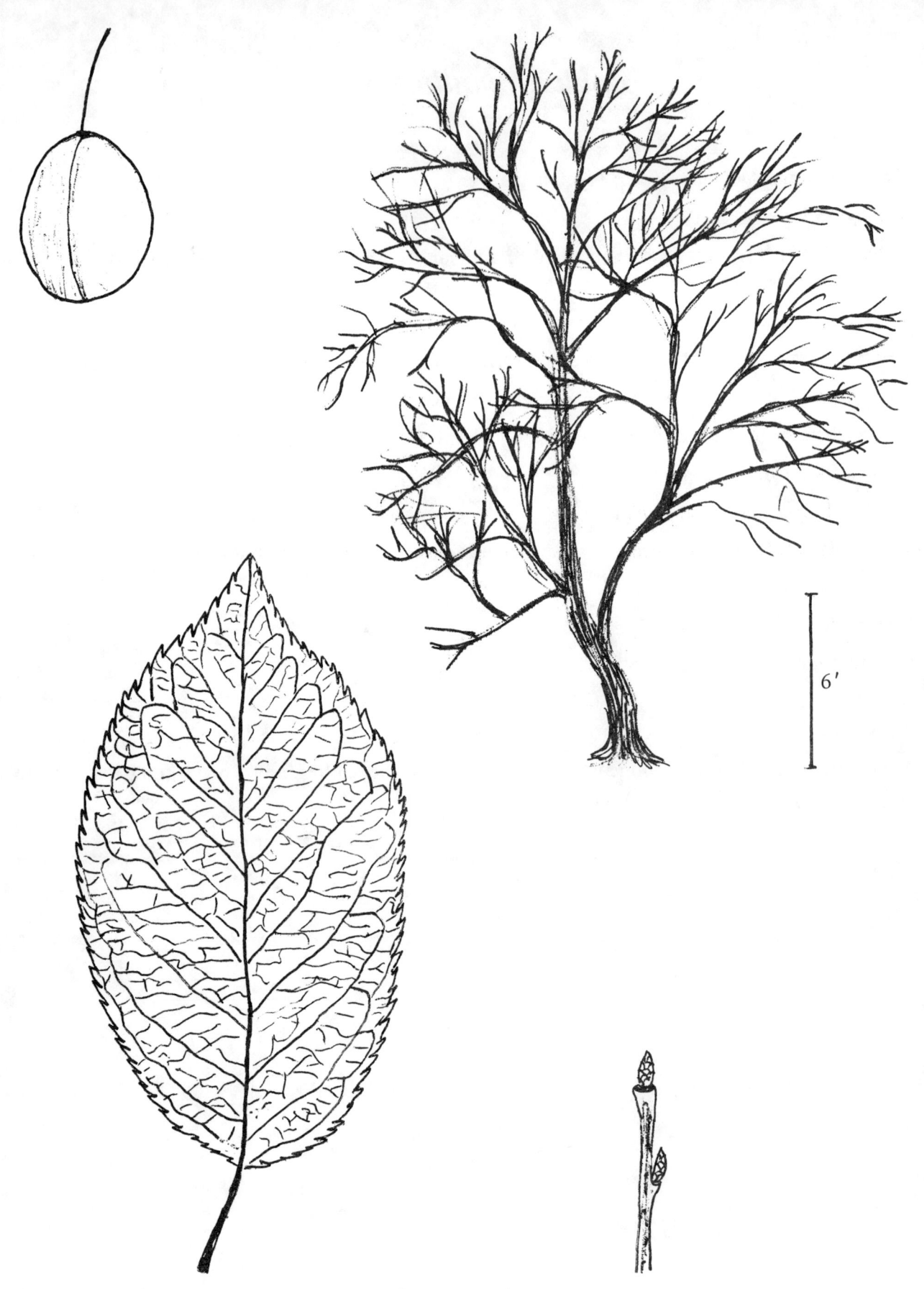

Prunus americana

Prunus americana

Common Name: Wild Plum

Family: Rosaceae

Foliage: 2-4 inches long; sharp, ragged teeth; thick; dark green above; paler below; yellow to red in autumn

Flowers: white clusters; fragrant; May

Fruit: 1 inch berry; thick, reddish skin; yellow flesh; edible; ripens September-October

Buds: pointed; brown

Twigs: slender; orange-brown; raised circular lenticels; sometimes spiny tipped

Bark: dark brown; shaggy scales

Roots: fibrous; spreading; transplants well

Growth Habit: 15-30 feet in height; low branching; dense, round crown; suckers freely

Hardiness: zone 3

Site: prefers rich, well-drained soil but tolerates dry; shade tolerant

Growth Rate: moderate-rapid

Maintenance: suckers; tolerant to pruning

Propagation: seed—stratify in a moist medium at 37-41° F up to 90 days then fall sow, or stratify for 90-150 days and spring sow

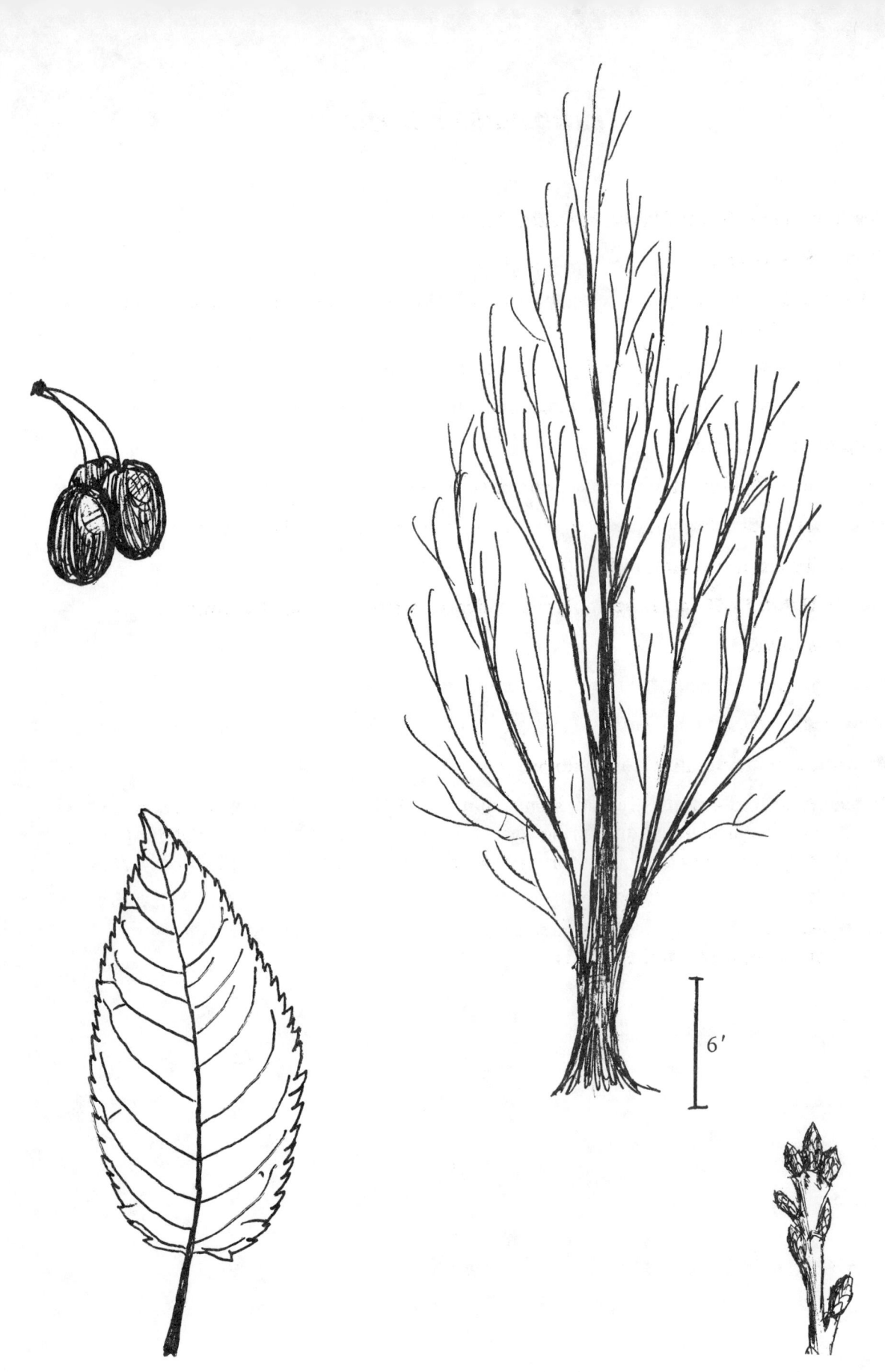

Prunus avium

Prunus avium

Common Name: Sweet Cherry; Mazzard Cherry

Family: Rosaceae

Foliage: 2-5 inches long; thin; coarse, rounded teeth; deep green above; hairy below; leaf stalk has small glands

Flowers: white; long, hairless stalks radiate from a central point; April-May

Fruit: 1 inch pomes clustered on spur shoots; red; sweet and edible; June-July

Buds: reddish brown

Twigs: moderately stout; reddish brown; smooth; shiny

Bark: dark reddish brown; smooth; horizontal, light colored lenticels; glossy

Roots: fibrous; transplants well

Growth Habit: 60-70 feet in height; upright, dense, narrowly pyramidal crown

Hardiness: zone 3

Site: rich, moist soil; sun

Growth Rate: rapid

Maintenance: clean; fairly tolerant to pruning

Propagation: seed—stratify in a moist medium at 37-41 °F for 60 days (from time of collection to time of sowing if fresh) then fall sow, or stratify at 32-41 °F for 120-180 (90-125 days if fruit is removed) and spring sow; graft or bud on *P. americana* or *P. besseyi* understock

Selections: 'Pendula' — weeping branches
'Plena' — double white flowers

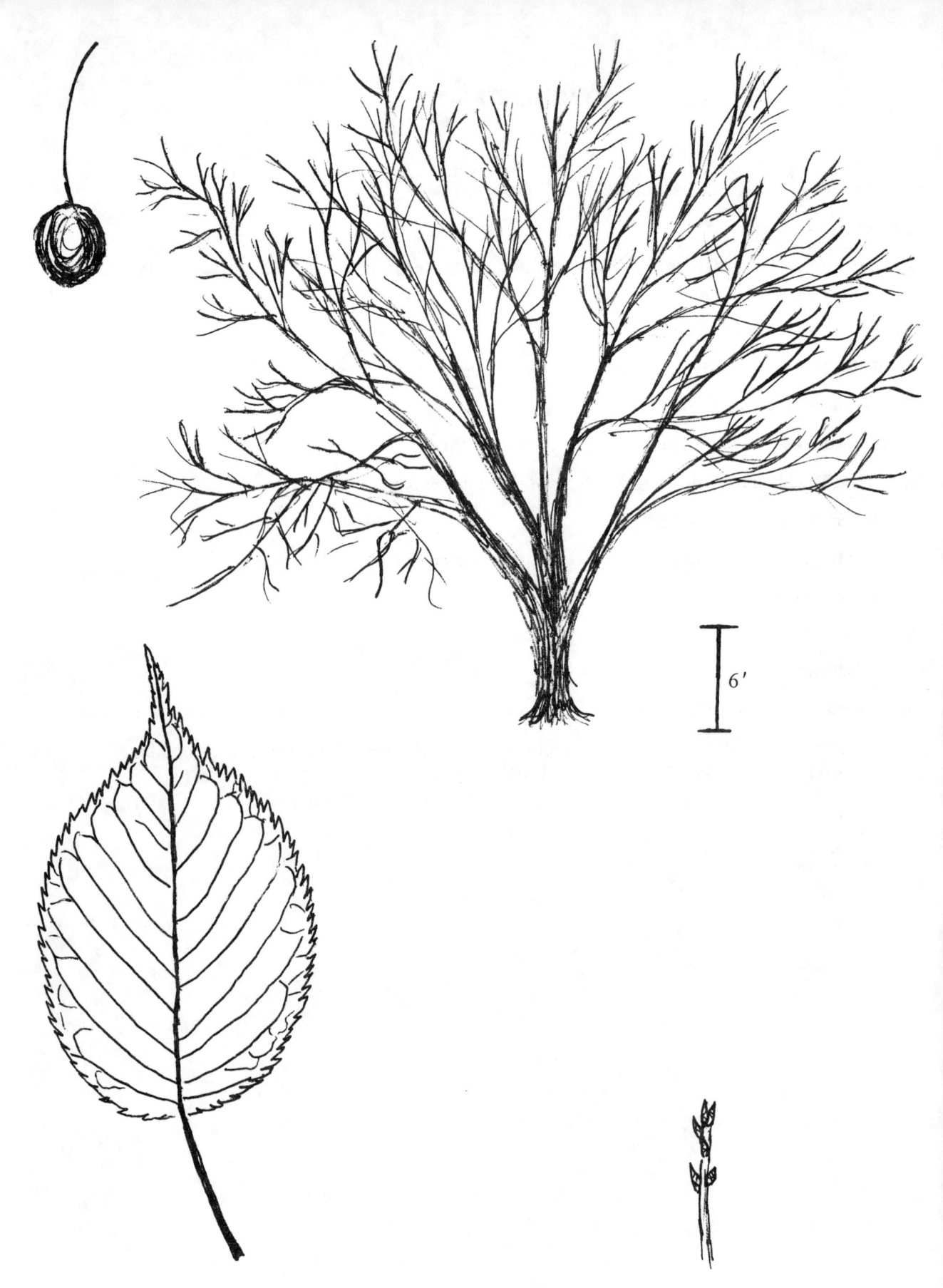

Prunus sargentii

Prunus sargentii

Common Name: Sargent Cherry

Family: Rosaceae

Foliage: 3-5 inches long; long, taper pointed apex; dark green above; grayish bloom below; 2 glands near base; teeth sharp and often double; red in autumn

Flowers: pink; bell shaped; late April

Fruit: small, round drupe; purplish black; ripens August

Buds: brown; hairy edges on scales

Twigs: slender; brown; distinct lenticels

Bark: dark purplish brown; smooth; large, rusty, horizontal lenticels

Roots: fibrous; transplants well

Growth Habit: 35-40 feet in height; upright, spreading crown

Hardiness: zone 4

Site: rich, moist, well-drained soil; sun

Growth Rate: moderate

Maintenance: clean; tolerant to pruning

Propagation: seed—stratify in a moist medium at 37-41°F for 90-120 days; graft or bud on *P. americana, P. besseyi,* or *P. sargentii* understock

Selections: 'Columnaris' — columnar habit

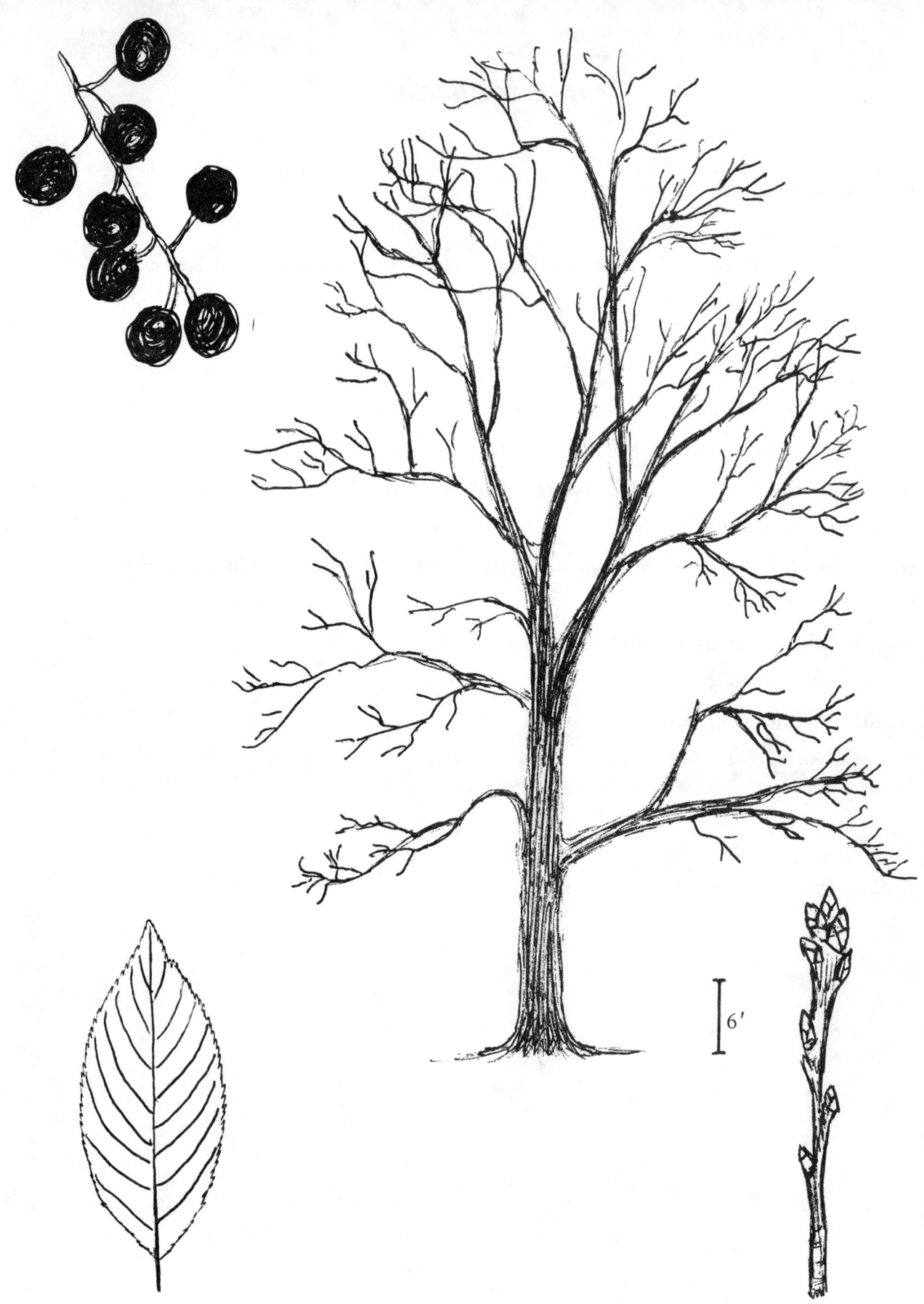

Prunus serotina

228

Prunus serotina

Common Name: Black Cherry

Family: Rosaceae

Foliage: 2-5 inches long; incurved teeth; shiny, bright green; underside of midrib fringed with white or brown hair; 2 glands at base of blade; yellow to orange-red in autumn

Flowers: white; on short stems; show clusters; May-June

Fruit: 1/3 inch, globose drupe; dark red to black; edible; ripens August-September

Buds: shiny; brown; many scales; sharp pointed

Twigs: slender; dark brown; often with peeling grayish skin; aromatic when broken

Bark: reddish brown to nearly black; shaggy; peeling in squarish flakes; large lenticels

Roots: fibrous; spreading; transplants well when young

Growth Habit: 70-100 feet in height; spreading; lower branches drooping; irregularly rounded crown

Hardiness: zone 3

Site: rich, moist soil; sun

Growth Rate: rapid

Maintenance: messy fruit; tolerant to pruning

Propagation: seed—fall sow and mulch, or stratify in a moist medium at 37-41° F for 170 days; graft or bud on *P. americana, P. besseyi,* or *P. serotina* understock

Selections: 'Asplenifolia' — cut leaves
'Pendula' — weeping branches

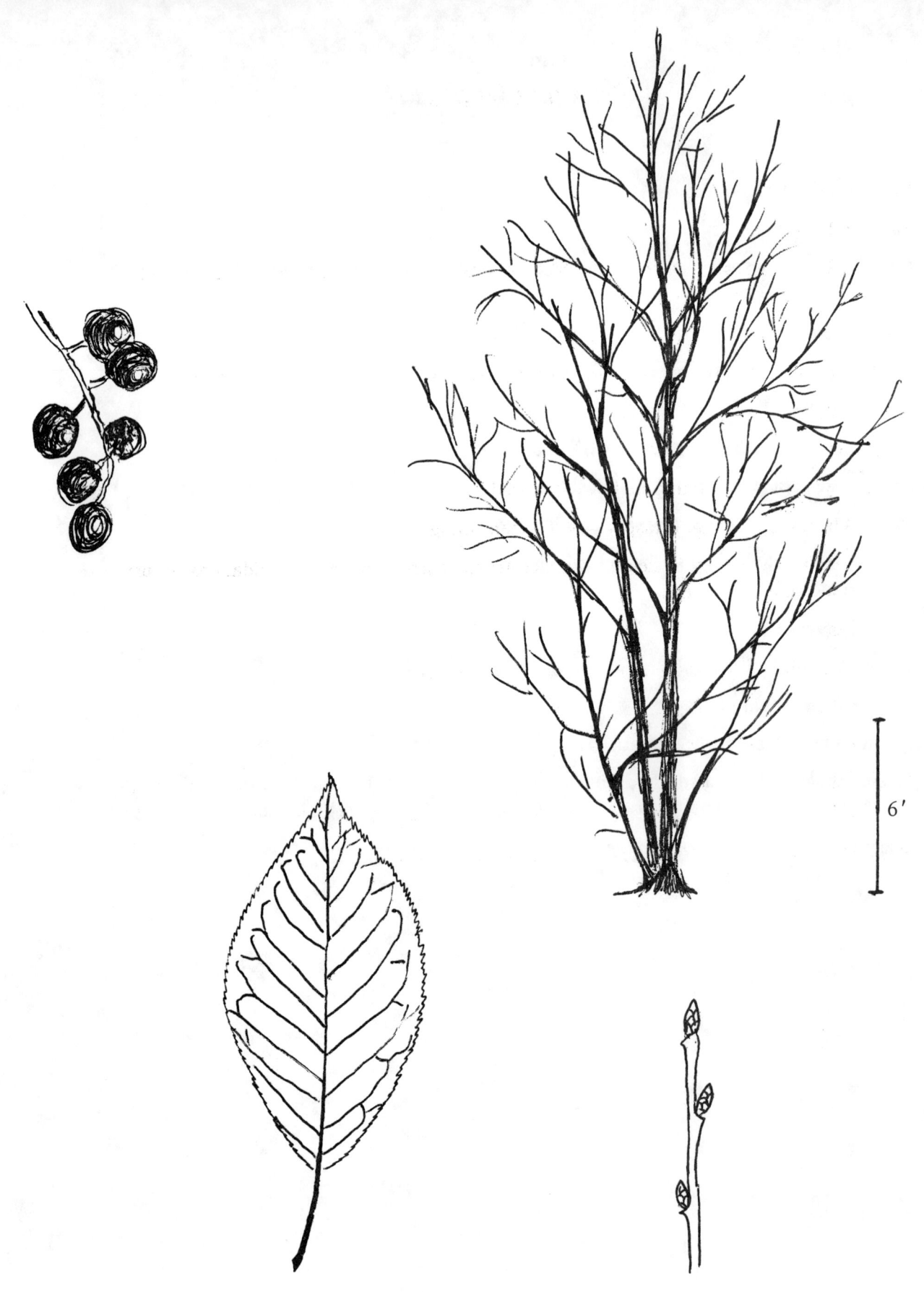

Prunus virginiana

Prunus virginiana

Common Name: Choke Cherry

Family: Rosaceae

Foliage: 2-4 inches long; sharp teeth which are not in-curved; bright green; glands at base; bronze to yellow in autumn

Flowers: drooping, elongated white clusters; late April—early June

Fruit: red drupe; in long clusters; bitter except when totally ripe; ripens July-August

Buds: tan; dull; gray margins

Twigs: slender; red-brown; glossy; bitter

Bark: gray; smooth becoming shallowly fissured

Roots: fibrous; spreading; transplants well when young

Growth Habit: 20-30 feet in height; crooked trunk; narrow, open, pyramidal crown; usually with multiple trunks

Hardiness: zone 2

Site: prefers moist, rich soil but tolerant to dry; sun or shade

Growth Rate: moderate-rapid

Maintenance: suckers; tolerant to pruning

Propagation: seed—fall sow fresh and mulch, or stratify in a moist medium at 37-41°F for 120-160 days; graft or bud on *P. americana* or *P. besseyi* understock

Selections: 'Shubert' — foliage green changing to purple in summer

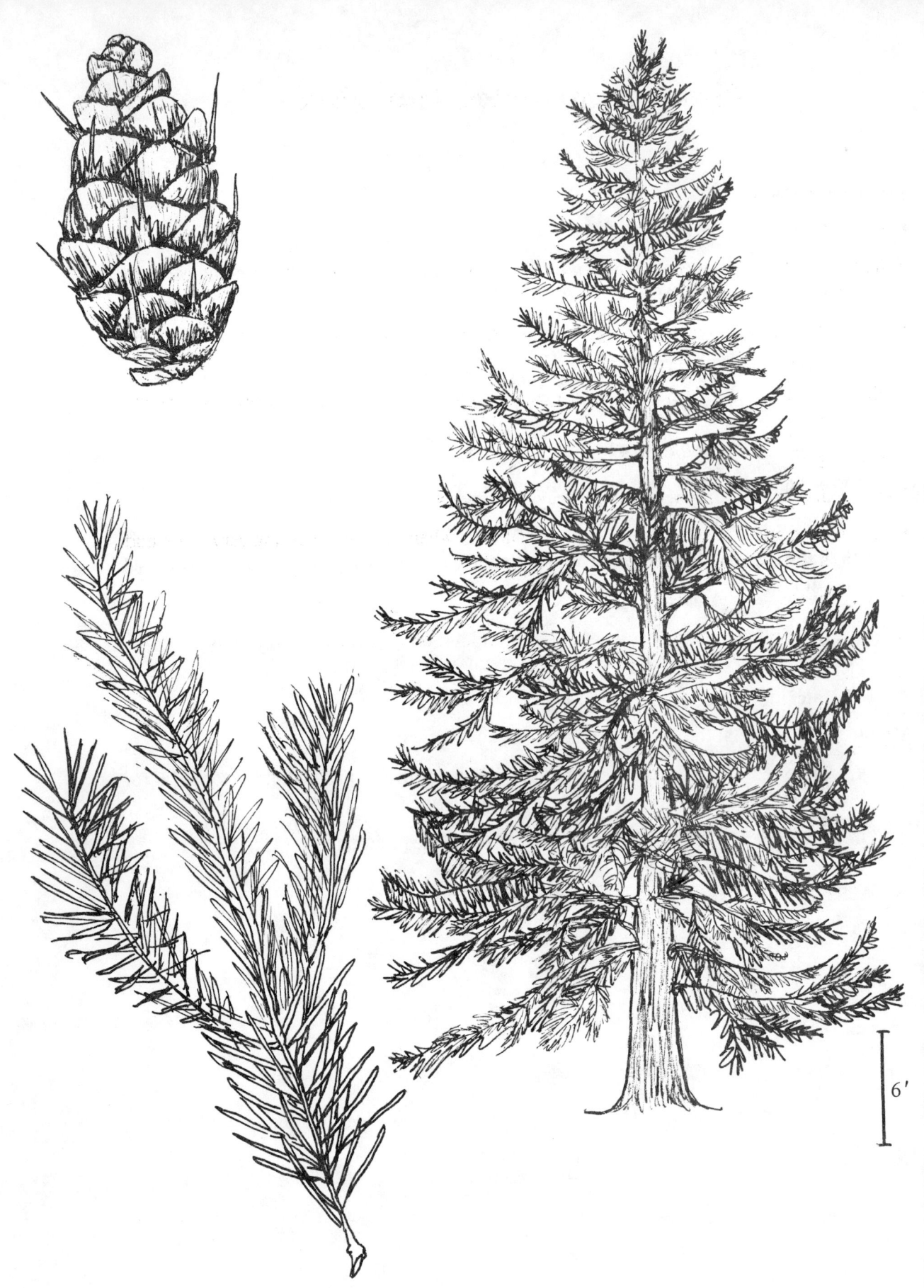

Pseudotsuga menziesii var. *glauca*

232

Pseudotsuga menziesii var. *glauca*

Common Name: Douglas Fir

Family: Pinaceae

Foliage: 1-1 1/4 inch, evergreen needles; flat with groove along upper midrib; short stalked; soft; bluish green; 2 ranked; flexible; persists 6-7 years

Flowers: male and female separate but on the same tree; male: orange-red; female: red to green with a 3 pointed bract; May-June

Fruit: 2-4 inch cone; oblong; thin, rounded scales; 3 parted bracts; pendent; light brown; ripens in autumn

Buds: long pointed terminals

Twigs: hairy; orange-brown becoming grayish brown

Bark: smooth and grayish brown with resin blisters when young; becoming very thick and rough with reddish brown ridges

Roots: deep taproot; transplants well if root pruned

Growth Habit: 60-80 feet in height; dense, pyramidal crown; horizontal branching

Hardiness: zone 4

Site: moist, well-drained soil; sun

Growth Rate: moderate-rapid

Maintenance: clean; tolerant to pruning

Propagation: seed—stratify in a moist medium at 32-41 ° F for 20-40 days; graft on *P. menziesii* var. *glauca* understock

Selections: 'Glauca Pendula' — drooping branches

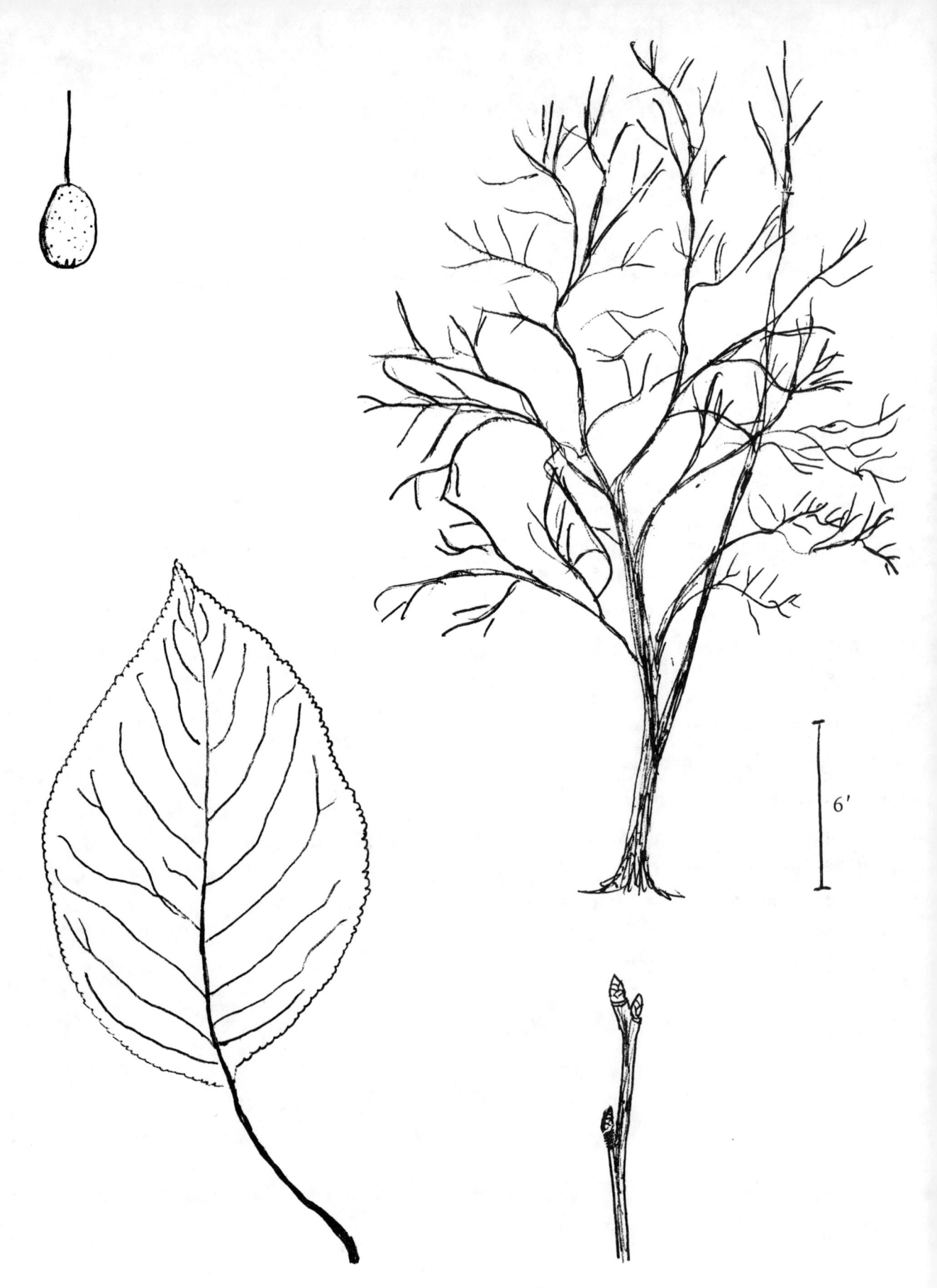

Pyrus calleryana

Pyrus calleryana

Common Name: Callery Pear

Family: Rosaceae

Foliage: 1 1/2-3 inches long; small teeth; bright green; glossy; long, slender leaf stalks; red in autumn

Flowers: white; April-May

Fruit: 1/2 inch pear; russet-brown; grit cells; slender stalks; ripens September-October; persists through winter

Buds: red; fine hairs

Twigs: slender; smooth; brown; spurs

Bark: gray; furrowed

Roots: fibrous; spreading; transplants well

Growth Habit: 25-30 feet in height; pyramidal crown

Hardiness: zone 4

Site: tolerant to many soils; sun

Growth Rate: moderate

Maintenance: clean; tolerant to pruning

Propagation: seed—fall sow, or soak in water 24 hours then stratify in moist vermiculite in plastic bags at 32-36° F for 60-90 days; bud or graft on *P. calleryana* or *P. communis* understock

Selections: 'Aristocrat' — horizontal branching
'Bradford' — fruitless; oval crown; foliage yellow to purple in autumn
'Chanticleer' — conical crown; glossy foliage
var. *faurei* — dwarf; round crown; long stem, russet colored fruit

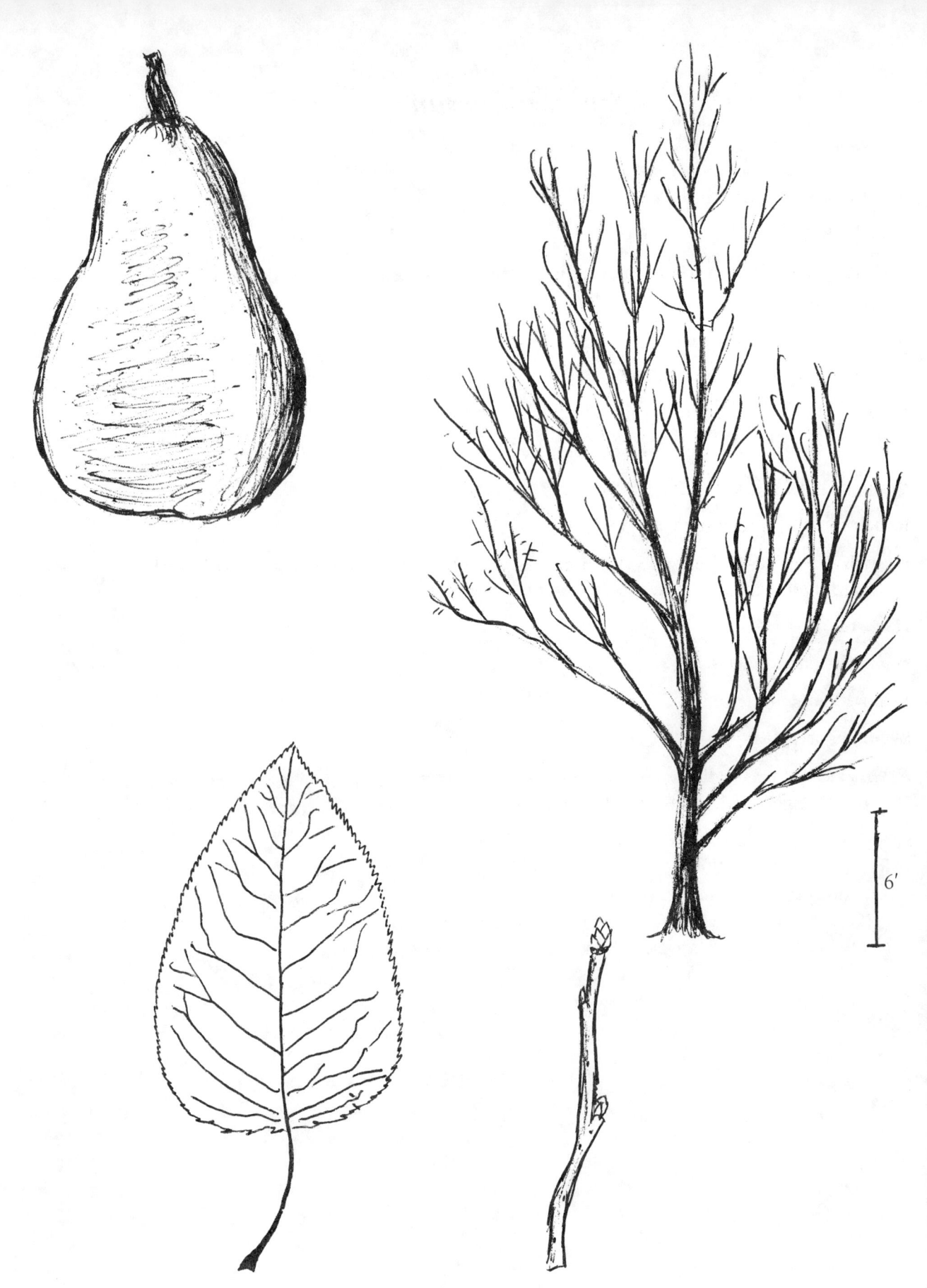

Pyrus communis

Pyrus communis

Common Name: Common Pear

Family: Rosaceae

Foliage: 1-4 inches long; small teeth; shiny; thick; smooth beneath

Flowers: clusters on short spurs; white; April-May

Fruit: at least 2 inches long; dry, gritty pear; yellowish green; black, smooth seeds; ripens late August-early October

Buds: gray-brown; sharp pointed

Twigs: moderately stout; yellowish green; with short spurs

Bark: grayish brown; fissured with flat top ridges

Roots: fibrous; spreading; transplants well

Growth Habit: 30-45 feet in height; branches with short, shiny spurs; ascending branches; pyramidal crown

Hardiness: zone 4

Site: rich, moist, well-drained soil; sun

Growth Rate: slow

Maintenance: clean; tolerant to pruning

Propagation: seed—fall sow, or soak in water for 24 hours then stratify in moist vermiculite at 32-36°F for 60-90 days; graft or bud on *P. calleryana* or *P. communis* understock

Selections: var. *pyraster* — thorny; small, round fruit

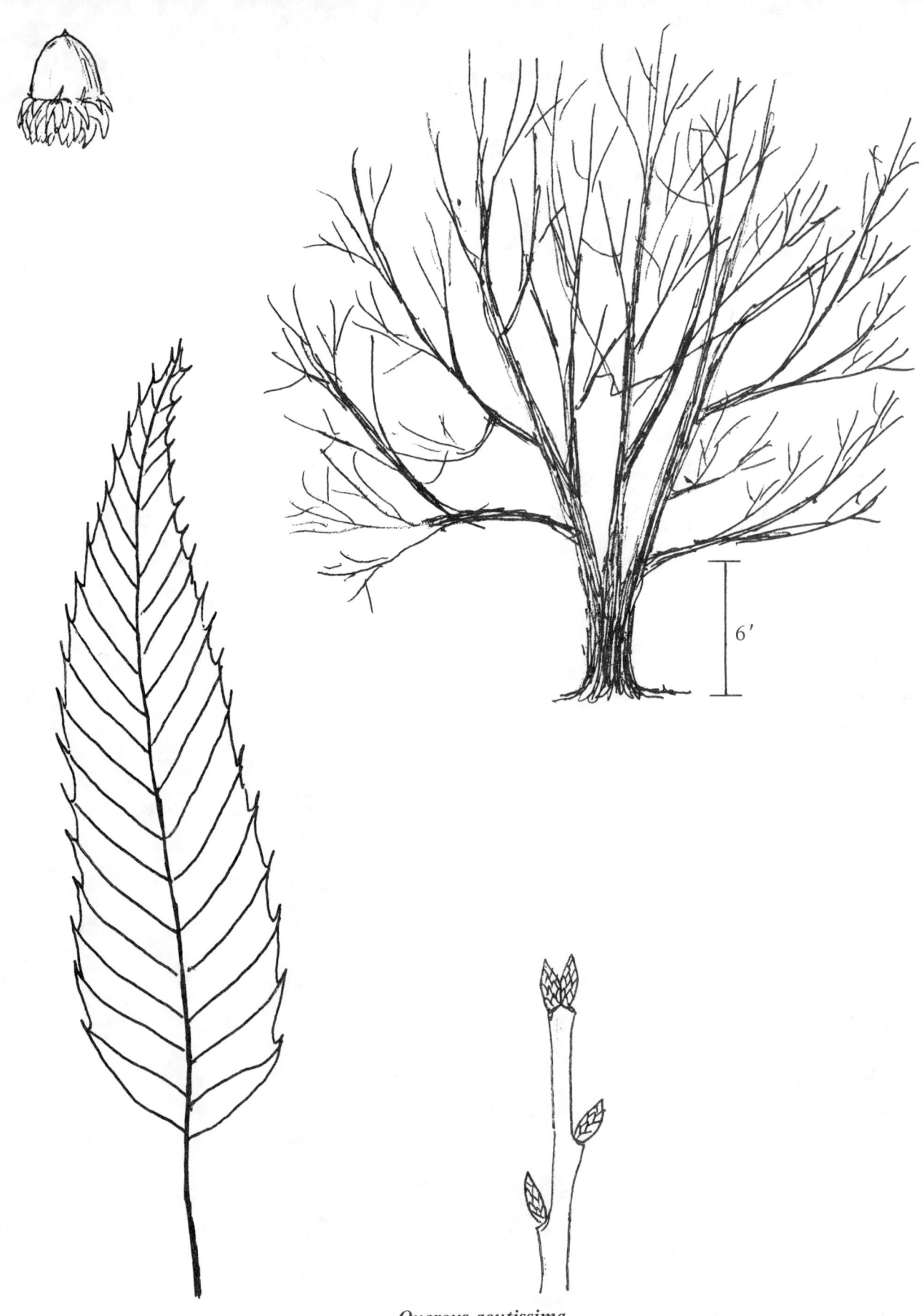

Quercus acutissima

Quercus acutissima

Common Name: Sawtooth Oak

Family: Fagaceae

Foliage: 3-7 inches long; chestnutlike; bristle tip teeth; each vein terminating in a tooth; deep, shiny green above; axillary tufts of hair beneath; remains green or turns brown in autumn; persistent

Flowers: male and female separate but on the same tree; spring

Fruit: 1 inch acorn; sessile; long, curving scales on cup; cup covers 2/3 of nut; 2 seasons to mature

Buds: pointed; terminals clustered; tan; hairy scale margin

Twigs: moderately stout; light brown; star-shaped pith

Bark: gray; shallowly fissured

Roots: semifibrous as compared to other oaks

Growth Habit: 35-50 feet in height; widespreading branches; broad, round crown

Hardiness: zone 3

Site: adaptable; sun

Growth Rate: moderate-rapid

Maintenance: clean; limited tolerance to pruning

Propagation: seed—sow fresh and mulch

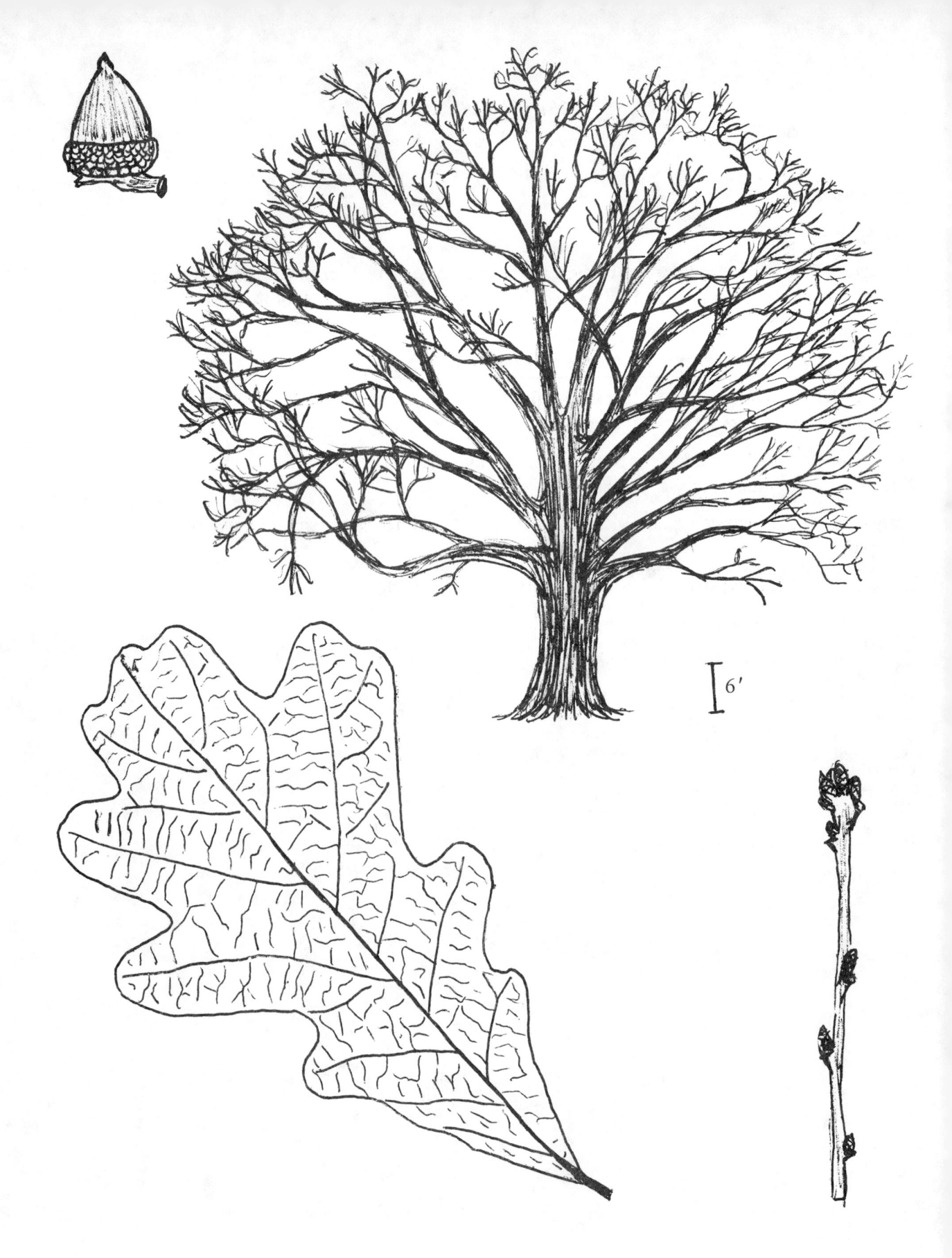

Quercus alba

Quercus alba

Common Name: White Oak

Family: Fagaceae

Foliage: 4-8 inches long; 5-9 round lobes; not lobed all the way to the base; smooth; pale below; purple-red in autumn; often persists through winter

Flowers: male and female separate but on the same tree; male: hairy, yellow catkins; female: short, red spikes; May-June

Fruit: 1/2-3/4 inch acorn; usually short stalked; covered 1/4 by cup; light brown; shallow cup with warty scales; nut with pointed tip and sweet kernel; ripens September-October of the first year

Buds: clustered; blunt; reddish brown

Twigs: moderate; lenticels light colored and small but distinct; gray; smooth; star-shaped pith

Bark: thick; light gray; shallow fissures with long, irregular ridges

Roots: taproot with few laterals; very difficult to transplant

Growth Habit: 60-100 feet in height; broad, widespreading crown; heavy branches

Hardiness: zone 4

Site: moist, well drained, rich soil; sun or partial shade

Growth Rate: slow

Maintenance: clean; tolerant to pruning

Propagation: seed—fall sow and mulch; no pretreatment

Quercus bicolor

Quercus bicolor

Common Name: Swamp White Oak

Family: Fagaceae

Foliage: 4-7 inches long; round teeth; shallow lobes; dark green above; white hair beneath; no teeth on lower portion; stout stalk; yellow, brown or red in autumn

Flowers: male and female separate but on the same tree; small; male: hairy catkins; female: short spikes; May-June

Fruit: 1 inch acorn; in pairs on hairy stalks; stalk 1-4 inches long; light brown; hairy apex; white kernel; cap encloses 1/3 of nut; roughened and fringed cap; nut is sweet and edible; ripens September-October of the first season

Buds: blunt; terminal clustered; brown; sometimes with hairy tips; many scales

Twigs: moderately stout; gray; smooth with pale, raised lenticels; star-shaped pith

Bark: thick; gray; furrowed into long plates

Roots: taproot with few laterals; difficult to transplant

Growth Habit: 60-100 feet in height; open, irregular or round crown; dense foliage; branches are penduluous and spreading

Hardiness: zone 4

Site: rich, moist soil; shade tolerant

Growth Rate: slow

Maintenance: clean; tolerant to pruning

Propagation: seed—fall sow and mulch; no pretreatment

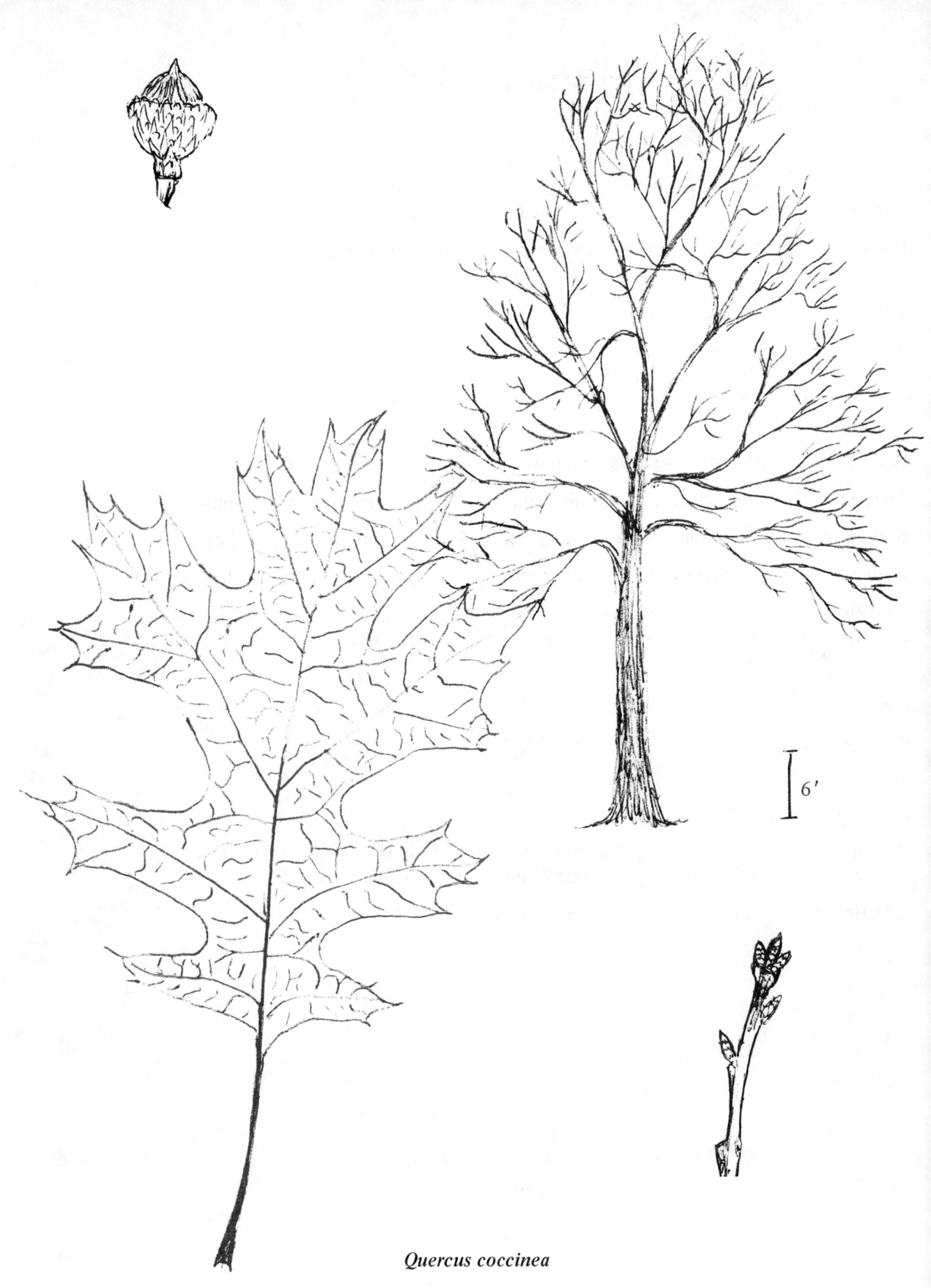

Quercus coccinea

244

Quercus coccinea

Common Name: Scarlet Oak

Family: Fagaceae

Foliage: 3-6 inches long; nearly as broad; 5-9 lobes; deep, wide, round sinuses; lobes bristle tipped; smooth; shiny; bright green above; paler below; scarlet red in autumn

Flowers: male and female separate on the same tree; male: catkins; female: spikes; May

Fruit: 1/2-3/4 inch acorn; sessile or short stalked; oval or oblong nut; light reddish brown; 1/2 covered by a thin, light brown cup; cup base constricted and cup is slight downy with flattened scales; often with concentric rings on apex of nut; kernel is pale yellow and bitter; ripens September-October of second season

Buds: terminals clustered; blunt; gray; hair only on upper portion; not angled

Twigs: slender; young are hairy; becoming smooth; brownish gray; star-shaped pith

Bark: thick; dark gray; shallow furrows and corky plates; inner bark is red; not bitter

Roots: taproot with more laterals than white oaks; difficult to transplant but less so than many oaks

Growth Habit: 60-100 feet in height; open, round crown; horizontal branches at bottom and ascending at top

Hardiness: zone 4

Site: moist to dry; prefers sandy, acid soil; sun

Growth Rate: slow

Maintenance: clean; tolerant to pruning

Propagation: seed—fall sow and mulch, or stratify in a moist medium at 32-41 °F for 30-60 days; graft on *Q. coccinea*, *Q. palustris* or *Q. velutina* understock

Selections: 'Splendens' — foliage more glossy

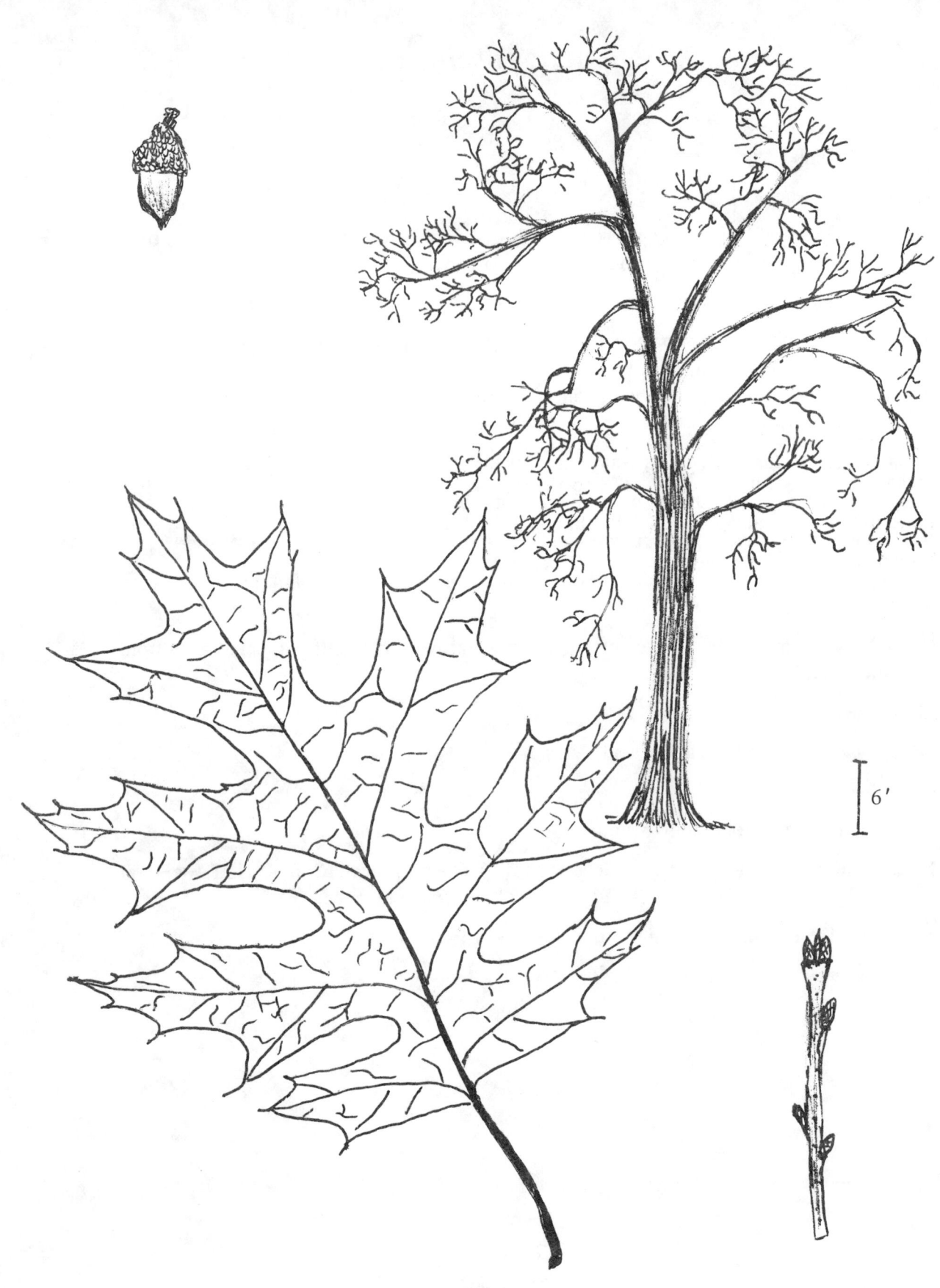

Quercus ellipsoidalis

Quercus ellipsoidalis

Common Name: Hill's Oak; Jack Oak; Northern Pin Oak

Family: Fagaceae

Foliage: 3-5 inches long; 3-8 oblong lobes; deep, wide, round sinuses; bristle tips; thin; bright green and shiny above; paler beneath; red to brown in autumn

Flowers: male and female separate but on the same tree; small; male: catkins; female: spikes; spring

Fruit: 1/2-3/4 inch acorn; cup covers 1/2 of nut; short stalked; bitter kernel; matures second season

Buds: sharp; smooth; reddish brown; clustered terminals

Twigs: slender; reddish brown; star-shaped pith

Bark: dark gray; shallow fissures with thin plates

Roots: taproot with fibrous laterals; difficult to transplant

Growth Habit: 60-70 feet in height; round crown

Hardiness: zone 3

Site: moist to dry, sandy soil; partial shade

Growth Rate: moderate

Maintenance: clean; fairly tolerant to pruning

Propagation: seed—fall sow and mulch, or stratify in a moist medium at 32-41°F for 60-90 days

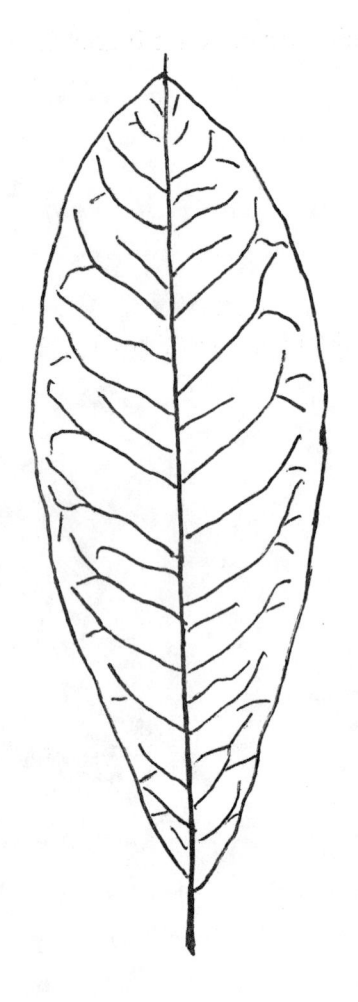

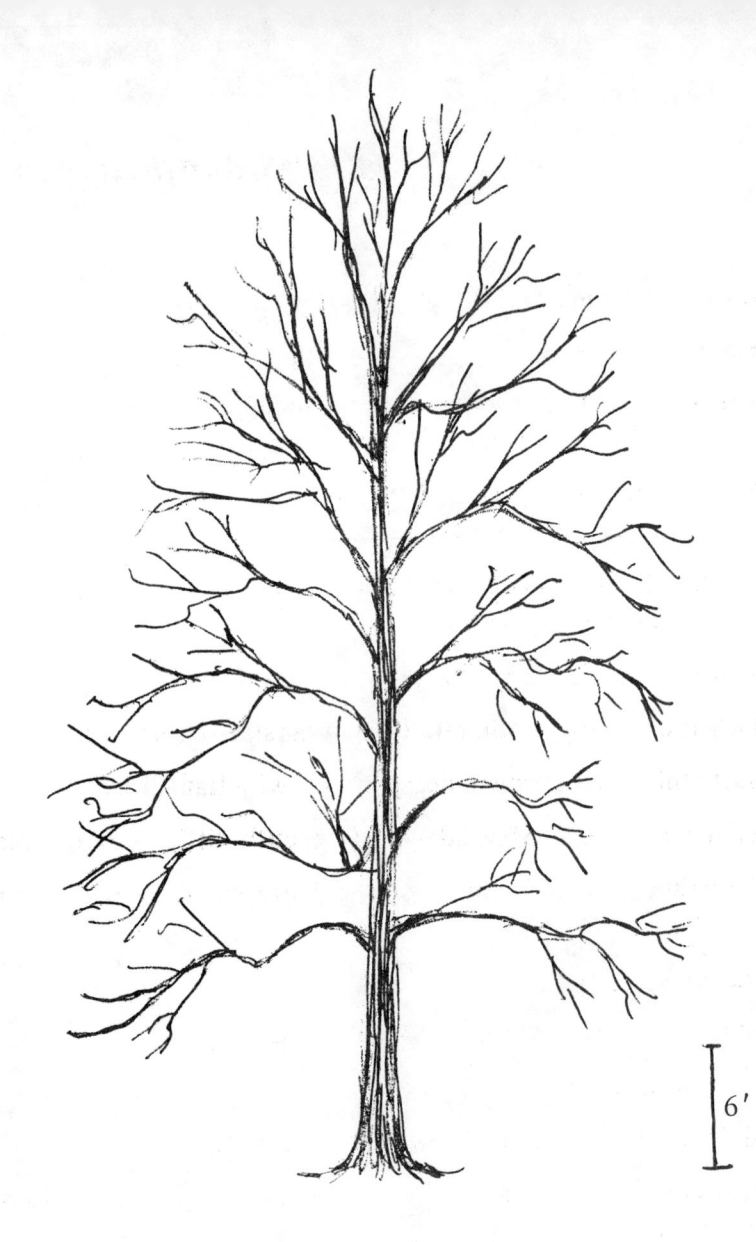

Quercus imbricaria

Quercus imbricaria

Common Name: Laurel Oak; Shingle Oak

Family: Fagaceae

Foliage: 3-6 inches long; wavy margin; bristle tipped; dark green and shiny above; pale and hairy beneath; thick and leathery; russet in autumn; persists through winter

Flowers: male and female separate but on the same tree; small; male: yellow catkins; female: short spikes; spring

Fruit: 1/2-1 inch acorn; enclosed 1/2-1/3 by cup; dark brown; short stalk; bitter kernel; matures second season

Buds: light chestnut brown; clustered terminals

Twigs: slender; smooth; reddish brown; star-shaped pith

Bark: thick; dark brown; deep furrows with flat ridges

Roots: taproot with few laterals; frequently difficult to transplant

Growth Habit: 50-60 feet in height; dense, round topped, pyramidal crown; lower branches droop

Hardiness: zone 4

Site: rich, moist soil; sun or partial shade

Growth Rate: slow

Maintenance: clean; fairly tolerant to pruning

Propagation: seed—fall sow and mulch, or stratify in a moist medium at 32-41 °F for 30-60 days

Leaf: ½ actual size

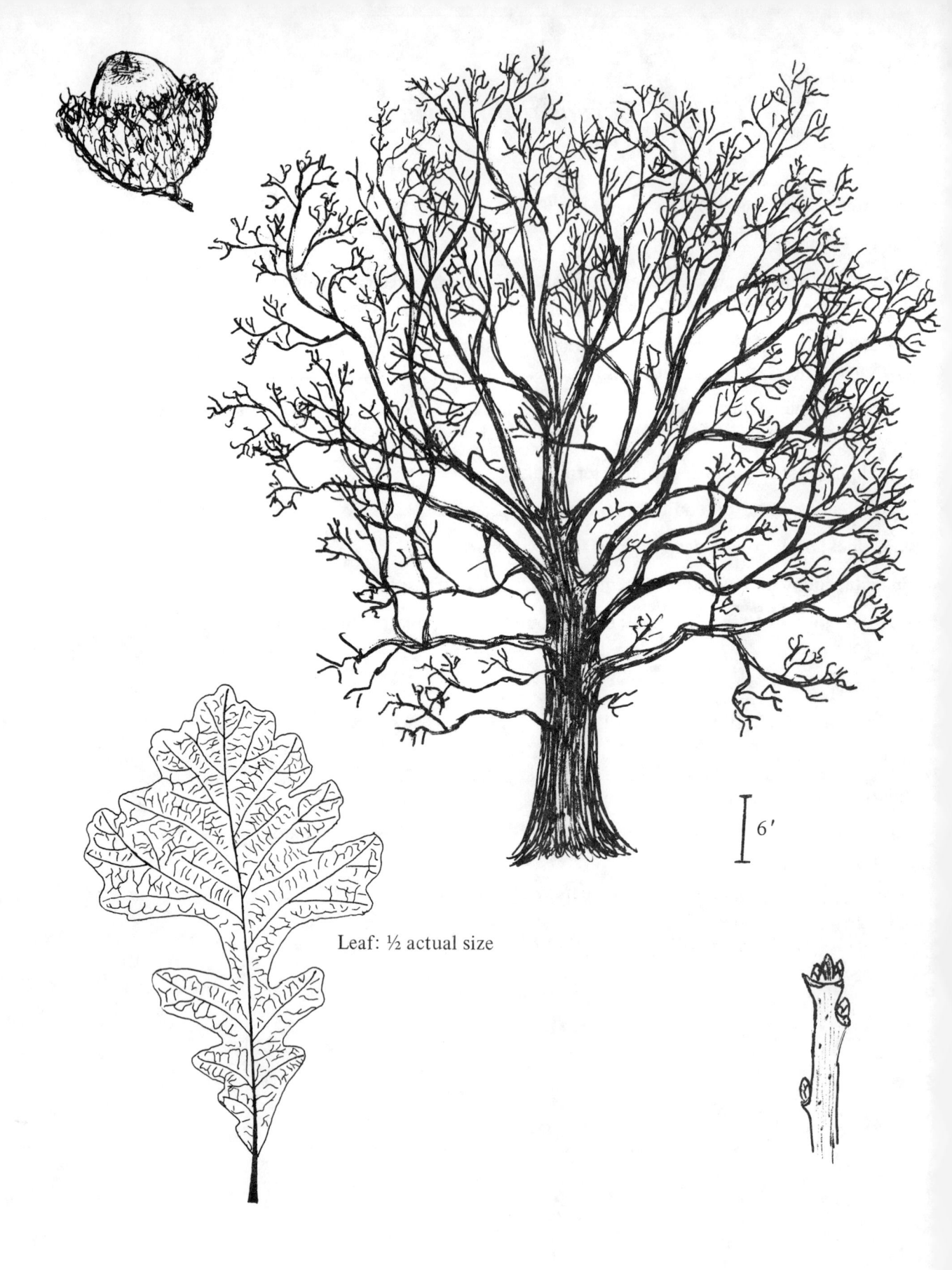

Quercus macrocarpa

Quercus macrocarpa

Common Name: Burr Oak; Mossy-cup Oak

Family: Fagaceae

Foliage: 5-10 inches long; deeply lobed in middle; shallow lobes at the top; broader toward the tip; 5-9 lobes; round sinuses; grayish hair beneath; yellow in autumn

Flowers: male and female separate but on the same tree; male: yellow-green catkins; female: reddish, hairy spikes; late May

Fruit: sessile or short-stalked acorn; 3/4-1 1/2 inches long; cup covers 1/2 of nut; cup rim fringed; cup with woolly scales which are thickened at the base with pointed tips; nut has brownish hairs with a white, sweet kernel; matures in one season

Buds: reddish brown; pale woolly covering; clustered terminals; many scales

Twigs: moderate; purplish brown; prominent lenticels; somewhat hairy; often with corky wings; star-shaped pith

Bark: thick; dark gray; young bark has corky ridges; older becomes deeply furrowed and ridged

Roots: taproot; difficult to transplant

Growth Habit: 60-100 feet in height; open, broad, irregularly rounded crown; massive, widespreading limbs

Hardiness: zone 3

Site: adaptable to many soil types; sun or partial shade

Growth Rate: slow-moderate

Maintenance: clean; tolerant to pruning

Propagation: seed—fall sow and mulch, or stratify in a moist medium at 32-41 °F for 30-60 days

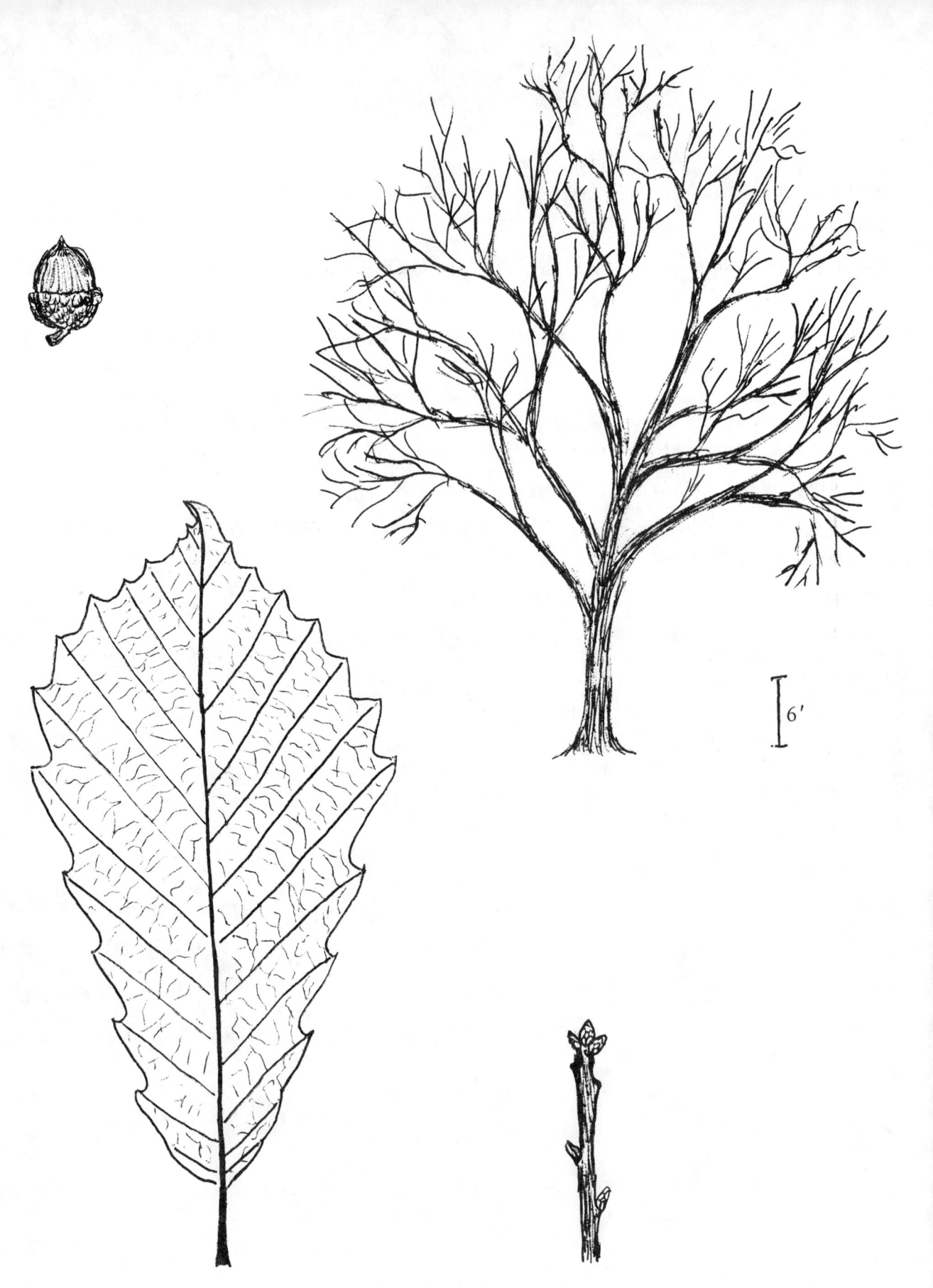

Quercus muehlenbergii

Quercus muehlenbergii

Common Name: Chinquapin Oak; Yellow Oak

Family: Fagaceae

Foliage: 4-8 inches long; coarse, sharp, incurved teeth with glandular tips; hairy beneath; slender stalks; bright orange or scarlet in autumn

Flowers: male and female separate on the same tree; small; male: catkins; female: spikes; May-June

Fruit: 1/2-3/4 inch acorn; short stalked or sessile; single or in pairs; 1/2 enclosed by cup; cup with pale brown scales that are woolly and knobby around the base; nut is dark brown and smooth; sweet kernel; ripens October-November of the first season

Buds: clustered terminals; sharp pointed; light brown; smooth

Twigs: slender; smooth; light orange-brown to reddish brown; star-shaped pith

Bark: gray; scaly ridges

Roots: taproot with fibrous laterals difficult to transplant

Growth Habit: 35-80 feet in height; open, rounded crown; ascending branches

Hardiness: zone 4

Site: rich soil; tolerant to alkaline soil; less shade tolerant as it ages

Growth Rate: rapid

Maintenance: clean; tolerant to pruning

Propagation: seed—fall sow and mulch; no pretreatment

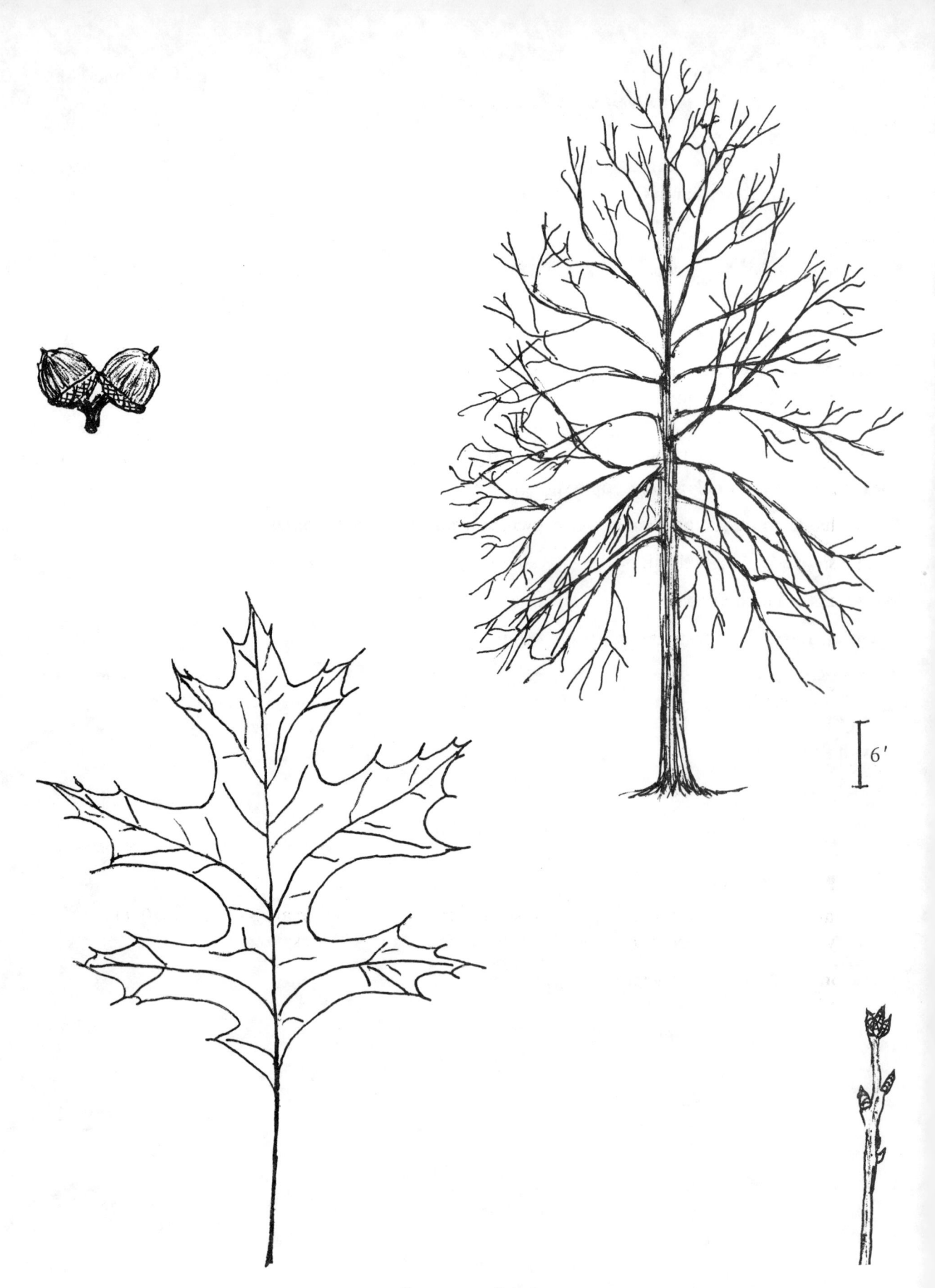

Quercus palustris

254

Quercus palustris

Common Name: Pin Oak

Family: Fagaceae

Foliage: 3-5 inches long; 5-7 deep lobes; round sinuses; bristle tipped; bright green and shiny above; paler beneath; tufts of hairs in vein axils; slender, yellowish leaf stalks; yellow, brown or deep scarlet in autumn; persists through winter

Flowers: male and female separate but on the same tree; small; male: catkins; female: spikes; May

Fruit: 1/2 inch acorn; usually sessile; 1-4 per cluster; light brown; wider than long; saucer shape, flat, shallow cup; pale yellow kernel that is only slightly bitter; ripens September-October of second season

Buds: sharp; pointed; smooth; reddish brown; conical; clustered terminals

Twigs: slender; shiny; reddish brown; star-shaped pith

Bark: gray; shallow furrows

Roots: shallow; fibrous; transplants the best of this genus

Growth Habit: 60-75 feet in height; straight trunk; pyramidal crown; slender limbs; lower limbs pendulous; upper limbs horizontal or ascending with short twigs; symmetrical; dense

Hardiness: zone 4

Site: moist, acid soil; sun

Growth Rate: rapid

Maintenance: clean; tolerant to pruning

Propagation: seed—fall sow and mulch, or stratify in a moist medium at 32-41 °F for 30-45 days; graft on *Q. coccinea, Q. palustris,* or *Q. velutina* understock

Selections: 'Pendula' — weeping branches
'Sovereign' — upright branching

Quercus prinus

Quercus prinus

Common Name: Basket Oak

Family: Fagaceae

Foliage: 4-8 inches long; round teeth; shiny and smooth above; paler with fine hairs below; dark green; crimson in autumn

Flowers: male and female separate but on the same tree; small; male: catkins; female: short spikes; May

Fruit: 1-1 1/2 inch acorn; chestnut brown; 1/3 enclosed by cup; thin, hairy cup; sweet, white kernel; short stalk; ripens in September-October of the first season

Buds: stout; clustered terminals; many scales; pointed; brown

Twigs: moderately stout; orange-brown; star-shaped pith

Bark: light gray; thick; deeply furrowed with round ridges

Roots: deep taproot with few laterals; difficult to transplant

Growth Habit: 50-90 feet in height; dense, round crown with low branching

Hardiness: zone 4

Site: does well in dry, well-drained soil; sun or partial shade

Growth Rate: rapid

Maintenance: clean; tolerant to pruning

Propagation: seed—fall sow and mulch; no pretreatment

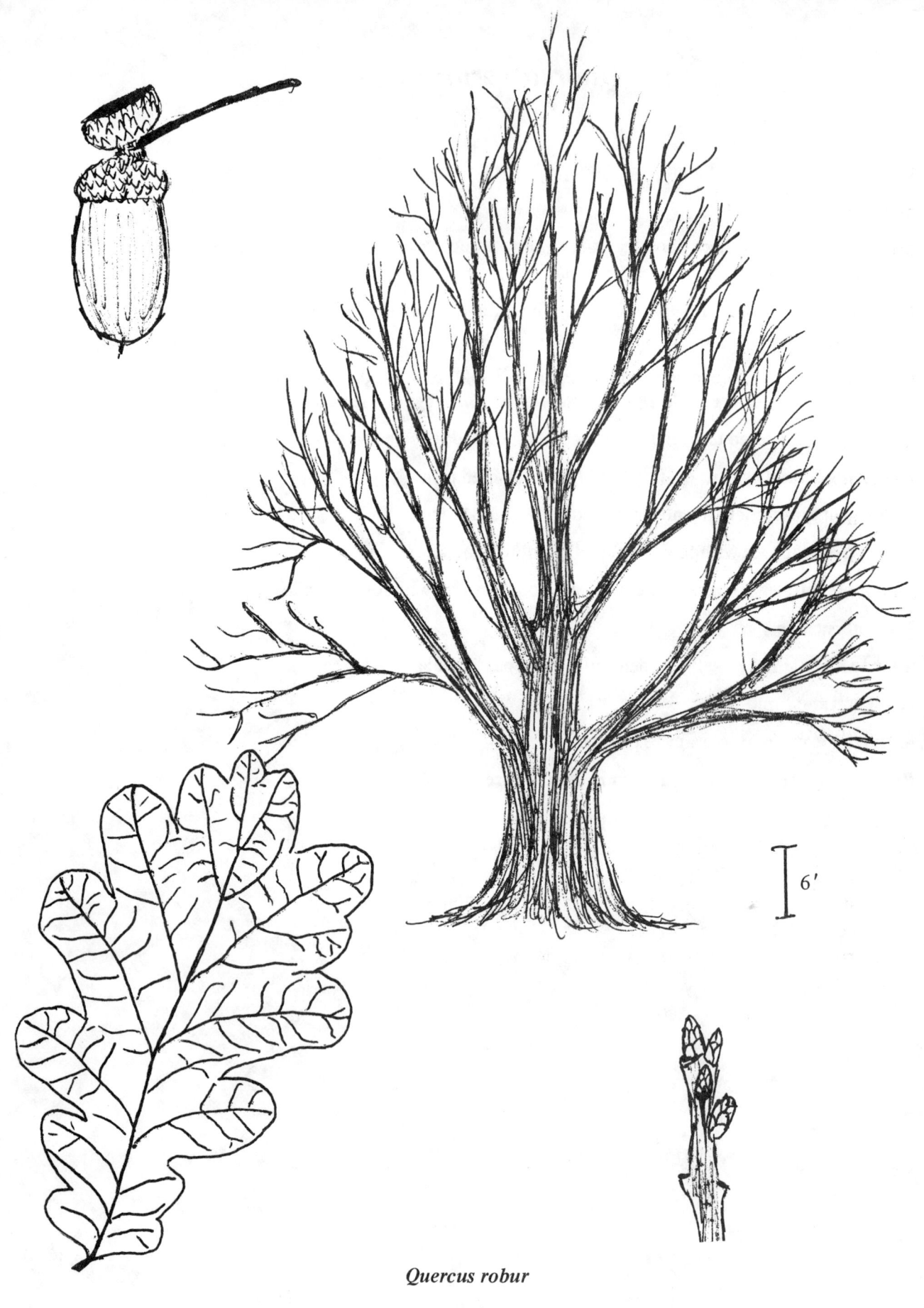

Quercus robur

258

Quercus robur

Common Name: English Oak

Family: Fagaceae

Foliage: 2-5 inches long; rounded lobes extend to leaf base; dark green; pale and downy beneath; hairless leaf stalk; green in autumn

Flowers: male and female separate but on the same tree; male: catkins; female: short spikes; spring

Fruit: 1-1 1/2 inch, oblong acorn; 2-3 per cluster; 1-3 inch stalk; cup encloses 1/3 of nut; ripens September-October of first season

Buds: rounded; light brown; clustered terminals

Twigs: moderate; hairless; rough; purplish brown with white lenticels

Bark: dark gray; deep furrows with irregular plates

Roots: taproot with few laterals; transplants rather well

Growth Habit: 75-100 feet in height; broad, oval to pyramidal crown; widespreading branches with a short trunk

Hardiness: zone 4

Maintenance: clean; tolerant to pruning

Propagation: seed—fall sow and mulch; no pretreatment; graft on *Q. alba* or *Q. robur* understock

Selections: 'Asplenifolia' — cut foliage
    'Atropurpurea' — dark purple foliage
    'Concordia' — young leaves yellowish
    'Fastigiata' — upright columnar; more hardy
    'Fastigiata Purpurea' — upright with purple foliage
    'Pendula' — weeping branches
    'Purpurascens' — young foliage purple

Quercus rubra

260

Quercus rubra

Common Name: Red Oak

Family: Fagaceae

Foliage: 5-9 inches long; 5-11 lobes with coarse teeth and bristle tips; wide sinuses; dull, dark green above; paler beneath; slightly hairy on vein axils; smooth; red in autumn

Flowers: male and female separate but on the same tree; small; male: catkins; female: short spikes; May-June

Fruit: 3/4-1 1/4 inch acorn; sessile or short stalked; very shallow cap with scales that closely overlap; reddish brown; white, bitter kernel; ripens October-November of second season

Buds: clustered terminals; pointed; reddish brown

Twigs: slender; reddish brown; star-shaped pith

Bark: thick; gray; deep fissures with broad, flat topped ridges; inner bark is light red

Roots: taproot with fibrous laterals; transplants better than many oaks

Growth Habit: 60-100 feet in height; dense and spreading; straight trunk; oval or rounded crown

Hardiness: zone 3

Site: moist, well-drained soil; humidity but not excessive heat; fairly shade tolerant

Growth Rate: rapid

Maintenance: clean; fairly tolerant to pruning

Propagation: seed—fall sow and mulch, or stratify in a moist medium at 32-41°F for 30-45 days

Quercus velutina

Quercus velutina

Common Name: Black Oak

Family: Fagaceae

Foliage: 5-7 inches long; glossy; shallow, broad sinuses; smooth; bristle tipped, coarse teeth; dark green above; hairy beneath; stout, yellow, long-leaf stalks; red or orange in autumn

Flowers: male and female separate but on the same tree; small; male: catkins; female: short spikes; May-June

Fruit: 1/3-3/4 inch acorn; sessile; cup encloses 1/2 of nut; cap scales are thin and ragged; nut is wider than long; reddish brown; often hairy; yellow, bitter kernel; ripens October-November of second season

Buds: clustered terminals; pointed; 5 angled; hairy; brown

Twigs: moderately stout; sometimes shiny; reddish brown; large lenticels; star-shaped pith

Bark: thick; dark brown to nearly black; deep fissures with round ridges and platelike scales; inner bark is orange-yellow

Roots: deep taproot; generally difficult to transplant

Growth Habit: 60-90 feet in height; open, irregular, oblong or round crown; spreading branches

Hardiness: zone 4

Site: well drained, sandy or moist soil; intolerant to shade

Growth Rate: moderate

Maintenance: clean; fairly tolerant to pruning

Propagation: seed—fall sow and mulch, or stratify in a moist medium at 32-41 °F for 30-60 days

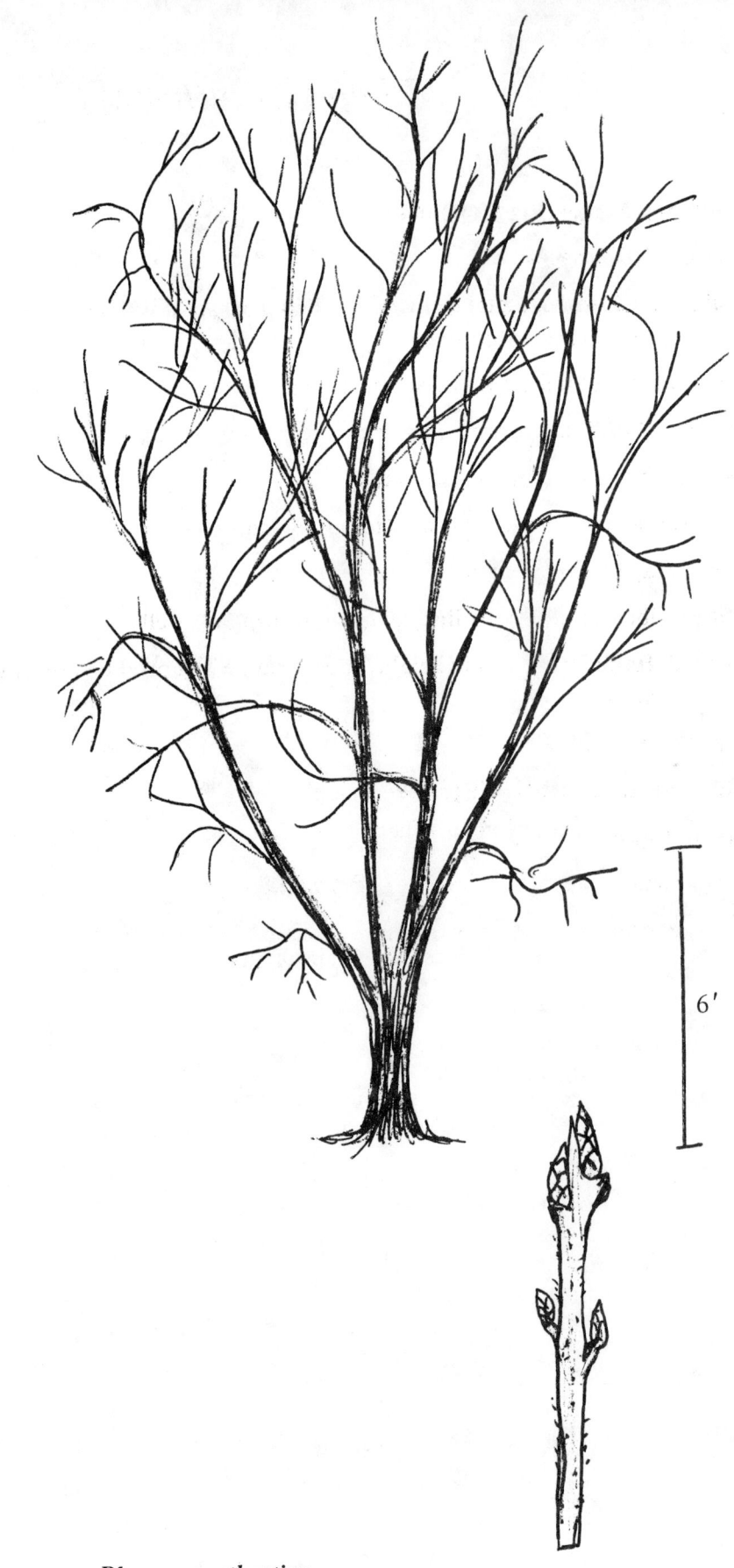

Rhamnus cathartica

Rhamnus cathartica

Common Name: Common Buckthorn

Family: Rhamnaceae

Foliage: 1-2 inches long; prominent, parallel veins; fine teeth; dull green above; lighter green beneath; smooth

Flowers: male and female separate on separate trees; fragrant; greenish; April-June

Fruit: 1/4 inch, black drupe; bitter; ripens September-October

Buds: subopposite; brown; smooth

Twigs: gray to brown; smooth; often ending in a spine; stiff

Bark: gray to brown rough

Roots: fibrous; widespreading; shallow; transplants well

Growth Habit: 10-25 feet in height; short trunk with upright, spreading branches; oblong or round crown

Hardiness: zone 2

Site: tolerant to many soils; sun or shade

Growth Rate: rapid

Maintenance: weedy; very tolerant to pruning

Propagation: seed—stratify in a moist medium at 34-41°F up to 15 days; suckers

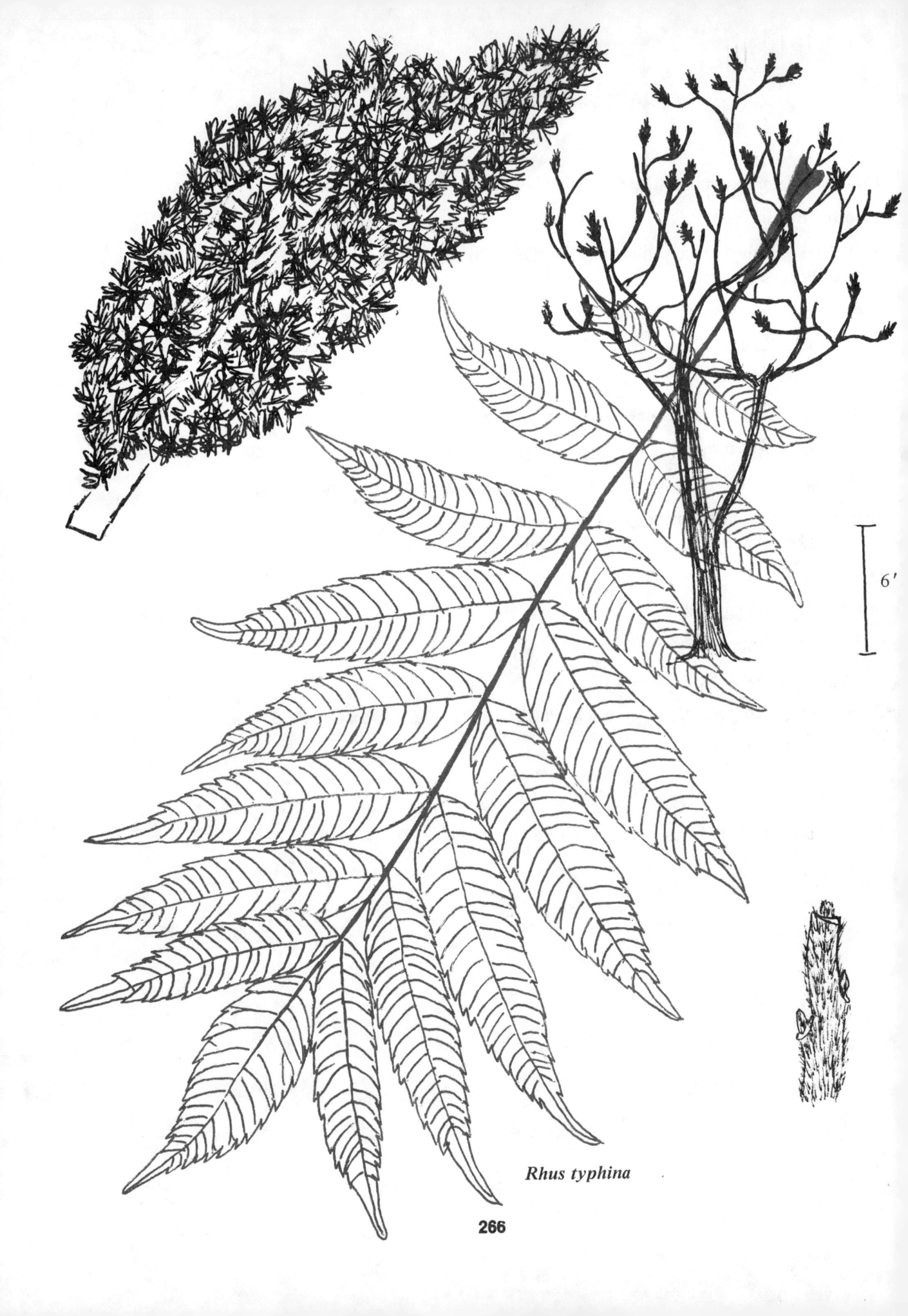

Rhus typhina

Rhus typhina

Common Name: Staghorn Sumac

Family: Anacardiaceae

Foliage: up to 25 inches long; 11-31 leaflets; sharp teeth; dark green above; white beneath; hairy leaf stalk with milky sap and an enlarged base; scarlet in autumn

Flowers: male and female in one flower or separate on separate trees; small; in hairy panicles 6-12 inches long; greenish; May-July

Fruit: cluster of dark red, hairy drupes; red hairs; dense; upright; sour; ripens August-October

Buds: round; brown; hairy

Twigs: stout; hairy; brown; milky sap

Bark: thin; dark brown scaly

Roots: widespreading; fibrous; transplants well

Growth Habit: 10-30 feet in height; irregular crown; gnarled texture; forms thickets

Hardiness: zone 3

Site: poor, dry or wet soil; sun or partial shade

Growth Rate: rapid

Maintenance: suckers freely; tolerant to moderate pruning

Propagation: seed—scarify in concentrated sulfuric acid for 4-6 hours if covering is attached (1-1 1/2 for seed that has been cleaned); fall or spring sow; root cuttings

Selections: 'Dissecta' — cut foliage

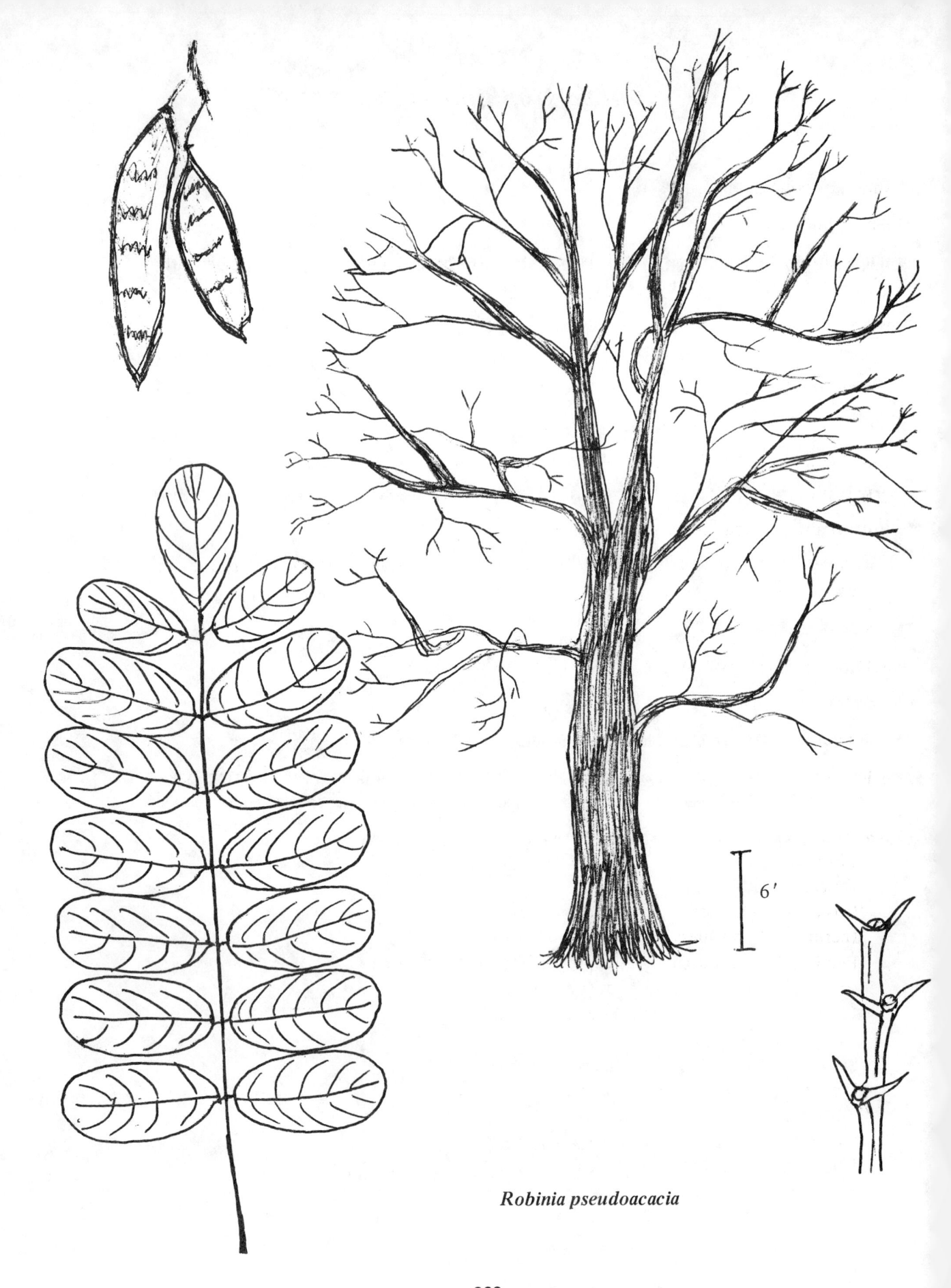

Robinia pseudoacacia

Robinia pseudoacacia

Common Name: Black Locust

Family: Leguminosae

Foliage: 6-14 inches long; 7-21, nearly round leaflets; without teeth; gray-green; yellow in autumn

Flowers: in pendulous clusters; very fragrant; white with a yellow spot; May-June

Fruit: 2-4 inch pod; dark brown; smooth; 4-8 brown seeds; ripens September-October; often persistent

Buds: no terminal; small; red; hairy; 3-4 superimposed within a leaf scar

Twigs: stout; dull brown; paired spines at nodes

Bark: brown to nearly black; furrowed with round, scaly ridges

Roots: shallow; spreading; transplants well

Growth Habit: 40-70 feet in height; few branches; irregular crown with a round top; suckers freely

Hardiness: zone 3

Site: prefers moist, rich soil but tolerant of poor, dry soils; sun

Growth Rate: rapid

Maintenance: can become rampant if unattended; tolerant to pruning

Propagation: seed—soak in sulfuric acid 10-120 minutes and wash in water, spring sow only; root cuttings; graft or bud on *R. pseudocacia* understock

Selections: 'Amorphaefolia' — narrow, oblong leaflets
'Bessoniana' — dense, oval crown; thornless
'Descaisneana' — pink flowers
'Frisia' — yellow foilage; dark red spines
'Inermis' — thornless
'Pendulifolia Purpurea' — weeping habit; purple foliage
'Purpurea' — young foliage purple
'Pyramidalis' — pyramidal; thornless
'Rectissima' — upright
'Semperflorens' — flowers throughout the summer
'Stricta' — pyramidal with ascending branches
'Tortuosa' — contorted branches
'Umbraculifera' — round crown; no flowers or thorns
'Unifoliola' — usually one large leaf

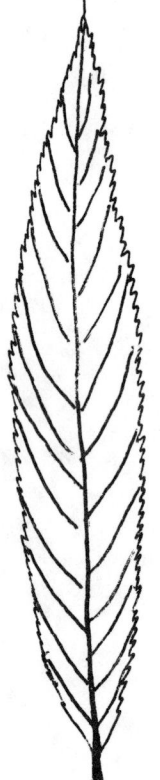

Salix alba

270

Salix alba

Common Name: White Willow

Family: Salicaceae

Foliage: 2-4 inches long; fine teeth; hairy; veins extend to margins without branching; dark green above; short leaf stalks; yellow in autumn

Flowers: male and female separate on separate trees; green catkins; April-May

Fruit: capsule in a long cluster; small seed with tufts of long, silky hair; ripens May-June

Buds: terminal absent; single, caplike scale

Twigs: slender; greenish to yellow; brittle at base

Bark: rough; gray; deep furrows and ridges; astringent

Roots: fibrous; spreading; transplants easily

Growth Habit: 60-100 feet in height; upright, spreading, irregular crown; low branching

Hardiness: zone 2

Site: moist or wet soil; adaptable; sun or partial shade

Growth Rate: rapid

Maintenance: brittle branches; tolerant to pruning

Propagation: seed—sow fresh; hardwood cuttings; root cuttings

Selections: 'Calva' — dark brown twigs
  'Chermesina' — bright red twigs
  'Sericea' — downy, grayish foliage
  'Tristis' — drooping branches, yellow twigs

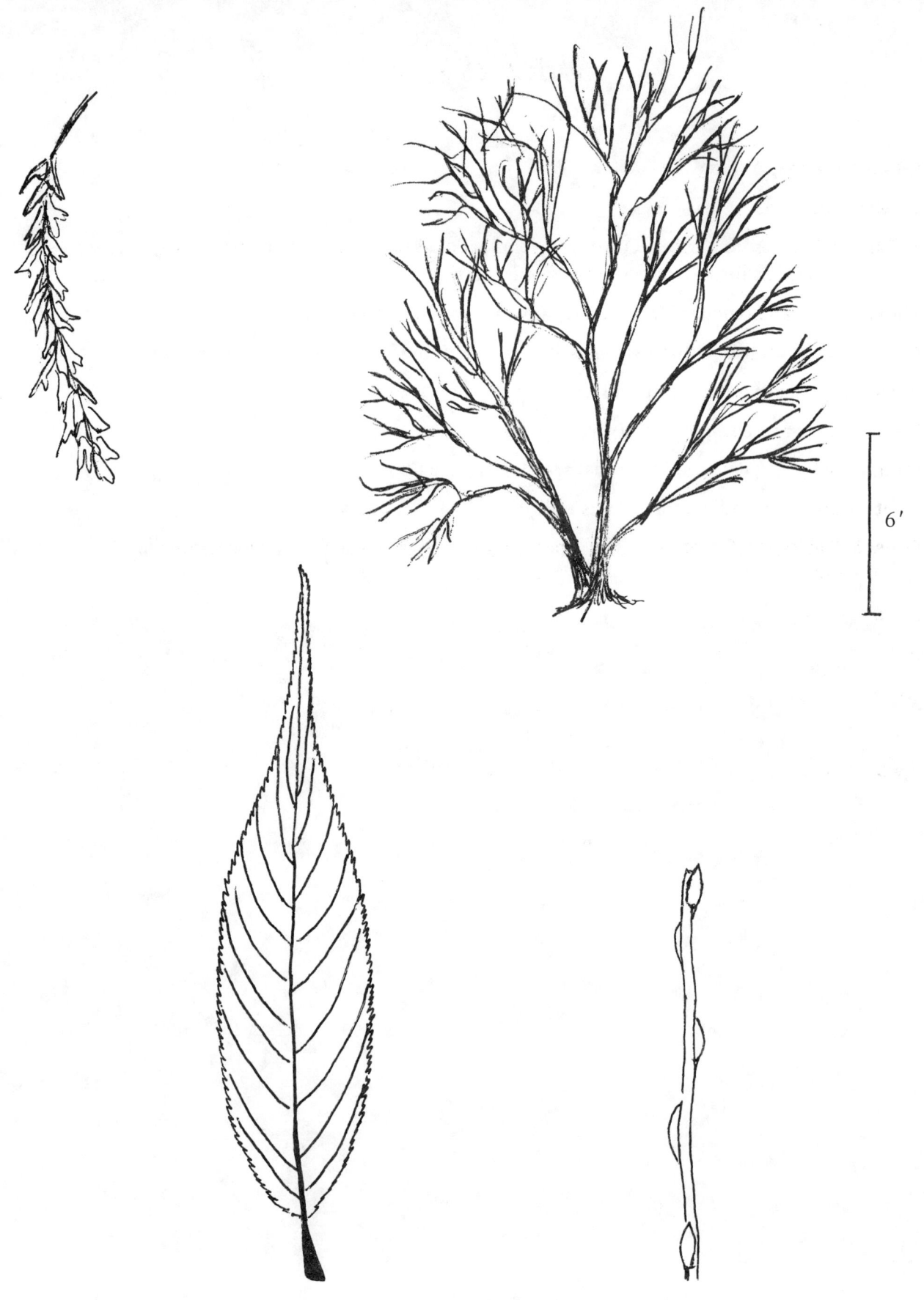

Salix lucida

272

Salix lucida

Common Name: Shining Willow

Family: Salicaceae

Foliage: 3-5 inches long; fine, glandular teeth; yellow-green above; paler below; shiny on both surfaces; long, pointed apex; stout leaf stalks

Flowers: male and female separate on separate trees; catkins; spring

Fruit: cluster of capsules; hairless; June

Buds: no terminal; reddish brown; caplike scales; short stalks

Twigs: yellow-brown; shiny; brittle where joined to branches

Bark: gray-brown; smooth; horizontal orange-brown lenticels

Roots: fibrous; spreading; transplants well

Growth Habit: 15-20 feet in height; open, round top crown; low branching; often with multiple trunks

Hardiness: zone 2

Site: moist, rich soil; sun

Growth Rate: rapid

Maintenance: brittle wood; tolerant to pruning

Propagation: seed—sow fresh; hardwood cuttings; root cuttings

Salix matsudana

Salix matsudana

Common Name: Hankow Willow

Family: Salicaceae

Foliage: 2-3 inches long; narrow; whitish below; sharp, glandular teeth

Flowers: male and female separate on separate trees; catkins; spring

Fruit: cluster of capsules; May-June

Buds: small; no terminal; green; caplike scales

Twigs: slender; olive green

Bark: gray; furrowed

Roots: fibrous; spreading; transplants well

Growth Habit: 30-40 feet in height; upright, spreading crown

Hardiness: zone 4

Site: adaptable to many soil types; sun

Growth Rate: rapid

Maintenance: tolerant to pruning

Propagation: seed—sow fresh; hardwood cuttings; root cuttings

Selections: 'Pendula' — weeping branches
    'Tortuosa' — contorted branches
    'Umbraculifera' — semi-globose crown

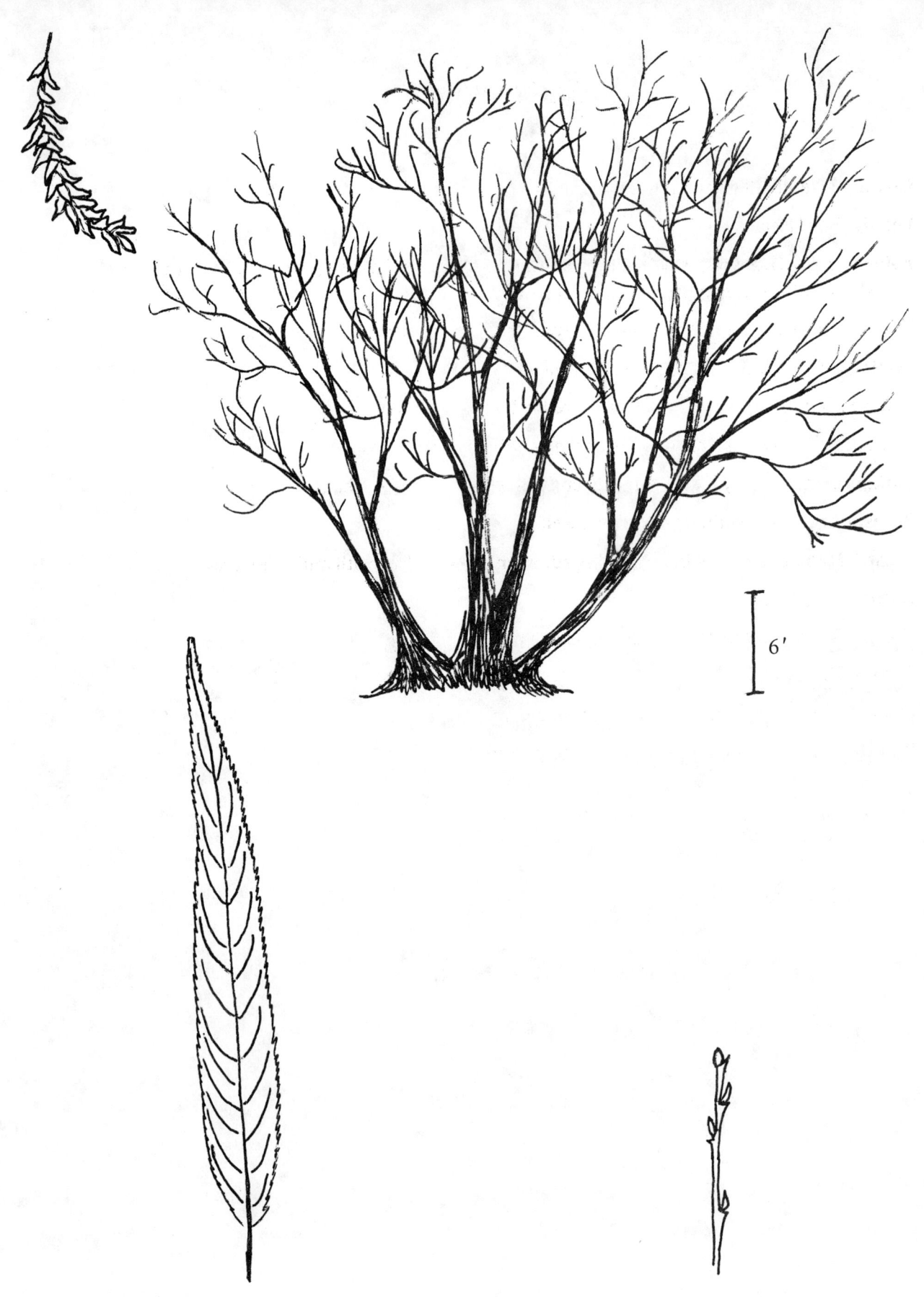

Salix nigra

276

Salix nigra

Common Name: Black Willow

Family: Salicaceae

Foliage: 3-6 inches long; small, incurved teeth; smooth, yellowish green above and below; short leaf stalk; stipules persist until autumn

Flowers: male and female separate on separate trees; green catkins; April-May

Fruit: cluster of capsules; ripens May-June

Buds: without terminal; caplike scales; reddish brown; bitter

Twigs: slender; reddish brown; brittle where joined to branches

Bark: brown to nearly black; thick; deep furrows with vertical, shaggy ridges

Roots: fibrous; spreading; transplants well

Growth Habit: 30-40 feet in height; broad, open crown; often with multiple stems

Hardiness: zone 3

Site: prefers moist soil but tolerant to dry; sun

Growth Rate: rapid

Maintenance: brittle branches; tolerant to pruning

Propagation: seed—sow fresh; tolerant to pruning

Sassafras albidum

Sassafras albidum

Common Name: Sassafras

Family: Lauraceae

Foliage: 3-7 inches long; 1-2 lobes; without teeth; thin; spicy fragrance when crushed; dull green; orange, red or yellow in autumn

Flowers: male and female separate on separate trees; greenish yellow; fragrant; March-April

Fruit: shiny, blue drupe; bright red, club shaped stalk; ripens August-September

Buds: green; scaly; fragrant when crushed

Twigs: moderately stout; smooth; green; fragrant when crushed

Bark: thick; gray; spicy fragrant; deep fissures with raised ridges

Roots: long and deep; fragrant; difficult to establish

Growth Habit: 30-50 feet in height; often with a crooked trunk; open, flat top crown; free suckering

Hardiness: zone 4

Site: sandy, well-drained soil; sun

Growth Rate: rapid

Maintenance: clean except for suckers; limited tolerance to pruning

Propagation: seed—fall sow and mulch, or stratify in a moist medium at 41° F for 120 days; root cuttings; graft on *S. albidum* understock

Selections: var. *molle* — hairy buds, twigs and underside of young leaves

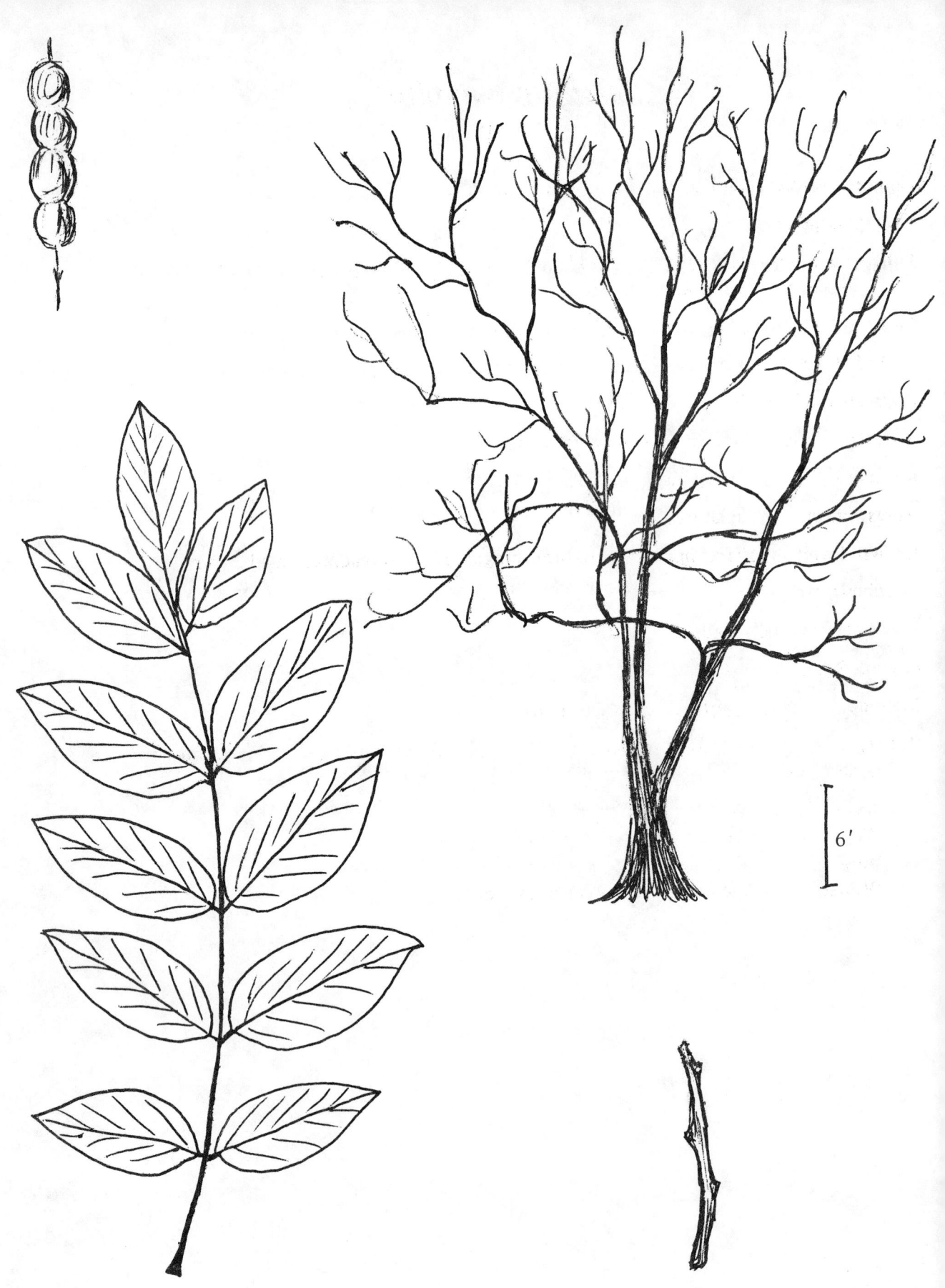

Sophora japonica

280

Sophora japonica

Common Name: Japanese Pagoda Tree; Scholar Tree

Family: Leguminosae

Foliage: 6-10 inches long; 7-17 stalked leaflets; without teeth; blue-green; bloomy beneath; remain blue-green in autumn

Flowers: large, upright panicles to 15 inches long; terminal; creamy white: July

Fruit: 2-3 inch, yellowish green pod; 1-6 seed; ripens October; persistent

Buds: small; fuzzy; brown

Twigs: dull green; smooth; triangular leaf scars

Bark: dull green to almost black; deep furrows with ridges

Roots: fibrous; transplants well

Growth Habit: 40-60 feet in height; low branching; upright, spreading, round crown

Hardiness: zone 4

Site: wet or dry soil; shade

Growth Rate: moderate

Maintenance: clean; fairly tolerant to pruning

Propagation: seed—stratify in sand at 41° F for 30-90 days; graft on *S. japonica* understock

Selections: 'Fastigiata' — upright habit
    'Pendula' — weeping branches; few flowers
    'Regent' — early flowering; oval crown
    'Violacea' — late flowering; purplish flowers

Sorbus aucuparia

Sorbus aucuparia

Common Name: European Mountain Ash; Rowan Tree

Family: Rosaceae

Foliage: 9-15 leaflets; light green; hairy below; no teeth on lower 1/3 of leaflet; hairy leaf stalk; reddish in autumn

Flowers: flat topped clusters; white; May

Fruit: 1/3-3/8 inch, orange-red berrylike pome; in clusters; acid flavor; ripens October; persistent through winter

Buds: large terminal; long, white hairs; sticky

Twigs: moderately stout; grayish brown; shiny; smooth

Bark: smooth; gray

Roots: fibrous; widespreading; transplants moderately well

Growth Habit: 30-40 feet in height; erect and spreading branches; round topped, oblong crown

Hardiness: zone 3

Site: tolerant to many soils; cool soil; sun

Growth Rate: moderate-rapid

Maintenance: clean; fairly tolerant to pruning

Propagation: seed—fall sow, or stratify in a moist medium at 33-41°F for 60-210 days; bud or graft on *S. americana* or *S. aucuparia* understock

Selections: 'Apricot Queen' — apricot colored fruit
  'Asplenifolia' — cut foliage
  'Black Hawk' — columnar; large fruit
  'Cardinal Royal' — upright; large fruit clusters
  'Carpet of Gold' — yellow to orange fruit
  'Cole's Columnar' — columnar
  'Fastigiata' — upright
  'Pendula' — weeping branches
  'Scarlet King' — oval crown; scarlet fruit
  'Wilson Columnar' — dense; columnar

Note: *Sorbus decora*, Showy Mountain Ash, is a small tree (25-30 feet in height) and has larger, more showy fruits than *S. aucuparia*

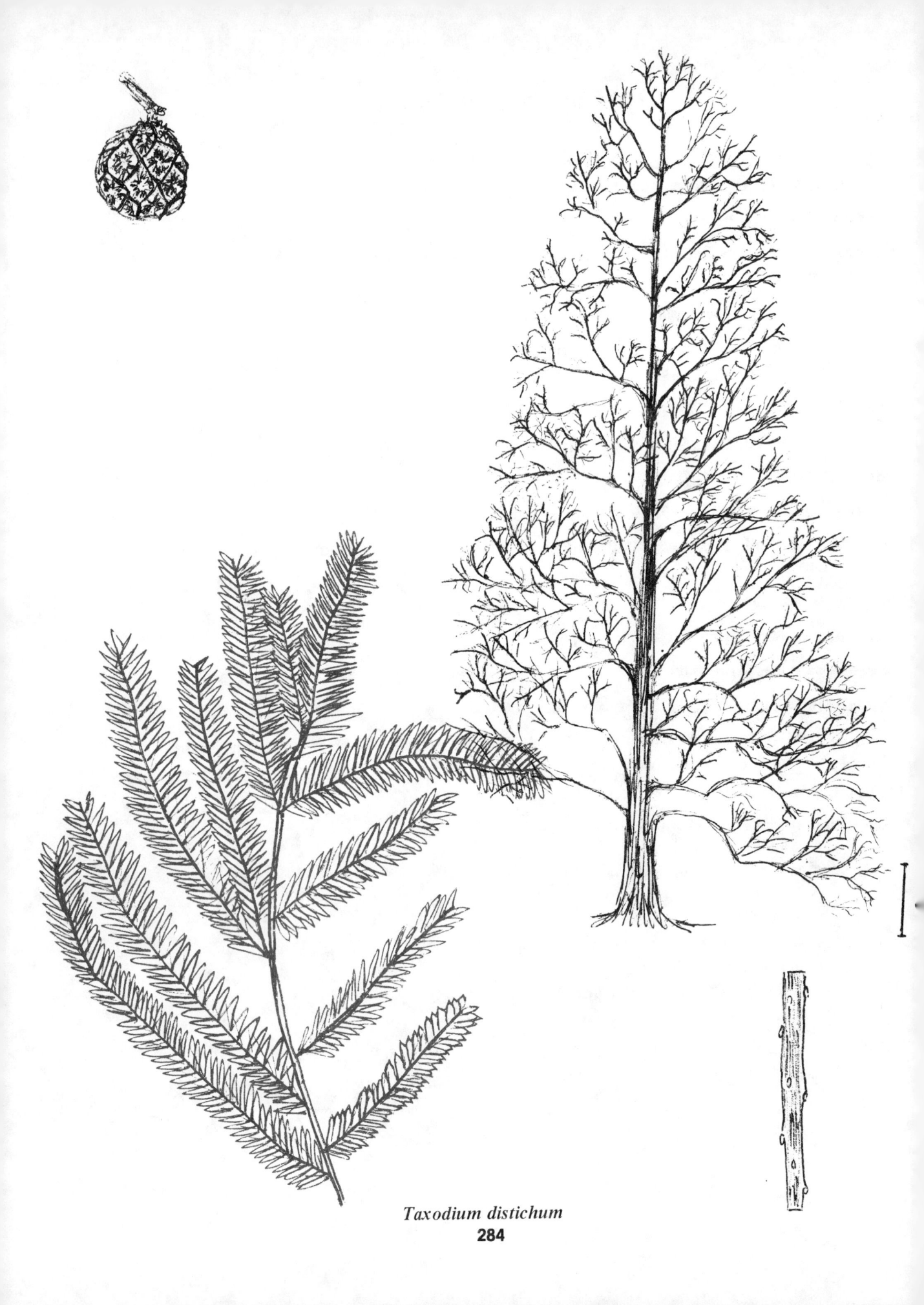

Taxodium distichum

Taxodium distichum

Common Name: Bald Cypress

Family: Taxodiaceae

Foliage: 1/2-3/4 inch, needlelike, deciduous leaves; soft; yellow-green to rust in autumn

Flowers: male and female separate but on the same tree; male: purplish clusters; female: single or in clusters, globular; March-April

Fruit: 1/2-1 1/4 inch, modified cone; globular; brown; wrinkled, thickened scales; ripens October-December

Buds: small; few scales

Twigs: slender; brown; no leaf scars visible

Bark: thin; brown; scaly and fibrous

Roots: shallow; widespreading; transplants well in the proper site

Growth Habit: 75-80 feet in height; narrowly pyramidal crown; "knees" produced at trunk base if the tree is growing in water

Hardiness: zone 4

Site: moist or wet, acid soil; sun

Growth Rate: slow-moderate

Maintenance: clean

Propagation: seed—fall sow and mulch, or soak in water at 38°F for 90 days, or soak 5 minutes in ethyl alcohol then stratify in a moist medium at 41°F for 90 days; cuttings; graft on *T. distichum* understock

Selections: 'Pendens' — weeping branchlets

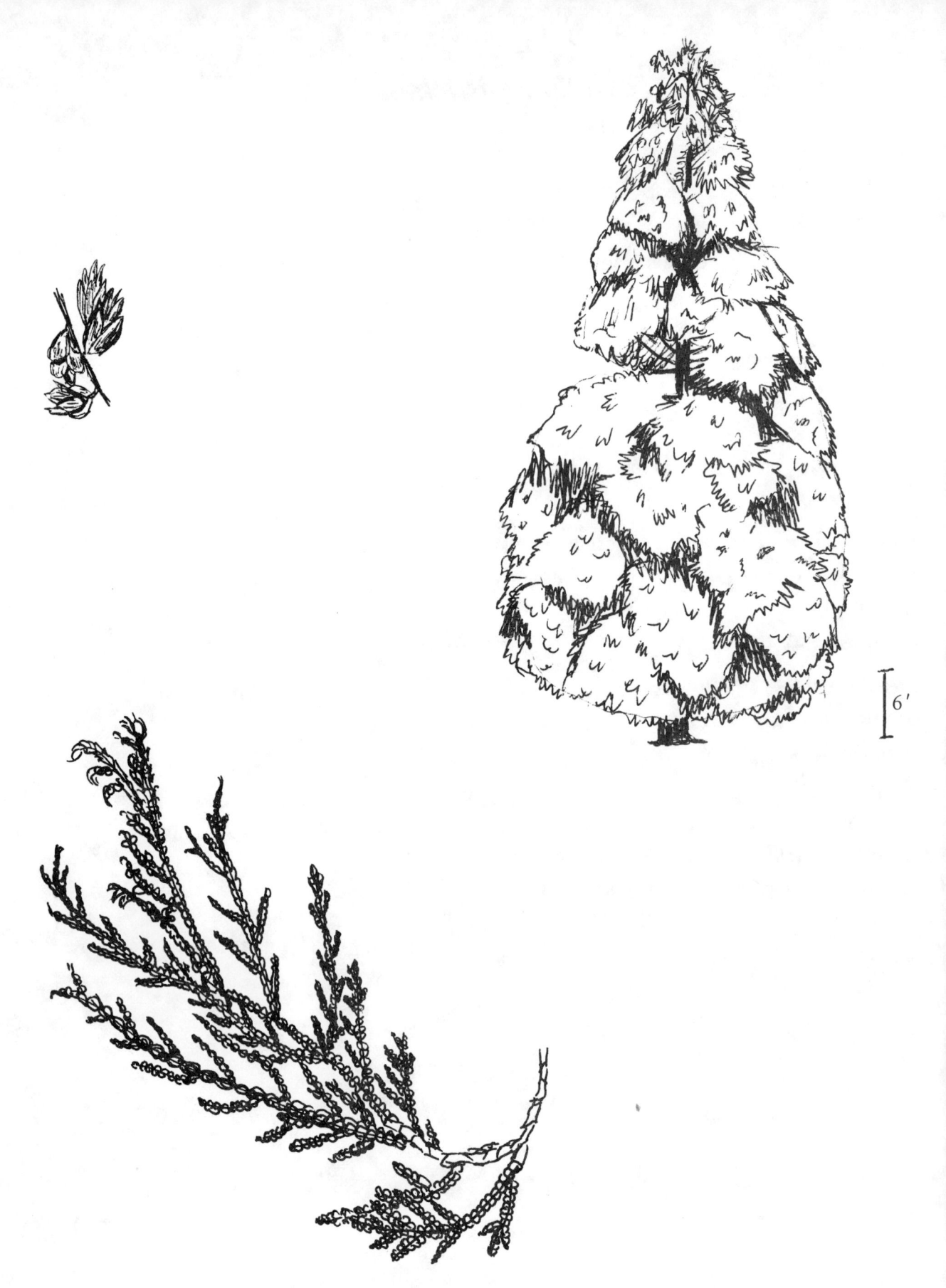

Thuja occidentalis

286

Thuja occidentalis

Common Name: American Arborvitae; Northern White Cedar

Family: Pinaceae

Foliage: scalelike; evergreen; small; scales overlap; tiny glands; in flat sprays; flexible; aromatic; persists 2 years

Fruit: 1/3-1/2 inch cone; erect; rounded scales; yellow-brown; ripens August-September

Twigs: slender; flattened

Bark: thin; reddish brown; shreddy or fibrous

Roots: taproot with fibrous laterals; transplants well

Growth Habit: 30-70 feet in height; flat branches; pyramidal crown; branches often extend to ground; sometimes with multiple trunks

Hardiness: zone 2

Site: moist, well-drained soil; somewhat shade tolerant

Growth Rate: slow-moderate

Maintenance: clean; tolerant to pruning

Propagation: seed—fall sow or stratify in a moist medium at 34-41°F for 30-60 days; cuttings

Selections: 'Alba' — white tips on foliage
    'Beaufort' — white, variegated foliage
    'Columbia' — columnar; white tips on foliage
    'Douglasii Aurea' — yellowish foliage
    'Fastigiata' — narrow, upright crown
    'Gracilis' — drooping branches
    'Lutea' — yellow foliage; shorter in height
    'Mastersii' — compact; foliage in a vertical plane
    'Nigra' — dark green foliage
    'Pendula' — weeping branches
    'Riversii' — compact; yellow foliage in summer
    'Semperaurea' — shorter; yellow foliage
    'Spiralis' — shorter; slender; dark green
    'Vervaeneana' — shorter; dense; light colored in summer becoming bronze in winter

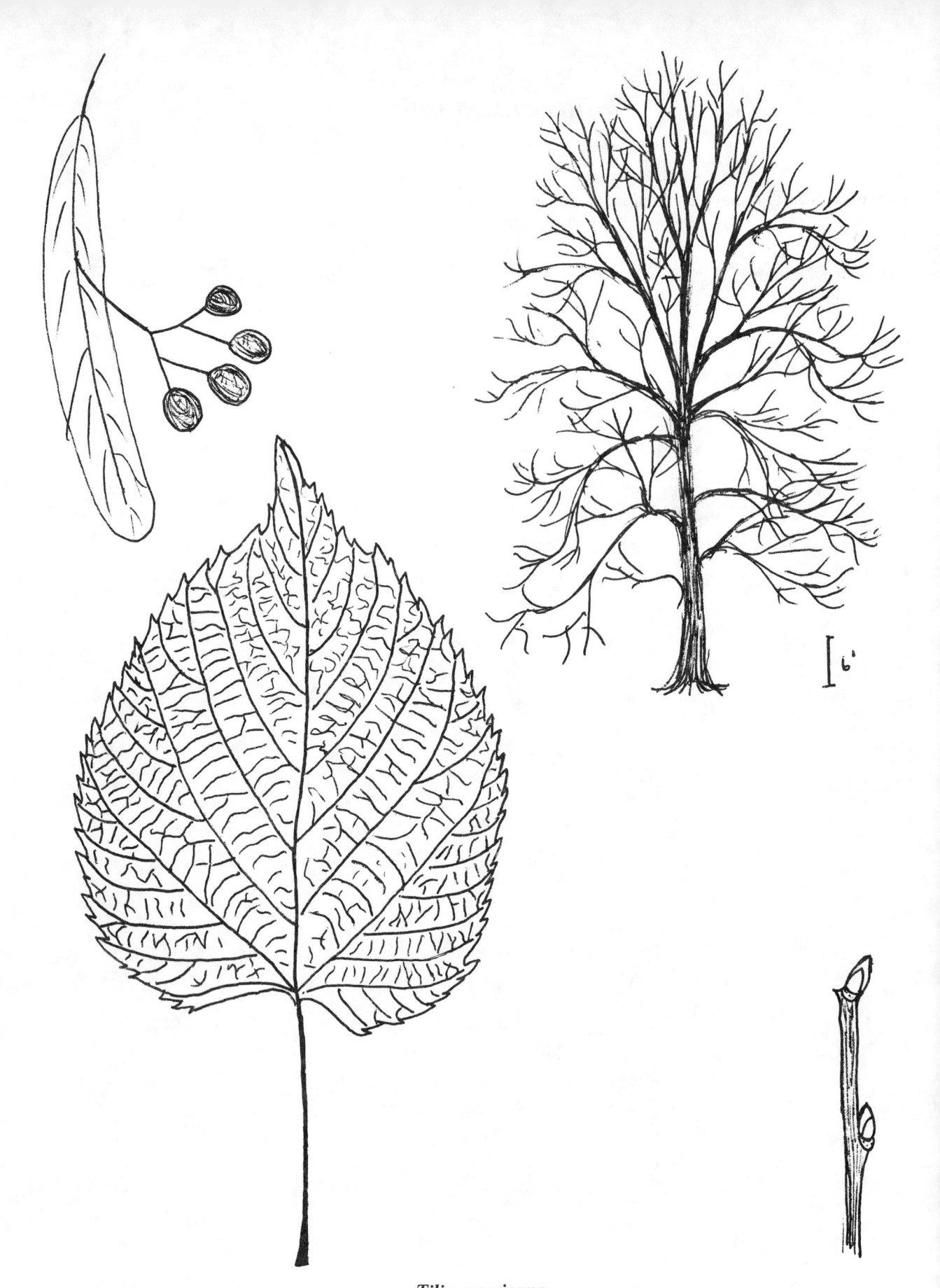

Tilia americana

Tilia americana

Common Name: American Linden; Basswood

Family: Tiliaceae

Foliage: 5-6 inches long; coarse teeth; heart-shape base; dull, dark green above; paler beneath; yellow in autumn

Flowers: clustered on a long stalk which is attached to a leafy bract; creamy-white; fragrant; June-July

Fruit: round, hairy nutlet; greenish brown; attached to a leafy bract; thick shell; edible; ripens September-October; often persistent

Buds: no terminal; stout; rounded; dark red; 2 scales; lopsided

Twigs: slender; red becoming dark gray

Bark: dark gray with vertical ridges

Roots: widespreading; transplants well when young

Growth Habit: 70-130 feet in height; low branching; drooping lower branches; upper branches ascending; broadly, oval or oblong crown; often suckers at base

Hardiness: zone 2

Site: rich, moist, well-drained soil; sun or partial shade

Growth Rate: rapid

Maintenance: clean; tolerant to pruning

Propagation: seed—scarify in sulfuric acid 40 minutes and force through a screen, then stratify in a moist medium at 34-38° F for 90 days; graft or bud on *T. americana* understock

Selections: 'Dentata' — large teeth
    'Fastigiata' — upright, compact crown
    'Macrophylla' — very large leaves

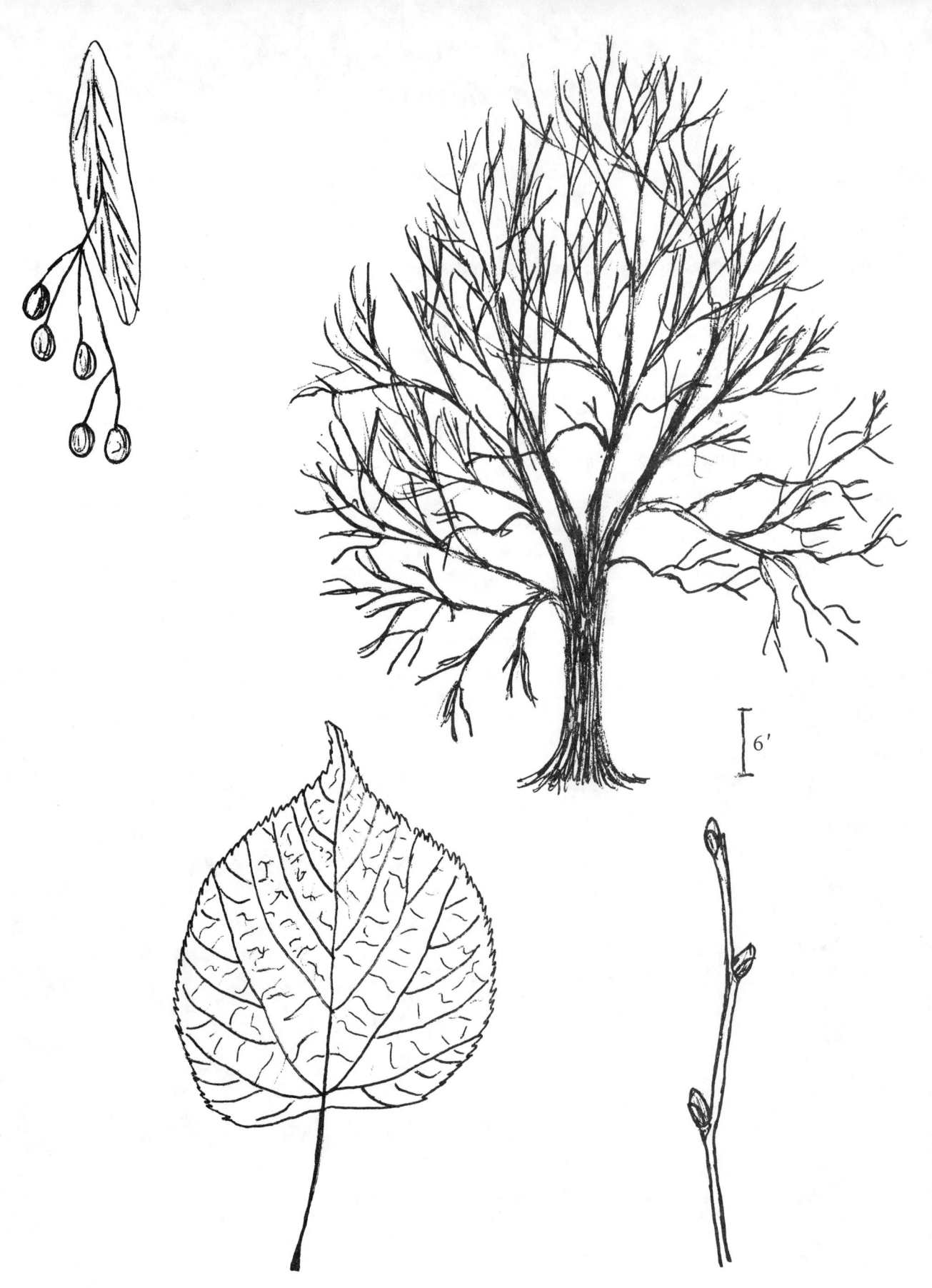

Tilia cordata

Tilia cordata

Common Name: Little-leaved Linden; Small-leaved European Linden

Family: Tiliaceae

Foliage: 2-2 1/2 inches long; fine teeth; heart shape; dark green and shiny above; bluish-gray beneath with axillary tufts of hair; pale yellow in autumn

Flowers: 5-7 inch cluster attached to a leafy bract; tiny; pale yellow to white; fragrant; June-July

Fruit: cluster of nutlets attached to a leafy bract; yellowish brown; ripens September-October

Buds: no terminal; lopsided; 2 scales; green

Twigs: slender; reddish brown

Bark: brown-gray; fine ridges and furrows

Roots: fibrous; transplants well

Growth Habit: 50-100 feet in height; dense, oval crown; massive, ascending, spreading branches

Hardiness: zone 3

Site: prefers moist, well-drained soil but tolerant; sun or partial shade

Growth Rate: moderate

Maintenance: clean; tolerant to pruning

Propagation: seed—scarify in sulfuric acid 40 minutes and force through a screen, then stratify in a moist medium at 34-38° F for 90 days; graft or bud on *T. cordata* understock

Selections: 'Chancellor' — compact, upright crown
  'De Groot' — pyramidal; slow growth rate
  'Fairview' — pyramidal; rapid growth rate
  'Greenspire' — upright, oval crown; rapid growth rate
  'Handsworth' — light yellow-green twigs
  'Pyramidalis' — pyramidal crown
  'Swedish Upright' — narrow, upright crown; short branches

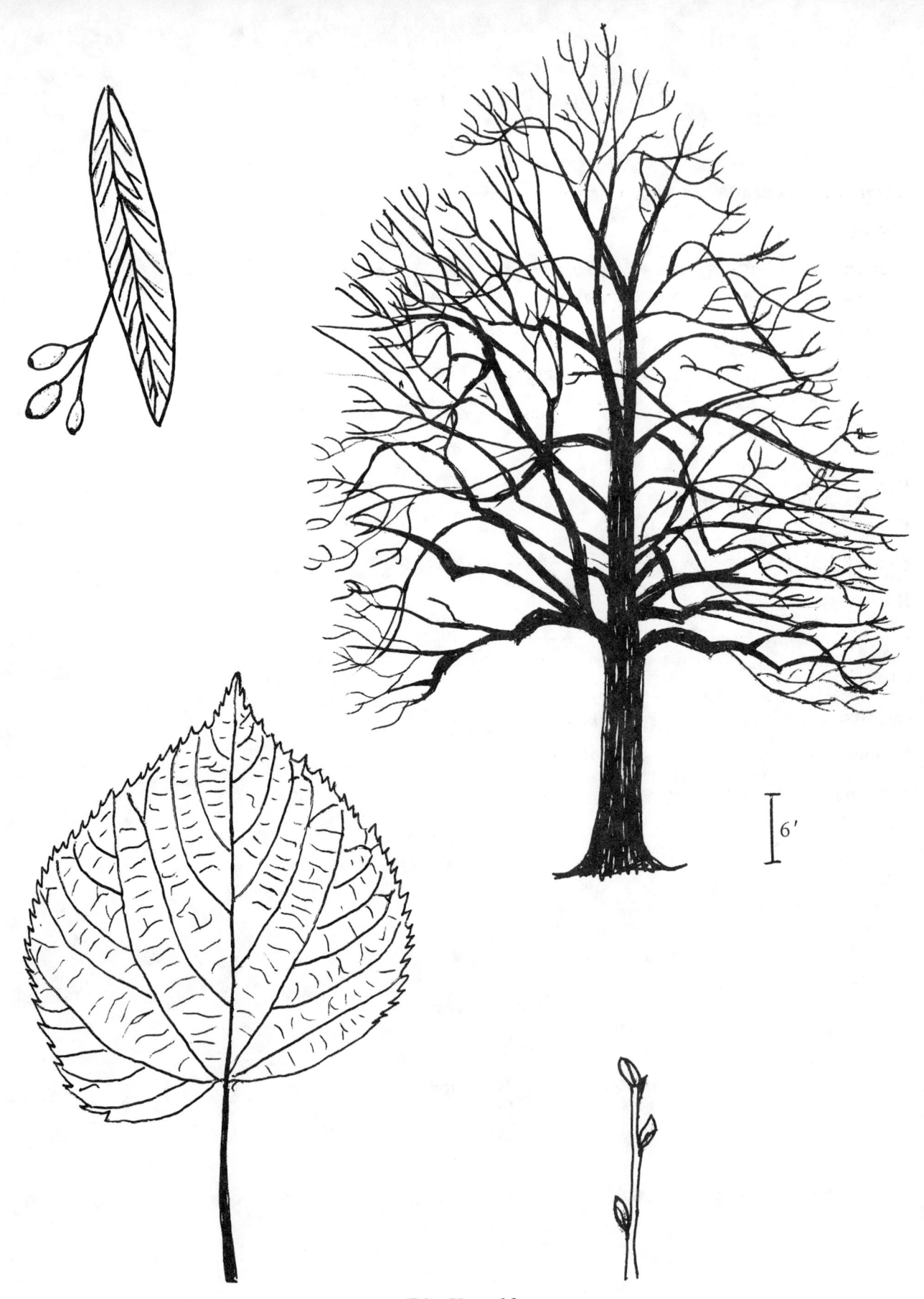

Tilia X *euchlora*

292

Tilia X *euchlora*

Common Name: Crimean Linden

Family: Tiliaceae

Foliage: 2-4 inches long; dense; dark green; sharp pointed; glossy; fine teeth; pale beneath with axillary tufts of brown hair

Flowers: in a pendulous cluster attached to a leafy bract; yellow; fragrant; early July

Fruit: short nutlets on a leafy bract; bract narrowed at ends; fuzzy; 5 ribs on nutlet

Buds: no terminal; stout; red; shiny; 2 scales; lopsided

Twigs: slender; smooth

Bark: thin; gray; vertical furrows

Roots: fibrous; transplants well

Growth Habit: 60-90 feet in height; slightly weeping branches; oval crown

Hardiness: zone 4

Site: moist, well-drained soil; full sun or partial shade

Growth Rate: moderate

Maintenance: clean; tolerant to pruning

Propagation: graft or bud on *T. americana* understock

Selections: 'Redmond' — densely pyramidal crown

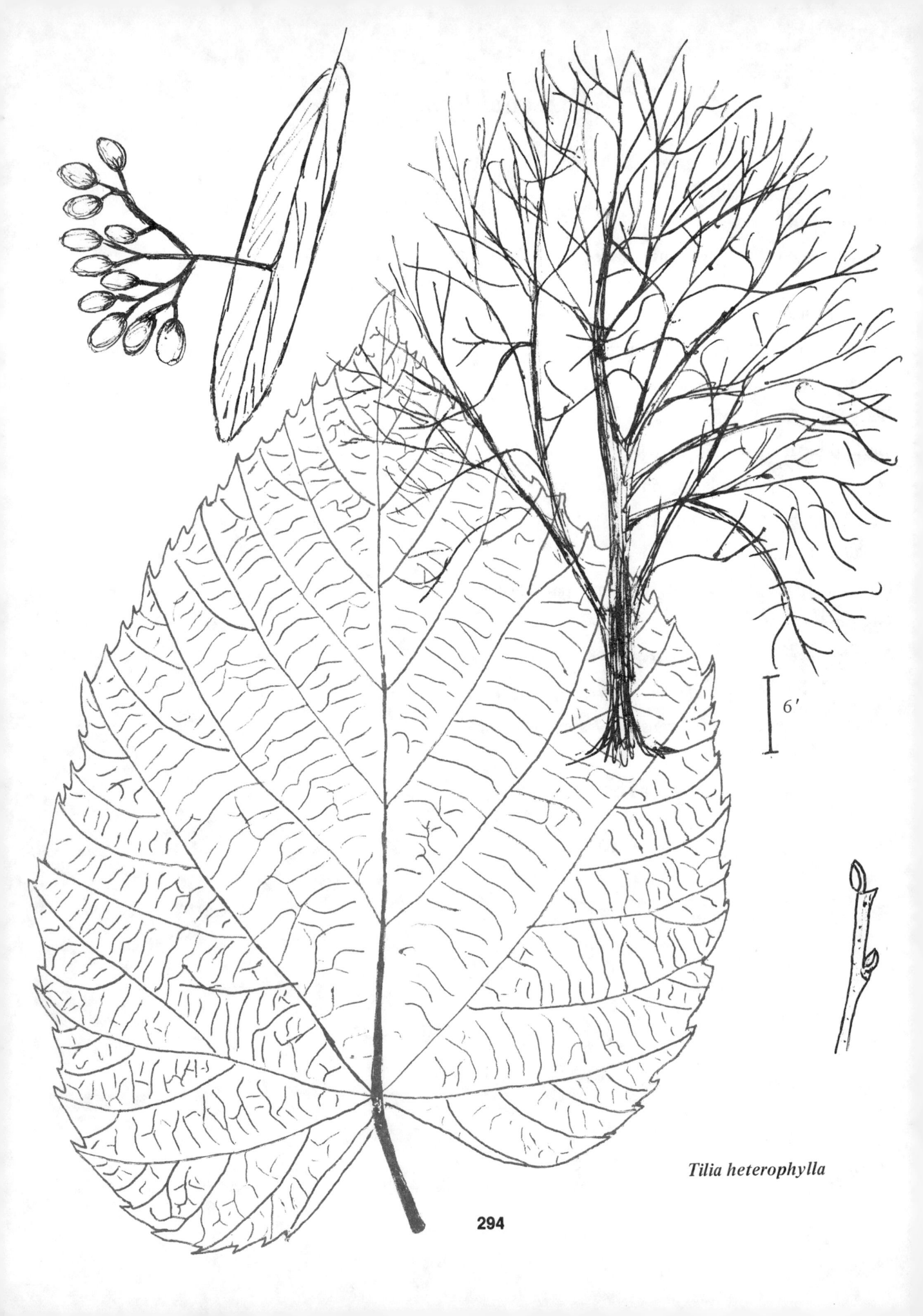

Tilia heterophylla

Tilia heterophylla

Common Name: White Basswood

Family: Tiliaceae

Foliage: 3-7 inches long; fine, bristle tipped teeth; dark green and smooth above; white down beneath with small tufts of reddish brown hair; shiny

Flowers: 10-20 flowered cluster on a leafy bract; fragrant; greenish-yellow; July

Fruit: cluster hard-shelled nutlets on a leafy bract; rusty hair

Buds: no terminal; red; smooth; 2 scales

Twigs: slender; reddish brown; smooth

Bark: dark gray; furrowed with flat ridges

Roots: fibrous; transplants well

Growth Habit: 50-60 feet in height; ascending, spreading branches; pyramidal crown

Hardiness: zone 4

Site: moist, rich soil; sun or partial shade

Growth Rate: moderate

Maintenance: clean; tolerant to pruning

Propagation: seed—scarify in sulfuric acid 40 minutes and force through a screen, then stratify in a moist medium at 34-38°F for 90 days

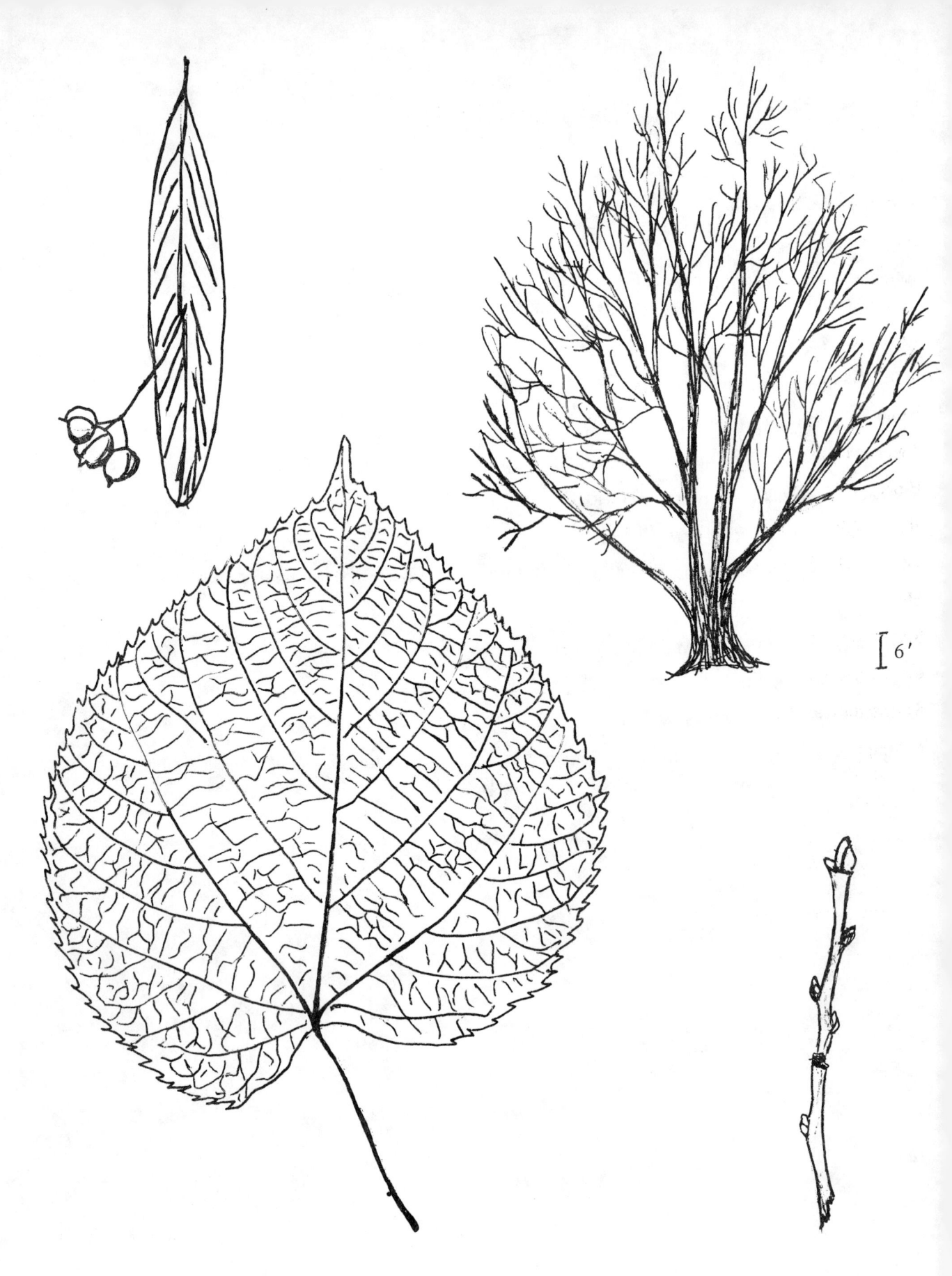

Tilia platyphyllos

296

Tilia platyphyllos

Common Name: Bigleaf Linden

Family: Tiliaceae

Foliage: 3-5 inches long; coarse teeth; hairy; dull green above; lighter green beneath; hairy leaf stalk; yellow in autumn

Flowers: cluster attached to a leafy bract; yellowish white; fragrant; June-July

Fruit: cluster of hard-shelled nutlets on a leafy bract; ribbed; hairy

Buds: lopsided; red; 2 scales

Twigs: slender; dark red

Bark: gray; rough

Roots: fibrous; spreading; transplants well

Growth Habit: 60-80 feet in height; widespreading, round or pyramidal crown

Hardiness: zone 3

Site: deep, rich, moist soil; tolerant to alkaline conditions; sun or partial shade

Growth Rate: moderate

Maintenance: clean; tolerant to pruning

Propagation: seed—scarify in sulfuric acid 40 minutes and force through a screen, then stratify in a moist medium at 34-38° F for 90 days; graft or bud on *T. cordata* understock

Selections: 'Aurea' — yellow twigs
   'Fastigiata' — narrowly columnar
   'Laciniata' — cut leaf
   'Vitifolia' — 3 small lobes on foliage

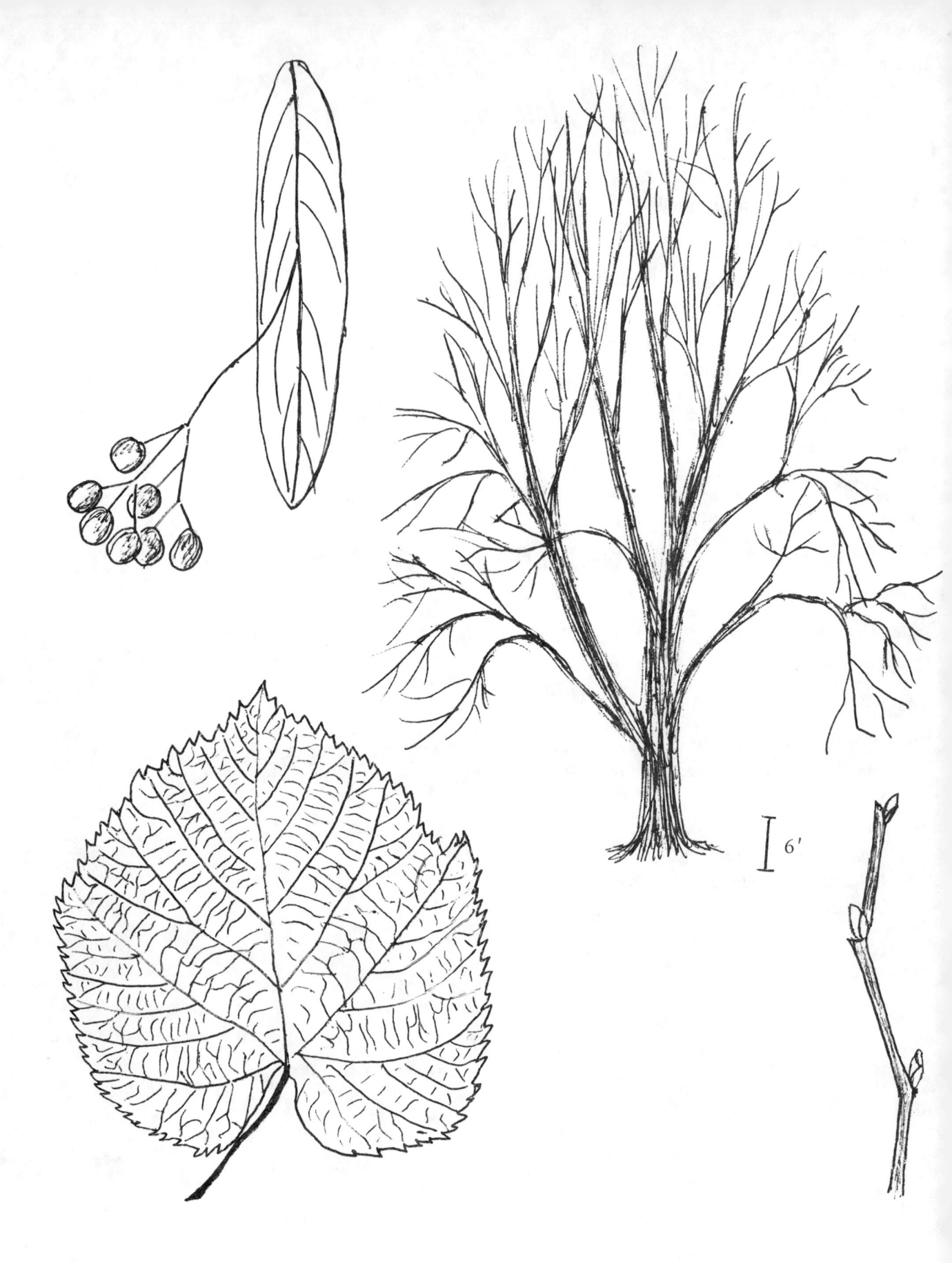

Tilia tomentosa

Tilia tomentosa

Common Name: Silver Linden

Family: Tiliaceae

Foliage: 2-5 inches long; sharp teeth; deep green and shiny above; white hair below; short, hairy leaf stalk; remains green in autumn

Flowers: clusters on a leafy bract; yellowish; fragrant; mid-July

Fruit: cluster of nutlets on a leafy bract; small warts; 5 angled

Buds: no terminal; lopsided; 2 scales; reddish

Twigs: slender; gray; woolly; smooth

Bark: gray; furrowed with flat ridges

Roots: fibrous; transplants well

Growth Habit: 50-60 feet in height; compact, oval crown; stiff, ascending branches

Hardiness: zone 4

Site: tolerant to many soil types; sun or partial shade

Growth Rate: moderate

Maintenance: clean; tolerant to pruning

Propagation: seed—scarify in sulfuric acid 40 minutes and force through a screen, then stratify in a moist medium at 34-38°F for 90 days

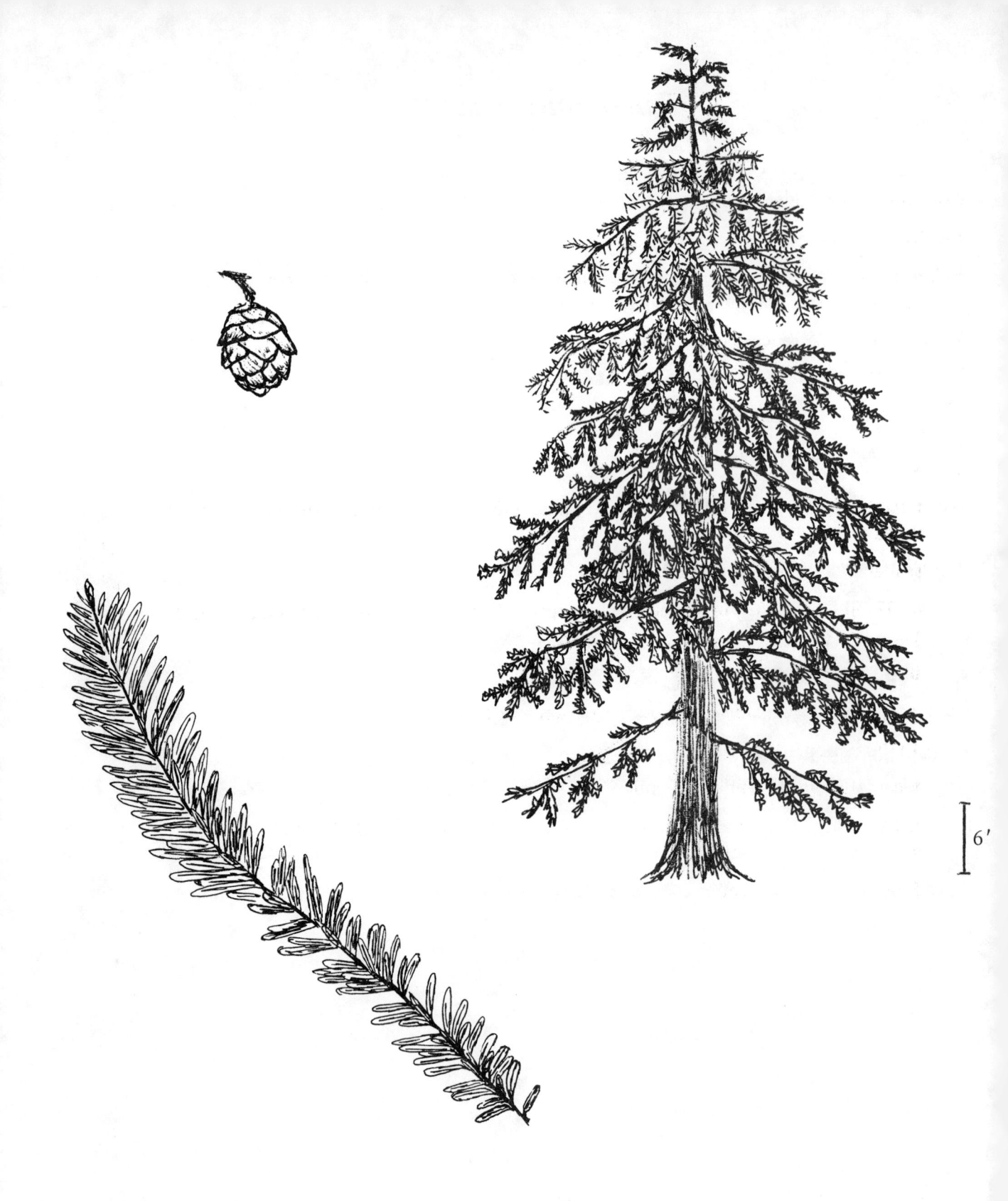

Tsuga canadensis

Tsuga canadensis

Common Name: Canadian Hemlock; Common Hemlock; Eastern Hemlock

Family: Pinaceae

Foliage: 1/3-3/4 inch, evergreen needles; slender leaf stalks; round or notched tips; flat; dark green above; 2, parallel, white lines below

Flowers: male and female separate but on the same tree; small cones; male: yellow; female; pale green with short bracts; June

Fruit: 1/2-3/4 inch, pendent cone; thin, rounded scales; light brown; ripens September-October

Twigs: slender; gray-brown; rough

Bark: reddish gray; deep fissures with irregular plates; if freshly cut will show purple streaks

Roots: shallow; fibrous; transplants well

Growth Habit: 60-100 feet in height; conical crown; dense; horizontal branches that extend nearly to the ground

Hardiness: zone 3

Site: moist, well-drained, acid soil; prefers partial shade; cool

Growth Rate: moderate

Maintenance: clean; tolerant to pruning

Propagation: seed—fall sow or stratify in moist sand or peat at 33-41° F for 30-120 days; graft on *T. canadensis* understock

Selections: 'Fremdii' — compact, pyramidal crown

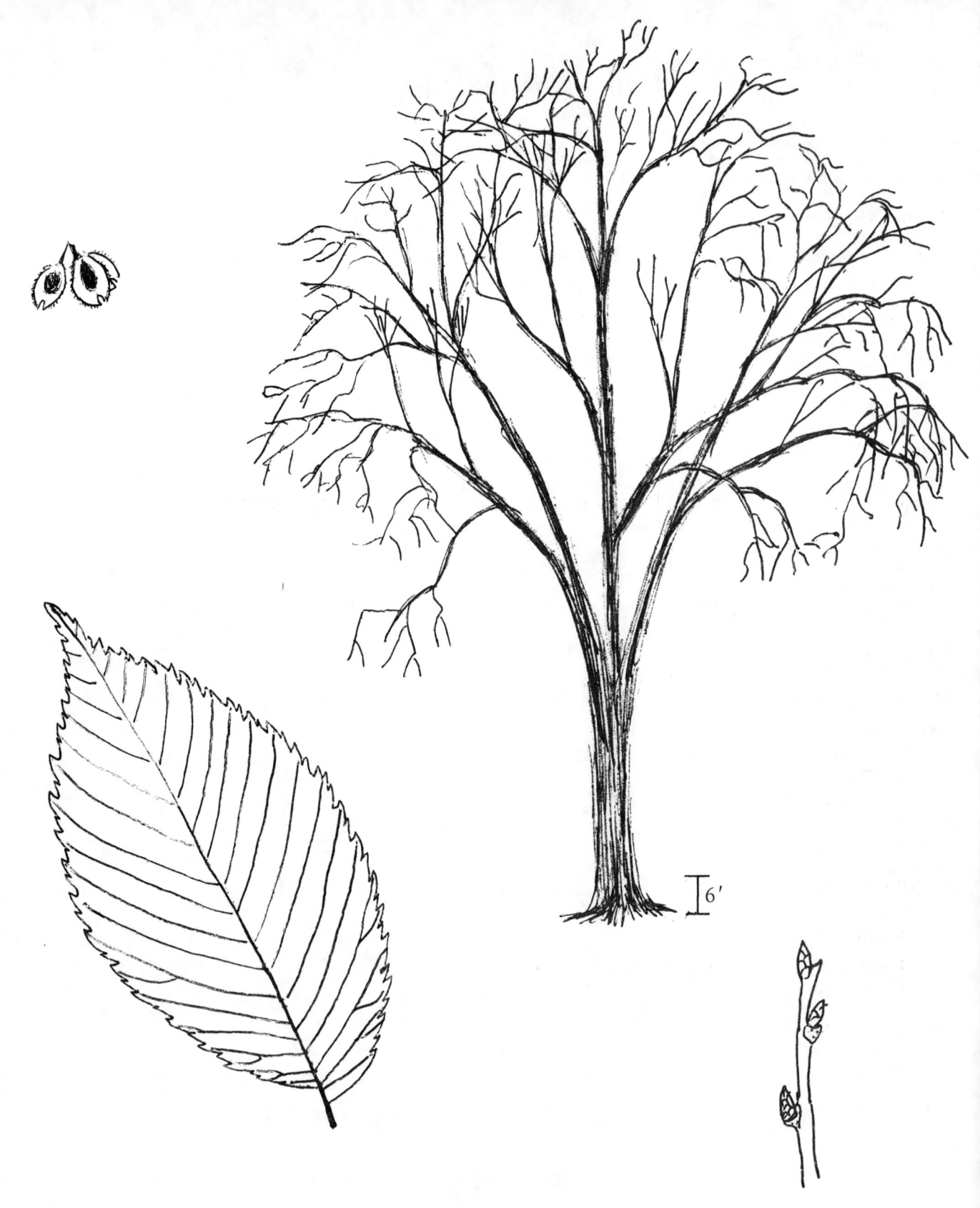

Ulmus americana

Ulmus americana

Common Name: American Elm; White Elm

Family: Ulmaceae

Foliage: 4-6 inches long; coarse, double teeth; taper pointed apex; uneven bases; dark green; hairy fringed; yellow to russet in autumn

Flowers: greenish red clusters; long, slender stems; February-April

Fruit: 1/4 inch samara; seed in center; notch at top of wings; hairy margins; ripens April-May

Buds: no terminal; brown

Twigs: slender; brown

Bark: dark gray; thick ridges and furrows; reddish brown and white stripe cork layers visible when broken

Roots: fibrous; shallow; widespreading; transplants well

Growth Habit: up to 125 feet in height; large arching branches with drooping branchlets; widespreading; vase-shaped crown with a round top

Hardiness: zone 2

Site: prefers deep, rich moist soil but will tolerate dry, alkaline soils; sun

Growth Rate: moderate-rapid

Maintenance: clean; tolerant to pruning

Propagation: seed—spring sow only; softwood cuttings; bud or graft on *U. americana* understock

Selections: 'Augustine Ascending' — columnar; rapid growth rate
    'Columnaris' — columnar
    'Fastigiata' — upright
    'Lake City' — upright; widespreading top
    'Littleford' — columnar
    'Moline' — more upright
    'Pendula' — weeping branches
    'Princeton' — large, leathery foliage; rapid growth rate

Note: Due to Dutch Elm Disease it is not advisable to plant the American Elm at this time

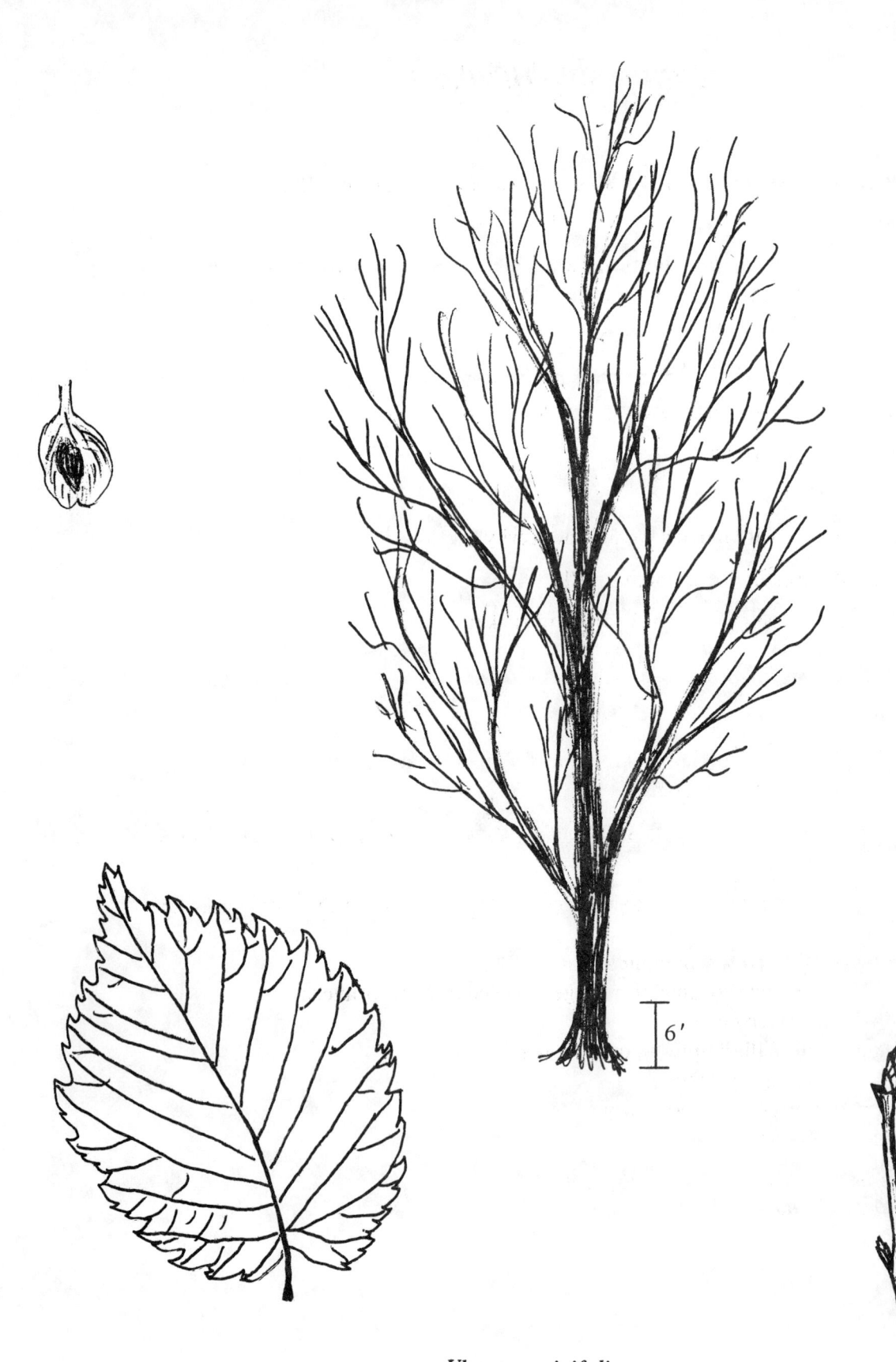

Ulmus carpinifolia

Ulmus carpinifolia

Common Name: European Field Elm; Small-leaved Elm; Smooth-leaved Elm

Family: Ulmaceae

Foliage: may be up to 2-3 1/2 inches long, although it is usually smaller; taper pointed apex; double teeth; uneven base; bright green; shiny; axillary tufts of hair beneath; hairy leaf stalk; yellow in autumn

Flowers: dense clusters; February-March

Fruit: samara; seed above middle; closed notch; April-May

Buds: no terminal; hairy; brown

Twigs: slender; brown

Bark: gray; deep fissures with narrow, sometimes corky ridges

Roots: fibrous; widespreading; transplants well

Growth Habit: 80 feet in height; narrowly upright; suckers

Hardiness: zone 4

Site: rich, moist soil; sun

Growth Rate: moderate-rapid

Maintenance: clean; tolerant to pruning

Propagation: seed—no pretreatment; softwood cuttings; suckers; graft or bud on *U. pumila* understock

Selections: 'Christine Buisman' — densely pyramidal; less susceptible to Dutch Elm Disease
'Cornubiensis' — narrowly pyramidal
'Dampieri' — narrowly pyramidal; foliage crowded on short branches
'Gracilis' — global crown
'Koopmannii' — smaller; upright, oval crown
'Pendula' — weeping branches
'Sarniensis' — upright, conical crown
'Umbraculifers' — global crown

Note: variable resistance to Dutch Elm Disease

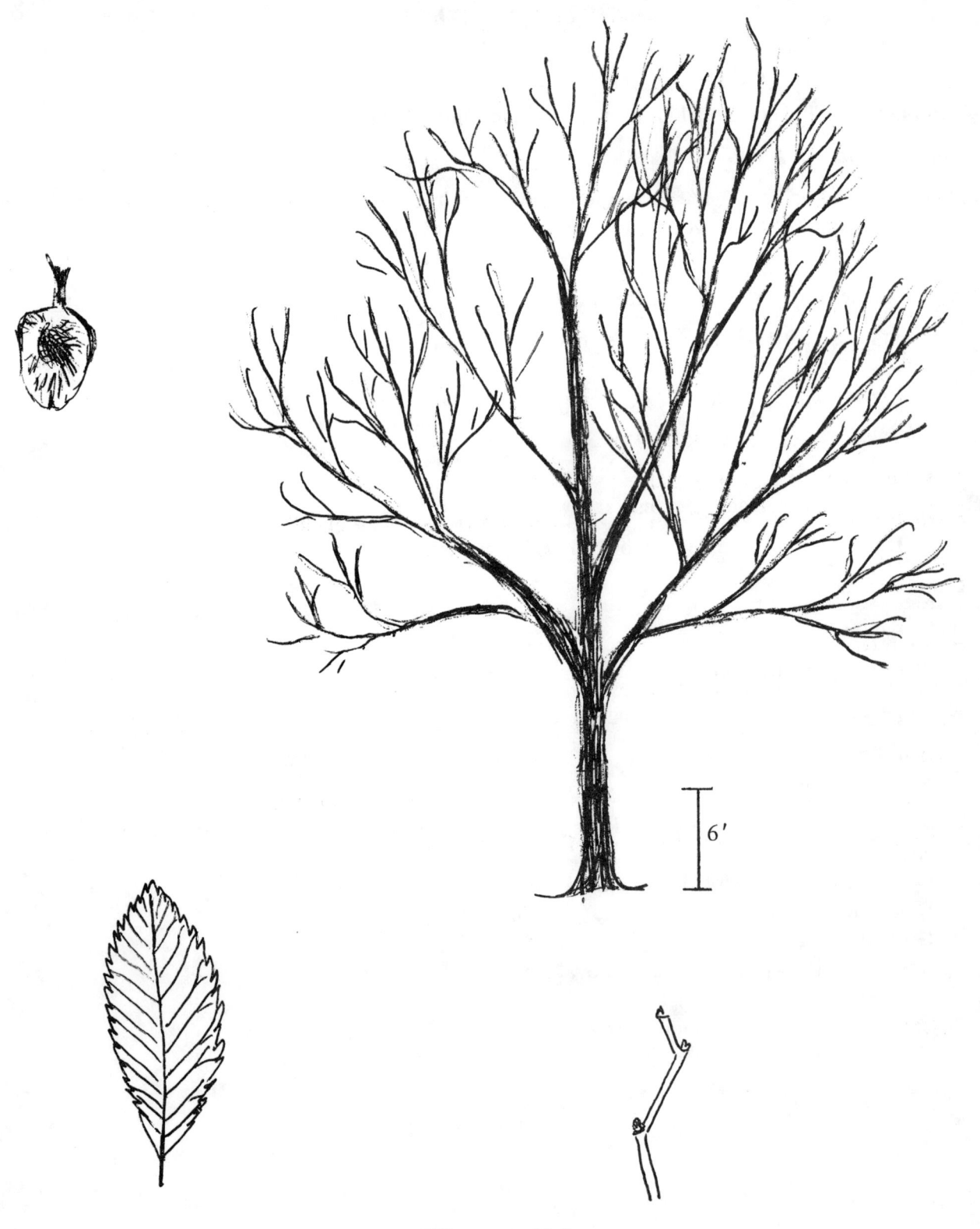

Ulmus parvifolia

Ulmus parvifolia

Common Name: Chinese Elm

Family: Ulmaceae

Foliage: 1-2 inches long; unequal bases; teeth; smooth, shiny, dark green above; young leaves hairy beneath; reddish in autumn

Flowers: axillary clusters; August-September

Fruit: samara with notched tip; seed in center; ripens September-October

Buds: small; chestnut-brown

Twigs: slender; hairy; zigzag; orange lenticels; brown

Bark: mottled, exfoliating scales; often marked with orange

Roots: fibrous; widespreading; transplants well

Growth Habit: 30-50 feet in height; broad, round crown; upright branching

Hardiness: zone 4

Site: rich, moist soil; sun

Growth Rate: moderate

Maintenance: clean; tolerant to pruning

Propagation: seed—fall sow; softwood cuttings; root cuttings; graft or bud on *U. pumila* understock

Selections: 'Pendens' — evergreen leaves in mild climates; pendant branches

Note: one of the most resistant species to Dutch Elm Dissase

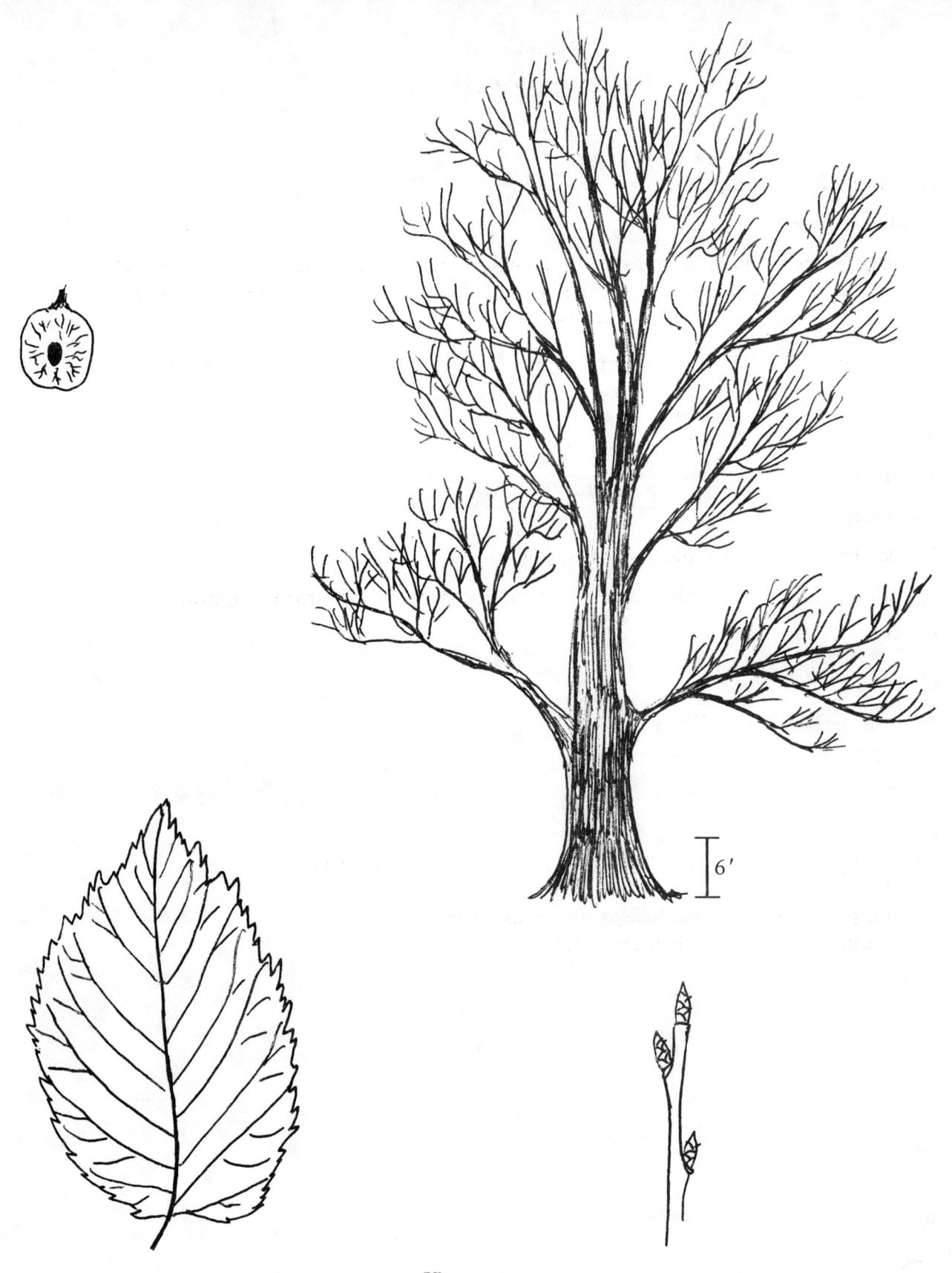

Ulmus procera

308

Ulmus procera

Common Name: English Elm

Family: Ulmaceae

Foliage: 2-3 inches long; lopsided base; double teeth; dark green; very rough above; soft tufts of hair in vein axils below; hairy leaf stalks; pale yellow to russet in autumn; persists longer into winter than most elms

Flowers: dense clusters; February-March

Fruit: circular samara; seed near apex; closed notch on apex; ripens April-May

Buds: conical; dark purplish; fuzzy

Twigs: thin; light brown; sometimes developing corky wings

Bark: gray; deep fissures

Roots: fibrous; spreading; shallow; transplants well

Growth Habit: 70-90 feet in height; usually a straight trunk; upright, round top crown

Hardiness: zone 5

Site: moist, rich soil; sun

Growth Rate: moderate-rapid

Maintenance: clean; tolerant to pruning

Propagation: seed—no pretreatment; softwood cuttings; root cuttings; suckers; graft or bud on *U. pumila* understock

Selections: 'Argenteo-variegata' — white spots and stripes on foliage
'Marginata' — white margin on foliage
'Purpurascens' — small foliage with purple tinges
'Purpurea' — foliage tinged with purple

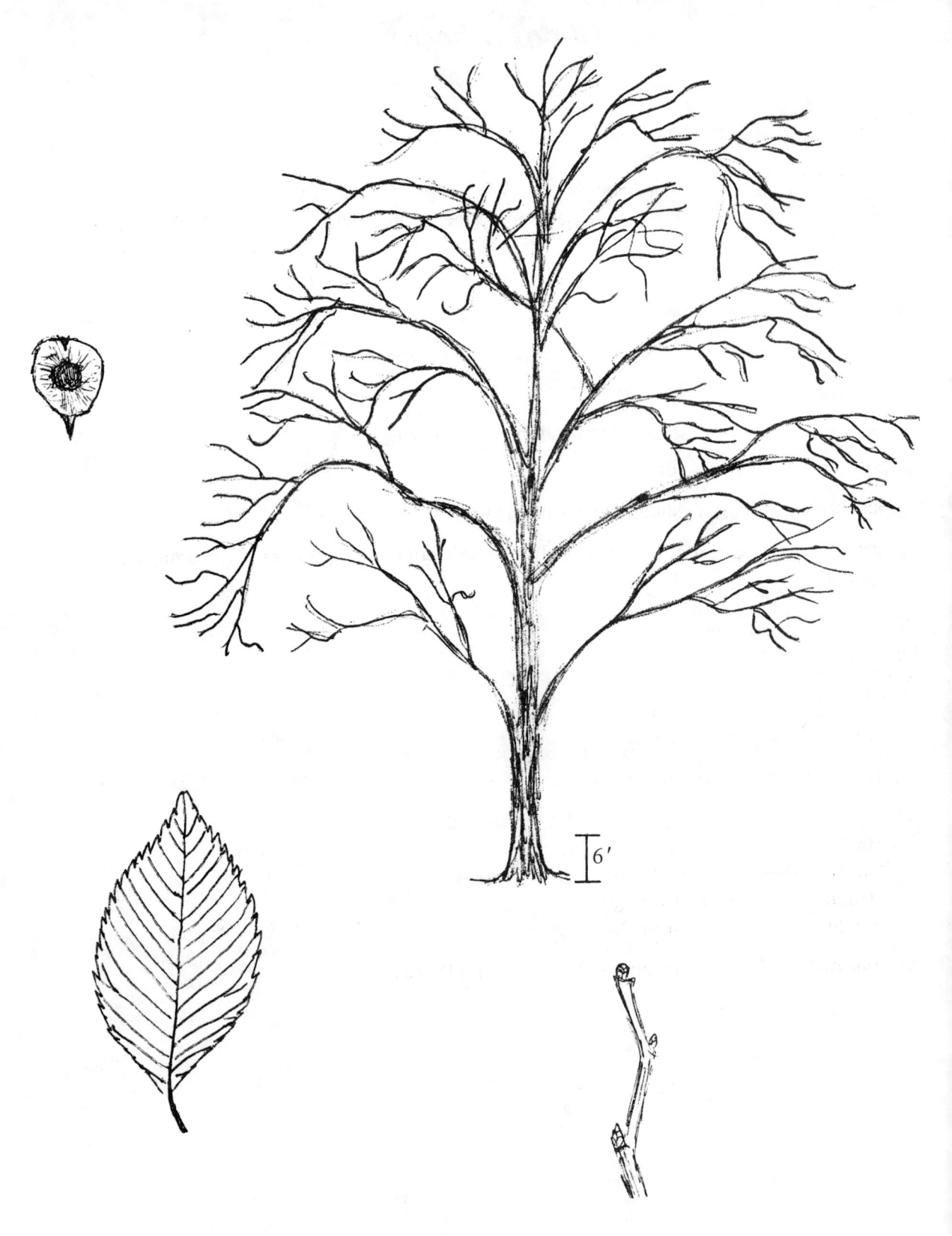

Ulmus pumila

Ulmus pumila

Common Name: Siberian Elm

Family: Ulmaceae

Foliage: 1-3 inches long; bases nearly equal; teeth; dark green and smooth above; young leaves hairy beneath; axillary tufts of hair on older leaves; short leaf stalks; yellow to russet in autumn

Flowers: clusters; March-April

Fruit: samara; seed often above center; closed notch; ripens April-May

Buds: round; black; somewhat hairy

Twigs: slender; gray; hairy when young

Bark: gray; fissures with rough plates

Roots: fibrous; spreading; shallow; transplants well

Growth Habit: 50-80 feet in height; large, ascending branches with drooping tips; spreading, round crown

Hardiness: zone 4

Site: rich, moist soil; sun

Growth Rate: rapid

Maintenance: weak wood; tolerant to pruning

Propagation: seed—no pretreatment; spring sow only; softwood cuttings; graft or bud on *U. pumila* understock

Selections: var. *arborea* — pyramidal crown
    'Chenkota' — stronger wood
    'Dropmore' — smaller foliage
    'Pendula' — weeping branches

Note: one of the most resistant species to Dutch Elm Disease

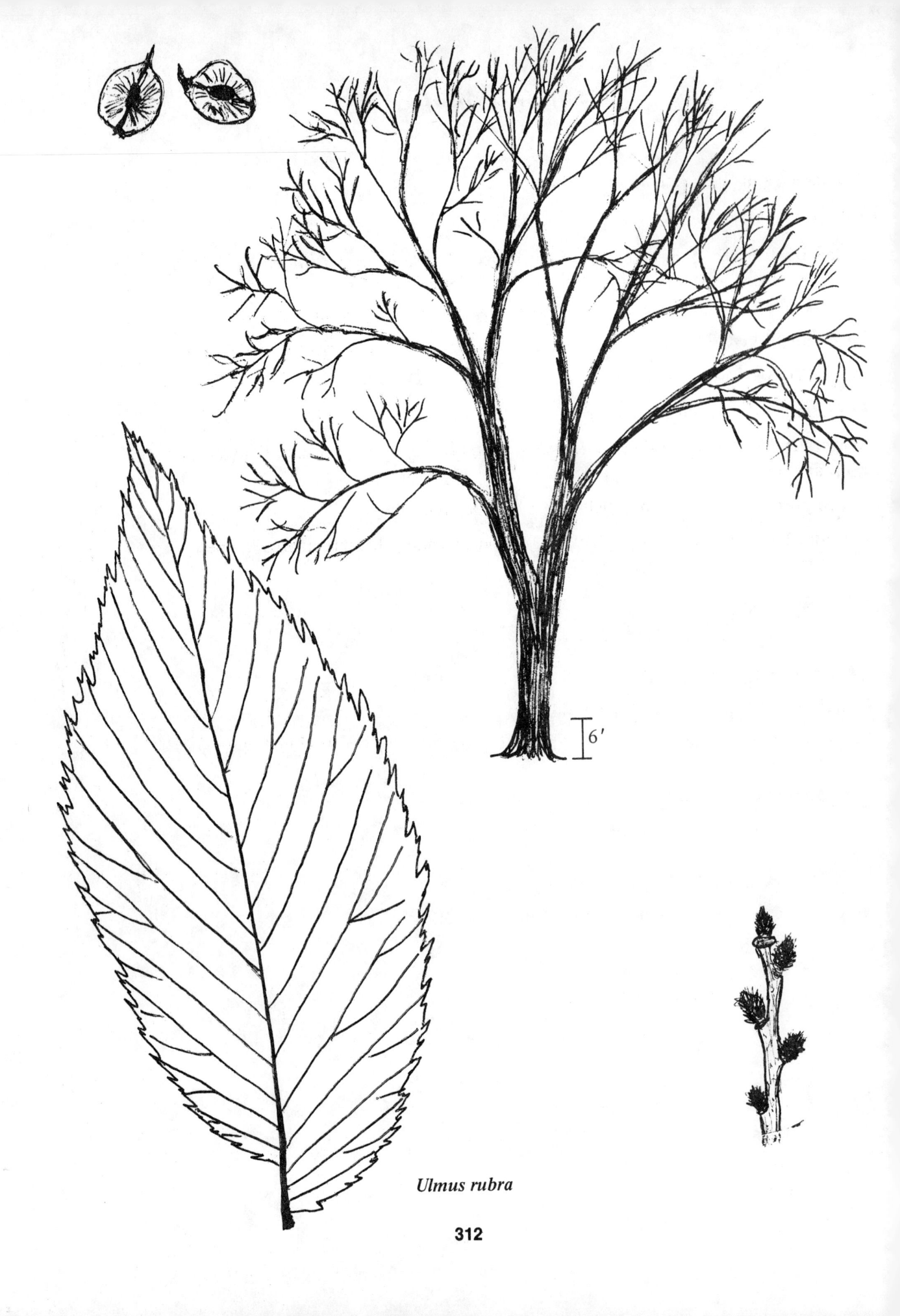

Ulmus rubra

Ulmus rubra (fulva)

Common Name: Red Elm; Slippery Elm

Family: Ulmaceae

Foliage: 4-7 inches long; coarse, double teeth; taper-pointed apex; uneven bases; dark green; rough; pale yellow to russet in autumn

Flowers: dense clusters; green; short stem on each flower; late February-April

Fruit: samara with a brown, woolly seed; smooth wing; short stalk; ripens April-June

Buds: no terminal; round; rust-red hair

Twigs: moderately stout; gray; rough

Bark: thick; red-brown; shallow, vertical furrows; inner bark slippery; no color variation in bark layers

Roots: fibrous; widespreading; shallow; transplants well

Growth Habit: 40-70 feet in height; high, widespreading branches; broad; open; vase shaped; round to irregular crown

Hardiness: zone 3

Site: rich, moist soil; sun to partial shade

Growth Rate: moderate-rapid

Maintenance: clean; tolerant to pruning

Propagation: seed—may be beneficial to stratify in a moist medium at 41 °F for 60-90 days; softwood cuttings

Note: susceptible to Dutch Elm Disease

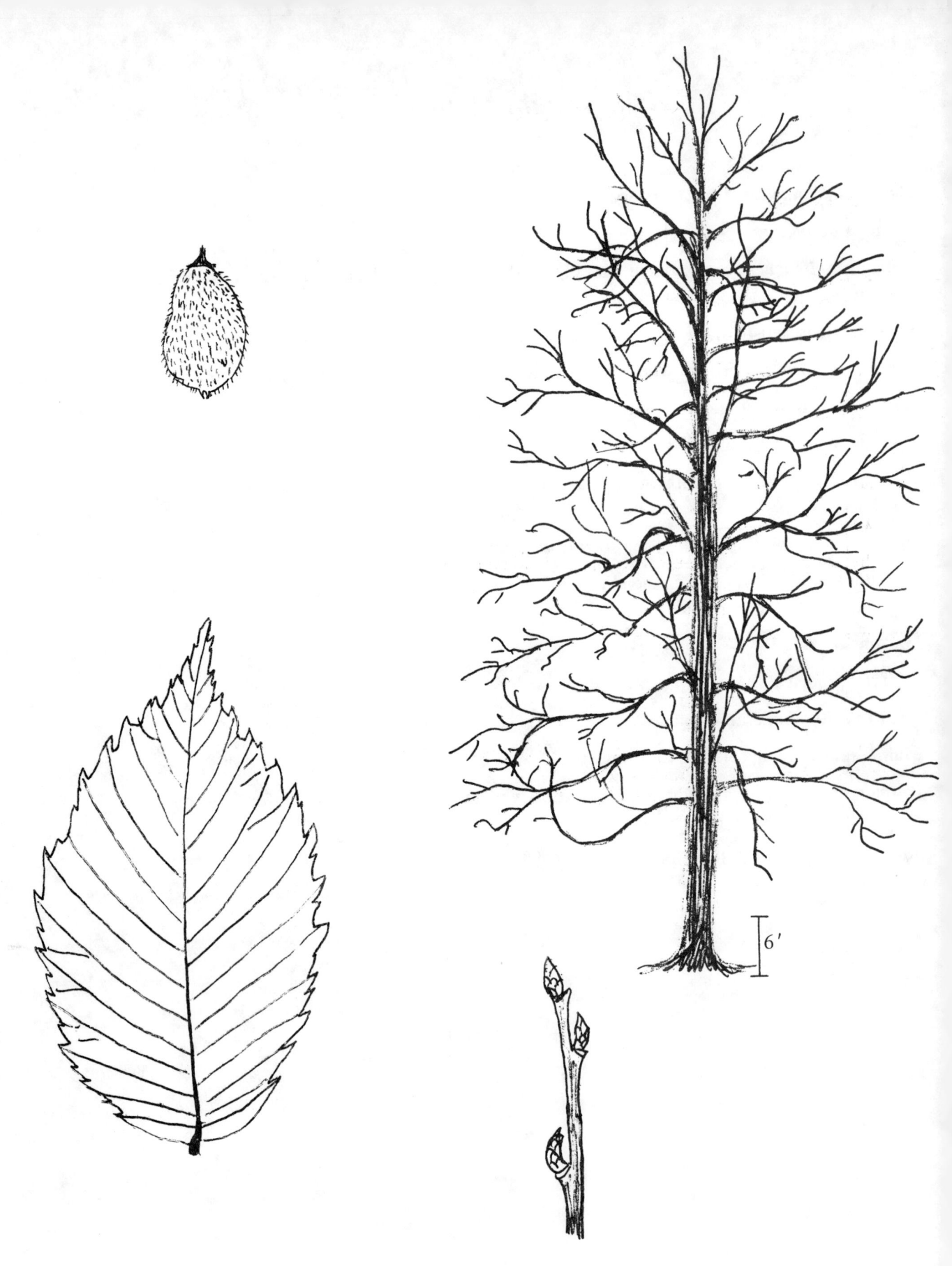

Ulmus thomasii

Ulmus thomasii

Common Name: Cork Elm; Rock Elm

Family: Ulmaceae

Foliage: 2-6 inches long; coarse, double teeth; thick; bases nearly equal; dark green; paler and hairy beneath; yellow to russet in autumn

Flowers: greenish red; clustered; hairy; March-May

Fruit: large, oval samara; hairy; shallowly notched on apex; indistinct seed cavity; ripens May-June

Buds: no terminal; pointed; downy; chestnut-brown

Twigs: moderately stout; hairy; red-brown; develops corky wings on second year wood

Bark: thick; gray; irregular fissures with corky patches; red and white striped cork layers visible when broken

Roots: fibrous; spreading; transplants well

Growth Habit: 60-90 feet in height; long, straight trunk; short, stiff, horizontal branching; oblong, round-topped crown

Hardiness: zone 2

Site: tolerant to many soils if well drained; sun

Growth Rate: slow-moderate

Maintenance: clean; tolerant to pruning

Propagation: seed—no pretreatment

Zelkova serrata

Zelkova serrata

Common Name: Japanese Zelkova

Family: Ulmaceae

Foliage: 1-5 inches long; scalloped teeth; dark green; rough above; yellow to reddish orange in autumn

Flowers: male and female in the same flower or separate on the same tree; April-May

Fruit: berrylike drupe; short stalk; ripens September-October

Buds: conical; many dark brown scales; sometimes 2 buds in axil

Twigs: slender; brown

Bark: fairly smooth; becoming loose plated with age; gray; horizontal lenticels

Roots: fibrous; widespreading; shallow

Growth Habit: 75-90 feet in height; low branching; ascending branches; vase-shape crown with a round top

Hardiness: zone 5

Site: moist, deep soil; sun

Growth Rate: moderate

Maintenance: clean; fairly tolerant to pruning

Propagation: root cuttings; softwood cuttings; graft or bud on *Ulmus pumila* understock

Selections: 'Parkview' — has the form of *Ulmus americana*
'Villiage Green' — has the form of *Ulmus americana*

BIBLIOGRAPHY

Archibald, David. 1967. Quick-key Guide to Trees. Doubleday, Inc. Garden City, N.Y.

Blakeslee, Albert and Chester D. Jarvis. 1972. Northeastern Trees in Winter. Dover Publications, Inc. N.Y.

Brooklyn Botanic Garden. 1970. Handbook on Conifers. Vol. XXV. No. 2. Brooklyn Botanic Garden. Brooklyn, N.Y.

Colvin, Brenda. 1972. Trees for Town and Country. Lund Humphries. London, England.

Eickhorst, Walter, Ray Schulenberg, and Floyd Swink. 1972. Woody Plants of the Morton Arboretum. Morton Arboretum. Lisle, IL.

Harlow, William M. 1959. Fruit Key and Twig Key to Trees and Shrubs. Dover Publications, Inc. N.Y.

———. 1957. Trees of the Eastern and Central United States and Canada. Dover Publications, Inc. N.Y.

Hartmann, Hudson T. and Dale E. Kester. 1968. Plant Propagation Principles and Practices. Prentice Hall, Inc. Englewood Cliffs, N.J.

Hosie, R. C. 1969. Native Trees of Canada. Queen's Printer for Canada.

Krüssman, Gerd. 1965. Der Nadelgehölze. Paul Parey. Berlin and Hamburg, Germany.

———. 1960. Handbuch der Laubgehölze. Vol. I, II. Paul Parey. Berlin and Hamburg, Germany.

Kurata, S. 1971. Illustrated Important Forest Trees of Japan. Vol. I. 2nd edition. Chikyo Shuppan Co., LTD. Tokyo, Japan.

Li, Hui-lin. 1972. Trees of Pennsylvania, the Atlantic States and the Lake States. Univ. of Pennsylvania Press. Philadelphia, PA.

Mohlenbrock, Robert H. 1972. Forest Trees of Illinois. Dept. of Conservation of Illinois, Division of Forestry.

Morton Arboretum. 1943. Morton Arboretum Bulletin of Popular Information-The Cones of the Arboretum. Vol. XVIII. No. 12. Morton Arboretum. Lisle, IL.

———. 1945. Morton Arboretum of Popular Information-The Evergreen Trees. Vol. XX. No. 6-7. Morton Arboretum, Lisle, IL.

Nichols, Lester P. 1976. Disease Resistant Crabapples-1976. Pennsylvania State Univ. University Park, PA

Ouden, Pieter den and B. K. Boom. 1965. Manual of Cultivated Conifers Hardy in the Cold and Warm Temperate Zone. Martinus Wijoff. The Hague. Netherlands.

Preston, Richard J. Jr. 1961. North American Trees. 2nd edition. Iowa State University Press. Ames, Iowa.

Rehder, Alfred. 1940. Manual of Cultivated Trees and Shrubs. 2nd edition. MacMillan Co. N.Y.

Robinson, Florence Bell. 1960. Useful Trees and Shrubs. Garrard Publishing Co. Champaign, IL.

Symonds, George. 1958. The Tree Identification Book. M. Barrows and Co. N.Y.

U.S.D.A.-Agricultural Research Service. 1970. History, Progeny and Location of Crabapples of Docunented Authentic Origin. National Arboretum Contribution 2. Supt. of Documents. U.S. Government Printing Office. Washington, D.C.

U.S.D.A.-Forest Service. Seeds of Woody Plants in the United States. Supt. of Documents. U.S. Government Printing Office. Washington, D.C.

Wyman, Donald. 1965. Trees for American Gardens. Macmillan Co. N.Y.

INDEX

Abies
  balsamea, xxii, 1
  concolor, 2, 3
  homolepis, 4, 5
Acer
  campestre, 6, 7
  ginnala, 8, 9
  griseum, 10, 11
  negundo, 12, 13
  nigrum, 14, 15
  palmatum, 16, 17
  pensylvanicum, 18, 19
  platanoides, 20, 21
  rubrum, 22, 23
  saccharinum, 24, 25
  saccharum, 26, 27
Aesculus
  glabra, 28, 29
  hippocastanum, 30, 31
  octandra, 32, 33
Ailanthus altissima, 34, 35
Alder
  Black, 36, 37
  European, 36, 37
Allegheny Serviceberry, 42, 43
Alnus glutinosa, 36, 37
Alternate-leaved Dogwood, 92, 93
Amelanchier
  arborea, 38, 39
  X grandiflora, 40, 41
  laevis, 42, 43
American Arborvitae, 286, 287
American
  Beech, 108, 109
  Chestnut, 76, 77
  Elm, 302, 303
  Hop Hornbeam, 172, 173
  Hornbeam, 64, 65
  Larch, 146, 147
  Linden, 288, 289
  Plane Tree, 215, 216
Amur
  Cork-tree, 176, 177
  Maple, 8, 9
Apple, 164, 165
Apple Serviceberry, 40, 41
Arborvitae, American, 286, 287
Ash
  Black, 116, 117
  Blue, 120, 121

European, 114, 115
Pumpkin, 122, 123
Red, 118, 119
White, 112, 113
Ash-leaved Maple, 12, 13
Asian White Birch, 54, 55
Asimina triloba, 44, 45
Aspen
  Quaking, 220, 221
  Trembling, 220, 221
Austrian Pine, 198, 199

Bald Cypress, 284, 285
Balsam Fir, xxii, 1
Basket Oak, 256, 257
Basswood, 288, 289
  White, 294, 295
Beech
  American, 108, 109
  Blue, 64, 65
  European, 110, 111
  Water, 64, 65
Betula
  alleghaniensis, 46, 47
  lenta, 48, 49
  lutea, 46, 47
  nigra, 50, 51
  papyrifera, 52, 53
  pendula, 60, 61
  platyphylla, 54, 55
  populifolia, 56, 57
  pubescens, 58, 59
  verrucosa, 60, 61
Big Shellbark Hickory, 72, 73
Bigleaf Linden, 296, 297
Birch
  Asian White, 54, 55
  Canoe, 52, 53
  Cherry, 48, 49
  European, 60, 61
  Gray, 56, 57
  Hairy, 58, 59
  Paper, 52, 53
  River, 50, 51
  Sweet, 48, 49
  White, 52, 53
  Yellow, 46, 47
Bitternut Hickory, 66, 67
Black Alder, 36, 37

Ash, 116, 117
Cherry, 228, 229
Gum, 170, 171
Locust, 268, 269
Maple, 14, 15
Oak, 262, 263
Spruce, 184, 185
Walnut, 134, 135
Willow, 276, 277
Blue
  Ash, 120, 121
  Beech, 64, 65
  Spruce, 188, 189
Bog Spruce, 184, 185
Box-Elder, 12, 13
Buckeye
  Ohio, 28, 29
  Sweet, 32, 33
Buckthorn, Common, 264, 265
Burr Oak, 250, 251
Butternut, 132, 133
Buttonwood, 214, 215

Callery Pear, 234, 235
Canadian Hemlock, 300, 301
Canoe Birch, 52, 53
Carolina Silverbell, 130, 131
Carpinus
  betulus, 62, 63
  caroliniana, 64, 65
Carya
  cordiformis, 66, 67
  glabra, 68, 69
  illinoensis, 70, 71
  laciniosa, 72, 73
  ovata, 74, 75
Castanea
  dentata, 76, 77
  mollissima, 78, 79
Castor-aralia, 140, 141
Catalpa speciosa, 80, 81
Catalpa, Western, 80, 81
Cedar
  Red, 138, 139
  Northern White, 286, 287
Celtis occidentalis, 82, 83
Cercidiphyllum japonicum, 84, 85
Cercis canadensis, 86, 87
Cherry Birch, 48, 49

Cherry
  Black, 228, 229
  Choke, 230, 231
  Mazzard, 224, 225
  Sargent, 226, 227
  Sweet, 224, 225
Chestnut
  American, 76, 77
  Chinese, 78, 79
  Horse, 30, 31
China-tree, 142, 143
Chinese
  Chestnut, 78, 79
  Elm, 306, 307
  Juniper, 136, 137
Chinquapin Oak, 252, 253
Chionanthus virginicus, 88, 89
Choke Cherry, 230, 231
Cigar-tree, 80, 81
Cladrastis lutea, 90, 91
Cockspur Thorn, 96, 97
Coffee-tree, Kentucky, 128, 129
Colorado
  Blue Spruce, 188, 189
  Fir, 2, 3
  Spruce, 188, 189
Common
  Buckthorn, 264, 265
  Hemlock, 300, 301
  Pear, 236, 237
  Persimmon, 104, 105
Cork Elm, 314, 315
Cork-tree, Amur, 176, 177
Cornus
  alternifolia, 92, 93
  florida, 94, 95
Cottonwood, 218, 219
Crabapples, 164, 165
Crataegus
  crus-galli, 96, 97
  mollis, 98, 99
  oxycantha, 100, 101
  phaenopyrum, 102, 103
Crimean Linden, 292, 293
Cucumber-tree, 156, 157
Cypress, Bald, 284, 285

Diospyros virginiana, 104, 105
Dogwood
  Alternate-leaved, 92, 93
  Flowering, 94, 95
  Pagoda, 93, 94
Douglas Fir, 232, 233
Downy
  Hawthorn, 98, 99
  Serviceberry, 38, 39

Eastern
  Hemlock, 300, 301
  Redbud, 86, 87
  White Pine, 206, 207
Elaeagnus angustifolia, 106, 107

Elm
  American, 302, 303
  Chinese, 306, 307
  Cork, 314, 315
  English, 308, 309
  European Field, 304, 305
  Red, 312, 313
  Rock, 314, 315
  Siberian, 310, 311
  Slippery, 312, 313
  Small-leaved, 304, 305
  Smooth-leaved, 304, 305
  White, 302, 303
English
  Elm, 308, 309
  Hawthorn, 100, 101
  Oak, 258, 259
Engelmann Spruce, 180, 181
European
  Alder, 36, 37
  Ash, 114, 115
  Beech, 110, 111
  Birch, 60, 61
  Field Elm, 304, 305
  Hornbeam, 62, 63
  Larch, 144, 145
  Mountain Ash, 282, 283

Fagus
  grandifolia, 108, 109
  sylvatica, 110, 111
Fir
  Balsam, xxii, 1
  Colorado, 2, 3
  Douglas, 232, 233
  Nikko, 4, 5
  White, 2, 3
Flowering Dogwood, 94, 95
Fraxinus
  americana, 112, 113
  excelsior, 114, 115
  nigra, 116, 117
  pensylvanica, 118, 119
  profunda, 122, 123
  quadrangulata, 120, 121
  tomentosa, 122, 123
Fringe Tree, White, 88, 89

Ginkgo biloba, 124, 125
Gleditsia triacanthos, 126, 127
Golden Rain Tree, 142, 143
Gray Birch, 56, 57
Gum
  Black, 170, 171
  Sour, 170, 171
  Sweet, 150, 151
Gymnocladus dioecus, 128, 129

Hackberry, 82, 83
Hairy Birch, 58, 59
Halesia carolina, 130, 131

Hankow Willow, 274, 275
Hawthorn
  Downy, 98, 99
  English, 100, 101
Heaven, Tree of, 34, 35
Hedge Maple, 6, 7
Hemlock
  Canadian, 300, 301
  Common, 300, 301
  Eastern, 300, 301
Hickory
  Big Shellbark, 72, 73
  Bitternut, 66, 67
  Sweet Pignut, 68, 69
  Shagbark, 74, 75
Hill's Oak, 246, 247
Honey Locust, 126, 127
Hop Hornbeam, American, 172, 173
Hornbeam
  American, 64, 65
  European, 62, 63
Horse Chestnut, 30, 31

Ironwood, 172, 173

Jack
  Oak, 246, 247
  Pine, 190, 191
Japanese
  Larch, 148, 149
  Maple, 16, 17
  Pagoda Tree, 280, 281
  Red Pine, 192, 193
  White Pine, 200, 201
  Zelkova, 316, 317
Jeffrey Pine, 196, 197
Jersey Pine, 210, 211
Judas Tree, 86, 87
Juglans
  cinerea, 132, 133
  nigra, 134, 135
Juniper, Chinese, 136, 137
Juniperus
  chinensis, 136, 137
  virginiana, 138, 139

Kalopanax pictus, 140, 141
Katsura Tree, 84, 85
Kentucky Coffee-tree, 128, 129
Kobus Magnolia, 158, 159
Koelreuteria paniculata, 142, 143

Larch
  American, 146, 147
  European, 144, 145
  Japanese, 148, 149
Larix
  decidua, 144, 145
  laricina, 146, 147
  leptolepis, 148, 149

Laurel Oak, 248, 249
Limber Pine, 194, 195
Linden
   American, 288, 289
   Bigleaf, 296, 297
   Crimean, 292, 293
   Little-leaved, 290, 291
   Silver, 298, 299
   Small-leaved European, 290, 291
Liquidambar styraciflua, 150, 151
Liriodendron tulipifera, 152, 153
Little-leaved Linden, 290, 291
Locust
   Honey, 126, 127
   Black, 268, 269
London Plane, 212, 213

Maclura pomifera, 154, 155
Magnolia
   acuminata, 156, 157
   kobus, 158, 159
   Saucer, 160, 161
   soulangeana, 160, 161
   Thurber's, 158, 159
   tripetala, 162, 163
   Umbrella, 162, 163
Maidenhair Tree, 124, 125
Malus species, 164, 165
Maple
   Amur, 8, 9
   Ash-leaved, 12, 13
   Black, 14, 15
   Hedge, 6, 7
   Japanese, 16, 17
   Moosewood, 18, 19
   Norway, 20, 21
   Paperbark, 10, 11
   Red, 22, 23
   Scarlet, 22, 23
   Silver, 24, 25
   Striped, 18, 19
   Sugar, 26, 27
   Swamp, 22, 23
Mazzard Cherry, 224, 225
Moosewood, 18, 19
Morus
   alba, 166, 167
   rubra, 168, 169
Mossy-cup Oak, 250, 251
Mountain Ash
   European, 282, 283
   Showy, 283
Mulberry
   Red, 168, 169
   White, 166, 167

Nikko Fir, 4, 5
Northern
   Pin Oak, 246, 247
   White Cedar, 286, 287
Norway
   Maple, 20, 21

   Pine, 204, 205
   Spruce, 178, 179
Nyssa sylvatica, 170, 171

Oak
   Basket, 256, 257
   Black, 262, 263
   Burr, 250, 251
   Chinquapin, 252, 253
   English, 258, 259
   Hill's, 246, 247
   Jack, 246, 247
   Laurel, 248, 249
   Mossy-cup, 250, 251
   Northern Pin, 246, 247
   Pin, 254, 255
   Red, 260, 261
   Sawtooth, 238, 239
   Scarlet, 244, 245
   Shingle, 248, 249
   Swamp White, 242, 243
   White, 240, 241
   Yellow, 252, 253
Ohio Buckeye, 28, 29
Old-Mans-Beard, 88, 89
Oleaster, 106, 107
Olive, Russian, 106, 107
Osage Orange, 154, 155
Ostrya virginiana, 172, 173
Oxydendrum arboreum, 174, 175

Pagoda Dogwood, 92, 93
Pagoda-tree, Japanese, 280, 281
Paper Birch, 52, 53
Paperbark Maple, 10, 11
Pawpaw, 44, 45
Pear
   Callery, 234, 235
   Common, 236, 237
Pecan, 70, 71
Persimmon, Common, 104, 105
Phellodendron amurense, 176, 177
Picea
   abies, 178, 179
   engelmannii, 180, 181
   glauca, 182, 183
   mariana, 184, 185
   omorika, 186, 187
   pungens, 188, 189
Pin Oak, 254, 255
Pine
   Austrian, 198, 199
   Eastern White, 206, 207
   Jack, 190, 191
   Japanese Red, 192, 193
   Japanese White, 200, 201
   Jeffrey, 196, 197
   Jersey, 210, 211
   Limber, 194, 195
   Norway, 204, 205
   Ponderosa, 202, 203
   Red, 204, 205

   Scotch, 208, 209
   Scrub, 210, 211
   Western Yellow, 202, 203
Pinus
   banksiana, 190, 191
   densiflora, 192, 193
   flexilis, 194, 195
   jeffreyi, 196, 197
   nigra, 198, 199
   parviflora, 200, 201
   ponderosa, 202, 203
   resinosa, 204, 205
   strobus, 206, 207
   sylvestris, 208, 209
   virginiana, 210, 211
Plane, London, 212, 213
Plane Tree, American, 214, 215
Platanus X
   acerifolia, 212, 213
   occidentalis, 214, 215
Plum, Wild, 222, 223
Ponderosa Pine, 202, 203
Populus
   alba, 216, 217
   deltoides, 218, 219
   tremuloides, 220, 221
Poplar
   Silver-leaved, 216, 217
   White, 216, 217
   Yellow, 152, 153
Prunus
   americana, 222, 223
   avium, 224, 225
   sargentii, 226, 227
   serotina, 228, 229
   virginiana, 230, 231
Pseudotsuga menziesii var. *glauca,* 232, 233
Pumpkin Ash, 122, 123
Pyrus
   calleryana, 234, 235
   communis, 235, 237

Quaking Aspen, 220, 221
Quercus
   acutissima, 238, 239
   alba, 240, 241
   bicolor, 242, 243
   coccinea, 244, 245
   ellipsoidalis, 246, 247
   imbricaria, 248, 249
   macrocarpa, 250, 251
   muehlenbergi, 252, 253
   palustris, 254, 255
   prinus, 256, 257
   robur, 258, 259
   rubra, 260, 261
   velutina, 262, 263

Rain Tree, Golden, 142, 143
Red
   Ash, 118, 119

Cedar, 138, 139
Elm, 312, 313
Oak, 260, 261
Pine, 204, 205
Maple, 22, 23
Mulberry, 168, 169
Redbud, Eastern, 86, 87
Rhamnus cathartica, 264, 265
Rhus typhina, 266, 267
River Birch, 50, 51
Robinia pseudoacacia, 268, 269
Rock Elm, 314, 315
Rowan Tree, 282, 283
Russian Olive, 106, 107

Salix
  alba, 270, 271
  lucida, 272, 273
  matsudana, 274, 275
  nigra, 276, 277
Sargent Cherry, 226, 227
Sassafras albidum, 278, 279
Saucer Magnolia, 160, 161
Sawtooth Oak, 238, 239
Scarlet
  Maple, 22, 23
  Oak, 244, 245
Scholar tree, 280, 281
Scotch Pine, 208, 209
Scrub Pine, 210, 211
Serbian Spruce, 186, 187
Serviceberry
  Allegheny, 42, 43
  Apple, 40, 41
  Downy, 38, 39
Shadbush, Smooth Northern, 42, 43
Shagbark Hickory, 74, 75
Shingle Oak, 248, 249
Shining Willow, 272, 273
Showy Mountain Ash, 283
Siberian Elm, 310, 311
Silver
  Linden, 298, 299
  Maple, 24, 25
Silverbell, Carolina, 130, 131
Silver-leaved Poplar, 216, 217
Slippery Elm, 312, 313
Small-leaved
  Elm, 304, 305
  European Linden, 290, 291

Smooth Northern Shadbush, 42, 43
Smooth-leaved Elm, 304, 305
Sophora japonica, 280, 281
Sorbus
  aucuparia, 282, 283
  decora, 283
Sorrel-tree, 174, 175
Sour Gum, 170, 171
Sourwood, 174, 175
Spruce
  Black, 184, 185
  Bog, 184, 185
  Colorado, 188, 189
  Colorado Blue, 188, 189
  Engelmann, 180, 181
  Norway, 178, 179
  Serbian, 186, 187
  White, 182, 183
Staghorn Sumac, 266, 267
Striped Maple, 18, 19
Sugar Maple, 26, 27
Sumac, Staghorn, 266, 267
Swamp
  Maple, 22, 23
  White Oak, 242, 243
Sweet
  Birch, 48, 49
  Buckeye, 32, 33
  Cherry, 224, 225
Sweet Gum, 150, 151
Sweet Pignut Hickory, 68, 69
Sycamore, 214, 215

Tamarack, 146, 147
Taxodium distichum, 284, 285
Thorn
  Cockspur, 96, 97
  Washington, 102, 103
Thuja occidentalis, 286, 287
Thurber's Magnolia, 158, 159
Tilia
  americana, 288, 289
  cordata, 290, 291
  X euchlora, 292, 293
  heterophylla, 294, 295
  platyphyllos, 296, 297
  tomentosa, 298, 299
Tree of Heaven, 34, 35
Trembling Aspen, 220, 221
Tsuga canadensis, 300, 301

Tulip Tree, 152, 153
Tupelo, 170, 171

Ulmus
  americana, 302, 303
  carpinifolia, 304, 305
  parvifolia, 306, 307
  procera, 308, 309
  pumila, 310, 311
  rubra, 312, 313
  thomasii, 314, 315
Umbrella Magnolia, 162, 163

Walnut, Black, 134, 135
Washington Thorn, 102, 103
Water Beech, 64, 65
Western
  Catalpa, 80, 81
  Yellow Pine, 202, 203
White
  Ash, 112, 113
  Basswood, 294, 295
  Birch, 52, 53
  Elm, 302, 303
  Fir, 2, 3
  Fringe Tree, 88, 89
  Mulberry, 166, 167
  Oak, 240, 241
  Poplar, 216, 217
  Spruce, 182, 183
  Willow, 270, 271
Wild Plum, 222, 223
Willow
  Black, 276, 277
  Hankow, 274, 275
  Shining, 272, 273
  White, 270, 271

Yellow
  Birch, 46, 47
  Oak, 252, 253
  Poplar, 152, 153
Yellowwood, 90, 91

Zelkova, Japanese, 316, 317
Zelkova serrata, 316, 317

```
QK        Stava, Pamela Sue
484
A1.5      Handbook of trees for the
S7        Midwest
c. 1
```

**NORMANDALE COMMUNITY
COLLEGE**
9700 FRANCE AVENUE S.
BLOOMINGTON, MN 55431